Beginning C++ Game Programming

Learn C++ from scratch and get started building your very own games

John Horton

BIRMINGHAM - MUMBAI

Beginning C++ Game Programming

First published: October 2016

Production reference: 3191016

Published by Packt Publishing Ltd.
Livery Place
35 Livery Street
Birmingham
B3 2PB, UK.

ISBN 978-1-78646-619-8

www.packtpub.com

Credits

Author

John Horton

Reviewer

Glen De Cauwsemaecker

Commissioning Editor

Wilson D'souza

Acquisition Editor

Tushar Gupta

Content Development Editor

Onkar Wani

Technical Editor

Rashil Shah

Copy Editor

Safis Editing

Project Coordinator

Ulhas Kambali

Proofreader

Safis Editing

Indexer

Tejal Daruwale Soni

Production Coordinator

Aparna Bhagat

Cover Work

Aparna Bhagat

About the Author

John Horton is a coding and gaming enthusiast based in the UK.

He has a passion for writing apps, games, books, and blog articles about programming, especially for beginners. He is the founder of Game Code School, `http://www.gamecodeschool.com`, which is dedicated to helping complete beginners get started coding using the language and platform that is best for them.

John sincerely believes that anyone can learn to code and that everybody has a game or an app inside of them, and that they just need to do enough work to bring it out.

He has authored around a dozen technology books, most recently the following:

Beginning C++ Game Programming: `https://www.packtpub.com/game-development/beginning-c-game-programming`

Android Programming for Beginners: `https://www.packtpub.com/application-development/android-programming-beginners`

Android Game programming by Example: `https://www.packtpub.com/game-development/android-game-programming-example`

Learning Java Building Android Games: `https://www.packtpub.com/game-development/learning-java-building-android-games`

About the Reviewer

Glen De Cauwsemaecker, commonly known as glendc, is an open source hacker from Belgium. Currently, he lives a nomadic life in South America, while working freelance for the UK games industry. Glen is passionate about open source technology, as much as exploring new cultures and countries. This is why he became in 2015 a digital nomad, after living and working in the UK for 2 years.

I would like to thank my girlfriend, Elizabeth Gonzales Belsuzarri, for her support and love. I would also like to thank Exient Ltd., my employer for the last 3 years, for providing me with the chance to work remotely, while living nomadically.

www.PacktPub.com

eBooks, discount offers, and more

Did you know that Packt offers eBook versions of every book published, with PDF and ePub files available? You can upgrade to the eBook version at www.PacktPub.com and as a print book customer, you are entitled to a discount on the eBook copy. Get in touch with us at customercare@packtpub.com for more details.

At www.PacktPub.com, you can also read a collection of free technical articles, sign up for a range of free newsletters and receive exclusive discounts and offers on Packt books and eBooks.

https://www.packtpub.com/mapt

Do you need instant solutions to your IT questions? PacktLib is Packt's online digital book library. Here, you can search, access, and read Packt's entire library of books.

Why subscribe?

- Fully searchable across every book published by Packt
- Copy and paste, print, and bookmark content
- On demand and accessible via a web browser

Dedicated to everyone who has no place to stay or insufficient strength to live. Especially to those who used up all their strength serving someone else.

Table of Contents

Preface

This book is about learning C++ programming the fun way. Starting from zero experience, you will learn the basics of C++, such as variables and loops, through to advanced topics, such as inheritance and polymorphism. Everything you learn will be put into practice building three fully-playable games.

These are our three projects for the book.

Timber!!!

The first game is an addictive, fast-paced clone of the hugely successful Timberman, `http:/` `/store.steampowered.com/app/398710/`. Our game, Timber!!!, will allow us to be introduced to all the C++ basics at the same time as building a genuinely playable game.

Zombie Arena

Next we will build a frantic, zombie survival-shooter, not unlike the Steam hit, Over 9,000 Zombies, `http://store.steampowered.com/app/273500/`. The player will have a machine gun, and must fight off ever growing waves of zombies. All this will take place in a randomly generated, scrolling world. To achieve this, we will learn about object-oriented programming and how it enables us to have a large code base (lots of code) that is easy to write and maintain. Expect exciting features such as hundreds of enemies, rapid-fire weaponry, pick-ups and a character that can be "leveled-up" after each wave.

Thomas was Late

The third game will be a stylish and challenging, single player and co-op puzzle platformer. It is based on the very popular game, Thomas was Alone, `http://store.steampowered.co` `m/app/220780/`. Expect to learn cool topics such as particle effects, OpenGL Shaders, and split-screen cooperative multiplayer.

What this book covers

Chapter 1, *C++, SFML, Visual Studio, and Starting the First Game,* this is quite a hefty first chapter, but we will learn absolutely everything we need in order to have the first part of our first game up and running. Here is what we will do:

- Find out more about the games we will build
- Learn a bit about C++
- Explore SFML and its relationship with C++
- Look at the software, Visual Studio, that we will use throughout the book
- Set up a game development environment
- Create a reusable project template, which will save a lot of time
- Plan and prepare for the first game project, Timber!!!
- Write the first C++ code of the book and make a runnable game that draws a background

Chapter 2, *Variables, Operators, and Decisions – Animating Sprites,* in this chapter, we will do quite a bit more drawing on the screen, and to achieve this we will need to learn some of the basics of C++. Here is what is in store:

- Learn all about C++ variables
- See how to manipulate the values stored in variables
- Add a static tree, ready for the player to chop
- Draw and animate a bee and three clouds

Chapter 3, *C++ Strings, SFML Time – Player Input, and HUD,* in this chapter, we will spend around half the time learning how to manipulate text and display it on the screen, and the other half looking at timing and how a visual time-bar can inform the player and create a sense of urgency in the game. We will cover:

- Pausing and restarting the game
- C++ strings
- SFML text and SFML font classes
- Adding a HUD to Timber!!!
- Adding a time-bar to Timber!!!

Chapter 4, *Loops, Arrays, Switch, Enumerations, and Functions – Implementing Game Mechanics,* this chapter probably has more C++ information than any other chapter in the book. It is packed with fundamental concepts that will move our understanding on enormously. It will also begin to shed light on some of the murky areas we have been skipping over a little bit like functions and the game loop. Once we have explored a whole list of C++ language necessities, we will then use everything we know to make the main game mechanic, the tree branches, move. By the end of this chapter, we will be ready for the final phase and the completion of Timber!!!. Get ready for the following topics:

- Loops
- Arrays
- Making decisions with switch
- Enumerations
- Getting started with functions
- Creating and moving the tree branches

Chapter 5, *Collisions, Sound, and End Conditions – Making the Game Playable,* this is the final phase of the first project. By the end of this chapter, you will have your first completed game. Once you have Timber!!! up and running, be sure to read the last section of this chapter as it will suggest ways to make the game better:

- Adding the rest of the sprites
- Handling the player input
- Animating the flying log
- Handling death
- Adding sound effects
- Adding features and improving Timber!!!

Chapter 6, *Object-Oriented Programming, Classes, and SFML Views,* this is the longest chapter of the book. There is a fair amount of theory, but the theory will give us the knowledge to start using OOP (object-oriented programming) to great effect. Furthermore, we will not waste any time in putting that theory to good use. Before we explore C++ OOP, we will find out about and plan our next game project. This is what we will do:

- Plan the Zombie Arena game
- Learn about OOP and classes
- Code the Player class
- Learn about the SFML View class

- Build the Zombie Arena game engine
- Put the Player class to work

Chapter 7, *C++ References, Sprite Sheets, and Vertex Arrays*, in this chapter, we will explore C++ references, which allow us to work on variables and objects that are otherwise out of scope. In addition, references will help us avoid having to pass large objects between functions, which is a slow process. It is a slow process because each time we do this, a copy of the variable or object must be made.

Armed with this new knowledge about references, we will take a look at the SFML VertexArray class, which allows us to build up a large image that can be very quickly and efficiently drawn to the screen using multiple images from a single image file. By the end of the chapter, we will have a scaleable, random, scrolling background, using references and a VertexArray object.

We will now talk about:

- C++ references
- SFML VertexArrays
- Coding a random, scrolling background

Chapter 8, *Pointers, the Standard Template Library, and Texture Management*, we will learn a lot, as well as get plenty done to the game, in this chapter. We will first learn about the fundamental C++ topic of pointers. Pointers are variables that hold memory addresses. Typically, a pointer will hold the memory address of another variable. This sounds a bit like a reference, but we will see how they are much more powerful and we will use a pointer to handle an ever-expanding horde of zombies.

We will also learn about the Standard Template Library (STL), which is a collection of classes that allow us to quickly and easily implement common data management techniques.

Once we understand the basics of the STL, we will be able to use that new knowledge to manage all the textures from the game, because if we have 1,000 zombies, we don't really want to load a copy of a zombie graphic into the GPU for each and every one.

We will also dig a little deeper into OOP and use a static function, which is a function of a class that can be called without an instance of the class. At the same time, we will see how we can design a class to ensure that only one instance can ever exist. This is ideal when we need to guarantee that different parts of our code will use the same data.

In this chapter we will:

- Learn about pointers
- Learn about the STL
- Implement the Texture Holder class using static functions and a singleton class
- Implement a pointer to a horde of zombies
- Edit some existing code to use the TextureHolder class for the player and background

Chapter 9, *Collision Detection, Pickups, and Bullets*, so far, we have implemented the main visual parts of our game. We have a controllable character running around in an arena full of zombies that chase him. The problem is that they don't interact with each other. A zombie can wander right through the player without leaving a scratch. We need to detect collisions between the zombies and the player.

If the zombies are going to be able to injure and eventually kill the player, it is only fair that we give the player some bullets for his gun. We will then need to make sure that the bullets can hit and kill the zombies.

At the same time, if we are writing collision detection code for bullets, zombies, and the player, it would be a good time to add a class for health and ammo pickups as well.

Here is what we will do and the order we will cover things:

- Shooting bullets
- Adding a crosshair and hiding the mouse pointer
- Spawning pickups
- Detecting collisions

Chapter 10, *Layering Views and Implementing the HUD*, in this chapter, we will get to see the real value of SFML Views. We will add a large array of SFML Text objects and manipulate them as we did before in the Timber!!! project. What is new is that we will draw the HUD using a second View instance. This way the HUD will stay neatly positioned over the top of the main game action, regardless of what the background, player, zombies, and other game objects are doing.

Here is what we will do:

- Add text and a background to the home/game over screen
- Add text to the level-up screen
- Create the second View
- Add a HUD

Chapter 11, *Sound Effects, File I/O, and Finishing the Game*, we are nearly there. This short chapter will demonstrate how we can easily manipulate files stored on the hard drive using the C++ standard library, and we will also add sound effects. Of course, we know how to add sound effects but we will discuss exactly where in the code the calls to play will go. We will also tie up a few loose ends to make the game complete. In this chapter we will do the following:

- Saving and loading the highscore
- Adding sound effects
- Allowing the player to levelup
- Creating, never-ending multiple waves

Chapter 12, *Abstraction and Code Management – Making Better Use of OOP*, in this chapter, we will take a first look at the final project of the book. The project will have advanced features, such as directional sound that comes out of the speakers relative to the position of the player. It will also have split-screen co-operative gameplay. In addition, this project will introduce the concept of Shaders which are programs written in another language that run directly on the graphics card. By the end of Chapter 16: *Extending SFML Classes, Particle Systems and Shaders*, you will have a fully functioning, multiplayer platform game built in the style of the hit classic Thomas Was Alone. This chapter's main focus will be getting the project started, especially exploring how the code will be structured to make better use of OOP. Here are the details of this chapter.

- Introduce the final project, Thomas Was Late, including the gameplay features and project assets
- A detailed discussion of how we will improve the structure of the code compared to previous projects
- Coding the Thomas Was Late game engine
- Implementing split-screen functionality

Chapter 13, *Advanced OOP – Inheritance and Polymorphism*, in this chapter, we will further extend our knowledge of OOP by looking at the slightly more advanced concepts of inheritance and polymorphism. We will then be able to use this new knowledge to implement the star characters of our game, Thomas and Bob. Here is what we will cover, in a little more detail:

- Learn how to extend and modify a class using inheritance
- Treat an object of a class as if it is more than one type of class by using polymorphism
- Learn about abstract classes and how designing classes that are never instantiated can actually be useful

- Build an abstract `PlayableCharacter` class
- Put inheritance to work with the `Thomas` and `Bob` classes
- Add Thomas and Bob to the game project

Chapter 14, *Building Playable Levels and Collision Detection*, this chapter will probably be one of the most satisfying of this project. The reason for this is that by the end of it we will have a playable game. Although there will be features still to implement (sound, particle effects, HUD, shader effects), Bob and Thomas will be able to run, jump, and explore the world. Furthermore, you will be able to create your very own level designs of almost any size or complexity, by simply making platforms and obstacles in a text file. We will achieve all this by covering these topics:

- Exploring how to design levels in a text file
- Building a `LevelManager` class that will load levels from a text file, convert them into data our game can use, and keep track of the level details such as spawn position, current level, and allowed time limit
- Update the game engine to use `LevelManager`
- Code a polymorphic function to handle the collision detection for both Bob and Thomas

Chapter 15, *Sound Spatialization and HUD*, in this chapter we will be adding all the sound effects and the HUD. We have done this in both of the previous projects, but we will do things a bit differently this time. We will explore the concept of sound spatialization and how SFML makes this otherwise complicated concept nice and easy; in addition, we will build a HUD class to encapsulate our code draws information to the screen.

We will complete these tasks in this order:

- What is spatialization?
- How SFML handles spatialization
- Building a `SoundManager` class
- Deploying emitters
- Using the `SoundManager` class
- Building a HUD class
- Using the HUD class

Chapter 16, *Extending SFML Classes, Particle Systems, and Shaders,* in this final chapter, we will explore the C++ concept of extending other people's classes. More specifically, we will look at the SFML Drawable class and the benefits of using it as a base class for our own classes. We will also scratch the surface of the topic of OpenGL Shaders and see how writing code in another language (GLSL), which can be run directly on the graphics card, can lead to smooth graphical effects that might otherwise be impossible. As usual, we will also use our new skills and knowledge to enhance the current project.

Here is a list of the topics in the order we will cover them:

- SFML Drawable
- Building a particle system
- OpenGl shaders and GLSL
- Using shaders in the Thomas Was Late game

Chapter 17, *Before You Go...,* a quick discussion of what you might like to do next.

What you need for this book

- Windows 7 Service Pack 1, Windows 8 or Windows 10
- 1.6 GHz or faster processor
- 1 GB of RAM (for x86) or 2 GB of RAM (for x64)
- 15 GB of available hard disk space
- 5400 RPM hard disk drive
- DirectX 9-capable video card that runs at 1024 x 768 or higher display resolution

All the software used in this book is free. Obtaining and installing the software is covered step by step within the book. The book uses Visual Studio for Windows throughout, but experienced Linux and Mac users will probably have no trouble running the code and following the instructions using their favorite programming environment.

Who this book is for

This book is perfect for you if any of the following describes you: You have no C++ programming knowledge whatsoever or need a beginner level refresher course, if you want to learn to build games or just use games as an engaging way to learn C++, if you have aspirations to publish a game one day, perhaps on Steam, or if you just want to have loads of fun and impress friends with your creations.

Conventions

In this book, you will find a number of text styles that distinguish between different kinds of information. Here are some examples of these styles and an explanation of their meaning.

Code words in text, database table names, folder names, filenames, file extensions, path names, dummy URLs, user input, and Twitter handles are shown as follows: "We can include other contexts through the use of the include directive."

A block of code is set as follows:

```
[default]
exten => s,1,Dial(Zap/1|30)
exten => s,2,Voicemail(u100)
exten => s,102,Voicemail(b100)
exten => i,1,Voicemail(s0)
```

When we wish to draw your attention to a particular part of a code block, the relevant lines or items are set in bold:

```
[default]
exten => s,1,Dial(Zap/1|30)
exten => s,2,Voicemail(u100)
exten => s,102,Voicemail(b100)
exten => i,1,Voicemail(s0)
```

Any command-line input or output is written as follows:

```
# cp /usr/src/asterisk-addons/configs/cdr_mysql.conf.sample
/etc/asterisk/cdr_mysql.conf
```

New terms and **important words** are shown in bold. Words that you see on the screen, for example, in menus or dialog boxes, appear in the text like this: "Clicking the **Next** button moves you to the next screen."

Warnings or important notes appear in a box like this.

Tips and tricks appear like this.

Reader feedback

Feedback from our readers is always welcome. Let us know what you think about this book-what you liked or disliked. Reader feedback is important for us as it helps us develop titles that you will really get the most out of. To send us general feedback, simply e-mail feedback@packtpub.com, and mention the book's title in the subject of your message. If there is a topic that you have expertise in and you are interested in either writing or contributing to a book, see our author guide at www.packtpub.com/authors.

Customer support

Now that you are the proud owner of a Packt book, we have a number of things to help you to get the most from your purchase.

Downloading the example code

You can download the example code files for this book from your account at http://www.packtpub.com. If you purchased this book elsewhere, you can visit http://www.packtpub.com/support and register to have the files e-mailed directly to you.

You can download the code files by following these steps:

1. Log in or register to our website using your e-mail address and password.
2. Hover the mouse pointer on the **SUPPORT** tab at the top.
3. Click on **Code Downloads & Errata**.
4. Enter the name of the book in the **Search** box.
5. Select the book for which you're looking to download the code files.
6. Choose from the drop-down menu where you purchased this book from.
7. Click on **Code Download**.

Once the file is downloaded, please make sure that you unzip or extract the folder using the latest version of:

- WinRAR / 7-Zip for Windows
- Zipeg / iZip / UnRarX for Mac
- 7-Zip / PeaZip for Linux

The code bundle for the book is also hosted on GitHub at `https://github.com/PacktPubl ishing/Beginning-Cpp-Game-Programming`. We also have other code bundles from our rich catalog of books and videos available at `https://github.com/PacktPublishing/`. Check them out!

Downloading the color images of this book

We also provide you with a PDF file that has color images of the screenshots/diagrams used in this book. The color images will help you better understand the changes in the output. You can download this file from `http://www.packtpub.com/sites/default/files/downl oads/BeginningCppGameProgramming_ColorImages.pdf`.

Errata

Although we have taken every care to ensure the accuracy of our content, mistakes do happen. If you find a mistake in one of our books-maybe a mistake in the text or the code-we would be grateful if you could report this to us. By doing so, you can save other readers from frustration and help us improve subsequent versions of this book. If you find any errata, please report them by visiting `http://www.packtpub.com/submit-errata`, selecting your book, clicking on the **Errata Submission Form** link, and entering the details of your errata. Once your errata are verified, your submission will be accepted and the errata will be uploaded to our website or added to any list of existing errata under the Errata section of that title.

To view the previously submitted errata, go to `https://www.packtpub.com/books/conten t/support` and enter the name of the book in the search field. The required information will appear under the **Errata** section.

Piracy

Piracy of copyrighted material on the Internet is an ongoing problem across all media. At Packt, we take the protection of our copyright and licenses very seriously. If you come across any illegal copies of our works in any form on the Internet, please provide us with the location address or website name immediately so that we can pursue a remedy.

Please contact us at `copyright@packtpub.com` with a link to the suspected pirated material.

We appreciate your help in protecting our authors and our ability to bring you valuable content.

Questions

If you have a problem with any aspect of this book, you can contact us at questions@packtpub.com, and we will do our best to address the problem.

1

C++, SFML, Visual Studio, and Starting the First Game

Welcome to Beginning C++ Game Programming. I will waste no time in getting you started on your journey to writing great games for the PC, using C++ and **OpenGL–powered SFML**.

This is quite a hefty first chapter, but we will learn absolutely everything we need to, in order to have the first part of our first game up-and-running. Here is what we will cover in this chapter:

- Find out about the games we will build
- Learn a bit about C++
- Explore SFML and its relationship with C++
- Look at the Visual Studio software, which we will use throughout the book
- Set up a game development environment
- Create a reusable project template, which will save a lot of time
- Plan and prepare for the first game project, Timber!!!
- Write the first C++ code of the book and make a runnable game that draws a background

The games

We will learn the fundamentals of the super-fast C++ language, a step at a time, and then put the new knowledge to use, so it should be fairly easy to add cool features to the three games we are building.

If you get stuck with any of the content in this chapter, take a look at the sections near the end Handling errors and FAQs.

These are our three projects for the book:

Timber!!!

The first game is an addictive, fast-paced clone of the hugely successful Timberman, which can be found at http://store.steampowered.com/app/398710/. Our game, Timber!!!, will introduce us to all the C++ basics at the same time as building a genuinely playable game. Here is what our version of the game will look like when we are done and we have added a few last-minute enhancements.

Zombie Arena

Next, we will build a frantic, zombie survival shooter, not unlike the Steam hit, Over 9000 Zombies, which can be found at `http://store.steampowered.com/app/273500/`. The player will have a machine gun, and must fight off ever-growing waves of zombies. All this will take place in a randomly generated, scrolling world. To achieve this we will learn about object-oriented programming and how it enables us to have a large code base (lots of code) that is easy to write and maintain. Expect exciting features such as hundreds of enemies, rapid-fire weaponry, pick-ups, and a character that can be "leveled-up" after each wave.

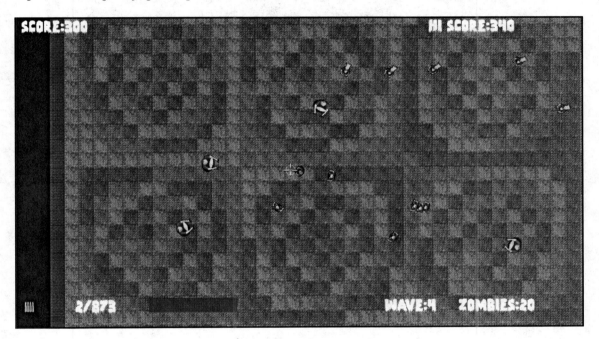

Thomas was Late

The third game will be a stylish and challenging puzzle platformer, which can be played as a single player and coop. It is based on the very popular game, Thomas was Alone, which can be found at `http://store.steampowered.com/app/220780/`. Expect to learn about cool topics such as particle effects, OpenGL Shaders, and split-screen cooperative multiplayer features.

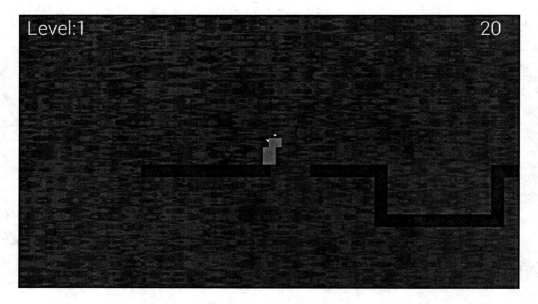

 If you want to play any of the games now, you can do so from the download bundle in the `Runnable Games` folder. Just double-click on the appropriate `.exe` file. Notice that in this folder you can either run the completed games or any game in its partially completed state from any chapter.

Let's get started by introducing C++, Visual Studio, and SFML!

Meet C++

One question you might have is, why use C++ at all? C++ is fast, very fast. What makes this the case is the fact that the code that we write is directly translated into machine executable instructions. These instructions make the game. The executable game is contained within an .exe file that the player can simply double-click to run.

There are a few steps in the process. First, the **pre-processor** looks to see if any other code needs to be included within our own code and adds it when necessary. Next, all the code is compiled into **object files** by the compiler program. Finally, a third program, called the **linker**, joins all the object files into the executable file, which is our game.

In addition, C++ is well established at the same time as being extremely up-to-date. C++ is an **object oriented programming (OOP)** language, which means we can write and organize our code in a proven way that makes our games efficient and manageable. The benefits, as well as the necessity for this, will reveal themselves as we progress through the book.

Most of the other code to which I referred is SFML, and we will find out more about SFML in just a minute. The pre-processor, compiler, and linker programs I have just mentioned, are all part of the Visual Studio **Integrated Development Environment(IDE)**.

Microsoft Visual Studio

Visual Studio hides away the complexity of the pre-processing, compiling, and linking. It wraps it all up into one press of a button. In addition to this, it provides a slick user interface for us to type our code and manage what will become a large selection of code files, and other project assets as well.

While there are advanced versions of Visual Studio that cost hundreds of dollars, we will be able to build all three of our games in the free **Express 2015 for Desktop** version.

SFML

Simple Fast Media Library (SFML) is not the only C++ library for games and multimedia. It is possible to make an argument for using other libraries, but SFML seems to be the best for me, every time. First it is written using object oriented C++. The benefits of this are numerous. Most of these benefits you will experience as you progress through the book.

SFML is so easy to get started and is therefore a good choice if you are a beginner. At the same time, it also has the potential to build the highest-quality 2D games if you are a professional. So a beginner can get started using SFML and not worry about having to start again with a new language/library as their experience grows.

Perhaps the biggest benefit is that most modern C++ programming uses OOP. Every C++ beginners guide I have ever read uses and teaches OOP. OOP is, in fact, the future (and the now) of coding in almost all languages. So why, if you're learning C++ from the beginning, would you want to do it any other way?

SFML has a module (code) for just about anything you would ever want to do in a 2D game. SFML works using OpenGL, which can also make 3D games. OpenGL is the de-facto free-to-use graphics library for games when you want them to run on more than one platform. When you use SFML, you are automatically using OpenGL.

SFML drastically simplifies:

- 2D graphics and animation including scrolling game worlds.
- Sound effects and music playback, including high-quality directional sound.
- Online multiplayer features
- The same code can be compiled and linked on all major desktop operating systems, and soon mobile, as well!

Extensive research has not uncovered any more suitable way to build 2D games for PC, even for expert developers, and especially if you are a beginner and want to learn C++ in a fun gaming environment.

Setting up the development environment

Now you know a bit more about how we will be making these games, it is time to set up a development environment so we can get coding.

What about Mac and Linux?

The games that we make can be built to run on Windows, Mac and Linux! The code we use will be identical for each. However, each version does need to be compiled and linked on the platform for which it is intended and Visual Studio will not be able to help us with Mac and Linux.

It would be unfair to say that this book is entirely suited for Mac and Linux users, especially complete beginners. Although, I guess, if you are an enthusiastic Mac or Linux user, and you are comfortable with your operating system, the vast majority of the extra challenges you will encounter will be in the initial setup of the development environment, SFML, and the first project.

To this end, I can highly recommend the following tutorials which will hopefully replace the next 10 pages (approximately), up to the section *Planning Timber!!!*, when this book should again become relevant to all operating systems.

For Linux, read this for an overview: `http://www.sfml-dev.org/tutorials/2.0/start-linux.php`.

For Linux, read this for step-by-step guidance: `http://en.sfml-dev.org/forums/index.php?topic=9808.0`.

On Mac, read this tutorial as well as the linked out articles: `http://www.edparrish.net/common/sfml-.osx.html`.

Installing Visual Studio Express 2015 on your desktop

Installing Visual Studio can be almost as simple as downloading a file and clicking a few buttons. It will help us, however, if we carefully run through exactly how we do this. For this reason, I will walk through the installation process a step at a time.

The Microsoft Visual Studio site says that you need 5 GB of hard disk space. From experience, however, I would suggest you need at least 10 GB of free space. In addition, these figures are slightly ambiguous. If you are planning to install it on a secondary hard drive, you will still need at least 5 GB on the primary hard drive because no matter where you choose to install Visual Studio, it will need this space too.

 To summarize this ambiguous situation: It is essential to have a full 10 GB space on the primary hard disk, if you intend to install Visual Studio to that primary hard disk. On the other hand, make sure you have 5 GB on the primary hard disk as well as 10 GB on the secondary, if you intend to install to a secondary hard disk. Yep, stupid, I know!

1. The first thing you need is a Microsoft account and the login details. If you have a Hotmail or MSN email address then you already have one. If not, you can sign up for a free one here: `https://login.live.com/`.

2. Visit this link: `https://www.visualstudio.com/en-us/downloads/download-vi sual-studio-vs.aspx`. Click on **Visual Studio 2015**, then **Express 2015 for desktop** then the **Downloads** button. The next screenshot shows the three places to click:

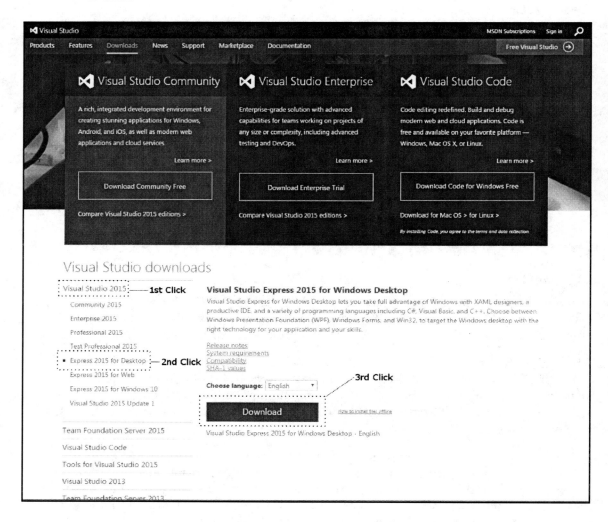

3. Wait for the short download to complete and then run the downloaded file. Now you just need to follow the on-screen instructions. However, make a note of the folder where you choose to install Visual Studio. If you want to do things exactly the same as me, then create a new folder called `Visual Studio 2015` on your preferred hard disk and install to this folder. This whole process could take a while depending on the speed of your Internet connection.

4. When you see the next screen, click on **Launch** and enter your Microsoft account login details.

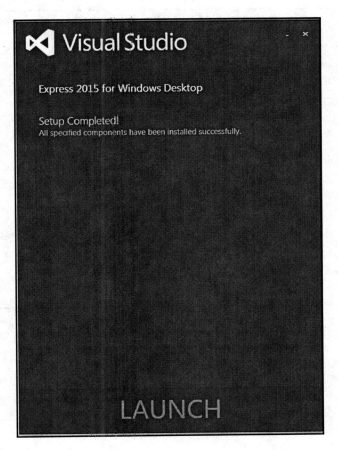

Now we can turn to SFML.

Setting up SFML

This short tutorial will take you through downloading the SFML files that allow us to include the functionality contained in the library. In addition, we will see how to use the SFML DLL files that will enable our compiled object code to run alongside SFML:

1. Visit this link on the SFML website: `http://www.sfml-dev.org/download.php`. Click on the button that says **Latest stable version** as shown next.

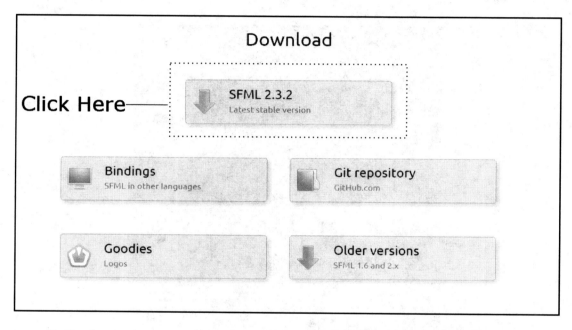

2. By the time you read this guide, the latest version will almost certainly have changed. That doesn't matter as long as you do the next step correctly. We want to download the 32-bit version for **Visual C++ 2014**. This might sound counter-intuitive because we have just installed Visual Studio 2015 and you probably (most commonly) have a 64-bit PC. The reason we choose this download is because Visual C++ 2014 is part of Visual Studio 2015 (Visual Studio offers more than just C++) and we will be building games in 32-bit so that they run on both 32- and 64- bit machines. To be clear, click the following download:

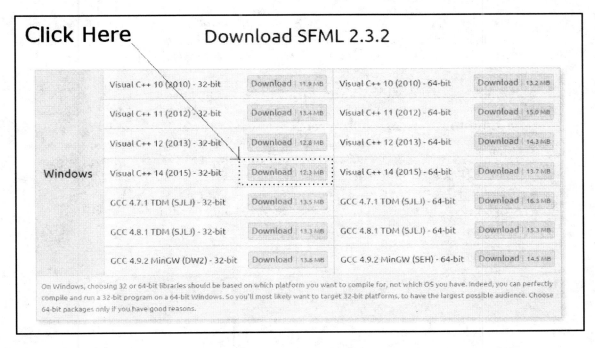

3. When the download completes, create a folder at the root of the same drive where you installed Visual Studio and name it SFML. Also create another folder at the root of the drive where you installed Visual Studio and call it `Visual Studio Stuff`. We will store all kinds of Visual Studio-related things here so `Visual Studio Stuff` seems like a good name. Just to be clear, here is what my hard drive looks like after this step:

4. Obviously, the folders you have in between the highlighted three folders in the screenshot will probably be totally different to mine. Now we are ready for all the projects we will soon be making, create a new folder inside `Visual Studio Stuff`. Name the new folder `Projects`.

5. Finally, unzip the SFML download. Do this on your desktop. When unzipping is complete you can delete the `zip` folder. You will be left with a single folder on your desktop. Its name will reflect the version of SFML that you downloaded. Mine is called `SFML-2.3.2-windows-vc14-32-bit`. Your file name will likely reflect a more recent version. Double-click this folder to see the contents, then double-click again into the next folder (mine is called `SFML-2.3.2`). The following screenshot shows what my `SFML-2.3.2` folder's contents looks like, when the entire contents have been selected. Yours should look the same.

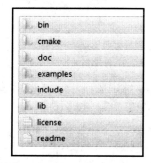

6. Copy the entire contents of this folder, as seen in the previous screenshot, and paste/drag all the contents into the `SFML` folder you created in Step 3. For the rest of the book I will refer to this folder simply as your SFML folder.

Now we are ready to start using C++ and SFML in Visual Studio.

Creating a reusable project template

As setting up a project is a fairly fiddly process, we will create a project and then save it as a Visual Studio template. This will save us quite a significant amount of work each time we start a new game. So, if you find the next tutorial a little tedious, rest assured that you will never need to do this again:

1. Start Visual Studio and, in the **New Project** window, click the little drop-down arrow next to **Visual C++** to reveal more options, then click **Win32,** and click **Win32 Console Application**. You can see all these selections in the next screenshot.

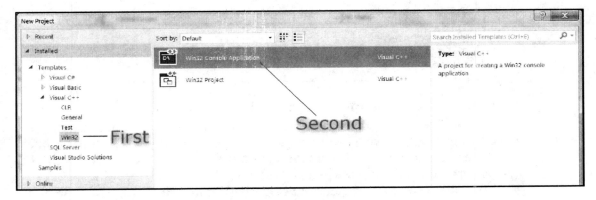

2. Now, at the bottom of the **New Project** window, type HelloSFML in the **Name:** field.

3. Next, browse to the Visual Studio Stuff\Projects\ folder that we created in the previous tutorial. This will be the location where all our project files will be kept. All templates are based on an actual project. So, we will have a project called HelloSFML but the only thing we will do with it is make a template from it.

4. When you have completed the steps above, click **OK**. The next screenshot shows the **Application Settings** window. Check the box for **Console application**, and leave the other options as shown below.

Application type:
  ◯ Windows application
  ◉ Console application
  ◯ DLL
  ◯ Static library

Additional options:
  ☐ Empty project
  ☐ Export symbols
  ☑ Precompiled header
  ☑ Security Development Lifecycle (SDL) checks

Add common header files for:
  ☐ ATL
  ☐ MFC

5. Click **Finish** and Visual Studio will create the new project.

6. Next, we will add some fairly intricate and important project settings. This is the laborious part but, as we will create a template, we will only need to do this once. What we need to do is tell Visual Studio, or more specifically the code compiler that is part of Visual Studio, where to find a special type of code file from SFML. The special type of file I am referring to is a header file. Header files are the files that define the format of the SFML code. So when we use the SFML code, the compiler knows how to handle it. Note that the header files are distinct from the main source code files and they are contained in files with the .hpp file extension. (All this will become clearer when we eventually start adding our own header files in the second project). In addition, we need to tell Visual Studio where it can find the SFML library files. From the Visual Studio main menu select **Project | HelloSFML properties**.

7. In the resulting **HelloSFML Property Pages** window, perform the following steps, flagged in the next screenshot.

8. Select **All Configurations** from the **Configuration:** drop-down.

9. Select **C/C++** then **General** from the left-hand menu.

10. Locate the **Additional Include Directories** edit box and type the drive letter where your SFML folder is located, followed by \SFML\include. The full path to type, if you located your SFML folder on your D drive, is as shown in the screenshot: D:\SFML\include. Vary your path if you installed SFML to a different drive.

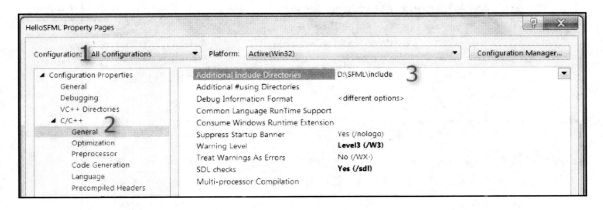

11. Click **Apply** to save your configurations so far.
12. Now, still in the same window, perform these next steps, again flagged in the next screenshot. Select **Linker** then **General**.
13. Find the **Additional Library Directories** edit box and type the drive letter where your SFML folder is, followed by \SFML\lib. So the full path to type if you located your SFML folder on your D drive is, as shown in the screenshot, D:\SFML\lib. Vary your path if you installed SFML to a different drive.

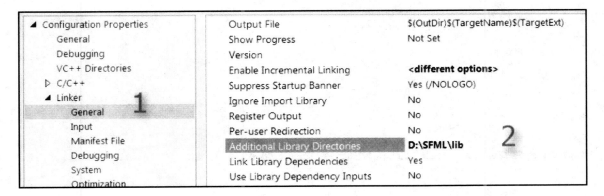

14. Click **Apply** to save your configurations so far.
15. Finally for this stage, still in the same window, perform these steps, which again refer to the next screenshot. Switch the **Configuration:** drop-down(1) to **Debug** as we will be running and testing our games in Debug mode.
16. Select **Linker** then **Input** (2).
17. Find the **Additional Dependencies** edit box (3) and click into it on the far left-hand side. Now copy and paste/type the following: `sfml-graphics-d.lib;sfml-window-d.lib;sfml-system-d.lib;sfml-network-d.lib;sfml-audio-d.lib;` at the indicated place. Again, be really careful to place the cursor precisely, and dont overwrite any of the text that is already there.
18. Click **OK**.

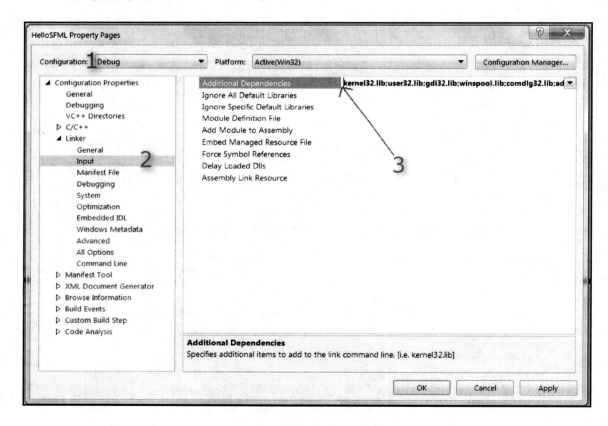

19. Let's make a template from our `HelloSFML` project so we never have to do this slightly mind-numbing task again. Creating a reusable project template is really easy. In Visual Studio select **File | Export Template...**. Then, in the **Export Template Wizard** window, make sure the **Project template** option is selected, and then select **HelloSFML** project for the **From which project do you want to create a template** option.

20. Click **Next** and then **Finish**.

Phew, that's it! Next time we create a project, I'll show you how to do it from this template. Now let's build Timber!!!

Planning Timber!!!

Whenever you make a game it is always best to start with a pencil and paper. If you don't know exactly how your game is going to work on the screen, how can you possibly make it work in code?

At this point, if you haven't already, I suggest you go and watch a video of Timberman in action, so you can see what we are aiming for. If you feel your budget can stretch to it, then grab a copy and give it a play. It is often on sale for under a dollar on Steam. `http://store.steampowered.com/app/398710/`.

The features and objects of a game, which define the gameplay, are known as the **mechanics**. The basic mechanics of the game are:

- Time is always running out.
- Get more time by chopping the tree.
- Chopping the tree causes the branches to fall.
- The player must avoid the falling branches.
- Repeat until the time runs out or the player is squished.

Expecting you to plan the C++ code at this stage is obviously a bit silly. This is, of course, the first chapter of a C++ beginner's guide. We can, however, take a look at all the assets we will use and an overview of what we will need to make our C++ do what we want it to.

Take a look at a annotated screenshot of the game:

You can see that we have the following features:

- **Player's current score:** Each time the player chops a log he will get one point. He can chop a log with either the left or the right arrow.
- **Player Character:** Each time the player chops, he will move/stay on the same side of the tree. Therefore the player must be careful which side he chooses to chop on. When the player chops, a simple ax graphic will appear in the player character's hands.
- **Shrinking time-bar:** Each time the player chops, a small amount of time will be added to the ever-shrinking time bar.
- **Lethal branches:** The faster the player chops, the more time he will get, but also the faster the branches will move down the tree, and therefore the more likely he is to get squished. The branches spawn randomly at the top of the tree and move down with each chop.
- When the player gets squished, which he will quite regularly, a gravestone graphic will appear.
- **Chopped log:** When the player chops, a chopped log graphic will whiz off away

from the player.
- There are three floating clouds that will drift at random heights and speeds as well as a bee that does nothing but fly around.
- All this takes place on a pretty background.

So, in nutshell the player must frantically chop to gain points and avoid running out of time. As a slightly perverse but fun consequence, the faster he chops, the more likely his squishy demise.

We now know what the game looks like, how it is played, and the motivation behind the game mechanics. We can go ahead and start to build it.

Creating a project from the template

Creating a new project is now extremely easy. Just follow these straightforward steps in Visual Studio:

1. Select **File | New Project** from the main menu.
2. Make sure that **Visual C++** is selected in the left-hand menu and then select **HelloSFML** from the list of presented options. This next screenshot should make this clear.

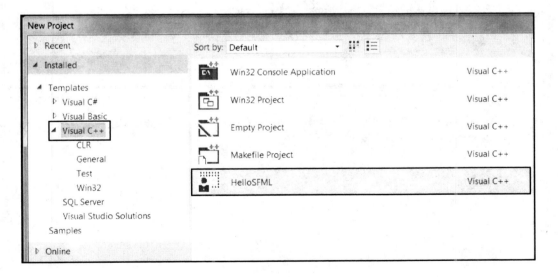

3. In the **Name:** field, type Timber and also make sure that the **Create directory for solution** option is checked. Now click **OK**.

4. Now we need to copy the SFML .dll files into the main project directory. My main project directory is D:\Visual Studio Stuff\Projects\Timber\Timber. It was created by Visual Studio in the previous step. If you put your Projects folder somewhere else, then perform this step there instead. The files we need to copy into the project folder are located in your SFML\bin folder. Open a window for each of the two locations and highlight the required files as shown in the next screenshot on the left.

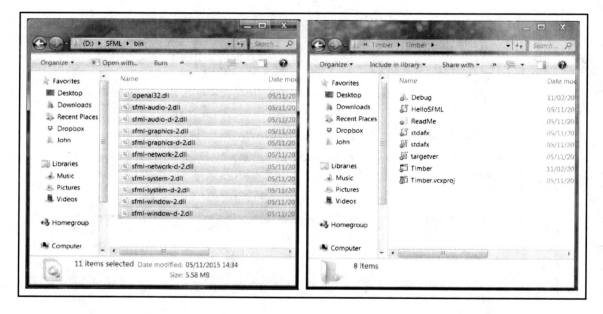

5. Now copy and paste the highlighted files into the project folder on the right of the previous screenshot.

The project is now set up and ready to go. You will be able to see the screen shown in this next screenshot. I have annotated the screenshot so you can start to familiarize yourself with Visual Studio. We will revisit all these areas, and others, soon.

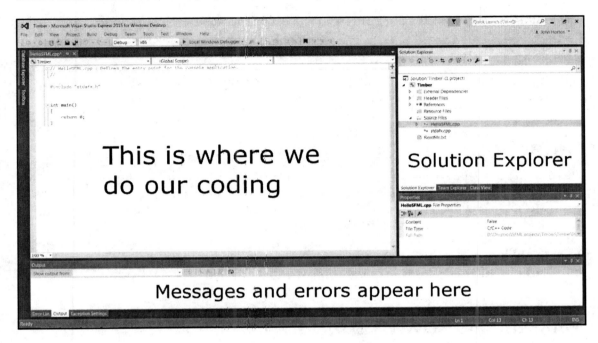

Your layout might look slightly different from the screenshot because the windows of Visual Studio, like most applications, are customizable. Take the time to locate the **Solution Explorer** window on the right and adjust it to make its contents nice and clear, such as they are in the previous screenshot.

We will be back here really soon to start coding.

Project assets

Assets are anything you need to make your game. In our case the assets include:

- A font for the writing on the screen
- Sound effects for different actions such as chopping, dying, and running out of time
- Graphics for the character, background, branches, and other game objects

All the graphics and sound required for the game are included in the download bundle. They can be found in the Chapter 1/graphics and Chapter 1/sound folders as appropriate.

The font that is required has not been supplied. This is because I wanted to avoid any possible ambiguity regarding licensing. This will not cause a problem though, as I will show you exactly where and how to choose and download fonts for yourself.

Although I will provide either the assets themselves or information on where to get them, you might like to create and acquire them for yourself.

Outsourcing assets

There are a number of websites that allow you to contract artists, sound engineers, and even programmers. One of the biggest is the www.upwork.com. You can join this site for free and post your jobs. You need to write a clear explanation of your requirements as well as state how much you are prepared to pay. Then you will probably get a good selection of contractors bidding to do the work. Be aware, there is a lot of unqualified contractors whose work might be disappointing, but if you choose carefully you will likely find a competent, enthusiastic, and great value person or company to do the job.

Making your own sound FX

Sound effects can be downloaded for free from sites like www.freesound.org but often the license won't allow you to use them if you are selling your game. Another option is to use an open source software called BFXR from www.bfxr.net, which can help you generate lots of different sound effects that are yours to keep and do as you like with.

Adding assets to the project

Once you have decided which assets you will use, it is time to add them to the project. These next instructions will assume you are using all the assets supplied in the book's download bundle. Where you are using your own, simply replace the appropriate sound or graphic file with your own, using exactly the same file name.

1. Browse to the Visual D:\Visual Studio Stuff\Projects\Timber\Timber.
2. Create three new folders within this folder and name them as graphics, sound, and fonts.

3. From the download bundle, copy the entire contents of `Chapter 1/graphics` into the `D:\Visual Studio Stuff\Projects\Timber\Timber\graphics` folder.

4. From the download bundle, copy the entire contents of `Chapter 1/sound` into the `D:\Visual Studio Stuff\Projects\Timber\Timber\sound` folder.

5. Now visit: `http://www.1001freefonts.com/komika_poster.font` in your web browser and download the **Komika Poster** font.

6. Extract the contents of the zipped download and add the `KOMIKAP_.ttf` file to the `D:\Visual Studio Stuff\Projects\Timber\Timber\fonts` folder.

Let's take a look at these assets, especially the graphics, so we can better visualize what is happening when we use them in our C++ code.

Exploring assets

Graphical assets form the individual parts of the screen in our Timber!!! game. Take a look at the graphical assets and it should be clear where, in our game, they will be used.

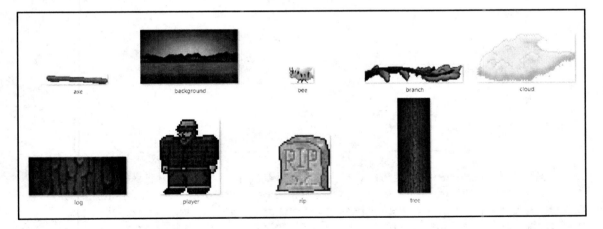

The sound files are all `.wav` format. These are files containing the sound effects that we will play at certain events throughout the game. They were all generated using BFXR. They are:

- `chop.wav`: A sound that is a bit like an ax (a retro ax) chopping a tree
- `death.wav`: A sound a bit like a retro "losing" sound.
- `out_of_time.wav`: Plays when the player loses by running out of time, as opposed to being squashed

Understanding screen and internal coordinates

Before we move on to the actual C++ coding, let's talk a little about coordinates. All the images that we see on our monitors are made out of pixels. Pixels are little tiny dots of light that combine to make the images we see.

There are many different monitor resolutions but, as an example, a fairly typical gamer's monitor might have 1920 pixels horizontally and 1080 pixels vertically.

The pixels are numbered starting at the top left of the screen. As you can see from the next diagram, our 1920 x 1080 example is numbered from 0 through to 1919 on the horizontal (x) axis and 0 through 1079 on the vertical (y) axis.

A specific and exact screen location can therefore be identified by x and y coordinate. We create our games by drawing game objects such as background, characters, bullets and, text, to specific locations on the screen. These locations are identified by the coordinates of the pixels. Take a look at this next hypothetical example of how we might draw at, approximately, the central coordinates of the screen. In the case of a 1920 x 1080 screen this would be at position 960, 540.

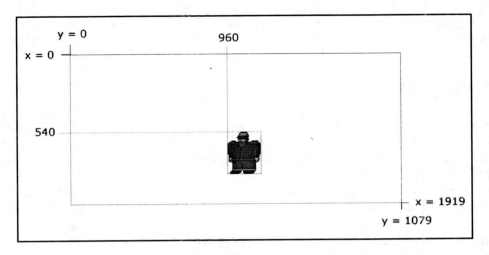

In addition to the screen coordinates, our game objects will each have their own similar coordinate system as well. As with the screen coordinate system, their **internal** or **local** coordinates start at 0,0 in the top left-hand corner.

We can see in the previous screenshot that 0,0 of the character is drawn at 960, 540 of the screen.

A visual, 2D game object, such as a character or perhaps a zombie, is called a **sprite**. A sprite is typically made from an image file. All sprites have what is known as an **origin**.

If we draw a sprite at a specific location on the screen, the origin will be located at this specific location. The 0,0 coordinates of the sprite are the origin. The next screenshot demonstrates this.

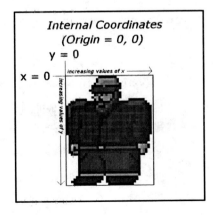

This is why, in the screenshot showing the character drawn to the screen, although we drew the image at the central position (960, 540) it appears off to the right and down a bit.

We just need to bear in mind how this works as we progress through the first project.

Note that, in the real world, gamers have a huge variety of screen resolutions and our games will need to work with as many of them as possible. In the second project we will see how we can make our games dynamically adapt to almost any resolution. In this first project we will need to assume that the screen resolution is 1920 x 1080. Don't worry if your screen is different to this, as I have provided a separate set of code for each chapter, for the Timber!!! game. The code files are nearly identical, apart from adding and swapping a few lines of code near the beginning. If you have a lower-resolution screen, then simply follow the code in the book that assumes a 1920 x 1080 resolution and when it comes to trying out the game you can copy and paste the code files from the `low res` folder in each of Chapters 1 to 5, as appropriate. In fact, once the extra lines have been added in this first chapter, all the rest of the code will be identical regardless of your screen resolution. I have supplied the low-res code for each chapter, just as a convenience. We will discuss how the few lines of code work their magic (scale the screen) in the second project. The alternative code will work on resolutions as low as 960 x 540 so should be good on almost any PC or laptop.

Now we can write our first C++ code, and very soon we will see it in action.

Starting to code the game

Open up Visual Studio if it isn't already, open up the Timber project (if it isn't already open) by left-clicking it from the **Recent** list on the main Visual Studio window.

The first thing we will do is to rename our main code file. It is currently called `HelloSFML.cpp` and we will rename it to the more appropriate `Timber.cpp`. The `.cpp` stands for C plus plus.

1. Find the **Solution Explorer** window on the right-hand side.
2. Locate the `HelloSFML.cpp` file under the **Source Files** folder.
3. Right-click `HelloSFML.cpp` and choose **Rename**.
4. Edit the filename to `Timber.cpp` and press *Enter*.

Make some minor edits in the code window so that you have exactly the same code as shown next. You can do so in exactly the same way that you would with any text editor or word processor; you could even copy and paste it if you prefer. After you have made the slight edits, we can talk about them:

```
// Include important C++ libraries here
#include "stdafx.h"
int main()
{
    return 0;
}
```

This simple C++ program is a good place to start. Let's go through it line by line

Making code clearer with comments

As you can see, the only code that needed to change was a little bit at the very top. The first line of code is this:

```
// Include important C++ libraries here
```

Any line of code that starts with // is a comment and is ignored by the compiler. As such, this line of code does nothing. It is used to leave any information that we might find useful when we come back to the code at a later date. The comment ends at the end of the line, so anything on the next line is not part of the comment. There is another type of comment called a **multi-line** or **c-style** comment, which can be used to leave comments that take up more than a single line. We will see some of them later in this chapter. Throughout this book I will leave hundreds of comments to help add context and further explain the code.

#including Windows essentials

Now that you know what comments are for, you can probably take a decent guess at what the next line of code does. Here it is again:

```
#include "stdafx.h"
```

The #include directive tells Visual Studio to include, or add the contents of another file before compiling. The effect of this is that some other code, that we have not written ourselves, will be a part of our program when we run it. The process of adding code from other files into our code is called **pre-processing** and, perhaps unsurprisingly, is performed by something called a **pre-processor**. The file extension .h stands for header file.

You might be wondering what this code will do? The stdafx.h file actually contains more #include directives itself. It adds into our program, all the necessary code that is required to run our program on Windows. We will never need to see this file and definitely don't need to concern ourselves with what is in it. We just need to add the line of code at the top of every game that we make.

What is more significant and relevant to us, and the reason it is worth discussing the #include directive, is that we will add many more #include directives at the top of our code files. This is to include code that we will use and take the trouble to understand.

The main files that we will be including are the SFML header files, which give us access to all the cool game coding features. We will also use #include to access the **C++ Standard Library** header files. These header files give us access to core features of the C++ language itself.

That's two lines squared away, so let's move on.

The main function

The next line we see in our code is this:

```
int main()
```

The code int is what is known as a **type**. C++ has many types and they represent different types of data. An int is an **integer** or whole number. Hold that thought and we will come back to it in a minute.

The main() code part is the name of the section of code that follows. This section of code is marked out between the opening curly brace { and the next closing curly brace }.

So, everything in between these curly braces { . . . } is a part of main. We call a section of code like this, a **function**.

Every C++ program has a `main` function and it is the place where the execution (running) of the entire program will start. As we progress through the book, eventually our games will have many code files. However, there will only ever be one `main` function, and no matter what code we write, our game will always begin execution from the first line of code inside the opening curly brace of the `main` function.

For now, don't worry about the strange brackets that follow the function name `()`. We will discuss them further in `Chapter 4`: *Loops, Arrays, Switch, Enumerations, and Functions–Implementing Game Mechanics*, where we will get to see functions in a whole new and more interesting light.

Let's look closely at the one single line of code within our `Main` function.

Presentation and syntax

Take a look at the entirety of our `Main` function again:

```
int main()
{
    return 0;
}
```

We can see that inside `Main` there is just one single line of code, `return 0;`. Before we move on to find out what this line of code does, let's look at how it is presented. This is useful because it can help us prepare to write code that is easy to read, and distinguish, from other parts of our code.

First notice that `return 0;` is indented to the right by one tab. This clearly marks it out as being internal to the `main` function. As our code grows in length we will see that indenting our code and leaving white space will be essential to maintaining readability.

Next, notice the punctuation on the end of the line. A semicolon `;` tells the compiler that it is the end of the instruction and whatever follows it is a new instruction. We call an instruction terminated by a semicolon, a `statement`.

Note that the compiler doesn't care whether you leave a new line or even a space between the semicolon and the next statement. However, not starting a new line for each statement will lead to desperately hard-to-read code, and missing the semicolon altogether will result in a syntax error so that the game will not compile or run.

A section of code together, often denoted by its indentation with the rest of the section, is called a **block**.

Now that you are comfortable with the idea of the `main` function, indenting your code to keep it tidy and putting a semicolon on the end of each statement, we can move on to find out exactly what the `return 0;` statement actually does.

Returning values from a function

Actually, `return 0;` does almost nothing in the context of our game. The concept, however, is an important one. When we use the `return` keyword, either on its own or followed by a value, it is an instruction for the program execution to jump/move back to the code that got the function started in the first place.

Often this code that got the function started will be yet another function somewhere else in our code. In this case, however, it is the operating system that started the `main` function. So, when the line `return 0;` is executed, the `main` function exits and the entire program ends.

As we have a 0 after the `return` keyword, that value is also sent to the operating system. We could change the value of zero to something else and that value would be sent back instead.

We say that the code that starts a function, **calls** the function, and that the function **returns** the value.

You don't need to fully grasp all this function information just yet. It is just useful to introduce it here. There's one last thing on functions before we move on. Remember the `int` from `int Main()`? That tells the compiler that the type of value returned from `Main` must be an `int` (integer/whole number). We can return any value that qualifies as an `int`. Perhaps 0, 1, 999, 6358, and so on. If we try and return something that isn't an int, perhaps 12.76, then the code won't compile and the game won't run.

Functions can return a big selection of different types, including types that we invent for ourselves! That kind of type, however, must be made known to the compiler in the way we have just seen.

This little bit of background information on functions will make things smoother as we progress.

Running the game

You can actually run the game at this point. Do so by clicking **the Local Windows Debugger** button in the quick-launch bar of Visual Studio, or you can use the F5 shortcut key.

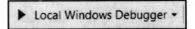

You will just get a flash of a black screen. This flash is the C++ console, which we can use for debugging our game. We don't need to do this for now. What is happening is that our program is starting, executing from the first line of Main, which of course is return 0; and then immediately exiting back to the operating system.

Opening a window using SFML

Now let's add some more code. The code that follows will open a window that Timber!!! will eventually run in. The window will be 1920 pixels wide by 1080 pixels high and will be full-screen (no border or title).

Enter the new code that is highlighted below amongst the existing code and then we will examine it. As you type (or copy and paste) try and work out what is going on:

```
// Include important C++ libraries here
#include "stdafx.h"
#include <SFML/Graphics.hpp>

// Make code easier to type with "using namespace"

using namespace sf;
int main()
{
    // Create a video mode object
    VideoMode vm(1920, 1080);
    // Create and open a window for the game RenderWindow
    window(vm, "Timber!!!", Style::Fullscreen);
    return 0;
}
```

#including SFML features

The first thing we notice in our new code is another, albeit slightly different, #include directive. #include <SFML/Graphics.hpp> tells the pre-processor to include the contents of the file Graphics.hpp contained within the folder named SFML which we created while setting up the project.

So what this line achieves is that it adds code from the aforementioned file, which gives us access to some of the features of SFML. Exactly how it achieves this will become clearer when we start writing our own separate code files and using #include to use them.

 If you are wondering about the difference between pre-processor directives where the file name is contained like this <filename.hpp> and "filename.h", <...> is for files contained within our folder structure, such as the SFML files or anything we code ourselves. The "..." is for files included with Visual Studio. Also the .hpp file extension is just a more C++-oriented version of a .h file, which is more of a C-style extension. Both styles and both file extensions end up doing exactly the same thing and will work fine in our games.

What matters, for now, is that we have a whole bunch of new functionality provided by SFML, available for use.The next new line is using namespace sf;. We will come back to what this line does in a few paragraphs-time.

OOP, classes, objects

We will more fully discuss OOP, classes, and objects as we proceed through the book. What follows is the briefest introduction, so we can understand what is happening.

We already know that OOP stands for object-oriented programming. OOP is a programming paradigm, a way of coding. OOP is generally accepted throughout the world of programming, in almost every language, as the best, if not the only, professional way to write code.

OOP introduces a lot of coding concepts, but fundamental to them all are **classes** and **objects**. When we write code, whenever possible we want to write code that is reusable. The way we do this is to structure our code as a class. We will learn how to do this in Chapter 6: *Object-Oriented Programming, Classes and SFML Views*.

All we need to know about classes, for now, is that once we have coded our class, we don't just execute that code as part of our game instead we create usable objects from the class.

For example, if we wanted a hundred zombie **Non-Player Characters (NPCs)** we could carefully design and code a class called `Zombie` and then, from that single class, create as many zombie objects as we like. Each and every zombie object would have the same functionality and internal data types, but each and every zombie object would be a separate and distinct entity.

To take the hypothetical zombie example further, but without showing any code for the `Zombie` class, we might create a new object based on the `Zombie` class like this:

```
Zombie z1;
```

The object, `z1`, is now a fully coded and functioning `Zombie` object. We could then do this:

```
Zombie z2;
Zombie z3;
Zombie z4;
Zombie z5;
```

We now have five separate zombies, but they are all based on one carefully coded class. Let's take things one step further before we get back to the code we have just written. Our zombies can contain both behaviors (defined by functions), as well as data that might represent things such as the zombie's health, speed, location, or direction of travel. As an example, we could code our `Zombie` class to enable us to use our zombie objects, perhaps like this:

```
z1.attack(player);
z2.growl();
z3.headExplode();
```

 Note again that all this zombie-code is hypothetical for the moment. Don't type this code in to Visual Studio; it will just produce a bunch of errors.

We will design our class to enable us to use the data and behaviors in the most appropriate manner to suit our game's objectives. For example, we could design our class so that we can assign values for the data for each zombie object at the time we create it.

Perhaps we need to assign a unique name and speed in meters per second, at the time we create each zombie. Careful coding of the `Zombie` class could enable us to write code like this:

```
// Dave was a 100 meter Olympic champion before infection
// He moves at 10 meters per second
Zombie z1("Dave", 10);
```

```
// Gill had both of her legs eaten before she was infected
// She drags along at .01 meters per second
Zombie z2("Gill", .01);
```

The point is that classes are almost infinitely flexible, and once we have coded the class, we can go about using them by creating an object from them. It is through classes and the objects that we create from them that we will harness the power of SFML. And yes, we will also write our own classes, including a `Zombie` class.

Let's get back to the real code we just wrote.

Using namespace sf

Before we move on to look more closely at `VideoMode` and `RenderWindow`, which, as you've probably guessed, are classes provided by SFML, we will learn what the `using namespace sf;` line of code does.

When we create a class, we do so in a **namespace**. We do this to distinguish our classes from those that others have written. Consider the `VideoMode` class. It is entirely possible that, in an environment like Windows, somebody has already written a class called `VideoMode`. By using a namespace, we, and the SFML programmers, can make sure that the names of classes never clash.

The full way of using the `VideoMode` class is like this:

```
sf::VideoMode...
```

The code `using namespace sf;` enables us to omit the prefix `sf::` from everywhere in our code. Without it, there would be over 100 instances of `sf::` in this simple game alone. It also makes our code more readable as well as shorter.

SFML VideoMode and RenderWindow

Inside the `Main` function we now have two new comments and two new lines of actual code. The first line of actual code is this:

```
VideoMode vm(1920, 1080);
```

This code creates an object called `vm` from the class called `VideoMode` and sets up two internal values of `1920` and `1080`. These values represent the resolution of the player's screen.

The next new line of code is this:

```
RenderWindow window(vm, "Timber!!!", Style::Fullscreen);
```

In the previous line of code, we were creating a new object called `window` from the SFML provided class called `RenderWindow`. Furthermore, we were setting up some values inside our window object.

Firstly, the `vm` object is used in order to initialize part of the `window`. At first this might seem confusing. Remember, however, that a class can be as varied and flexible as its creator wants to make it. And yes, some classes can contain other classes.

It is not necessary to fully understand how this works at this point, just as long as you appreciate the concept. We code a class and then make usable objects from that class. A bit like an architect might draw a blueprint. You certainly can't move all your furniture, kids, and dog into the blueprint; but you could build a house (or many houses) from the blueprint. In this analogy, a class is like the blueprint and an object is like a house.

Next we use the value Timber!!! to give the window a name. And we use the predefined value `Style::FullScreen` to make our `window` object full screen.

`Style::FullScreen` is a value defined in SFML. It is useful so that we don't need to remember the integer number that the internal code uses to represent a full screen. The coding term for this type of value is a `constant`. Constants and their close C++ relatives, **variables**, are covered in the next chapter.

Let's see our window object in action.

Running the game

You can run the game again at this point. You will see a bigger black screen flash on then disappear. This is the 1920 x 1080 full-screen window that we just coded. Unfortunately, what is still happening is that our program is starting, executing from the first line of `Main`, creating the cool new game window, then coming to `return 0;`, and immediately exiting back to the operating system.

The main game loop

We need a way to stay in the program until the player wants to quit. At the same time, we should clearly mark out where the different parts of our code will go as we progress with Timber!!!. Furthermore, if we are going to stop our game from exiting, we had better provide a way for the player to exit when they are ready. Otherwise the game will go on forever!

Add the highlighted code, inside the existing code, and then we will go through and discuss it all:

```cpp
int main()
{
    // Create a video mode object
    VideoMode vm(1920, 1080);

    // Create and open a window for the game
    RenderWindow window(vm, "Timber!!!", Style::Fullscreen);
    while (window.isOpen())
    {
        /*
        ****************************************
        Handle the players input
        ****************************************
        */
        if (Keyboard::isKeyPressed(Keyboard::Escape))
        {
            window.close();
        }
        /*
        ****************************************
        Update the scene
        ****************************************
        */

        /*
        ****************************************
        Draw the scene
        ****************************************
        */
        // Clear everything from the last frame
        window.clear();

        // Draw our game scene here

        // Show everything we just drew
        window.display();
```

```
    }

    return 0;
}
```

While loops

The very first thing we see in the new code is this:

```
while (window.isOpen())
{
```

The very last thing we see in the new code is a closing }. We have created a `while` loop. Everything between the opening { and closing } of the `while` loop will continue to execute, over and over, potentially forever.

Look closely between the parentheses (...) of the `while` loop as shown highlighted in the next code:

```
while (window.isOpen())
```

The full explanation of this code will have to wait until we discuss loops and conditions in `Chapter 4`: *Loops, Arrays, Switch, Enumerations, and Functions–Implementing Game Mechanics*. What is important for now is that, when the `window` object is set to closed, the execution of the code will break out of the `while` loop and onto the next statement. Exactly how a window is closed will be covered soon.

The next statement is of course `return 0;`, which ends our game.

We now know that our `while` loop will whiz round and round, repeatedly executing the code within it, until our window object is set to closed.

C-style code comments

Just inside the while loop we see what, at first glance, might look a bit like ASCII art:

```
/*
*****************************************
Handle the player's input
*****************************************
*/
```

ASCII art is a niche but fun way of creating images with computer text. You can read more about it here: `https://en.wikipedia.org/wiki/ASCII_art`.

This previous code is simply another type of comment. This type of comment is known as a C-style comment. The comment begins with `/*` and ends with `*/`. Anything in between is just for information and is not compiled. I have used this slightly elaborate text to make it absolutely clear what we will be doing in this part of the code file. And of course you can now work out that any code that follows will be related to handling the player's input.

Skip over a few lines of code and you will see that we have another C-style comment announcing that, in that part of the code, we will be updating the scene.

Jump to the next C-style comment and it is plain where we will be drawing all the graphics.

Input, update, draw, repeat

Although this first project uses the simplest possible version of a **game loop**, every game will need these phases in the code:

1. Get the player's input (if any).
2. Update the scene based on things such as artificial intelligence, physics, or the player's input.
3. Draw the current scene.
4. Repeat the above at a fast enough rate to create a smooth and animated game world.

Now let's look at the code that actually does something within the game loop.

Detecting a key press

Firstly, within the section labeled `Handle the player's input` we have the following code:

```
if (Keyboard::isKeyPressed(Keyboard::Escape))
{
    window.close();
}
```

This code checks whether the Escape key is currently pressed. If it is, the highlighted code uses the `window` object to close itself. Now, the next time the `while` loop begins, it will see that the `window` object is closed and jump to the code immediately after the closing curly brace } of the `while` loop and the game will exit. We will discuss `if` statements more fully in `Chapter 2`: *Variables, Operators, and Decisions-Animating Sprites*.

Clearing and drawing the scene

At the moment there is no code in the `Update the scene` section, so let's move on to the `Draw the scene` section.

The first thing we do is to rub out the previous frame of animation using the code:

```
window.clear();
```

What we do now is draw each and every object from the game. At the moment, however, we don't have any game objects.

The next line of code is this:

```
window.display();
```

When we draw all the game objects, we are drawing them to a hidden surface ready to be displayed. The code `window.display()` flips from the previously displayed surface to the newly updated (previously hidden) one. This way, the player will never see the drawing process as the surface has all the sprites added to it. It also guarantees that the scene will be complete before it is flipped. This prevents a graphical glitch known as **tearing**. The process is called **double buffering**.

Also, notice that all this drawing and clearing functionality is performed using our `window` object, which was created from the SFML `RenderWindow` class.

Running the game

Run the game and you will get a blank, full-screen window that remains until you press the *Esc* keyboard key.

Drawing the game background

At last we will get to see some real graphics in our game. What we need to do is create a sprite. The first one we will create will be the game background. We can then draw it in between clearing the window and displaying/flipping it.

Preparing the sprite using a texture

The SFML `RenderWindow` class allowed us to create our `window` object to take care of all the functionality that our game's window needs.

We will now explore two more SFML classes, which will take care of drawing sprites to the screen. One of these classes, perhaps unsurprisingly, is called `Sprite`. The other class is called `Texture`. A texture is a graphic stored in memory on the **Graphics Processing Unit (GPU)**.

An object made from the `Sprite` class needs an object made from the `Texture` class in order to display itself as an image. Add the following highlighted code. Try and work out what is going on as well. Then we will go through it one line at a time:

```cpp
int main()
{
    // Create a video mode object
    VideoMode vm(1920, 1080);

    // Create and open a window for the game
    RenderWindow window(vm, "Timber!!!", Style::Fullscreen);

    // Create a texture to hold a graphic on the GPU
    Texture textureBackground;

    // Load a graphic into the texture
    textureBackground.loadFromFile("graphics/background.png");

    // Create a sprite
    Sprite spriteBackground;

    // Attach the texture to the sprite
    spriteBackground.setTexture(textureBackground);

    // Set the spriteBackground to cover the screen
    spriteBackground.setPosition(0, 0);

    while (window.isOpen())
```

```
{
```

First, we create an object called `textureBackground` from the SFML `Texture` class.

```
Texture textureBackground;
```

Once this is done, we can use the `textureBackground` object to load a graphic from our `graphics` folder, into the `textureBackground`, like this:

```
textureBackground.loadFromFile("graphics/background.png");
```

 We only need to specify `graphics/background` as the path is relative to the Visual Studio working directory where we created the folder and added the image.

Next, we create an object called `spriteBackground` from the SFML `Sprite` class with this code:

```
Sprite spriteBackground;
```

Then, we can associate the texture object `textureBackground` with the Sprite object `spriteBackground`, like this:

```
spriteBackground.setTexture(textureBackground);
```

Finally, we can position the `spriteBackground` object in the `window` object at coordinates `0,0`:

```
spriteBackground.setPosition(0,0);
```

As the `background.png` graphic in the `graphics` folder is 1920 pixels wide by 1080 pixels high, it will neatly fill the entire screen. Just note that this previous line of code doesn't actually show the sprite. It just sets its position ready for when it is shown.

The object, `backgroundSprite`, can now be used to display the background graphic. Of course you are almost certainly wondering why we had to do things in such a convoluted way. The reason is because of the way that graphics cards and OpenGL work.

Textures take up graphics memory and this memory is a finite resource. Furthermore, the process of loading a graphic into the GPU's memory is very slow. Not so slow that you can watch it happen, or that you will see your PC noticeably slow down while it is happening, but slow enough that you can't do it every frame of the game loop. So it is useful to dissociate the actual texture `textureBackground` from any code that we will manipulate during the game loop.

As you will see when we start to move our graphics, we will do so using the sprite. Any objects made from the `Texture` class will sit happily on the GPU, just waiting for an associated `Sprite` object to tell them where to show themselves. In later projects we will also reuse the same `Texture` object with multiple different `Sprite` objects, which makes efficient use of GPU memory.

In summary:

- Textures are very slow to load onto the GPU
- Textures are very fast to access once they are on the GPU
- We associate a sprite object with a texture
- We manipulate the position and orientation of sprite objects (usually in the `Update the scene` section)
- We draw the `Sprite` object, which in turn displays the texture that is associated with it (usually in the `Draw the scene` section).

So all we need to do now is use our double-buffering system, provided by our `window` object, to draw our new `Sprite` object (`spriteBackground`), and we should actually get to see our game in action.

Double-buffering the background sprite

Finally we need to draw that sprite, and its associated texture, in the appropriate place in the game loop.

 Note that, when I present code that is all from the same block, I don't add the indenting because it lessens the instances of line wraps in the text of the book. The indenting is implied. Check out the code file in the download bundle to see the full use of indenting.

Add the highlighted code:

```
/*
****************************************
Draw the scene
****************************************
*/
// Clear everything from the last run frame
window.clear();

// Draw our game scene here
window.draw(spriteBackground);
```

```
// Show everything we just drew
window.display();
```

The new line of code simply uses the `window` object to draw the `spriteBackground` object, in between clearing the display and showing the newly drawn scene.

Running the game

Run the program now and you will see the first signs that we have a real game in progress.

It's not going to get **Greenlit** on Steam in its current state, but we are on our way at least!

Let's take a look at some of the things that might go wrong in this chapter, and as we proceed through the book.

Handling errors

There will always be problems and errors in every project you make, that is guaranteed! The tougher a problem is, the more satisfying it is when you solve it. When, after hours of struggling, a new game feature finally bursts into life, it can cause a genuine high. Without the struggle, it would somehow be less worthwhile.

At some point in this book there will probably be some struggle. Remain calm, be confident that you will overcome it, and then set to work.

Remember that, whatever your problem, it is very unlikely you are the first person in the world to have ever had this same problem. Think of a concise sentence that describes your problem or error and then type it in to Google. You will be surprised how quickly, precisely, and often, someone else will already have solved your problem for you.

Having said that, here are a few pointers (pun intended; see `Chapter 8`: *Pointers, Standard Template Library, and Texture Management*) to get you started, in the event you are struggling with making this first chapter work.

Configuration errors

The most likely cause of problems in this chapter will be configuration errors. As you probably noticed during the process of setting up Visual Studio, SFML, the project template, and the project itself, there are an awful lot of filenames, folders, and settings that need to be just right. Just one wrong setting could cause one of a number of errors in which the text doesn't make it clear exactly what is wrong.

If you can't get the empty project with the black screen working in the **Creating a reusable template** section, it might be easier to start that section again. Make sure all the filenames and folders are appropriate for your specific setup and then get the simplest part of the code running (the part where the screen flashes black and then closes). If you can get to this stage, then configuration is probably not the issue.

Compile errors

Compile errors are probably the most common error we will experience going forward. Check that your code is identical to mine, especially semicolons on the ends of lines and subtle changes in upper and lower case for class and object names. If all else fails, open the code files in the download bundle and copy and paste it. While it is always possible that a code typo made it into the book, the code files were made from actual working projects – they definitely work!

Link errors

Link errors are most likely caused by missing SFML .dll files. Did you copy all of them into the project folder in the section *Creating a project from the template?*

Bugs

Bugs are what happen when your code works, but not as you expect it to. Debugging can actually be fun. The more bugs you squash the better your game and the more satisfying your day's work will be. The trick to solving bugs is to find them early! To do this I recommend running and playing your game every time you implement something new. The sooner you find the bug, the more likely the cause will be fresh in your mind. In this book we will run the code to see the results at every possible stage.

FAQ

Here are some questions that might be on your mind:

Q) I am struggling with the content presented so far. Am I cut out for programming?

A) Setting up a development environment and getting your head round OOP as a concept is probably the toughest thing you will do in this book. As long as your game is functioning (drawing the background), you are ready to proceed with the next chapter.

Q) All this talk of OOP, classes, and objects is too much and kind of spoiling the whole learning experience.

A) Don't worry. We will keep returning to OOP, classes, and objects constantly. In Chapter 6: *Object-Oriented Programming, Classes, and SFML Views*, we will really begin to get grip with the whole OOP thing. All you need to understand for now is that SFML has written a whole load of useful classes and we get to use this code by creating usable objects from those classes.

Q) I really don't get this function stuff.

A) It doesn't matter, we will return to it again and will learn about functions more thoroughly. You just need to know that, when a function is called, its code is executed, and when it is done (reaches a return statement), then the program jumps back to the code that called it.

Summary

That was quite a challenging chapter. It is true that configuring an IDE to use a C++ library can be a bit awkward and time-consuming. Also, it is well known that the concept of classes and objects is slightly awkward for people who are new to coding.

Now that we are at this stage, however, we can totally focus on C++, SFML, and games. As the chapters progress, we will learn more and more C++, as well as how to implement increasingly interesting game features. As we do so, we will take a further look at things such as functions, classes, and objects, to help demystify them a little more. Next up we will learn all the C++ we need to draw some more sprites and animate them as well.

2
Variables, Operators, and Decisions – Animating Sprites

In this chapter we will do quite a bit more drawing on the screen and to achieve this we will need to learn some of the basics of C++.

Here is what is in store:

- Learning all about C++ variables
- Seeing how to manipulate the values stored in variables
- Adding a static tree, ready for the player to chop
- Drawing and animating a bee and three clouds

C++ variables

Variables are the way that our C++ games store and manipulate values. If we want to know how much health the player has then we need a variable. Perhaps you want to know how many zombies are left in the current wave? That is a variable as well. If you need to remember the name of the player who got a particular high score, you guessed it, we need a variable for that. Is the game over or still playing? Yep, that's a variable too.

Variables are named identifiers to locations in memory. So we might name a variable `numberOfZombies` and that variable could refer to a place in the memory that stores a value representing the number of zombies that are left in the current wave.

The way that computer systems address locations in memory is complex. Programming languages use variables to give a human-friendly way to manage our data in memory.

Our brief discussion about variables implies that there must be different types of variable.

Types of variable

There are a wide variety of C++ variable types (see the next tip about variables). It would easily be possible to spend an entire chapter discussing them. What follows is a table of the most commonly used types in this book. Then we will look at how to actually use each of these variable types.

Type	Examples of values	Explanation
int	`-42, 0, 1, 9826`, and so on.	Integer whole numbers.
float	`-1.26f, 5.8999996f, 10128.3f`	Floating point values with precision up to 7 digits.
double	`925.83920655234, 1859876.94872535`	Floating point values with precision up to 15 digits.
char	a, b, c, 1, 2, 3 (a total of 128 symbols including ?, ~, #, and so on...)	Any symbol from the ASCII table (see next tip about variables).
bool	True or false	Bool stands for Boolean and can be only `true` or `false`.
string	Hello everyone! I am a string.	Any text value from a single letter or digit up to perhaps an entire book.

The compiler must be told what type a variable is, so that it can allocate the right amount of memory for it. It is good practice to use the best and most appropriate type for each and every variable you use. In practice, however, you will often get away with promoting a variable. Perhaps you need a floating-point number with just five significant digits? The compiler won't complain if you store it as a `double`. However, if you try to store a `float` or a `double` in an `int`, it will change/cast the value to fit the `int`. As we progress through the book, I clarify what is the best variable type to use in each case, and we will even see a few instances where we deliberately convert/cast between variable types.

A few extra details worth noticing, in the table above, include the `f` postfix next to all the `float` values. This `f` tells the compiler that the value is a `float` type not a `double`. A floating-point value without the `f` prefix is assumed to be a `double`. See the next tip about variables for more about this.

As mentioned previously, there are many more types. If you want to find out more about types see the next tip about variables.

Constants

Sometimes we need to make sure that a value can never be changed. To achieve this we can declare and initialize a **constant** using the `const` keyword:

```
const float PI = 3.141f;
const int PLANETS_IN_SOLAR_SYSTEM = 8;
const int NUMBER_OF_ENEMIES = 2000;
```

It is conventional to declare constants in all upper case. The value of the preceding constants can never be altered. We will see some constants in action in `Chapter 4`: *Loops, Arrays, Switch, Enumerations, and Functions – Implementing Game Mechanics*.

User-defined types

User-defined types are way more advanced than the types we have just seen. When we talk about user-defined types in C++ we are usually talking about classes. We briefly talked about classes and their related objects in the previous chapter. We can write code in a separate file, sometimes in two separate files. From these we will then be able to declare, initialize, and use them. We will leave how we define/create our own types until `Chapter 6`: *Object-Oriented Programming, Classes, and SFML Views*.

Declaring and initializing variables

So far we know that variables are for storing the data/values that our games need in order to work. For example, a variable could represent the number of lives a player has or the player's name. We also know that there is a wide selection of different types of values that these variables can represent, such as `int`, `float`, `bool`, and so on. Of course what we haven't seen yet is how we would actually go about using a variable.

There are two stages for creating and preparing a new variable. The stages are called **declaration** and **initialization**.

Declaring variables

We can declare variables in C++ like this:

```cpp
// What is the player's score?
int playerScore;

// What is the players first initial
char playerInitial;

// What is the value of pi
float valuePi;

// Is the player alive or dead?
bool isAlive;
```

Initializing variables

Now we have declared the variables with meaningful names, we can initialize those same variables with appropriate values, like this:

```cpp
playerScore = 0;
playerInitial = 'J';
valuePi = 3.141f;
isAlive = true;
```

Declaring and initializing in one step

When it suits us, we can combine the declaration and initialization steps into one:

```cpp
int playerScore = 0;
char playerInitial = 'J';
float valuePi = 3.141f;
bool isAlive = true;
```

Variables tip

As promised, here is the tip on variables. If you want to see a complete list of C++ types then check this web page: http://www.tutorialspoint.com /cplusplus/cpp_data_types.htm. If you want a deeper discussion on floats, doubles, and the f postfix then read this: http://www.cplusplus.c om/forum/beginner/24483/. And if you want to know the ins and out of ASCII character codes then there is some more information here: http://w ww.cplusplus.com/doc/ascii/. Note that these links are for the curious reader and we have already discussed enough in order to proceed.

Declaring and initializing user-defined types

We have already seen examples of how we declare and initialize some SFML defined types. Because the way we can create/define these types (classes) is so flexible, the way we declare and initialize them is also highly varied. Here are a couple of reminders for declaring and initializing user-defined types, from the previous chapter.

Create an object of type `VideoMode`, called `vm`, and initialize it with two `int` values, `1920` and `1080`:

```
// Create a video mode object
VideoMode vm(1920, 1080);
```

Create an object of type `Texture`, called `textureBackground` but don't do any initialization:

```
// Create a texture to hold a graphic on the GPU
Texture textureBackground;
```

Note that it is possible (in fact very likely) that even though we are not suggesting any specific values with which to initialize `textureBackground`, some variables may be set up internally. Whether or not an object needs/has the option of giving initialization values at this point is entirely dependent on how the class is coded and is almost infinitely flexible. This further suggests that when we get to write our own classes there will be some complexity. Fortunately, it also means we will have significant power to design our types/classes, so they are just what we need to make our games! Add this huge flexibility to SFML-designed classes and the potential for our games is almost limitless.

We will see a few more user-created types/classes provided by SFML in this chapter too and loads more throughout the book.

Manipulating variables

At this point we know exactly what variables are, the main types, and how to declare and initialize them, but we still can't do that much with them. We need to manipulate our variables, add them, take them away, multiply, divide, and test them.

First we will deal with how we can manipulate them and later we will look at how and why we test them.

C++ arithmetic and assignment operators

In order to manipulate variables, C++ has a range of **arithmetic operators** and **assignment operators**. Fortunately, most arithmetic and assignment operators are quite intuitive to use, and those that aren't are quite easy to explain. To get us started, let's look at a table of arithmetic operators followed by a table of assignment operators that we will regularly use throughout this book:

Arithmetic operator	Explanation
+	The addition operator can be used to add together the values of two variables or values.
−	The subtraction operator can be used to take away the value of one variable or value from another variable or value.
*	The multiplication operator can multiply the value of variables and values.
/	The division operator can divide the value of variables and values.
%	The modulo operator divides a value or variable by another value or variable to find the remainder of the operation.

And now for the assignment operators:

Assignment operators	Explanation
=	We have already seen this one. It is *the* assignment operator. We use it to initialize/set a variable's value.
+=	Add the value on the right-hand side to the variable on the left.
-=	Take away the value on the right-hand side from the variable on the left.
*=	Multiply by the value on the right-hand side by the variable on the left.
/=	Divide the value on the right-hand side by the variable on the left.
++	**Increment** operator; add 1 to a variable
--	**Decrement** operator; take away 1 from a variable

Technically, all the above operators except for =, -- and ++ are called **compound assignment operators** because they comprise more than one operator.

Now that we have seen a good range of arithmetic and assignment operators we can actually see how to manipulate our variables by combining operators, variables, and values to form **expressions**.

Getting things done with expressions

Expressions are combinations of variables, operators, and values. Using expressions we can arrive at a result. Furthermore, as we will soon see, we can use an expression in a test. These tests can be used to decide what our code should do next. First, let's look at some simple expressions we might see in our game code:

```
// Player gets a new high score
hiScore = score;
```

or

```
// Set the score to 100
score = 100;
```

Take a look at the addition operator, used in conjunction with the assignment operator:

```
// Add to the score when an alien is shot
score = aliensShot + wavesCleared;
```

or

```
// Add 100 to whatever the score currently is
score = score + 100;
```

Notice that it is perfectly acceptable to use the same variable on both sides of an operator.

Take a look at the subtraction operator in conjunction with the assignment operator. This next code subtracts the value on the right side of the subtraction operator from the value on the left. It is usually used in conjunction with the assignment operator, for example:

```
// Uh oh lost a life
lives = lives - 1;
```

or

```
// How many aliens left at end of game
aliensRemaining = aliensTotal - aliensDestroyed;
```

This is how we might use the division operator. This next code divides the number on the left by the number on the right. Again, it is usually used with the assignment operator, like this:

```
// Make the remaining hit points lower based on swordLevel
hitPoints = hitPoints / swordLevel;
```

or

```
// Give player something back for recycling a block
recycledValueOfBlock = originalValue / .9f;
```

Obviously, in the previous example, the variable recycledValueOfBlock will need to be of the type float to accurately store the answer to a calculation like that.

Perhaps unsurprisingly, we could use the multiplication operator like this:

```
// answer is equal to 100 - of course
answer = 10 * 10;
```

or

```
// biggerAnswer = 1000 - of course
biggerAnswer = 10 * 10 * 10;
```

 As an aside, have you ever wondered how C++ got its name? C++ is an extension of the C language. Its inventor, Bjarne Stroustrup, originally called it *C with classes* but the name evolved. If you are interested, read the C++ story at : http://www.cplusplus.com/info/history/.

Now, let's take a look at the increment operator in action. This is a really neat way to add 1 to the value of one of our game's variables.

Take a look at this code:

```
// Add one to myVariable
myVariable = myVariable + 1;
```

It gives the same result as this code:

```
// Much neater and quicker
myVariable ++;
```

The decrement operator -- is, you guessed it, a really neat way to subtract 1 from something:

```
playerHealth = playerHealth -1;
```

It is the same as this:

```
playerHealth --;
```

Let's look at a few more operators in action and then we can get back to building the Timber!!! game:

```
someVariable = 10;

// Multiply the variable by 10 and put the answer back in variable
someVariable *= 10;
// someVariable now equals 100

// Divide someVariable by 5 put the answer back into the variable
someVariable /= 5;
// someVariable now equals 20

// Add 3 to someVariable and put the answer back into the variable
someVariable += 3;
// someVariable now equals 23

// Take 25 from someVariable and put the answer back into the variable
someVariable -= 25;
// someVariable now equals -2
```

Now it's time to add some more sprites to our game.

Adding clouds, a tree, and a buzzing bee

First we will add a tree. This is going to be really easy. The reason it's easy is because the tree doesn't move. We will use exactly the same procedure that we used in the previous chapter when we drew the background.

Preparing the tree

Add the following highlighted code. Notice the un-highlighted code, which is the code that we have already written. This should help you identify that the new code should be typed immediately after we set the position of the background, but before the start of the main game loop. We will recap what is actually going on in the new code after you have added it:

```
int main()
{

    // Create a video mode object
```

```
VideoMode vm(1920, 1080);

// Create and open a window for the game
RenderWindow window(vm, "Timber!!!", Style::Fullscreen);

// Create a texture to hold a graphic on the GPU
Texture textureBackground;

// Load a graphic into the texture
textureBackground.loadFromFile("graphics/background.png");

// Create a sprite
Sprite spriteBackground;

// Attach the texture to the sprite
spriteBackground.setTexture(textureBackground);

// Set the spriteBackground to cover the screen
spriteBackground.setPosition(0, 0);

// Make a tree sprite
Texture textureTree;
textureTree.loadFromFile("graphics/tree.png");
Sprite spriteTree;
spriteTree.setTexture(textureTree);
spriteTree.setPosition(810, 0);

while (window.isOpen())
{
```

The five lines of code (excluding the comment) that we just added do the following:

- First, we create an object of the type `Texture` called `textureTree`.
- Next, we load a graphic into the texture from the `tree.png` graphics file.
- Next, we declare an object of the type `Sprite` called `spriteTree`
- Now, we associate `textureTree` with `spriteTree`. Whenever we draw `spriteTree` it will show the `textureTree` texture, which is a neat tree graphic.
- Finally we set the position of the tree using the coordinates `810` on the x axis and 0 on the y axis.

Let's move on to the bee object, which is handled in an almost identical manner.

Preparing the bee

The difference between this next code and the tree code is small but important. As the bee needs to move, we also declare two bee-related variables. Add the highlighted code in the place shown, and see if you can work out how we might use the variables `beeActive` and `beeSpeed`:

```
// Make a tree sprite
Texture textureTree;
textureTree.loadFromFile("graphics/tree.png");
Sprite spriteTree;
spriteTree.setTexture(textureTree);
spriteTree.setPosition(810, 0);

// Prepare the bee
Texture textureBee;
textureBee.loadFromFile("graphics/bee.png");
Sprite spriteBee;
spriteBee.setTexture(textureBee);
spriteBee.setPosition(0, 800);

// Is the bee currently moving?
bool beeActive = false;

// How fast can the bee fly
float beeSpeed = 0.0f;

while (window.isOpen())
{
```

We create a bee in exactly the same way we created a background and a tree. We use a `Texture` and a `Sprite`, and associate the two. Note that in the previous bee code there was some new code we haven't seen before. There is a `bool` variable for determining whether or not the bee is active. Remember that a `bool` variable can be either `true` or `false`. We initialize `beeActive` to `false`, for now.

Next, we declare a new `float` variable called `beeSpeed`. This will hold the speed, in pixels per second, at which our bee will fly across the screen.

Soon we will see how we use these two new variables to move the bee. Before we do, let's set up some clouds in an almost identical manner.

Preparing the clouds

Add the highlighted code shown next. Study the new code and try and work out what it will do:

```
// Prepare the bee
Texture textureBee;
textureBee.loadFromFile("graphics/bee.png");
Sprite spriteBee;
spriteBee.setTexture(textureBee);
spriteBee.setPosition(0, 800);

// Is the bee currently moving?
bool beeActive = false;

// How fast can the bee fly
float beeSpeed = 0.0f;

// make 3 cloud sprites from 1 texture
Texture textureCloud;

// Load 1 new texture
textureCloud.loadFromFile("graphics/cloud.png");

// 3 New sprites with the same texture
Sprite spriteCloud1;
Sprite spriteCloud2;
Sprite spriteCloud3;
spriteCloud1.setTexture(textureCloud);
spriteCloud2.setTexture(textureCloud);
spriteCloud3.setTexture(textureCloud);

// Position the clouds off screen
spriteCloud1.setPosition(0, 0);
spriteCloud2.setPosition(0, 250);
spriteCloud3.setPosition(0, 500);

// Are the clouds currently on screen?
bool cloud1Active = false;
bool cloud2Active = false;
bool cloud3Active = false;

// How fast is each cloud?
float cloud1Speed = 0.0f;
float cloud2Speed = 0.0f;
float cloud3Speed = 0.0f;

while (window.isOpen())
```

```
{
```

The only thing about the code we have just added that might seem a little odd is that we have only one object of the type `Texture`. It's completely normal for multiple `Sprite` objects to share a texture. Once a `Texture` is stored in the GPU memory it can be associated with a `Sprite` object very quickly. It is only the initial loading of the graphic in the `loadFromFile` code that is a relatively slow operation. Of course, if we wanted three different-shaped clouds then we would need three textures.

Apart from the minor texture issue, the code we have just added is nothing new compared to the bee. The only difference is that there are three cloud sprites, three `bool` variables to determine if each cloud is active and three `float` variables to hold the speed for each cloud.

Drawing the tree, the bee, and the clouds

Finally we can draw them all onto the screen by adding this highlighted code in the drawing section:

```
/*
******************************************
Draw the scene
******************************************
*/

// Clear everything from the last run frame
window.clear();

// Draw our game scene here
window.draw(spriteBackground);

// Draw the clouds
window.draw(spriteCloud1);
window.draw(spriteCloud2);
window.draw(spriteCloud3);

// Draw the tree
window.draw(spriteTree);

// Draw the insect
window.draw(spriteBee);

// Show everything we just drew
window.display();
```

Drawing the three clouds, the bee, and the tree is done in exactly the same way that the background was drawn. Notice, however, the order in which we draw the different objects to the screen. We must draw all the graphics after the background or they will be covered, and we must draw the clouds before the tree or they will look a bit odd drifting in front of the tree. The bee would look OK either in front or behind the tree. I opted to draw the bee in front of the tree so that it can try and distract our lumberjack, a bit like a real bee might.

Run Timber!!! and gaze in awe at the tree, three clouds, and a bee, which don't do anything! They look like they are lining up for a race, where the bee goes backwards.

Using what we know about operators, we could try and move the graphics around that we have just added, but there are a couple of problems. Firstly, real clouds and bees move in a non-uniform manner. They don't have a set speed or location. Although their location and speed are determined by factors such as wind speed or how much of a hurry the bee might be in, to the casual observer the path they take, and their speed, appear random.

Random numbers

Random numbers are useful for lots of reasons in games. Perhaps you could use them for determining what card the player is dealt, or how much damage within a certain range is subtracted from an enemy's health. As hinted at, we will use random numbers to determine the starting location and the speed of the bee and the clouds.

Generating random numbers in C++

To generate random numbers we will need to use some more C++ functions, two more to be precise. Don't add any code to the game yet. Let's just take a look at the syntax and the steps required with some hypothetical code.

Computers can't actually pick random numbers. They can only use algorithms/calculations to pick a number that *appears* to be random. So that this algorithm doesn't constantly return the same value, we must **seed** the random number generator. The seed can be any integer number, although it must be a different seed each time you require a unique random number. Take a look at this code, which seeds the random number generator:

```
// Seed the random number generator with the time
srand((int)time(0));
```

The code above gets the time from the PC using the `time` function like this `time(0)`. The call to the `time` function is enclosed as the value to be sent to the `srand` function. The result of this is that the current time is used as the seed.

The previous code is made to look a little more complicated because of the slightly unusual-looking `(int)` syntax. What this does is convert/cast the value returned from `time` to an `int`. This is required by the `srand` function in this situation.

 A conversion from one type to another is called a **cast**.

So, in summary, this is what happens in the previous line of code:

- It gets the time using `time`
- It converts it to type `int`
- It sends this resulting value to `srand`, which seeds the random number generator

The time is, of course, always changing. This makes the `time` function a great way to seed the random number generator. However, think about what might happen if we seed the random number generator more than once and in such quick succession that `time` returns the same value? We will see and solve this problem when we animate our clouds.

At this stage we can create a random number between a range, and save it to a variable for later use:

```
// Get the random number & save it to a variable called number
int number = (rand() % 100);
```

Notice the odd-looking way we assign a value to number. By using the Modulo operator % and the value of 100, we are asking for the remainder, after dividing the number returned from rand by 100. When you divide by 100, the highest number you can possibly have as a remainder is 99. The lowest number possible is 0. Therefore the previous code will generate a number between 0 and 99 inclusive. This knowledge will be really useful for generating a random speed and starting location for our bees and clouds.

We will do this soon, but we first need to learn how to make decisions in C++.

Making decisions with if and else

The C++ if and else keywords are what enable us to make decisions. Actually, we have already seen if in action in the previous chapter when we detected, in each frame, whether the player had pressed the *Esc* key:

```
if (Keyboard::isKeyPressed(Keyboard::Escape))
{
    window.close();
}
```

So far we have seen how we can use arithmetic and assignment operators to create expressions. Now we can see some new operators.

Logical operators

Logical operators are going to help us make decisions by building expressions that can be tested for a value of either true or false. At first this might seem like quite a narrow choice and insufficient for the kind of choices that might be needed in an advanced PC game. Once we dig a little deeper, we will see that we can actually make all the required decisions we will need, with just a few logical operators.

Here is a table of the most useful logical operators. Take a look at them and their associated examples, and then we will see how to put them to use.

Logical operator	Name and example
==	The **comparison operator** tests for equality and is either true or false. An expression such as (10 == 9), for example, is false. 10 is obviously not equal to 9.
!	This is the logical**NOT** operator. The expression (! (2 + 2 == 5)). This is true because 2 + 2 is NOT 5
!=	This is another comparison operator but is different to the = comparison operator. This tests if something is **NOT equal**. For example, the expression (10 != 9) is true. 10 is not equal to 9.
>	Another comparison operator – actually there are a few more as well. This tests if something is greater than something else. The expression (10 > 9) is true.
<	You guessed it. This tests for values less than. The expression (10 < 9) is false.
>=	This operator tests for whether one value is greater than or equal to the other, and if either is true, the result is true. For example, the expression (10 >= 9) is true. The expression (10 >= 10) is also true.
<=	Like the previous operator, this one tests for two conditions, but this time less than or equal to. The expression (10 <= 9) is false. The expression (10 <= 10) is true.
&&	This operator is known as logical **AND**. It tests two or more separate parts of an expression and both parts must be true in order for the result to be true. Logical AND is usually used in conjunction with the other operators to build more complex tests. The expression ((10 > 9) && (10 < 11)) is true because both parts are true, so the expression is true. The expression ((10 > 9) && (10 < 9)) is false because only one part of the expression is true and the other is false.
||	This operator is called logical **OR**, and it is just like logical AND except that at least one, of two or more parts of an expression, needs to be true for the expression to be true. Let's look at the last example we used above but replace the && with ||. The expression ((10 > 9) || (10 < 9)) is now true because one part of the expression is true.

Let's meet the C++ if and else keywords which will enable us to put all these logical operators to good use.

C++ if and else

Let's make the previous examples less abstract. Meet the C++ if keyword. We will use if and a few operators along with a small story to demonstrate their use. Next follows a made-up military situation that will hopefully be less abstract than the previous examples.

If they come over the bridge, shoot them!

The captain is dying and, knowing that his remaining subordinates are not very experienced, he decides to write a C++ program to convey his last orders for after he has died. The troops must hold one side of a bridge while awaiting reinforcements.

The first command the captain wants to make sure his troops understand is this:

"If they come over the bridge, shoot them!"

So, how do we simulate this situation in C++? We need a bool variable: isComingOverBridge. The next bit of code assumes that the isComingOverBridge variable has been declared and initialized to either true or false.

We can then use if like this:

```
if(isComingOverBridge)
{
    // Shoot them
}
```

If the isComingOverBridge variable is equal to true, the code inside the opening and closing curly braces { ... } will run. If not, the program continues after the if block and without running the code within it.

Or do this instead

The captain also wants to tell his troops to stay put, if the enemy is not coming over the bridge.

Now we can introduce another C++ keyword, else. When we want to explicitly do something when the if does not evaluate to true, we can use else.

For example, to tell the troops to stay put if the enemy is not coming over the bridge, we could write this code:

```
if(isComingOverBridge)
{
    // Shoot them
}

else
{
    // Hold position
}
```

The captain then realized that the problem wasn't as simple as he first thought. What if the enemy comes over the bridge, but has too many troops? His squad would be overrun and slaughtered. So, he came up with this code (we'll use some variables as well this time.):

```
bool isComingOverBridge;
int enemyTroops;
int friendlyTroops;

// Initialize the previous variables, one way or another

// Now the if
if(isComingOverBridge && friendlyTroops > enemyTroops)
{
    // shoot them
}

else if(isComingOverBridge && friendlyTroops < enemyTroops)
{
    // blow the bridge
}

else
{
    // Hold position
}
```

The above code has three possible paths of execution. The first one is if the enemy is coming over the bridge, and the friendly troops are greater in number:

```
if(isComingOverBridge && friendlyTroops > enemyTroops)
```

The second is if the enemy troops are coming over the bridge but outnumber the friendly troops:

```
else if(isComingOveBridge && friendlyTroops < enemyTroops)
```

Then the third and final possible outcome, which will execute if neither of the others is true, is captured by the final else, without an if condition.

Reader challenge

Can you spot a flaw with the preceding code? One that might leave a bunch of inexperienced troops in complete disarray? The possibility of the enemy troops and friendly troops being exactly equal in number has not been handled explicitly, and would therefore be handled by the final else. The final else is meant for when there are no enemy troops. I guess any self-respecting captain would expect his troops to fight in this situation. He could change the first if statement to accommodate this possibility:

```
if(isComingOverBridge && friendlyTroops >=  enemyTroops)
```

And finally, the captain's last concern was that, if the enemy came over the bridge waving the white flag of surrender and were promptly slaughtered, then his men would end up as war criminals. The C++ code needed was obvious. Using the wavingWhiteFlag Boolean variable he wrote this test:

```
if (wavingWhiteFlag)
{
    // Take prisoners
}
```

But the issue of where to put this code was less clear. In the end, the captain opted for the following nested solution and for changing the test for wavingWhiteFlag to logical NOT, like this:

```
if (!wavingWhiteFlag)
{
    // not surrendering so check everything else
    if(isComingOverTheBridge && friendlyTroops >= enemyTroops)
    {
        // shoot them
    }
    else if(isComingOverTheBridge && friendlyTroops < enemyTroops)
    {
        // blow the bridge
    }
```

```
}

else
{
   // this is the else for our first if
   // Take prisoners
{

// Holding position
```

This demonstrates that we can nest `if` and `else` statements inside one another to create quite deep and detailed decisions.

We could go on making more and more complicated decisions with `if` and `else` but what we have seen is more than sufficient as an introduction. It is probably worth pointing out that, very often there is more than one way to arrive at a solution to a problem. The right way will usually be the way that solves the problem in the clearest and simplest manner.

We are getting closer to having all the C++ knowledge we need to be able to animate our clouds and bee. We have one final animation issue to discuss and then we can get back to the game.

Timing

Before we can move the bee and the clouds, we need to consider timing. As we already know, the main game loop executes over and over again, until the player presses the *Esc* key.

We have also learnt that C++ and SFML are exceptionally fast. In fact, my ageing laptop executes a simple game loop (such as the current one) at around five thousand times per second.

The frame-rate problem

Let's consider the speed of the bee. For the purpose of discussion we could pretend that we are going to move it at 200 pixels per second. On a screen that is 1920 pixels wide, it would take, very approximately, 10 seconds to cross the entire width, because 10 x 200 is 2000 (near enough to 1920).

Furthermore, we know that we can position any of our sprites with
`setPosition(...,...)`. We just need to put the x and the y coordinates in the
parentheses.

In addition to setting the position of a sprite, we can also **get** the position of a sprite. To get
the horizontal x coordinate of the bee, for example, we would use this code:

```
int currentPosition = spriteBee.getPosition().x;
```

The current x coordinate of the bee is now stored in `currentPosition`. To move the bee to
the right, we could then add the appropriate fraction of 200 (our intended speed) divided
by 5000 (the approximate frames per second on my laptop) to `currentPosition` like this:

```
currentPosition += 200/5000;
```

Now we could use `setPosition` to move our bee. It would smoothly move from left to
right by 200 divided by 5000 pixels each frame. But there are two big problems with this
approach.

Frame rate is the number of times per second that our game loop is processed. That is, the
number of times that we handle the player's input, update the game objects, and draw them
onto the screen. We will expand on and discuss frame rate implications now and
throughout the rest of the book.

The frame rate on my laptop might not always be constant. The bee might look like it is
intermittently **boosting** its way across the screen.

And of course, we want a wider audience for our game than just my laptop! Every PC's
frame rate will vary, at least slightly. If you have a really old PC, the bee will appear to be
weighed down with lead and if you have the latest gaming rig it will probably be
something of a blurry turbo bee.

Fortunately, this problem is the same for every game and SFML has provided a solution.
The easiest way to understand the solution is to implement it.

The SFML frame-rate solution

We will now measure and use the frame rate to control our game. To get started with
implementing this, add this code just before the main game loop:

```
// How fast is each cloud?
float cloud1Speed = 0;
float cloud2Speed = 0;
float cloud3Speed = 0;
```

```
// Variables to control time itself
Clock clock;

while (window.isOpen())
{
```

In the previous code we declare an object of the type `Clock` and we name it `clock`. The class name starts with a capital letter and the object name (that we will actually use) starts with a lower-case letter. The object name is arbitrary but `clock` seems like an appropriate name for, well, a clock. We will add some more time-related variables here soon as well.

Now in the update section of our game code add this highlighted code:

```
/*
*****************************************
Update the scene
*****************************************
*/

// Measure time
Time dt = clock.restart();

/*
*****************************************
Draw the scene
*****************************************
*/
```

The `clock.restart()` function, as you might expect, restarts the clock. We want to restart the clock each and every frame so that we can time how long each and every frame takes. In addition, however, it returns the amount of time that has elapsed since the last time we restarted the clock.

As a result of this, in the previous code, we are declaring an object of the type `Time`, called `dt`, and using it to store the value returned by the `clock.restart()` function.

Now, we have a `Time` object, called `dt`, which holds the amount of time that elapsed since the last time we updated the scene and restarted the clock. Maybe you can see where this is going.

Let's add some more code to the game and then we will see what we can do with `dt`.

 `dt` stands for **delta time**, the time between two updates.

Moving the clouds and the bee

Let's use the elapsed time since the last frame, to breathe life into the bee and the clouds. This will solve the problem of having a consistent frame rate across different PCs.

Giving life to the bee

The first thing we want to do is to set up the bee at a certain height and a certain speed. We only want to do this when the bee is inactive. So we wrap the next code in an `if` block. Examine and add the highlighted code, then we will discuss it:

```
/*
****************************************
Update the scene
****************************************
*/

// Measure time
Time dt = clock.restart();

// Setup the bee
if (!beeActive)
{
    // How fast is the bee
    srand((int)time(0));
    beeSpeed = (rand() % 200) + 200;

    // How high is the bee
    srand((int)time(0) * 10);
    float height = (rand() % 500) + 500;
    spriteBee.setPosition(2000, height);
    beeActive = true;
}

/*
****************************************
Draw the scene
****************************************
*/
```

Now, if the bee is not active, just like it won't be when the game first starts, `if(!beeActive)` will be `true` and the code above will do the following things, in this order:

- Seed the random number generator
- Get a random number between 199 and 399 and assign the result to `beeSpeed`
- Seed the random number generator again
- Get a random number between 499 and 999 and assign the result to a new `float` variable called `height`
- Set the position of the bee to `2000` on the x axis (just off-screen to the right) and to whatever `height` equals on the y axis
- Set `beeActive` to true

Note that the `height` variable is the first variable we have ever declared inside the game loop. Furthermore, because it was declared inside an `if` block, it is actually "invisible" outside the `if` block. This is fine for our use because once we have set the height of the bee we don't need it any more. This phenomenon, which affects variables, is called **scope**. We will explore this more fully in `Chapter 4`: *Loops, Arrays, Switch, Enumerations, and Functions – Implementing Game Mechanics.*

If we run the game, nothing will actually happen to the bee yet, but now the bee is active we can write some code that runs when `beeActive` is `true`.

Add the following highlighted code, which, as you can see, executes whenever `beeActive` is `true`. This is because it follows with an `else` after the `if(!beeActive)` block:

```
// Set up the bee
if (!beeActive)
{

    // How fast is the bee
    srand((int)time(0) );
    beeSpeed = (rand() % 200) + 200;

    // How high is the bee
    srand((int)time(0) * 10);
    float height = (rand() % 1350) + 500;
    spriteBee.setPosition(2000, height);
    beeActive = true;

}
else
```

```
// Move the bee
{
  spriteBee.setPosition(
    spriteBee.getPosition().x -
    (beeSpeed * dt.asSeconds()),
    spriteBee.getPosition().y);

  // Has the bee reached the right hand edge of the screen?
  if (spriteBee.getPosition().x < -100)
  {
    // Set it up ready to be a whole new cloud next frame
    beeActive = false;
  }
}

/*
******************************************
Draw the scene
******************************************
*/
```

In the `else` block the following things happen.

The bee position is changed using the following criteria. The `setPosition` function uses the `getPosition` function to get the current x coordinate of the bee. It then adds `beeSpeed * dt.asSeconds()` to that coordinate.

The `beeSpeed` variable value is many pixels per second and was randomly assigned in the previous `if` block. The value of `dt.asSeconds()` will be a fraction of 1 that represents how long the previous frame of the game took.

Assume that the bee's current x coordinate is 1000. Now suppose a fairly basic PC loops at 5000 frames per second. This would mean that `dt.asSeconds` would be 0.0002. And further suppose that `beeSpeed` was set to the maximum 399 pixels per second. Then the code that determines the value that `setPosition` uses for the x coordinate can be explained like this:

```
1000 - 0.0002 x 399
```

So the new position on the x axis for the bee would be 999.9202. We can see that the bee is, very smoothly drifting to the left, at well under a pixel per frame. If the frame rate fluctuates then the formula will produce a new value to suit. If we run the same code on a PC that only achieves 100 frames per second or a PC that achieves a million frames per second, the bee will move at the same speed.

The `setPosition` function uses `getPosition().y` to keep the bee in exactly the same y coordinate throughout this cycle of being active.

The final code in the `else` block we just added is this:

```
// Has the bee reached the right hand edge of the screen?
if (spriteBee.getPosition().x < -100)
{
    // Set it up ready to be a whole new cloud next frame
    beeActive = false;
}
```

This code tests each and every frame (when `beeActive` is `true`), whether the bee has disappeared off the left-hand side of the screen. If the `getPosition` function returns less than -100, it will certainly be out of view of the player. When this has occurred, `beeActive` is set to `false` and, on the next frame, a new bee will be set flying at a new random height and a new random speed.

Try running the game and watch our bee dutifully fly from right to left and then come back to the right again at a new height and speed. It's almost like a new bee every time.

 Of course a real bee would stick around for ages and pester you while you're trying to concentrate on chopping the tree. We will make some smarter game characters in the next project.

Now we will get the clouds moving in a very similar way.

Blowing the clouds

The first thing we want to do is set up the first cloud at a certain height and a certain speed. We only want to do this when the cloud is inactive. So we wrap the next code in an `if` block. Examine and add the highlighted code, just after the code we added for the bee, then we will discuss it. It is almost identical to the code we used for the bee:

```
else
// Move the bee
{

    spriteBee.setPosition(
        spriteBee.getPosition().x -
        (beeSpeed * dt.asSeconds()),
        spriteBee.getPosition().y);
```

```
    // Has the bee reached the right hand edge of the screen?
    if (spriteBee.getPosition().x < -100)
    {
        // Set it up ready to be a whole new bee next frame
        beeActive = false;
    }
}

// Manage the clouds
// Cloud 1
if (!cloud1Active)
{
    // How fast is the cloud
    srand((int)time(0) * 10);
    cloud1Speed = (rand() % 200);

    // How high is the cloud
    srand((int)time(0) * 10);
    float height = (rand() % 150);
    spriteCloud1.setPosition(-200, height);
    cloud1Active = true;
}

/*
****************************************
Draw the scene
****************************************
*/
```

The only difference between the code we have just added and the bee code is that we work on a different sprite and use different ranges for our random numbers. Also, we use `*10` to the result returned by `time(0)` so we are always guaranteed to get a different seed for each of the clouds. When we code the other cloud movement next you will see that we use `*20` and `*30` respectively.

Now we can take action when the cloud is active. We will do so in the `else` block. As with the `if` block, the code is identical to that of the bee, except that all the code works on the cloud and not the bee:

```
// Manage the clouds
if (!cloud1Active)
{

    // How fast is the cloud
    srand((int)time(0) * 10);
    cloud1Speed = (rand() % 200);
```

```
    // How high is the cloud
    srand((int)time(0) * 10);
    float height = (rand() % 150);
    spriteCloud1.setPosition(-200, height);
    cloud1Active = true;


}
else
{
    spriteCloud1.setPosition(
        spriteCloud1.getPosition().x +
        (cloud1Speed * dt.asSeconds()),
        spriteCloud1.getPosition().y);

    // Has the cloud reached the right hand edge of the screen?
    if (spriteCloud1.getPosition().x > 1920)
    {
        // Set it up ready to be a whole new cloud next frame
        cloud1Active = false;
    }
}

/*
****************************************
Draw the scene
****************************************
*/
```

Now we know what to do, we can duplicate the same code for the second and third clouds.
Add this highlighted code that handles the second and third clouds, immediately after the
code for the first cloud:

```
    ...

    // Cloud 2
    if (!cloud2Active)
    {
        // How fast is the cloud
        srand((int)time(0) * 20);
        cloud2Speed = (rand() % 200);
        // How high is the cloud
        srand((int)time(0) * 20);
        float height = (rand() % 300) - 150;
        spriteCloud2.setPosition(-200, height);
        cloud2Active = true;
    }
    else
```

```
{
  spriteCloud2.setPosition(
    spriteCloud2.getPosition().x +
    (cloud2Speed * dt.asSeconds()),
    spriteCloud2.getPosition().y);
  // Has the cloud reached the right hand edge of the screen?
  if (spriteCloud2.getPosition().x > 1920)
  {
    // Set it up ready to be a whole new cloud next frame
    cloud2Active = false;
  }
}
if (!cloud3Active)
{
  // How fast is the cloud
  srand((int)time(0) * 30);
  cloud3Speed = (rand() % 200);
  // How high is the cloud
  srand((int)time(0) * 30);
  float height = (rand() % 450) - 150;
  spriteCloud3.setPosition(-200, height);
  cloud3Active = true;
}
else
{
  spriteCloud3.setPosition(
    spriteCloud3.getPosition().x +
    (cloud3Speed * dt.asSeconds()),
    spriteCloud3.getPosition().y);

  // Has the cloud reached the right hand edge of the screen?
  if (spriteCloud3.getPosition().x > 1920)
  {
    // Set it up ready to be a whole new cloud next frame
    cloud3Active = false;
  }
}

/*
****************************************
Draw the scene
****************************************
*/
```

Now you can run the game and the clouds will randomly and continuously drift across the screen, and the bee will buzz from right to left before re-spawning once more back on the right.

Does all this cloud and bee handling seem a little bit repetitious? We will see how we could save lots of typing and make our code more readable. In C++ there are ways of handling multiple instances of the same type of variable or object. These are called **arrays** and we will learn about them in Chapter 4: *Loops, Arrays, Switch, Enumerations, and Functions – Implementing Game Mechanics*. At the end of the project, once we have learnt about arrays, we will discuss how we could improve our cloud code.

Take a look at a few frequently asked questions related to the topics in this chapter.

FAQ

Q) Why do we set the bee to inactive when it gets to -100? Why not just zero because zero is the left-hand side of the window?

A) The bee graphic is 60 pixels wide and its origin is at the top left pixel. So when the bee is drawn with its origin at x equals zero, the entire bee graphic is still on screen for the player to see. By waiting until it is at -100, we can be sure it is definitely out of the player's view.

Q) How do I know how fast my game loop is?

A) To measure this we will need to learn a few more things. We will add the ability to measure and display the current frame rate in Chapter 5: *Collisions, Sound, and End Conditions – Making the Game Playable*.

Summary

In this chapter we learnt that a variable is a named storage location in memory, in which we can keep values of a specific type. Types include `int`, `float`, `double`, `bool`, `String`, and `char`.

We can declare and initialize all the variables we need, to store the data for our game. Once we have our variables, we can manipulate them using the arithmetic and assignment operators and use them in tests with the logical operators. Used in conjunction with the `if` and `else` keywords, we can branch our code dependent upon the current situation in the game.

Using all this new knowledge, we animated some clouds and a bee. In the next chapter we will continue to use these skills to add a **Heads Up Display(HUD)** and add more input options for the player, as well as representing time visually via a time bar.

3
C++ Strings, SFML Time, Player Input, and HUD

In this chapter we will spend around half the time learning how to manipulate text and display it on the screen, and the other half looking at timing and how a visual time bar can create a sense of urgency in the game.

We will cover the following topics:

- Pausing and restarting the game
- C++ strings
- SFML Text and SFML font classes
- Adding a HUD to Timber!!!
- Adding a time bar to Timber!!!

Pausing and restarting the game

As we progress with this game over the next three chapters, the code will obviously get longer and longer. So, now it seems like a good time to think ahead and add a little bit more structure into our code. We will add this structure to give us the ability to pause and restart the game.

We will add code so that when the game is first run, it will be paused. The player will be able to press the *Enter* key to get the game started. Then the game will run until either the player gets squished or runs out of time. At this point the game will pause and wait for the player to press *Enter* key, to restart again.

Let's step through setting this up a bit at a time. First, declare a new `bool` variable called `paused`, outside the main game loop, and initialize it to `true`:

```
// Variables to control time itself
Clock clock;

// Track whether the game is running
bool paused = true;

while (window.isOpen())
{

    /*
    ****************************************
    Handle the players input
    ****************************************
    */
```

Now, whenever the game is run we have a variable, `paused`, that will be `true`.

Next, we will add another `if` statement where the expression will check to see whether the *Enter* key is currently being pressed. If it is being pressed it sets `paused` to `false`. Add the highlighted code just after our other keyboard-handling code:

```
/*
****************************************
Handle the players input
****************************************
*/

if (Keyboard::isKeyPressed(Keyboard::Escape))
{
    window.close();
}

// Start the game
if (Keyboard::isKeyPressed(Keyboard::Return))
{
  paused = false;
}

/*
****************************************
Update the scene
****************************************
*/
```

Now we have a `bool` called `paused`, which starts off `true` but changes to `false` when the player presses the *Enter* key. At this point, we have to make our game loop respond appropriately, based on whatever the current value of `paused` might be.

This is how we will proceed. We will wrap the entire, update part of the code, including the code we wrote in the last chapter to move the bee and clouds, in an `if` statement.

Notice that, in the next code, the `if` block will only execute when `paused` is not equal to `true`. Or to put it another way, the game won't move/update when it is paused.

This is exactly what we want. Look carefully at the exact place to add the new `if` statement and its corresponding opening and closing curly braces { . . . }. If they are put in the wrong place, things will not work as expected.

Add the highlighted code to wrap the update part of the code, paying close attention to the context shown next. I have added . . . on a few lines to represent hidden code. Obviously the . . . is not real code and should not be added to the game. You can identify where to place the new code (highlighted), at the start and the end, by the un-highlighted code surrounding it:

```
/*
****************************************
Update the scene
****************************************
*/

if (!paused)
{

    // Measure time
       ...
       ...
       ...
    // Has the cloud reached the right hand edge of the screen?
    if (spriteCloud3.getPosition().x > 1920)
    {
        // Set it up ready to be a whole new cloud next frame
        cloud3Active = false;
    }

}

} // End if (!paused)

/*
****************************************
Draw the scene
```

```
* * * * * * * * * * * * * * * * * * * * * * * * * * * * * * * * * * * *
*/
```

Notice that, when you place the closing curly brace of the new `if` block, Visual Studio neatly adjusts all the indenting, to keep the code tidy.

Now you can run the game and everything will be static until you press the *Enter* key. It is now possible to go about adding features to our game and we just need to remember when the player dies or runs out of time, we need to set `paused` to `true`.

In the previous chapter we had a first glimpse of C++ strings. We need to learn a bit more about them so we can implement the player's HUD.

C++ strings

In the previous chapter we briefly mentioned strings and we learned that a string can hold alphanumeric data in anything from a single character to a whole book. We didn't look at declaring, initializing, or manipulating strings. So let's do that now.

Declaring strings

Declaring a string variable is simple. We state the type, followed by the name:

```
String levelName;
String playerName;
```

Once we have declared a string we can assign a value to it.

Assigning a value to strings

To assign a value to a string, as with regular variables, we simply put the name, followed by the assignment operator, then the value:

```
levelName = "Dastardly Cave";
playerName = "John Carmack";
```

Note that the values need to be enclosed in quotation marks. As with regular variables we can also declare and assign values in a single line:

```
String score = "Score = 0";
String message = "GAME OVER!!";
```

This is how we can change our string variables.

Manipulating strings

We can use the `#include <sstream>` directive to give us some extra power with our strings. The `sstream` class enables us to add some strings together. When we do so it is called **concatenation**:

```
String part1 = "Hello ";
String part2 = "World";

sstream ss;
ss << part1 << part2;

// ss now holds "Hello World"
```

In addition to using `sstream` objects, a string variable can even be concatenated with a variable of a different type. This next code starts to reveal how strings might be quite useful to us:

```
String scoreText = "Score = ";
int score = 0;

// Later in the code
score ++;

sstream ss;
ss << scoreText << score;
// ss now holds "Score = 1"
```

The << operator is a bitwise operator. C++ however, allows you to write your own classes and override what a specific operator does, within the context of your class. The `sstream` class has done this to make the << operator work the way it does. The complexity is hidden in the class. We can use its functionality without worrying about how it works. If you are feeling adventurous you can read about operator overloading at: http://www.tutorialspoint.com/cplusplus/cpp_overloading.htm. You don't need any more information in order to continue with the project.

Now we know the basics of C++ strings, and how we can use `sstream`, we can see how to use some SFML classes to display them on the screen.

SFML Text and Font

Let's briefly discuss the `Text` and `Font` classes with some hypothetical code, before we actually go ahead and add code to our game.

The first step to drawing text on the screen is to have a font. In the first chapter we added a font file to the project folder. Now we can load the font, ready for use, into an SFML `Font` object.

The code to do so looks like this:

```
Font font;
font.loadFromFile("myfont.ttf");
```

In the previous code we first declare the `Font` object and then load an actual font file. Note that `myfont.ttf` is a hypothetical font and we could use any font that is in the project folder.

Once we have loaded a font we need an SFML `Text` object:

```
Text myText;
```

Now we can configure our `Text` object. This includes the size, the color, the position on screen, the string that holds the message, and, of course, associating it with our `font` object:

```
// Assign the actual message
myText.setString("Press Enter to start!");

// assign a size
myText.setCharacterSize(75);

// Choose a color
myText.setFillColor(Color::White);

// Set the font to our Text object
myText.setFont(font);
```

Let's add a HUD to Timber!!!

Adding a score and a message

Now we know enough about strings, SFML `Text`, and SFML `Font` to go about implementing the HUD.

The next thing we need to do is to add another `#include` directive to the top of the code file. As we have learned, the `sstream` class adds some really useful functionality for combining strings, and other variable types, together into a string.

Add the following line of highlighted code:

```
#include "stdafx.h"
#include <sstream>
#include <SFML/Graphics.hpp>

using namespace sf;

int main()
{
```

Next we will set up our SFML `Text` objects. One will hold a message that we will vary to suit the state of the game, and the other will hold the score and needs to be regularly updated.

The next code that declares the `Text` and `Font` objects loads the font, assigns the font to the `Text` objects, and then adds the string messages, color, and size. This should look familiar from our discussion in the previous section. In addition, we add a new `int` variable called `score` which we can manipulate to hold the player's score.

 Remember that if you chose a different font from `KOMIKAP_.ttf`, back in `Chapter 1`: C++, *SFML, Visual Studio, and Starting the First Game,* you will need to change that part of the code to match the `.ttf` file that you have in the `Visual Studio Stuff/Projects/Timber/Timber/fonts` folder.

Add the highlighted code and we will be ready to move on to updating the HUD:

```
// Track whether the game is running
bool paused = true;

// Draw some text
int score = 0;

sf::Text messageText;
sf::Text scoreText;
```

```
// We need to choose a font
Font font;
font.loadFromFile("fonts/KOMIKAP_.ttf");

// Set the font to our message
messageText.setFont(font);
scoreText.setFont(font);

// Assign the actual message
messageText.setString("Press Enter to start!");
scoreText.setString("Score = 0");

// Make it really big
messageText.setCharacterSize(75);
scoreText.setCharacterSize(100);

// Choose a color
messageText.setFillColor(Color::White);
scoreText.setFillColor(Color::White);

while (window.isOpen())
{

    /*
    ***************************************
    Handle the players input
    ***************************************
    */
```

The next code might look a little convoluted, even complex. It is, however, really straightforward when you break it down a bit. Examine and add the new code, then we will go through it:

```
// Choose a color
messageText.setFillColor(Color::White);
scoreText.setFillColor(Color::White);

// Position the text
FloatRect textRect = messageText.getLocalBounds();

messageText.setOrigin(textRect.left +
  textRect.width / 2.0f,
  textRect.top +
  textRect.height / 2.0f);

messageText.setPosition(1920 / 2.0f, 1080 / 2.0f);

scoreText.setPosition(20, 20);
```

```
while (window.isOpen())
{

    /*
    ******************************************
    Handle the players input
    ******************************************
    */
```

We have two objects of the type `Text` that we will display on the screen. We want to position `scoreText` on the top left with a little bit of padding. This is not a challenge; we simply use `scoreText.setPosition(20, 20)` and that positions it in the top left with 20 pixels of horizontal and vertical padding.

Positioning `messageText`, however, was not so easy. We want to position it in the exact center of the screen. Initially this might not seem like a problem, but then we remember that the origin of everything we draw is the top left-hand corner. So, if we simply divide the screen width and height by two and use the results in `mesageText.setPosition...`, then the top left of the text will be in the center of the screen and it will spread out untidily to the right.

What we need is a way to be able to set the center of `messageText` to the center of the screen. The rather nasty looking bit of code that you just added repositions the origin of `messageText` to the center of itself. Here is the code under current discussion again for convenience:

```
// Position the text
FloatRect textRect = messageText.getLocalBounds();

messageText.setOrigin(textRect.left +
    textRect.width / 2.0f,
    textRect.top +
    textRect.height / 2.0f);
```

First, in this code, we declare a new object of type `FloatRect`, called `textRect`. A `FloatRect` object, as the name suggests, holds a rectangle with floating point coordinates.

The code then uses the `messageText.getLocalBounds` function to initialize `textRect` with the coordinates of the rectangle that wraps `messageText`.

The next line of code, spread over four lines as it is quite long, uses the `messageText.setOrigin` function to change the origin (the point at which we draw) to the center of `textRect`. Of course, `textRect` holds a rectangle, which exactly matches the coordinates that wrap `messageText`. Then, this next line of code executes:

```
messageText.setPosition(1920 / 2.0f,    1080 / 2.0f);
```

Now, `messageText` will be neatly positioned in the exact center of the screen. We will use this exact same code each time we change the text of `messageText`, because changing the message changes the size of `messageText`, so its origin will need recalculating.

Next we declare an object of type `stringstream` called `ss`. Note that we use the full name including the namespace `std::stringstream`. We could avoid this syntax by adding `using namespace std` to the top of our code file. We don't, however, because we use it infrequently. Take a look at the code and add it to the game, then we can go through it in more detail. As we only want this code to execute when the game is not paused, be sure to add it with the other code, inside the `if(!paused)` block, as shown:

```
else
    {

        spriteCloud3.setPosition(
            spriteCloud3.getPosition().x +
            (cloud3Speed * dt.asSeconds()),
            spriteCloud3.getPosition().y);

        // Has the cloud reached the right hand edge of the screen?
        if (spriteCloud3.getPosition().x > 1920)
        {
            // Set it up ready to be a whole new cloud next frame
            cloud3Active = false;
        }
    }

    // Update the score text
    std::stringstream ss;
    ss << "Score = " << score;
    scoreText.setString(ss.str());

}// End if(!paused)

/*
*****************************************
Draw the scene
*****************************************
*/
```

We use `ss` and the special functionality provided by the << operator, which concatenates variables into a `stringstream`. So the code, `ss << "Score = " << score`, has the effect of creating a string with `"Score = "` and whatever the value of `score` is, it is concatenated together. For example, when the game first starts, `score` is equal to zero, so `ss` will hold the value `"Score = 0"`. If `score` ever changes, `ss` will adapt each frame.

The next line of code simply displays/sets the string contained in `ss` to `scoreText`.

```
scoreText.setString(ss.str());
```

It is now ready to be drawn onto the screen.

This next code draws both `Text` objects (`scoreText` and `messageText`), but notice that the code that draws `messageText` is wrapped in an `if` statement. This `if` statement causes `messageText` only to be drawn when the game is paused.

Add the highlighted code shown next:

```
// Now draw the insect
window.draw(spriteBee);

// Draw the score
window.draw(scoreText);
if (paused)
{
    // Draw our message
    window.draw(messageText);
}

// Show everything we just drew
window.display();
```

We can now run the game and see our HUD drawn on the screen. You will see the **SCORE = 0** and PRESS ENTER TO START! messages. The latter will disappear when you press *Enter*.

If you want to see the score updating, add a temporary line of code, `score ++;` anywhere in the `while(window.isOpen)` loop. If you add this temporary line you will see the score go up fast, very fast!

If you added the temporary code `score ++;`, be sure to delete it before continuing.

Adding a time bar

As time is a crucial mechanic in the game, it is necessary to keep the player aware of it. He needs to know if his allotted six seconds are about to run out. It will give him a sense of urgency as the end of the game draws near, and a sense of accomplishment if he performs well enough to maintain or increase his remaining time.

Drawing the number of seconds remaining on the screen is not easy to read (when concentrating on the branches) or a particularly interesting way to achieve the objective.

What we need is a time bar. Our time bar will be a simple red rectangle, prominently displayed on the screen. It will start off nice and wide, but rapidly shrink as time runs out. When the player's remaining time reaches zero, the time bar will be gone completely.

At the same time as adding the time bar, we will add the necessary code to keep track of the player's remaining time, as well as to respond when he runs out. Let's go through it a step at a time.

Find the Clock clock; declaration from earlier and add the highlighted code:

```
// Variables to control time itself
Clock clock;

// Time bar
RectangleShape timeBar;
float timeBarStartWidth = 400;
float timeBarHeight = 80;
timeBar.setSize(Vector2f(timeBarStartWidth, timeBarHeight));
timeBar.setFillColor(Color::Red);
timeBar.setPosition((1920 / 2) - timeBarStartWidth / 2, 980);

Time gameTimeTotal;
float timeRemaining = 6.0f;
float timeBarWidthPerSecond = timeBarStartWidth / timeRemaining;

// Track whether the game is running
bool paused = true;
```

First we declare an object of the type RectangleShape and call it timeBar. RectangleShape is an SFML class that is perfect for drawing simple rectangles.

Next we add a few float variables, timeBarStartWidth and timeBarHeight. We initialize them to 400 and 80 respectively. These variables will help us keep track of the size we need to draw the timeBar each frame.

Next we set the size of the timeBar using the timeBar.setSize function. We don't just pass in our two new float variables. First we create a new object of type Vector2f. What is different here, however, is that we don't give the new object a name. We simply initialize it with our two float variables and it is passed straight in to the setSize function.

> Vector2f is a class which holds two float variables. It also has some other functionality that will be introduced throughout the book.

After that we color the `timeBar` red by using the `setFillColor` function.

The last thing we do to the `timeBar`, in the previous code, is to set its position. The y coordinate is completely straightforward, but the way we set the x coordinate is slightly convoluted. Here is the calculation again:

```
(1920 / 2) - timeBarStartWidth / 2
```

The code first divides `1920` by 2. Then it divides `timeBarStartWidth` by 2. Finally it subtracts the latter from the former.

The result makes the `timeBar` sit nice and horizontally centered on the screen.

The final three lines of code that we are talking about declare a new `Time` object called `gameTimeTotal`, a new `float` called `timeRemaining` that is initialized to 6, and a curious-sounding `float` named `timeBarWidthPerSecond` which we will discuss further.

The `timeBarWidthPerSecond` variable is initialized with `timeBarStartWidth` divided by `timeRemaining`. The result is exactly the amount of pixels that the `timeBar` needs to shrink by, each second of the game. This will be useful when we resize the `timeBar` in each frame.

Obviously we need to reset the time remaining each time the player starts a new game. The logical place to do this is the *Enter* key press. We can also set the `score` back to zero at the same time. Let's do that now by adding this highlighted code:

```
// Start the game
if (Keyboard::isKeyPressed(Keyboard::Return))
{
    paused = false;

    // Reset the time and the score
    score = 0;
    timeRemaining = 5;
}
```

Now, each frame we must reduce the amount of time remaining and resize the `timeBar` accordingly. Add the following highlighted code in the update section as shown here:

```
/*
****************************************
Update the scene
****************************************
*/
if (!paused)
{
```

```
// Measure time
Time dt = clock.restart();

// Subtract from the amount of time remaining
timeRemaining -= dt.asSeconds();
// size up the time bar
timeBar.setSize(Vector2f(timeBarWidthPerSecond *
  timeRemaining, timeBarHeight));

// Set up the bee
if (!beeActive)
{

    // How fast is the bee
    srand((int)time(0) * 10);
    beeSpeed = (rand() % 200) + 200;

    // How high is the bee
    srand((int)time(0) * 10);
    float height = (rand() % 1350) + 500;
    spriteBee.setPosition(2000, height);
    beeActive = true;

}
else
    // Move the bee
```

First we subtracted the amount of time the player has left by however long the previous frame took to execute with this code:

```
timeRemaining -= dt.asSeconds();
```

Then we adjusted the size of the timeBar with the following code:

```
timeBar.setSize(Vector2f(timeBarWidthPerSecond *
        timeRemaining, timeBarHeight));
```

The x value of the Vector2F is initialized with timebarWidthPerSecond multiplied by timeRemaining. This produces exactly the correct width, relative to how long the player has left. The height remains the same and timeBarHeight is used without any manipulation.

And, of course, we must detect when time has run out. For now, we will simply detect that time has run out, pause the game, and change the text of the `messageText`. Later we will do more work here. Add the highlighted code right after the previous code we added, and we will look at it in more detail:

```cpp
// Measure time
Time dt = clock.restart();

// Subtract from the amount of time remaining
timeRemaining -= dt.asSeconds();

// resize up the time bar
timeBar.setSize(Vector2f(timeBarWidthPerSecond *
    timeRemaining, timeBarHeight));

if (timeRemaining <= 0.0f)
{
    // Pause the game
    paused = true;

    // Change the message shown to the player
    messageText.setString("Out of time!!");

    //Reposition the text based on its new size
    FloatRect textRect = messageText.getLocalBounds();
    messageText.setOrigin(textRect.left +
        textRect.width / 2.0f,
        textRect.top +
        textRect.height / 2.0f);

    messageText.setPosition(1920 / 2.0f, 1080 / 2.0f);
}

// Set up the bee
if (!beeActive)
{

    // How fast is the bee
    srand((int)time(0) * 10);
    beeSpeed = (rand() % 200) + 200;

    // How high is the bee
    srand((int)time(0) * 10);
    float height = (rand() % 1350) + 500;
    spriteBee.setPosition(2000, height);
    beeActive = true;
```

```
}
else
    // Move the bee
```

Stepping through the previous code:

- First we test whether time has run out with if(timeRemaining <= 0.0f)
- Then we set paused to true so this will be the last time the update part of our code is executed (until the player presses *Enter* again).
- Then we change the message of messageText, calculate its new center to set it as its origin, and position it in the center of the screen.

Finally, for this part of the code, we need to draw the timeBar. There is nothing new in this code that we haven't seen many times before. Just note that we draw the timeBar after the tree, so it is visible. Add the highlighted code to draw the time bar:

```
// Draw the score
window.draw(scoreText);

// Draw the timebar
window.draw(timeBar);

if (paused)
{
    // Draw our message
    window.draw(messageText);
}

// Show everything we just drew
window.display();
```

Now you can run the game. Press *Enter* to start, and watch the time bar smoothly disappear down to nothing.

The game then pauses and the **OUT OF TIME!!** message will appear.

You can, of course, press *Enter* again to start the whole thing running from the start.

FAQ

Q) I can foresee that positioning sprites by their top left corner could sometimes be inconvenient.

A) Fortunately, you can choose what point of a sprite is used as the positioning/origin pixel, just as we did with `messageText`, using the `setOrigin` function.

Q) The code is getting rather long and I am struggling to keep track of where everything is.

A) Yes, I agree. In the next chapter we will look at the first of a few ways we can organize our code and make it more readable. We will see this when we learn about writing C++ functions. In addition, we will learn a new way for handling multiple objects/variables of the same type (such as the clouds), when we learn about C++ arrays.

Summary

In this chapter we learnt about strings, SFML `Text`, and SFML `Font`. Between them they enabled us to draw text to the screen, which provided the player with a HUD. We also used `sstream`, which allows us to concatenate strings and other variables to display the score.

We explored the SFML `RectangleShape` class, which does exactly what its name suggests. We used an object of the type `RectangleShape`, and some carefully planned variables, to draw a time bar that visually displays how much time a player has left. Once we have implemented chopping, and moving branches that can squash the player, the time bar will create tension and urgency.

Next we are going to learn about a whole range of new C++ features, including loops, arrays, switching, enumerations, and functions. This will enable us to move the tree branches, keep track of their locations, and squash the player.

4

Loops, Arrays, Switch, Enumerations, and Functions – Implementing Game Mechanics

This chapter probably has more C++ information than any other chapter in the book. It is packed with fundamental concepts that will move our understanding on enormously. It will also begin to shed light on some of the murky areas that we have been skipping over a little bit, such as functions and game loops.

Once we have explored a whole list of C++ language necessities we will then use everything we know to make the main game mechanic, the tree branches, move. By the end of this chapter we will be ready for the final phase and the completion of Timber!!!.

We will be looking at the following topics:

- Loops
- Arrays
- Making decisions with switch
- Enumerations
- Getting started with functions
- Creating and moving the tree branches

Loops

In programming, we often need to do the same thing more than once. The obvious example that we have seen so far is our game loop. With all the code stripped out, our game loop looks like this:

```
while (window.isOpen())
{

}
```

There are a few different types of loop and we will look at the most commonly used. The correct term for this type of loop is a `while` loop.

while loops

The `while` loop is quite straightforward. Think back to the `if` statements and their expressions that evaluated to either `true` or `false`. We can use the exact same combination of operators and variables in the conditional expression of our `while` loops.

As with `if` statements, if the expression is `true` the code executes. The difference in comparison a `while` loop, however, is that the C++ code within it will continue to execute until the condition is `false`. Take a look at this code:

```
int numberOfZombies = 100;

while(numberOfZombies > 0)
{
    // Player kills a zombie
    numberOfZombies--;

    // numberOfZombies decreases each pass through the loop
}

// numberOfZOmbies is no longer greater than 0
```

This is what is happening in the previous code. Outside of the `while` loop, `int numberOfZombies` is declared and initialized to `100`. Then the `while` loop begins. Its conditional expression is `numberOfZombies > 0`. Therefore the `while` loop will continue looping through the code in its body until the condition evaluates to `false`. This means that the code above will execute `100` times.

On the first pass through the loop, `numberOfZombies` equals `100` then `99` then `98` and so on. But once `numberOfZOmbies` is equal to zero, it is of course, no longer greater than zero. Then the code will break out of the `while` loop and continue to run, after the closing curly brace.

Just like an `if` statement, it is possible that the `while` loop will not execute even once. Take a look at this:

```
int availableCoins = 10;

while(availableCoins > 10)
{
    // more code here.
    // Won't run unless availableCoins is greater than 10
}
```

Moreover, there is no limit to the complexity of the expression or the amount of code that can go in the loop body. Consider this hypothetical variation of a game loop:

```
int playerLives = 3;
int alienShips = 10;

while(playerLives !=0 && alienShips !=0 )
{
    // Handle input
    // Update the scene
    // Draw the scene
}

// continue here when either playerLives or alienShips equals 0
```

The previous `while` loop would continue to execute until either `playerLives` or `alienShips` was equal to zero. As soon as one of those conditions occurred, the expression would evaluate to `false`, and the program would continue to execute from the first line of code after the `while` loop.

It is worth noticing that, once the body of the loop has been entered, it will always complete at least once, even if the expression evaluates to `false`, part way through, as it is not tested again until the code tries to start another pass. For example:

```
int x = 1;

while(x > 0)
{
    x--;
    // x is now 0 so the condition is false
```

```
    // But this line still runs
    // and this one
    // and me!
}

// Now I'm done!
```

The previous loop body will execute once. We can also set up a `while` loop that will run forever, unsurprisingly called an **infinite loop**. Here is an example:

```
int y = 0;

while(true)
{
    y++; // Bigger... Bigger...
}
```

If you find the above loop confusing, just think of it literally. A loop executes when its condition is `true`. Well, `true` is always `true` and will therefore keep executing.

Breaking out of a while loop

We might use an infinite loop so that we can decide when to exit the loop from within its body, rather than in the expression. We would do this by using the `break` keyword, when we are ready to leave the loop body. Perhaps it would look like this:

```
int z = 0;

while(true)
{
    z++; // Bigger... Bigger...
    break; // No you're not
    // Code doesn't reach here
}
```

You might also have been able to guess that we can combine any of the C++ decision making tools such as `if`, `else`, and another we will learn shortly, `switch`, within our `while` loops and other loop types as well. Consider this example:

```
int x = 0;
int max = 10;

while(true)
{
    x++; // Bigger... Bigger...
```

```
if(x == max)
{
   break;
} // No you're not

// code reaches here only until x = 10
}
```

We could go on for a long time looking at the various permutations of C++ `while` loops, but at some point we want to get back to making games. So let's move on to another type of loop.

for loops

The `for` loop has a slightly more complicated syntax than a `while` loop, because it takes three parts to set one up. Have a look at the code first then we will break it apart:

```
for(int x = 0; x < 100; x ++)
{
    // Something that needs to happen 100 times goes here
}
```

Here is what all the parts of the `for` loop condition do.

`for`(declaration and initialization; condition; change before each iteration)

To clarify further, here is a table to explain all of the three key parts as they appear in the previous `for` loop example.

Part	Description
Declaration and initialization	We create a new `int` variable `i` and initialize it to 0
Condition	Just like the other loops, it refers to the condition that must be `true` for the loop to execute
Change after each pass through loop	In the example, `x  ++` means that 1 is added/incremented to `x` on each pass

We can vary `for` loops to do many more things. Here is another simple example that counts down from 10:

```
for(int i = 10; i > 0; i--)
{
    // countdown
}

// blast off
```

The `for` loop takes control of initialization, condition evaluation, and the control variable upon itself. We will use `for` loops in our game, later this chapter.

Arrays

If a variable is a box in which we can store a value of a specific type, like `int`, `float`, or `char`, then we can think of an array as a whole row of boxes. The row of boxes can be of almost any size and type, including objects of classes. However, all the boxes must be of the same type.

The limitation of having to use the same type in each box can be circumvented, to an extent, once we learn some more advanced C++ in the final project.

This array sounds like it could have been useful for our clouds from Chapter 2: *Variables, Operators, and Decisions – Animating Sprites*. So how do we go about creating and using an array?

Declaring an array

We can declare an array of `int` type variables like this:

```
int someInts[10];
```

Now we have an array called `someInts` that can store ten `int` values. At the moment, however, it is empty.

Initializing the elements of an array

To add values into the elements of an array, we can use the type of syntax we are already familiar with, combined with some new syntax, known as **array notation**. In this next code, we store the value of 99 into the first element of the array:

```
someInts[0] = 99;
```

To store a value of 999 at the second element we write this code:

```
someInts[1] = 999;
```

We can store a value of 3 at the last element as follows:

```
someInts[9] = 3;
```

Note that the elements of an array always start at zero and go up to the size of the array minus 1. Similarly to ordinary variables, we can manipulate the values stored in an array. The only difference is that we would use the array notation to do so as, although our array has a name, someInts, the individual elements do not have names.

In this next code we add the first and second elements together and store the answer in the third:

```
someInts[2] = someInts[0] + someInts[1];
```

Arrays can also interact seamlessly with regular variables, such as in this following example:

```
int a = 9999;
someInts[4] = a;
```

Quickly initializing the elements of an array

We can quickly add values to elements such as this example using a float array:

```
float myFloatingPointArray[3] {3.14f, 1.63f, 99.0f};
```

Now the values 3.14, 1.63 and 99.0 are stored in the first, second, and third positions respectively. Remember that when using array notation to access these values we would use [0], [1] and [2].

There are other ways to initialize the elements of an array. This slightly abstract example shows using a `for` loop to put the values 0 through 9 into the `uselessArray` array:

```
for(int i = 0; i < 10; i++)
{
    uselessArray[i] = i;
}
```

The code assumes that `uslessArray` had previously been initialized to hold at least `10 int` variables.

So what do these arrays really do for our games?

We can use arrays anywhere that a regular variable can be used. For example, they could be used in an expression such as in the following:

```
// someArray[] is declared and initialized with 9999 values

for(int i = 0; i < 9999; i++)
{
    // Do something with each entry in the array
}
```

Perhaps the biggest benefit of arrays in game code was hinted at the start of this section. Arrays can hold objects (instances of classes). Imagine that we have a `Zombie` class and we want to store a whole bunch of them. We could do so as we do in this hypothetical example:

```
Zombie horde [5] {zombie1, zombie2, zombie3}; // etc...
```

The `horde` array now holds a load of instances of the `Zombie` class. Each one is a separate, living (kind of), breathing, and self-determining `Zombie` object. We could then loop through the `horde` array, each pass through the game loop, moving the zombies, checking if their heads have met with an ax, or if they have managed to catch the player.

Arrays, had we known about them at the time, would have been perfect for handling our clouds. We could have had as many clouds as we wanted and written less code than we did for our three measly clouds.

 To check out this improved cloud code in full, and in action, look at the enhanced version of Timber!!! (the code and the playable game) in the download bundle. Or you can try to implement the clouds using arrays yourself before looking at the code.

The best way to get a feel for all this array stuff is to see it in action. And we will, when we implement our tree branches.

For now we will leave our cloud code as it is so that we can get back to adding features to the game as soon as possible. But first let's look at a bit more C++ decision making with switch.

Making decisions with switch

We have already seen if, which allows us to make a decision whether to execute a block of code based upon the result of its expression. Sometimes a decision in C++ can be better made in other ways.

When we have to make a decision based on a clear list of possible outcomes, which doesn't involve complex combinations or wide ranges of values, then switch is usually the way to go. We start a switch decision as we can see in the following code:

```
switch(expression)
{

    // More code here

}
```

In the previous example, expression could be an actual expression or just a variable. Then, within the curly braces, we can make decisions based on the result of the expression or the value of the variable. We do this with the case and break keywords:

```
case x:
    //code for x
    break;
case y:
    //code for y
    break;
```

You can see in the previous abstract example that, each case states a possible result and each break denotes the end of that case and the point at which execution leaves the switch block.

We can also, optionally, use the default keyword without a value, to run some code in case none of the case statements evaluate to true. Here is an example:

```
default: // Look no value
    // Do something here if no other case statements are true
    break;
```

As a final and less abstract example for `switch`, consider a retro text adventure where the player enters a letter such as `'n'`, `'e'`, `'s'`, or `'w'` to move North, East, South, or West. A `switch` block could be used to handle each possible input from the player, as we can see in this example:

```
// get input from user in a char called command

switch(command){

    case 'n':
        // Handle move here
        break;

    case 'e':
        // Handle move here
        break;

    case 's':
        // Handle move here
        break;

    case 'w':
        // Handle move here
        break;
    // more possible cases

    default:
        // Ask the player to try again
        break;

}
```

The best way of understanding everything we have learned about `switch` will be when we put it into action along with all the other new concepts we are learning.

Class enumerations

An enumeration is a list of all the possible values in a logical collection. C++ enumerations are a great way of, well, enumerating things. For example, if our game uses variables, which can only be in a specific range of values, and if those values could logically form a collection or a set, then enumerations are probably appropriate to use. They will make your code clearer and less error-prone.

To declare a class enumeration in C++ we use two keywords, enum and class, together, followed by the name of the enumeration, followed by the values the enumeration can contain, enclosed in a pair of curly braces {...}.

As an example, examine this enumeration declaration. Note that it is conventional to declare the possible values from the enumeration all in uppercase:

```
enum class zombieTypes {REGULAR, RUNNER, CRAWLER, SPITTER, BLOATER };
```

Note, at this point, we have not declared any instances of zombieType, just the type itself. If that sounds odd, think about it like this: SFML created the Sprite, RectangleShape, and RenderWindow classes, but to use any of those classes we had to declare an object/instance of the class.

At this point we have created a new type called zombieTypes, but we have no instances of it. So let's create them now:

```
zombieType dave = zombieTypes::CRAWLER;
zombieType angela = zombieTypes::SPITTER
zombieType jose = zombieTypes::BLOATER

/*
    Zombies are fictional creatures and any resemblance
    to real people is entirely coincidental
*/
```

Next is a sneak preview of the type of code we will soon be adding to Timber!!!. We will want to track which side of the tree a branch or the player is on, so we will declare an enumeration called side, as in the following example:

```
enum class side { LEFT, RIGHT, NONE };
```

We could position the player on the left as follows:

```
// The player starts on the left
side playerSide = side::LEFT;
```

We could make the fourth level (arrays start from zero) of an array of branch positions have no branch at all, as follows:

```
branchPositions[3] = side::NONE;
```

We can use enumerations in expressions as well:

```
if(branchPositions[5] == playerSide)
{
    // The lowest branch is the same side as the player
    // SQUISHED!!
}
```

We will look at one more vital C++ topic and then we will get back to coding the game.

Getting started with functions

So what exactly are C++ functions? A function is a collection of variables, expressions, and **control flow statements** (loops and branches). In fact, any of the code we have learnt about in the book so far can be used in a function. The first part of a function that we write is called the **signature**. Here is an example function signature:

```
public void bombPlayer(int power, int direction)
```

If you add an opening and closing pair of curly braces { . . . } with some code that the function actually performs then we have a complete function, a definition:

```
void shootLazers(int power, int direction)
{
    // ZAPP!
}
```

We could then use our new function in another part of our code, as follows:

```
// Attack the player
bombPlayer(50, 180) // Run the code in the function
//  I'm back again - code continues here after the function ends
```

When we use a function we say that we **call** it. At the point where we call `bombPlayer`, our program's execution branches to the code contained within that function. The function will run until it reaches the end or is told to `return`. Then the code will continue running from the first line after the function call. We have already been using the functions that SFML provides. What is different here is that we will learn to write and call our own functions.

Here is another example of a function, complete with the code to make the function return to the code that called it:

```
int addAToB(int a, int b)
{
    int answer = a + b;
    return answer;
}
```

The call to use the above function could look like the following:

```
int myAnswer = addAToB(2, 4);
```

Obviously, we don't need to write functions to add two variables together, but the example helps us see a little further into the workings of functions. First we pass in the values 2 and 4. In the function signature the value 2 is assigned to `int a`, and the value 4 is assigned to `int b`.

Within the function body, the variables `a` and `b` are added together and used to initialize the new variable `int answer`. The line `return answer;` does just that. It returns the value stored in `answer` to the calling code, causing `myAnswer` to be initialized with the value 6.

Notice that each of the function signatures in the examples above varies a little. The reason for this is that the C++ function signature is quite flexible, allowing us to build exactly the functions we require.

Exactly how the function signature defines how the function must be called and if/how the function must return a value, deserves further discussion. Let's give each part of that signature a name so we can break it into parts and learn about them.

Here is a function signature with its parts described by their formal, technical terms:

```
return type | name of function | (parameters)
```

And here are a few examples we can use for each of those parts:

- **Return-type**: `bool`, `float`, `int` and so on, or any C++ type or expression
- **Name of function**: `bombPlayer`, `shootLazers`, `setCoordinates`, `addAToB` and so on
- **Parameters**: `(int number, bool hitDetected)`, `(int x, int y)` `(float a, float b)`

Now let's look at each part in turn.

Function return types

The return type, as the name suggests, is the type of the value that will be returned from the function to the calling code:

```
int addAToB(int a, int b)
{
    int answer = a + b;
    return answer;
}
```

In our slightly dull, but useful, addAtoB example previously, the return type in the signature is int. The function addAToB sends back, or returns, to the code that called it, a value that will fit in an int variable. The return type can be any C++ type we have seen so far, or one of the ones we haven't seen yet.

A function does not have to return a value at all however. In this case the signature must use the void keyword as the return type. When the void keyword is used, the function body must not attempt to return a value as this will cause an error. It can, however, use the return keyword without a value. Here are some combinations of return type and the use of the return keyword that are valid:

```
void doWhatever()
{
    // our code
    // I'm done going back to calling code here
    // no return is necessary
}
```

Another possibility is as follows:

```
void doSomethingCool()
{
    // our code
    // I can do this as long as I don't try and add a value
    return;
}
```

The following code gives us yet more examples of possible functions. Be sure to read the comments as well as the code:

```
void doYetAnotherThing()
{
    // some code
    if(someCondition)
    {
```

```
        // if someCondition is true returning to calling code
        // before the end of the function body
        return;
    }
    // More code that might or might not get executed
    return;
    // As I'm at the bottom of the function body
    // and the return type is void, I'm
    // really not necessary but I suppose I make it
    // clear that the function is over.
  }

bool detectCollision(Ship a, Ship b)
{
    // Detect if collision has occurred
    if(collision)
    {
        // Bam!!!
        return true;
    }
    else
    {
        // Missed
        return false;
    }
}
```

The last function example above, detectCollision is a glimpse into the near future of our C++ code, and demonstrates that we can also pass in user-defined types, called **objects**, into functions to perform calculations on them.

We could call each of the functions above, in turn, like this:

```
// OK time to call some functions
doWhatever();
doSomethingCool();
doYetAnotherThing();
if (detectCollision(milleniumFalcon, lukesXWing))
{
    // The jedi are doomed!
    // But there is always Leia.
    // Unless she was on the Falcon?
}
else
{
    // Live to fight another day
}
//continue with code from here
```

Don't worry about the odd-looking syntax regarding the `detectCollision` function, we will see real code like this, quite soon. Simply, we are using the return value (`true` or `false`) as the expression, directly in an `if` statement.

Function names

The function name, when we design our own function, can be almost anything at all. But it is best to use words, usually verbs, to clearly explain what the function will do. For example, look at this function:

```
void functionaroonieboonie(int blibbityblob, float floppyfloatything)
{
    //code here
}
```

The above is perfectly legal, and will work, but these next function names are much clearer:

```
void doSomeVerySpecificTask()
{
    //code here
}

void getMySpaceShipHealth()
{
    //code here
}

void startNewGame()
{
    //code here
}
```

Next, let's take a closer look at how we share some values with a function.

Function parameters

We know that a function can return a result to the calling code. What if we need to share some data values from the calling code with the function? **Parameters** allow us to share values with the function. We have actually already seen examples of parameters while looking at return types. We will look at the same example but a little more closely:

```
int addAToB(int a, int b)
{
    int answer = a + b;
```

```
    return answer;
}
```

Above, the parameters are int a and int b. Notice that, in the first line of the function body, we use a + b as if they are already declared and initialized variables. Well, that's because they are. The parameters in the function signature are their declaration and the code that calls the function initializes them.

Important jargon note

Notice that we are referring to the variables in the function signature brackets (int a, int b) as parameters. When we pass values into the function from the calling code, these values are called arguments. When the arguments arrive they are called parameters and are used to initialize real, usable variables:

```
int returnedAnswer = addAToB(10,5);
```

Also, as we have partly seen in previous examples, we don't have to just use int in our parameters. We can use any C++ type. We can also use as many parameters as necessary to solve our problem, but it is good practice to keep the parameter list as short and therefore manageable as possible.

As we will see in future chapters, we have left a few of the cooler uses of functions out of this introductory tutorial, so that we can learn about related C++ concepts before we take the topic of functions further.

The function body

The body is the part we have been kind of avoiding with comments such as:

```
// code here
// some code
```

But actually, we know exactly what to do here already! Any C++ code we have learned about so far will work in the body of a function.

Function prototypes

We have seen how to code a function and we have seen how to call one as well. There is one more thing we need to do, however, to make them work. All functions must have a **prototype**. A prototype is what makes the compiler aware of our function; without a prototype, the entire game will fail to compile. Fortunately, prototypes are straightforward.

We can simply repeat the function's signature, followed by a semicolon. The caveat is that the prototype must appear before any attempt to call or define the function. So the absolutely simplest example of a fully usable function in action is as follows. Look carefully at the comments and where in the code the different parts of the function appear:

```
// The prototype
// Notice the semicolon
int addAToB(int a, int b);

int main()
{
   // Call the function
   // Store the result in answer
   int answer = addAToB(2,2);
   // Called before the definition
   // but that's OK because of the prototype
   // Exit main
   return 0;
}// End of main

// The function definition
int addAToB(int a, int b)
{
    return a + b;
}
```

What the previous code demonstrates is the following:

- The prototype is before the `main` function
- The call to use the function is, as we might expect, inside the `main` function
- The definition is after/outside the `main` function

 Note that we can omit the function prototype and go straight to the definition when the definition occurs before the function is used. As our code becomes longer and spreads across multiple files, however, this will almost never happen. We will use separate prototypes and definitions all the time.

Let's see how we can keep our functions organized.

Organizing functions

It's well worth pointing out that, if we have multiple functions, especially if they are fairly long, our .cpp file will quickly become unwieldy. This defeats part of the objective that functions are intended for. The solution that we will see in the next project, is that we can add all of our function prototypes to our very own header file (.hpp or .h). Then we can code all of our functions in another .cpp file, and then simply add another #include... directive in our main .cpp file. In this way we can use any number of functions without adding any of their code (prototype or definition) to our main code file.

Function gotcha!

Another point that we should discuss about functions is **scope**. If we declare a variable in a function, either directly or as one of the parameters, then that variable is not usable/visible outside the function. Furthermore, any variables declared outside the function cannot be seen/used inside the function.

The way we should share values between function code and calling code is through the parameters/arguments and the return value.

When a variable is not available, because it is from another function, it is said to be out of scope. When it is available and usable, it is said to be in scope.

Actually, variables declared within any block in C++, are only in scope within that block! This includes loops and if blocks as well. A variable declared at the top of main is in scope anywhere in main. A variable declared in the game loop is only in scope within the game loop, and so on. A variable declared within a function or other block is called a **local** variable. The more code we write, the more this will make sense. Every time we come across an issue in our code regarding scope, I will discuss it to make things clear. There will be one such issue coming up in the next section. And there are some more C++ staples that blow this issue wide open. They are called **references** and **pointers** and we will learn about them in Chapter 7: *C++ References, Sprite Sheets, and Vertex Arrays* and Chapter 8: *Pointers, the Standard Template Library, and Texture Management*, respectively.

Final word on functions – for now

There is a lot more we could learn about functions but we know enough about them already to implement the next part of our game. And don't worry if all the technical terms such as parameters, signatures and definitions, and so on have not completely sunk in. The concepts will become clearer when we start to use them.

Absolute final word on functions – for now

It has probably not escaped your attention that we have been calling functions, especially SFML functions, by appending the name of an object, and a period before the function name, as in the following example:

```
spriteBee.setPosition...
window.draw...
// etc
```

And yet, our entire discussion of functions saw us calling functions without any objects. We can write functions as part of a class or simply as a standalone function. When we write a function as part of a class, we need an object of that class to call the function, and when we have a standalone function we don't.

We will write a standalone function in a minute and we will write classes with functions starting in Chapter 6: *Object-Oriented Programming, Classes, and SFML Views*. Everything we know so far about functions is relevant in both cases.

Growing the branches

Next, as I have been promising for around the last seventeen pages, we will use all the new C++ techniques to draw and move some branches on our tree.

Add this code outside the `main` function. Just to be absolutely clear, I mean before the code `int main()`:

```
#include "stdafx.h"
#include <sstream>
#include <SFML/Graphics.hpp>

using namespace sf;

// Function declaration
void updateBranches(int seed);
```

```
const int NUM_BRANCHES = 6;
Sprite branches[NUM_BRANCHES];

// Where is the player/branch?
// Left or Right
enum class side { LEFT, RIGHT, NONE };
side branchPositions[NUM_BRANCHES];

int main()
{
```

We just achieved quite a few things with that new code:

- First, we wrote a function prototype for a function called `updateBranches`. We can see that it does not return a value (`void`) and it takes an `int` argument called `seed`. We will write the function definition soon and we will then see exactly what it does.
- Next, we declare a constant `int` called `NUM_BRANCHES` and initialize it to 6. There will be six moving branches on the tree and we will soon see how `NUM_BRANCHES` will be useful to us.
- Following this, we declare an array of `Sprite` objects called `branches` that can hold six Sprites.
- After that, we declare a new enumeration called `side` with three possible values, `LEFT`, `RIGHT`, and `NONE`. This will be used to describe the position of individual branches as well as the player, in a few places throughout our code.
- Finally, in the previous new code, we initialize an array of `side` types, with a size of `NUM_BRANCHES` (6). To be clear about what this achieves; we will have an array called `branchPositions` with six values in it. Each of these values is of the type `side`, which can be either, `LEFT`, `RIGHT`, or `NONE`.

 Of course, what you really want to know is why the constant, the two arrays, and the enumeration were declared outside the `main` function. By declaring them above `main` they now have **global scope**. Or, describing it another way, the constant, the two arrays, and the enumeration have scope for the entire game. This will mean we can access and use them all anywhere in the `main` function and in the `updateBranches` function. Note that it is good practice to make all variables as local to where they are actually used as possible. It might seem useful to make everything global but this leads to hard-to-read and error-prone code.

Preparing the branches

Now we will prepare our six `Sprite` objects and load them into the `branches` array. Add the highlighted code just before our game loop:

```
// Position the text
FloatRect textRect = messageText.getLocalBounds();
messageText.setOrigin(textRect.left +
    textRect.width / 2.0f,
    textRect.top +
    textRect.height / 2.0f);

messageText.setPosition(1920 / 2.0f, 1080 / 2.0f);

scoreText.setPosition(20, 20);

// Prepare 6 branches
Texture textureBranch;
textureBranch.loadFromFile("graphics/branch.png");

// Set the texture for each branch sprite
for (int i = 0; i < NUM_BRANCHES; i++)
{
  branches[i].setTexture(textureBranch);
  branches[i].setPosition(-2000, -2000);
  // Set the sprite's origin to dead center
  // We can then spin it round without changing its position
  branches[i].setOrigin(220, 20);
}

while (window.isOpen())
{
```

The previous code does not use any new concepts. First we declare an SFML `Texture` object and load the `branch.png` graphic into it.

Next, we create a `for` loop, which sets `i` to zero and increments `i` by one each pass through the loop until `i` is no longer less than `NUM_BRANCHES`. This is exactly right because `NUM_BRANCHES` is 6 and the `branches` array has positions 0 through 5.

Inside the `for` loop we set the `Texture` for each `Sprite` in the `branches` array with `setTexture` and then hide it off screen with `setPosition`.

Finally, we set the origin (the point which is located when it is drawn), with `setOrigin`, to the center of the sprite. Soon, we will be rotating these sprites and having the origin in the center means they will spin nicely around, without moving the sprite out of position.

Updating the branch sprites each frame

In this next code we set the position of all the sprites in the `branches` array, based upon their position in the array and the value of `side` in the corresponding `branchPositions` array. Add the highlighted code and try to understand it, then we can go through it in detail:

```
// Update the score text
std::stringstream ss;
ss << "Score: " << score;
scoreText.setString(ss.str());

// update the branch sprites
for (int i = 0; i < NUM_BRANCHES; i++)
{
    float height = i * 150;
    if (branchPositions[i] == side::LEFT)
    {
        // Move the sprite to the left side
        branches[i].setPosition(610, height);

        // Flip the sprite round the other way
        branches[i].setRotation(180);
    }

    else if (branchPositions[i] == side::RIGHT)
    {
        // Move the sprite to the right side
        branches[i].setPosition(1330, height);
        // Set the sprite rotation to normal
        branches[i].setRotation(0);
    }
    else
    {
        // Hide the branch
        branches[i].setPosition(3000, height);
    }
}
} // End if(!paused)

/*
****************************************
Draw the scene
****************************************
```

The code we just added is one big `for` loop that sets `i` to zero, increments `i` by 1 each time through the loop, and keeps going until `i` is no longer less than 6.

Inside the `for` loop a new `float` variable called `height` is set to `i * 150`. This means that the first branch will have a height of 0, the second of 150, and the sixth of 750.

Next we have a structure of `if` and `else` blocks. Look at the structure with the code stripped out:

```
if()
{
}
else if()
{
}
else
{
}
```

The first `if` uses the `branchPositions` array to see whether the current branch should be on the left. If it is, it sets the corresponding `Sprite` from the `branches` array to a position on the screen, appropriate for the left (610 pixels) and whatever the current `height` is. It then flips the sprite by `180` degrees because the `branch.png` graphic hangs to the right by default.

The `else if` only executes if the branch is not on the left. It uses the same method to see if it is on the right. If it is then the branch is drawn on the right (`1330` pixels). Then the sprite rotation is set to 0 degrees, just in case it had previously been at `180` degrees. If the x coordinate seems a little bit strange, just remember that we set the origin for the branch sprites to their center.

The final `else` assumes, correctly, that the current `branchPosition` must be NONE and hides the branch off screen at `3000` pixels.

At this point, our branches are in position, ready to be drawn.

Drawing the branches

Here we use another `for` loop, to step through the entire `branches` array from 0 to 5 and draw each branch sprite. Add the following highlighted code:

```
// Draw the clouds
window.draw(spriteCloud1);
window.draw(spriteCloud2);
window.draw(spriteCloud3);

// Draw the branches
```

```
for (int i = 0; i < NUM_BRANCHES; i++)
{
    window.draw(branches[i]);
}

// Draw the tree
window.draw(spriteTree);
```

Of course we still haven't written the function that actually moves all the branches. Once we have written that function, we will also need to work out when and how to call it. Let's solve the first problem and write the function.

Moving the branches

We have already added the function prototype above the main function. Now we code the actual definition of the function that will move all the branches down by one position each time it is called. We will code this function in two parts so we can more easily examine what is happening.

Add the first part of the updateBranches function after the closing curly brace of the main function:

```
// Function definition
void updateBranches(int seed)
{
    // Move all the branches down one place
    for (int j = NUM_BRANCHES-1; j > 0; j--)
    {
        branchPositions[j] = branchPositions[j - 1];
    }
}
```

In this first part of the function, we simply move all the branches down one position, one at a time, starting with the sixth branch. This is achieved by making the for loop count from 5 through to 0. The code branchPositions[j] = branchPositions[j - 1]; makes the actual move.

The other thing to note, with the previous code, is that, after we have moved the branch in position 4 to position 5, then the branch in position 3 to position 4, and so on, we will need to add a new branch at position 0, which is the top of the tree.

Now we can spawn a new branch at the top of the tree. Add the highlighted code and then we will talk about it:

```
// Function definition
void updateBranches(int seed)
{
    // Move all the branches down one place
    for (int j = NUM_BRANCHES-1; j > 0; j--)
    {
        branchPositions[j] = branchPositions[j - 1];
    }

    // Spawn a new branch at position 0
    // LEFT, RIGHT or NONE
    srand((int)time(0)+seed);
    int r = (rand() % 5);
    switch (r)
    {
    case 0:
      branchPositions[0] = side::LEFT;
      break;

    case 1:
      branchPositions[0] = side::RIGHT;
      break;

    default:
      branchPositions[0] = side::NONE;
      break;
    }
}
```

In the final part of the `updateBranches` function, we use the integer `seed` variable that gets passed in with the function call. We do this to guarantee that the random number `seed` is always different and we will see how this value is arrived at in the next chapter.

Next, we generate a random number between zero and four and store the result in the `int` variable r. Now we `switch` using r as the expression.

The `case` statements mean that, if r is equal to zero then we add a new branch on the left-hand side at the top of the tree. If r is equal to 1 then the branch goes on the right. If r is anything else, (2, 3, or 4) then the `default` ensures that no branch will be added at the top. This balance of left, right, and none makes the tree seem realistic and the game works quite well. You could easily change the code to make the branches more frequent or less so.

Even after all this code for our branches, we still can't glimpse a single one of them in the game. This is because we have more work to do before we can actually call `updateBranches`.

If you want to see some branches now, you can add some temporary code and call the function five times with a unique seed each time, just before the game loop:

```
updateBranches(1);
updateBranches(2);
updateBranches(3);
updateBranches(4);
updateBranches(5);

while (window.isOpen())
{
```

You can now see the branches in their place. But if the branches are to actually move we will need to call `updateBranches` on a regular basis.

 Don't forget to remove the temporary code before moving on.

Now we can turn our attention to the player and call the `updateBranches` function for real.

FAQ

Q) You mentioned there were a few types of C++ loop.

A) Yes, take a look at this tutorial and explanation for `do...while` loops:

`http://www.tutorialspoint.com/cplusplus/cpp_do_while_loop.htm`

Q) Can I assume I am an expert on arrays?

A) As with many topics in this book there is always more to learn. You know enough about arrays to proceed, but if you're hungry for more take a look at this fuller array tutorial:
`http://www.cplusplus.com/doc/tutorial/arrays/`.

Q) Can I assume I am an expert on functions?

A) As with many topics in this book there is always more to learn. You know enough about functions to proceed but if want to know even more, take a look at this tutorial:
`http://www.cplusplus.com/doc/tutorial/functions/`.

Summary

Although this wasn't the longest chapter it was probably the chapter where we covered the most C++. We looked at the different types of loop we can use, such as `for` and `while` loops. We studied arrays for handling large amounts of variables and objects without breaking a sweat. We also learnt about enumerations and `switch`. Probably the biggest concept in this chapter, was functions that allow us to organize and abstract our game's code. We will be looking more deeply at functions in a few more places as the book continues.

Now that we have a fully working tree, we can finish the game off in the last chapter for this project.

5
Collisions, Sound, and End Conditions – Making the Game Playable

This is the final phase of the first project. By the end of this chapter you will have your first completed game. Once you have Timber!!! up-and-running, be sure to read the last section of this chapter as it will suggest ways to make the game better. We will be looking at the following topics:

- Adding the rest of the sprites
- Handling the player input
- Animating the flying log
- Handling death
- Adding sound effects
- Adding features and improving Timber!!!

Preparing the player (and other sprites)

Let's add the code for the player's sprite, as well as a few more sprites and textures at the same time. This next, quite large, block of code also adds a gravestone sprite for when the player gets squished, an ax sprite to chop with, and a log sprite that can whiz away each time the player chops.

Notice that after the `spritePlayer` object we also declare a `side` variable, `playerSide`, to keep track of where the player is currently standing. Furthermore, we add some extra variables for the `spriteLog` object, including, `logSpeedX`, `logSpeedY`, and `logActive` to store how fast the log will move, and whether it is currently moving. The `spriteAxe` also has two related `float` constant variables to remember where the ideal pixel position is on both the left and the right.

Add this next block of code just before the `while(window.isOpen())` code as we have done so often before. Note that all the code in this next listing is new, not just the highlighted code. I haven't provided any extra context for the next block of code as `while(window.isOpen())` should be easy to identify. The highlighted code is the code we have just specifically discussed.

Add the entirety of this code, just before the `while(window.isOpen())` line, and make a mental note of the highlighted lines we have briefly discussed. It will make the rest of the chapter's code easier to understand:

```
// Prepare the player
Texture texturePlayer;
texturePlayer.loadFromFile("graphics/player.png");
Sprite spritePlayer;
spritePlayer.setTexture(texturePlayer);
spritePlayer.setPosition(580, 720);

// The player starts on the left
side playerSide = side::LEFT;

// Prepare the gravestone
Texture textureRIP;
textureRIP.loadFromFile("graphics/rip.png");
Sprite spriteRIP;
spriteRIP.setTexture(textureRIP);
spriteRIP.setPosition(600, 860);

// Prepare the axe
Texture textureAxe;
textureAxe.loadFromFile("graphics/axe.png");
Sprite spriteAxe;
spriteAxe.setTexture(textureAxe);
spriteAxe.setPosition(700, 830);

// Line the axe up with the tree
const float AXE_POSITION_LEFT = 700;
const float AXE_POSITION_RIGHT = 1075;

// Prepare the flying log
```

```
Texture textureLog;
textureLog.loadFromFile("graphics/log.png");
Sprite spriteLog;
spriteLog.setTexture(textureLog);
spriteLog.setPosition(810, 720);
```

```
// Some other useful log related variables
bool logActive = false;
float logSpeedX = 1000;
float logSpeedY = -1500;
```

Now we can draw all our new sprites.

Drawing the player and other sprites

Before we add the code to move the player and use all our new sprites, let's draw them. This is so that, as we add code to update/change/move the sprites, we will be able to see what is happening.

Add the highlighted code to draw the four new sprites:

```
// Draw the tree
window.draw(spriteTree);

// Draw the player
window.draw(spritePlayer);

// Draw the axe
window.draw(spriteAxe);

// Draraw the flying log
window.draw(spriteLog);

// Draw the gravestone
window.draw(spriteRIP);

// Draw the bee
window.draw(spriteBee);
```

Run the game and you will see our new sprites in the scene.

We are really close to a working game now.

Handling the player's input

Lots of different things depend on the movement of the player, such as when to show the ax, when to begin animating the log, and when to move all the branches down a place. It therefore makes sense to set up the keyboard handling for the player chopping. Once this is done, we can put all the features we just mentioned into the same part of the code.

Let's think for a moment about how we detect keyboard presses. In each frame we test whether a particular keyboard key is currently being held down. If it is, we take action. If the *Esc* key is being held down, we quit the game, or if the *Enter* key is being held down we restart the game. So far, this has been sufficient for our needs.

There is, however, a problem with this approach when we try and handle the chopping of the tree. The problem has always been there, it just didn't matter until now. Depending on how powerful your PC is, the game loop could be executing thousands of times per second. Each and every pass through the game loop during which a key is held down, it is detected and the related code will execute.

So actually, every time you press *Enter* to restart the game, you are most likely restarting it well in excess of a hundred times. This is because even the briefest of presses will last a significant fraction of a second. You can verify this by running the game and holding down the *Enter* key. Note that the time bar doesn't move. This is because the game is being restarted over and over again, hundreds, or even thousands, of times a second.

If we don't use a different approach for the player chopping, then just one attempted chop will bring the entire tree down in a mere fraction of a second. We need to be a bit more sophisticated. What we will do is allow the player to chop then, when he does so, disable the code that detects a key press. We will then detect when the player removes his finger from a key and then re-enable the detection of key presses. Here are the steps laid out clearly:

1. Wait for the player to use the left or right arrow keys to chop a log.
2. When the player chops, disable key press detection.
3. Wait for the player to remove their finger from a key.
4. Re enable chop detection.
5. Repeat from step 1.

This might sound complicated, but with SFML's help it will be really straightforward. Let's implement this now, one step at a time.

Add the highlighted line of code, which declares a `bool` variable called `acceptInput`, which will be used to determine when to listen for chops and when to ignore them:

```
float logSpeedX = 1000;
float logSpeedY = -1500;

// Control the player input
bool acceptInput = false;

while (window.isOpen())
{
```

Now we have our Boolean set up we can move on to the next step.

Handling setting up a new game

Now we're ready to handle chops, add the highlighted code to the `if` block that starts a new game:

```
/*
****************************************
Handle the players input
****************************************
*/

if (Keyboard::isKeyPressed(Keyboard::Escape))
{
  window.close();
}

// Start the game
if (Keyboard::isKeyPressed(Keyboard::Return))
{
  paused = false;

  // Reset the time and the score
  score = 0;
  timeRemaining = 6;

  // Make all the branches disappear
  for (int i = 1; i < NUM_BRANCHES; i++)
  {
    branchPositions[i] = side::NONE;
  }

  // Make sure the gravestone is hidden
  spriteRIP.setPosition(675, 2000);

  // Move the player into position
  spritePlayer.setPosition(580, 720);

  acceptInput = true;
}

/*
****************************************
Update the scene
****************************************
*/
```

In the previous code we used a `for` loop to set the tree with no branches. This is fair to the player because, if the game started with a branch right above his head, it would be considered unsporting. Then we simply move the gravestone off the screen and the player into his starting location on the left. The last thing this new code does is to set `acceptInput` to `true`. We are now ready to receive chopping key presses.

Detecting the player chopping

Now we can prepare to handle the left and right cursor key presses. Add this simple `if` block, which only executes when `acceptInput` is `true`:

```
// Start the game
if (Keyboard::isKeyPressed(Keyboard::Return))
{
  paused = false;

  // Reset the time and the score
  score = 0;
  timeRemaining = 5;

  // Make all the branches disappear
  for (int i = 1; i < NUM_BRANCHES; i++)
  {
    branchPositions[i] = side::NONE;
  }

  // Make sure the gravestone is hidden
  spriteRIP.setPosition(675, 2000);

  // Move the player into position
  spritePlayer.setPosition(675, 660);

  acceptInput = true;

}

// Wrap the player controls to
// Make sure we are accepting input
if (acceptInput)
{
  // More code here next...
}


/*
```

```
*****************************************
Update the scene
*****************************************
*/
```

Now, inside the `if` block that we just coded, add the highlighted code to handle what happens when the player presses the right cursor key (→) on the keyboard:

```
// Wrap the player controls to
// Make sure we are accepting input
if (acceptInput)
{
    // More code here next...
    // First handle pressing the right cursor key
    if (Keyboard::isKeyPressed(Keyboard::Right))
    {
        // Make sure the player is on the right
        playerSide = side::RIGHT;
        score ++;

        // Add to the amount of time remaining
        timeRemaining += (2 / score) + .15;

        spriteAxe.setPosition(AXE_POSITION_RIGHT,
            spriteAxe.getPosition().y);

        spritePlayer.setPosition(1200, 720);

        // update the branches
        updateBranches(score);

        // set the log flying to the left
        spriteLog.setPosition(810, 720);
        logSpeedX = -5000;
        logActive = true;

        acceptInput = false;
    }

    // Handle the left cursor key
}
```

Quite a bit is happening in that previous code, so let's go through it. First we detect if the player has chopped on the right hand side of the tree. If he has, then we set `playerSide` to `side::RIGHT`. We will respond to the value of `playerSide` later in the code.

Then we add 1 to the score with `score ++`. The next line of code is slightly mysterious, but all that is happening is that we are adding to the amount of time remaining. We are rewarding the player for taking action. The problem for the player, however, is that the bigger the score gets, the less additional time is added on. You can play with this formula to make the game easier or harder.

Then, the ax is moved into its right-hand side position with `spriteAxe.setPosition` and the player sprite is also moved into its right-hand position.

Next, we call `updateBranches` to move all the branches down one place and spawn a new random branch (or space) at the top of the tree.

Then, `spriteLog` is moved into its starting position, camouflaged against the tree, and its `speedX` variable is set to a negative number, so that it whizzes off to the left. Also, `logActive` is set to true so that the log-moving code, which we will write soon, animates the log each frame.

Finally, `acceptInput` is set to `false`. At this point, the player can make no more chops. We have solved the problem of the presses being detected too frequently and we will see how we re-enable chopping soon.

Now, still inside the `if(acceptInput)` block that we just coded, add the highlighted code to handle what happens when the player presses the left cursor key (←) on the keyboard:

```
// Handle the left cursor key

if (Keyboard::isKeyPressed(Keyboard::Left))
{
  // Make sure the player is on the left
  playerSide = side::LEFT;
  score++;

  // Add to the amount of time remaining
  timeRemaining += (2 / score) + .15;

  spriteAxe.setPosition(AXE_POSITION_LEFT,
    spriteAxe.getPosition().y);

  spritePlayer.setPosition(580, 720);

  // update the branches
  updateBranches(score);

  // set the log flying
  spriteLog.setPosition(810, 720);
```

```
        logSpeedX = 5000;
        logActive = true;

        acceptInput = false;
    }

}
```

The previous code is just the same as the code that handles the right-hand side chop, except that the sprites are positioned differently and the `logSpeedX` variable is set to a positive value, so that the log whizzes to the right.

Detecting a key being released

To make the above work beyond the first chop, we need to detect when the player releases a key and set `acceptInput` back to `true`.

This is slightly different to the key handling we have seen so far. SFML has two different ways of detecting keyboard input from the player. The first way we have already seen. It is dynamic and instantaneous, exactly what we need to respond immediately to a key press.

This next code uses the other method. Enter the next highlighted code at the top of the `Handle the players input` section and then we will go through it:

```
/*
****************************************
Handle the players input
****************************************
*/

Event event;

while (window.pollEvent(event))
{
    if (event.type == Event::KeyReleased && !paused)
    {
        // Listen for key presses again
        acceptInput = true;

        // hide the axe
        spriteAxe.setPosition(2000,
            spriteAxe.getPosition().y);
    }
}
```

```
if (Keyboard::isKeyPressed(Keyboard::Escape))
{
  window.close();
}
```

First we declare an object of the type `Event` called `event`. Then we call the `window.pollEvent` function, passing in our new object, `event`. The `pollEvent` function puts data into the `event` object, which describes an operating system event. This could be a key press, key release, mouse movement, mouse click, game controller action or something that happened to the window itself (it could be resized and so on).

The reason that we wrap our code in a `while` loop is because there might be many events stored in a queue. The `window.pollEvent` function will load them, one at a time, into `event`. We will see each pass through the loop, if we are interested in the current event, and respond if we are. When `window.pollEvent` returns `false`, that means there are no more events in the queue and the `while` loop will exit.

This `if` condition (`event.type == Event::KeyReleased && !paused`) is `true` when both a key has been released and also the game is not paused.

Inside the `if` block we set `acceptInput` back to `true` and hide the ax sprite off screen.

You can run the game now and gaze in awe at the moving tree, swinging ax, and animated player. It won't, however, squash the player, and the log needs to move when chopped as well.

Animating the chopped logs and the ax

When the player chops, `logActive` is set to `true`, so we can wrap some code in a block that only executes when `logActive` is `true`. Furthermore, each chop sets `logSpeedX` to either a positive or negative number, so the log is ready to fly away from the tree in the correct direction.

Add this next highlighted code, right after we update the branch sprites:

```
// update the branch sprites
for (int i = 0; i < NUM_BRANCHES; i++)
{

  float height = i * 150;

  if (branchPositions[i] == side::LEFT)
  {
```

```
        // Move the sprite to the left side
        branches[i].setPosition(610, height);

        // Flip the sprite round the other way
        branches[i].setRotation(180);
    }
    else if (branchPositions[i] == side::RIGHT)
    {
        // Move the sprite to the right side
        branches[i].setPosition(1330, height);

        // Flip the sprite round the other way
        branches[i].setRotation(0);

    }
    else
    {
        // Hide the branch
        branches[i].setPosition(3000, height);
    }
}

// Handle a flying log
if (logActive)
{

    spriteLog.setPosition(
        spriteLog.getPosition().x +
        (logSpeedX * dt.asSeconds()),
        spriteLog.getPosition().y +
        (logSpeedY * dt.asSeconds()));

    // Has the log reached the right hand edge?
    if (spriteLog.getPosition().x < -100 ||
        spriteLog.getPosition().x > 2000)
    {
        // Set it up ready to be a whole new log next frame
        logActive = false;
        spriteLog.setPosition(810, 720);
    }
}


} // End if(!paused)

/*
****************************************
Draw the scene
```

```
* * * * * * * * * * * * * * * * * * * * * * * * * * * * * * * * * * *
*/
```

The code sets the position of the sprite by getting its current x and y location with `getPosition`, and then adding to it using `logSpeedX` and `logSpeedY`, respectively, multiplied by `dt.asSeconds`.

After the log sprite has been moved in each frame, the code uses an `if` block to see if the sprite has disappeared out of view on either the left or the right. If it has, the log is moved back to its starting point ready for the next chop.

If you run the game you will be able to see the log flying off to the appropriate side of the screen.

Now for a more sensitive subject.

Handling death

Every game has to end badly, with either the player running out of time (which we have already handled), or getting squished by a branch.

Detecting the player getting squished is really simple. All we want to know is whether the last branch in the `branchPositions` array equals `playerSide`. If it does, the player is dead.

Add the highlighted code that detects this and then we will talk about everything we do when the player is squished:

```cpp
// Handle a flying log
if (logActive)
{

  spriteLog.setPosition(
    spriteLog.getPosition().x + (logSpeedX * dt.asSeconds()),
    spriteLog.getPosition().y + (logSpeedY * dt.asSeconds()));

  // Has the log reached the right hand edge?
  if (spriteLog.getPosition().x < -100 ||
    spriteLog.getPosition().x > 2000)
  {
    // Set it up ready to be a whole new cloud next frame
    logActive = false;
    spriteLog.setPosition(800, 600);
  }
}

// Has the player been squished by a branch?
if (branchPositions[5] == playerSide)
{
  // death
  paused = true;
  acceptInput = false;

  // Draw the gravestone
  spriteRIP.setPosition(525, 760);

  // hide the player
  spritePlayer.setPosition(2000, 660);

  // Change the text of the message
  messageText.setString("SQUISHED!!");

  // Center it on the screen
  FloatRect textRect = messageText.getLocalBounds();

  messageText.setOrigin(textRect.left +
    textRect.width / 2.0f,
    textRect.top + textRect.height / 2.0f);

  messageText.setPosition(1920 / 2.0f,
    1080 / 2.0f);

}
```

```
} // End if(!paused)

/*
*****************************************
Draw the scene
*****************************************
*/
```

The first thing the code does, after the player's demise, is to set `paused` to `true`. Now the loop will complete this frame and won't run the update part of the loop again until a new game is started by the player.

Then we move the gravestone into position, near where the player was standing, and hide the player sprite off-screen.

We set the string of `messageText` to `"SQUISHED!!"` and then use the usual technique to center it on the screen.

You can now run the game and play it for real. This image shows the player's final score and his gravestone, as well as the **SQUISHED** message.

There is just one more problem. Is it just me, or is it a little bit quiet?

Simple sound FX

We will add three sounds. Each sound will be played on a particular game event. A simple thud sound whenever the player chops, a gloomy losing sound when the player runs out of time, and a retro crushing sound when the player is squished to death.

How SFML sound works?

SFML plays sound effects using two different classes. The first class is the `SoundBuffer` class. This is the class that holds the actual audio data from the sound file. It is the `SoundBuffer` that is responsible for loading the `.wav` files into the PC's RAM in a format that can be played without any further decoding work.

In a minute, when we write code for the sound effects, we will see that, once we have a `SoundBuffer` object with our sound stored in it, we will then create another object of the type `Sound`. We can then associate this `Sound` object with a `SoundBuffer` object. Then, at the appropriate moment in our code, we will be able to call the `play` function of the appropriate `Sound` object.

When to play the sounds

As we will see very soon, the C++ code to load and play sounds is really simple. What we need to consider, however, is *when* to call the `play` function. Where in our code will we put the function calls to `play`? Following are some of the features we want to achieve:

- The chop sound can be called from the key presses of the left and right cursor keys
- The death sound can be played from the `if` block that detects that a tree has mangled the player
- The out-of-time sound can be played from the `if` block that detects that the `timeRemaining` is less than zero

Now we can write our sound code.

Adding the sound code

First we add another #include directive to make the SFML sound-related classes available. Add the following highlighted code:

```
#include "stdafx.h"
#include <sstream>
#include <SFML/Graphics.hpp>
#include <SFML/Audio.hpp>

using namespace sf;
```

Now we declare three different SoundBuffer objects, load three different sound files into them, and associate three different objects of the type Sound with the related objects of the type SoundBuffer. Add the following highlighted code:

```
// Control the player input
bool acceptInput = false;

// Prepare the sound
SoundBuffer chopBuffer;
chopBuffer.loadFromFile("sound/chop.wav");
Sound chop;
chop.setBuffer(chopBuffer);

SoundBuffer deathBuffer;
deathBuffer.loadFromFile("sound/death.wav");
Sound death;
death.setBuffer(deathBuffer);

// Out of time
SoundBuffer ootBuffer;
ootBuffer.loadFromFile("sound/out_of_time.wav");
Sound outOfTime;
outOfTime.setBuffer(ootBuffer);

while (window.isOpen())
{
```

Now we can play our first sound effect. Add the single line of code as shown next to the if block that detects that the player has pressed the left cursor key:

```
// Wrap the player controls to
// Make sure we are accepting input
if (acceptInput)
{
    // More code here next...
```

```
// First handle pressing the right cursor key
if (Keyboard::isKeyPressed(Keyboard::Right))
{
  // Make sure the player is on the right
  playerSide = side::RIGHT;
  score++;

  timeRemaining += (2 / score) + .15;

  spriteAxe.setPosition(AXE_POSITION_RIGHT,
    spriteAxe.getPosition().y);

  spritePlayer.setPosition(1120, 660);

  // update the branches
  updateBranches(score);
  // set the log flying to the left
  spriteLog.setPosition(800, 600);
  logSpeedX = -5000;
  logActive = true;


  acceptInput = false;

  // Play a chop sound
  chop.play();
}
```

 Add exactly the same code at the end of the next block of code that starts `if (Keyboard::isKeyPressed(Keyboard::Left))` to make a chopping sound when the player chops on the left-hand side of the tree.

Find the code that deals with the player running out of time and add the highlighted code, shown next, to play the out-of-time-related sound effect:

```
if (timeRemaining <= 0.f) {
  // Pause the game
  paused = true;

  // Change the message shown to the player
  messageText.setString("Out of time!!");

  //Reposition the text based on its new size
  FloatRect textRect = messageText.getLocalBounds();
  messageText.setOrigin(textRect.left +
    textRect.width / 2.0f,
    textRect.top +
```

```
        textRect.height / 2.0f);

    messageText.setPosition(1920 / 2.0f, 1080 / 2.0f);

    // Play the out of time sound
    outOfTime.play();

}
```

Finally, to play the death sound when the player is squished, add the highlighted code to the `if` block that executes when the bottom branch is on the same side as the player:

```
// has the player been squished by a branch?
if (branchPositions[5] == playerSide)
{
    // death
    paused = true;
    acceptInput = false;
    // Draw the gravestone
    spriteRIP.setPosition(675, 660);

    // hide the player
    spritePlayer.setPosition(2000, 660);

    messageText.setString("SQUISHED!!");
    FloatRect textRect = messageText.getLocalBounds();

    messageText.setOrigin(textRect.left +
        textRect.width / 2.0f,
        textRect.top + textRect.height / 2.0f);

    messageText.setPosition(1920 / 2.0f, 1080 / 2.0f);

    // Play the death sound
    death.play();
}
```

That's it! We have finished the first game. Let's discuss some possible enhancements before we move on to the second project.

Improving the game and the code

Take a look at these suggested enhancements for the Timber!!! project. You can see the enhancements in action in the `Runnable` folder of the download bundle:

1. **Speeding up the code**: There is a part of our code that is slowing down our game. It doesn't matter for this simple game, but we can speed things up by putting the `sstream` code in a block that only executes occasionally. After all, we don't need to update the score hundreds of times a second!

2. **Debugging console**: Let's add some more text so we can see the current frame rate. As with the score, we don't need to update this too often. Once every hundred frames will do.

3. **Adding more trees in the background**: Simply add some more tree sprites and draw them in whatever position looks good (you could have some nearer the camera, some further away).

4. **Improving the visibility of the HUD text**: We can draw simple `RectangleShape` objects behind the score and the FPS counter; black with a bit of transparency will look quite good.

5. **Making the cloud code more efficient**: As we alluded to a few times already, we can use our knowledge of arrays to make the cloud code a lot shorter.

Take a look at the game in action with extra trees, clouds, and a transparent background for the text.

To see the code for these enhancements, take a look in the `Timber Enhanced Version` folder for the download bundle.

FAQ

Q) I admit that the array solution for the clouds was more efficient. But do we really need three separate arrays, one for active, one for speed, and one for the sprite itself?

A) If we look at the properties/variables that various objects have, for example `Sprite` objects, we will see they are numerous. Sprites have position, color, size, rotation, and many more as well. But it would be just perfect if they had `active`, `speed`, and perhaps more as well. The problem is that the coders at SFML can't possibly predict all the ways that we will use their `Sprite` class. Fortunately, we can make our own classes. We could make a class called `Cloud` that has a Boolean for `active` and an `int` for speed. We can even give our `Cloud` class an SFML `Sprite` object. We could then simplify our cloud code even further. We will look at designing our own classes in the next chapter.

Summary

In this chapter we added the finishing touches and graphics to the Timber!!! game. If, prior to this book, you had never coded a single line of C++ then you can give yourself a big pat on the back. In just five modest chapters you have gone from zero knowledge to a working game.

However, we will not be congratulating ourselves for too long because in the next chapter we will move straight on to some slightly more hardcore C++, which we can use to build more complicated and fuller-featured games.

6
Object-Oriented Programming, Classes, and SFML Views

This is the longest chapter of the book. There is a fair amount of theory, but the theory will give us the knowledge to start using **Object-Oriented Programming (OOP)** to powerful effect. Furthermore, we will not waste any time bfore putting that theory to good use. Before we explore C++ OOP, we will find out about and plan our next game project.

This is what we will do in this chapter:

- Plan the **Zombie Arena** game
- Learn about OOP and classes
- Code the `Player` class
- Learn about the SFML `View` class
- Build the Zombie Arena game engine
- Put the `Player` class to work

Planning and starting the Zombie Arena game

At this point, if you haven't already, I suggest you go and watch a video of Over 9,000 Zombies (`http://store.steampowered.com/app/273500/`) and Crimson Land (`http://store.steampowered.com/app/262830/`).

Our game will obviously not be as in-depth or advanced as either of the examples but we will have the same basic set of features and game mechanics:

- A **Heads-up Display (HUD)** that shows details such as score, high score, bullets in clip, total bullets left, player health, and zombies left to kill
- The player will shoot zombies while frantically running away from them
- Move around a scrolling world using the *W*, *A*, *S*, and *D* keys while aiming the gun using the mouse
- In between each level, choose a **level up** that will affect the way the game needs to be played to succeed
- Collect **pick-ups** to restore health and ammunition
- Each wave brings more zombies and a bigger arena

There will be three types of zombie to splatter. They will have different attributes such as appearance, health, and speed. We will call them chasers, bloaters, and crawlers. Take a look at this annotated screenshot of the game to see some of the features in action and the components and assets that make up the game:

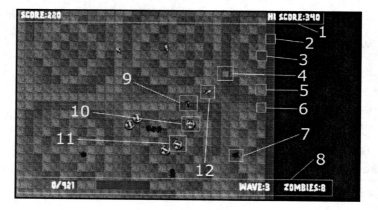

Here is a little bit more information about each of the numbered points:

1. The **SCORE** and **HI SCORE**. These, along with the other parts of the HUD, will be drawn in a separate layer, known as a **View**. The hi-score will be saved and loaded to a file.
2. This is a texture that will build a wall around the arena. This texture is contained in a single graphic called a **sprite-sheet**, along with the other background textures (3, 5, and 6).
3. The first of two mud textures from the sprite-sheet.
4. This is an **ammo pick-up**. When the player gets this they will be given more

ammunition. There is a **health pick-up** as well. The players can choose to upgrade these pick-ups in between waves of zombies.

5. A grass texture, also from the sprite-sheet.
6. The second mud texture from the sprite-sheet.
7. A blood splat where there used to be a zombie.
8. The bottom part of the HUD. From left to right there is an icon to represent ammo, the number of bullets in the clip, the number of spare bullets, a health bar, the current wave of zombies, and the number of zombies remaining in this wave.
9. The player character.
10. A crosshair which the player aims with the mouse.
11. A slow-moving but strong bloater zombie
12. A slightly faster-moving but weaker crawler zombie. There is also a chaser zombie who is very fast and weak. Unfortunately, I couldn't manage to get one in the screenshot before they were all killed.

We have a lot to do and new C++ skills to learn. Let's start by creating a new project.

Creating a project from the template

Creating a new project is now extremely easy. Just follow these straightforward steps in Visual Studio:

1. Select **File** | **New Project** from the main menu.
2. Make sure that **Visual C++** is selected in the left-hand menu and then select **HelloSFML** from the list of presented options. This next image should make this clear:

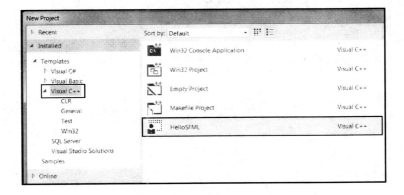

3. In the **Name:** field, type ZombieArena and also make sure that the **Create directory for solution** option is checked. Now click **OK**.

4. Now we need to copy the SFML .dll files into the main project directory. My main project directory is D:\Visual Studio Stuff\Projects\ ZombieArena\ZombieArena. This folder was created by Visual Studio in the previous step. If you put your Projects folder somewhere else then perform this step there instead. The files we need to copy in to the Projects folder are located in your SFML\bin folder. Open a window for each of the two locations and highlight the required .dll files.

Now copy and paste the highlighted files into the project. The project is now set up and ready to go.

The project assets

The assets in this project are more numerous and diverse than the previous game. The assets include:

- A font for the writing on the screen
- Sound effects for different actions such as shooting, reloading, or getting hit by a zombie

All the graphics for the character, zombies, background, and sound required for the game are included in the download bundle. They can be found in the Chapter 6/graphics, and Chapter 6/sound folders, respectively.

The font that is required has not been supplied. This is because I wanted to avoid any possible ambiguity regarding the license. This will not cause a problem though, as I will show you exactly where and how to choose and download fonts for yourself.

Although I will provide either the assets themselves or information on where to get them, you might like to create and acquire them for yourself.

Exploring the assets

The graphical assets make up the parts of the scene that is our Zombie Arena game. Take a look at the graphical assets and it should be clear where in our game they will be used:

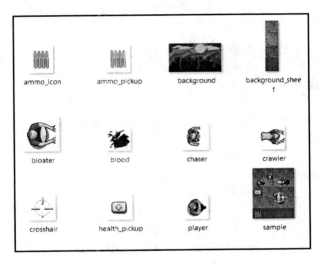

What might be less obvious, however, is the background_sheet.png which contains four different images. This is the sprite-sheet I mentioned previously, and we will see how we can use one to save memory and increase the speed of our game in Chapter 7, *C++ References, Sprite Sheets, and Vertex Arrays.*

The sound files are all .wav format. These are files which contain the sound effects that we will play at certain events throughout the game. They are:

- hit.wav: A sound that plays when a zombie comes into contact with the player
- pickup.wav: A sound that plays when the player touches (collects) a health boost (pick-up)
- powerup.wav: A sound that plays when the player chooses an attribute to increase (power-up) in between each wave of zombies
- reload.wav: A satisfying click to let the player know they have loaded a fresh clip of ammunition
- reload_failed.wav: A less satisfying sound that indicates failure to load new bullets
- shoot.wav: A shooting sound
- splat.wav: A sound like a zombie being hit by a bullet

Adding the assets to the project

Once you have decided which assets you will use, it is time to add them to the project. These next instructions will assume you are using all the assets supplied in the book's download bundle. Where you are using your own, simply replace the appropriate sound or graphic file with your own, using exactly the same file name that is used in this book:

1. Browse to `D:\Visual Studio Stuff\Projects\ZombieArena\ZombieArena`.
2. Create three new folders within this folder and name them `graphics`, `sound`, and `fonts`.
3. From the download bundle, copy the entire contents of `Chapter 6/graphics` into the `D:\Visual Studio Stuff\Projects\ZombieArena\ZombieArena\graphics` folder.
4. From the download bundle, copy the entire contents of `Chapter 6/sound` into the `D:\Visual Studio Stuff\Projects\ZombieArena\ZombieArena\sound` folder.
5. Now visit `http://www.1001freefonts.com/zombie_control.font` in your web browser and download the **Zombie Control** font.

Extract the contents of the zipped download and add the `zombiecontrol.ttf` file to the `D:\Visual Studio Stuff\Projects\ZombieArena\ZombieArena\fonts` folder. Now it's time to learn some more C++, so we can start writing the code for Zombie Arena.

OOP

OOP is a programming paradigm that we could consider almost the standard way to code. It is true there are non-OOP ways to code and there are even some non-OOP game coding languages and libraries. However, starting from scratch, as this book does, there is no reason to do things any other way. When the benefits of OOP become apparent you will never look back.

OOP will:

- Make our code easier to manage, change, or update
- Make our code quicker and more reliable to write
- Make it possible to easily use other people's code (such as SFML)

We have already seen the third benefit in action. Let's look at the first two benefits by introducing a problem that needs solving. The problem we are faced with is the complexity of the current project. Let's consider just a single zombie and what we need to make it function in the game:

- Horizontal and vertical position
- Size
- Direction it is facing
- Different textures for each zombie type
- Sprites
- Different speeds for each zombie type
- Different health for each zombie type
- Keeping track of the type of each zombie
- Collision-detection data
- Intelligence (to chase the player)
- Is the zombie alive or dead?

This list suggests perhaps a dozen variables for just one zombie! We would need, perhaps, whole arrays of each of these variables for managing a zombie horde. And what about all the bullets from the machine gun, the pick-ups, and the different level ups? The simple Timber!!! game was starting to get a bit unmanageable by the end, and it is easy to speculate that this more complicated shooter could be many times worse!

Fortunately, handling complexity is not a new problem, and C++ was designed from the start to be the solution for this complexity.

What is OOP?

OOP is a way of programming that involves breaking our requirements down into chunks that are more manageable than the whole.

Each chunk is self-contained, yet potentially reusable by other programs, while working together with the other chunks as a whole.

These chunks are what we have been referring to as objects. When we plan and code an object, we do so with a **class**.

A class can be thought of as the blueprint for an object.

We implement an object of a class. This is called an **instance** of a class. Think about a house blueprint. You can't live in it, but you can build a house from it. You build an instance of it. Often when we design classes for our games, we write them to represent real world things. In this project, we will write classes for the player, a zombie, a bullet, and more as well. However, OOP is more than this.

OOP is a way of doing things, a methodology that defines best practices.

The three core principles of OOP are **encapsulation**, **polymorphism**, and **inheritance**. This might sound complex, but actually, taken a step at a time, it is reasonably straightforward.

Encapsulation

Encapsulation means keeping the internal workings of your code safe from interference from the code that uses it. You can achieve this by allowing only the variables and functions, which you choose, to be accessed. This means your code can always be updated, extended, or improved without affecting the programs that use it, as long as the exposed parts are still accessed in the same way.

As an example, with proper encapsulation, it wouldn't matter if the SFML team needed to update the way their Sprite class works. As long as the function signatures remain the same, we don't have to worry about what goes on inside. Our code written before the update will still work after the update.

Polymorphism

Polymorphism allows us to write code that is less dependent on the types we are trying to manipulate. This will make our code clearer and more efficient. Polymorphism means different forms. If the objects that we code can be more than one type of thing, then we can take advantage of this. Polymorphism might sound a little bit like black magic at this point. We will use polymorphism in the final project starting in Chapter 12, *Abstraction and Code Management – Making Better Use of OOP*. Everything will then become clearer.

Inheritance

Just like it sounds, inheritance means we can harness all the features and benefits of other people's classes, including the encapsulation and polymorphism, while further refining their code specifically to our situation. We will use inheritance in the final project starting in Chapter 12, *Abstraction and Code Management - Making Better Use of OOP.*

Why do it like this?

When written properly, all this OOP allows you to add new features without worrying as much about how they interact with existing features. When you do have to change a class, its self-contained (encapsulated) nature means fewer or perhaps even zero consequences for other parts of the program.

You can use other people's code (such as the SFML classes) without knowing or perhaps even caring how it works inside.

OOP, and by extension SFML, allows you to write games that use complicated concepts, such as multiple cameras, multiplayer, OpenGL, directional sound, and more besides. All this without breaking a sweat.

Using inheritance you can create multiple similar, yet different, versions of a class without starting the class from scratch.

You can still use the functions intended for the original type of object with your new object because of polymorphism.

All this makes sense, really. And, as we know, C++ was designed from the start with all of this OOP in mind.

The ultimate key to success with OOP and making games (or any other type of app), other than the determination to succeed, is planning and design. It is not so much just knowing all the C++, SFML, and OOP topics that will help you write great code, but rather applying all that knowledge to write code that is well structured and designed. The code in this book is presented in an order and manner appropriate to learning the various C++ topics in a gaming context. The art and science of structuring your code is called **design patterns**. As your code gets longer and more complex, effective use of design patterns will become more important. The good news is that we don't need to invent these design patterns ourselves. We will need to learn about them as our projects get more complex. More on design patterns in the final chapter.

In this project we will learn about and use basic classes and encapsulation, and in the final project we will get a bit more daring and use inheritance, polymorphism, and other OOP-related C++ features too.

What is a class?

A class is a bunch of code that can contain functions, variables, loops, and all the other C++ syntax we have already learned about. Each new class will be declared in its own .h code file with the same name as the class and its functions will be defined in their own .cpp file. This will become clearer when we actually look at writing some classes.

Once we have written a class, we can use it to make as many objects from it as we want. Remember, the class is the blueprint and we make objects based on the blueprint. The house isn't the blueprint just as the object isn't the class. It is an object made from the class.

 You can think of an object as a variable and the class as a type.

Of course, with all this talk of OOP and classes we haven't actually seen any code. So let's fix that now.

The class, variable, and function declarations

Let's use a different game example to Zombie Arena. Consider the most basic game of all, Pong. A paddle/bat that bounces a ball. The paddle would be an excellent candidate for a class.

 If you don't know what Pong is, then take a look at this link: https://en. wikipedia.org/wiki/Pong

Take a look at a hypothetical Paddle.h file:

```
class Paddle
{
    private:

        // Length of the pong paddle
        int m_Length = 100;
```

```
    // Height of the pong paddle
    int m_Height = 10;

    // Location on x axis
    int m_XPosition;

    // Location on y axis
    int m_YPosition;

  public:

    void moveRight();
    void moveLeft();
};
```

At first glance the code might appear a little complex, but when it is explained we will see there are very few new concepts.

The first thing to notice is that a new class is declared using the `class` keyword followed by the name of the class, and that the entire declaration is enclosed in curly braces followed by a closing semicolon:

```
class Paddle
{

};
```

Now look at the variable declarations and their names:

```
// Length of the pong paddle
int m_Length = 100;

// Height of the pong paddle
int m_Height = 10;

// Location on x axis
int m_XPosition;

// Location on Y axis
int m_YPosition;
```

All the names are prefixed with m_. This is not necessary, but it is a good convention. Variables declared as part of the class are called **member variables**. Prefixing with an m_ makes it absolutely plain when we are dealing with a member variable. When we write functions for our classes, we will start to see local variables and parameters as well. The m_ convention will then prove itself useful.

Notice also that all the variables are in a section of the code headed with the `private:` keyword. Scan your eyes over the previous sample code and notice that the body of the class code is separated into two sections:

```
private:
    // more code here

public:
    // More code here
```

The `public` and `private` keywords control the encapsulation of our class. Anything that is private cannot be accessed directly by the user of an instance or object of the class. If you are designing a class for others to use, you don't want them being able to alter anything at will.

This means that our four member variables cannot be accessed directly by our game engine in `main`. They can be accessed indirectly by the code of the class. For the `m_Length` and `m_Height` variables this is fairly easy to accept, as long as we don't need to change the size of the paddle. The `m_XPosition` and `m_YPosition` member variables, however, do need to be accessed, or how on earth will we move the paddle?

This problem is solved in the `public:` section of the code as follows:

```
void moveRight();
void moveLeft();
```

The class provides two functions which are public and will be usable with an object of type `Paddle`. When we have seen the definition of these functions, we will see exactly how these functions manipulate the private variables.

In summary, we have a bunch of inaccessible (private) variables that cannot be used from the `main` function. This is good because encapsulation makes our code less error prone and more maintainable. We then solve the problem of moving the paddle by providing indirect access to the `m_XPosition` and `m_YPosition` variables by providing two public functions.

The code in `main` can call these functions, but the code inside the functions controls exactly how the variables are altered.

Let's take a look at the function definitions.

The class function definitions

The function definitions we will write in this book will all go in a separate file to the class and function declarations. We will use files with the same name as the class and the .cpp file extension. So, in our hypothetical example, this next code would go in a file called Paddle.cpp. Take a look at this really simple code that has just one new concept:

```
#include "stdafx.h"
#include "Paddle.h"

void Paddle::moveRight()
{
    // Move the paddle a pixel to the right
    m_XPosition ++;
}

void Paddle::moveLeft()
{
    // Move the paddle a pixel to the left
    m_XPosition --;
}
```

The first thing to note is that we must use an include directive to include the class and function declarations from the Paddle.h class.

The new concept we see here is the use of the **scope resolution** operator, ::. As the functions belong to a class, we must write the signature part by prefixing the function name with the class name and ::. void Paddle::moveLeft() and void Paddle::moveRight.

 Actually, we have briefly seen the scope resolution operator before. Whenever we declare an object of a class and we have not previously used using namespace...

Note also that we could have put the function definitions and declarations in one file like this:

```
class Paddle
{
    private:

        // Length of the pong paddle
        int m_Length = 100;

        // Height of the pong paddle
        int m_Height = 10;
```

```
        // Location on x axis
        int m_XPosition;

        // Location on y axis
        int m_YPosition;

    public:

        void Paddle::moveRight()
        {
            // Move the paddle a pixel to the right
            m_XPosition ++;
        }

        void Paddle::moveLeft()
        {
            // Move the paddle a pixel to the left
            m_XPosition --;
        }

};
```

However, when our classes get longer (as they will with our first Zombie Arena class) it is more organized to separate the function definitions into their own file. Furthermore, header files are considered public, and are often used for documentation purposes if other people will be using the code that we write.

Using an instance of a class

Despite all the code we have seen related to classes, we haven't actually used the class. We already know how to do this as we have used the SFML classes many times already.

First, we would create an instance of Paddle like this:

```
Paddle paddle;
```

The paddle object has all the variables we declared in Paddle.h. We just can't access them directly. We can, however, move our paddle using its public functions, like this:

```
paddle.moveLeft();
```

Or like this:

```
paddle.moveRight();
```

Remember that `paddle` is a `Paddle`, and as such it has all the member variables and all the functions available to it.

We could decide at a later date to make our **Pong** game multiplayer. In the `main` function, we could change the code to have two paddles. Perhaps like this:

```
Paddle paddle;
Paddle paddle2;
```

It is vitally important to realize that each of these instances of `Paddle` are separate objects with their very own set of variables.

Constructors and getter functions

The simple Pong paddle example was a good way of introducing the basics of classes. Classes can be simple and short like `Paddle`, but they can also be longer, more complicated, and themselves contain other objects.

When it comes to making games, there is a vital thing missing from the hypothetical `Paddle` class. It might be fine for all these private member variables and public functions, but how will we draw anything? Our Pong paddles need a sprite and a texture too.

We can include other objects in our class in exactly the same way that we include them in `main`.

Here is an updated version of the `private:` section of `Paddle.h` code which includes a member `Sprite` and a member `Texture` too. Note that the file would also need the relevant SFML include directive for this code to compile.

```
private:

    // Length of a pong paddle
    int m_Length = 100;

    // Height of a pong paddle
    int m_Height = 10;

    // Location on x axis
    int m_XPosition;

    // Location on y axis
    int m_YPosition;
```

```
// Of course we will need a sprite
Sprite m_Sprite;

// And a texture
Texture m_Texture;
```

The new problem is immediately upon us. If m_Sprite and m_Texture are private, then how on earth will we draw them in the main function?

We will need to provide a function that allows access to m_Sprite so it can be drawn. Look carefully at the new function declaration in the public section of Paddle.h.

```
public:

    void moveRight();
    void moveLeft();

    // Send a copy of the sprite to main
    Sprite getSprite();
```

The previous code declares a function called getSprite. The significant thing to notice is that getSprite returns a Sprite object. We will see the definition of getSprite very soon.

If you are sharp minded, you will also have noticed that at no point have we loaded the texture or called m_Sprite.setTexture(m_Texture) to associate the texture with the sprite.

When a class is coded, a special function is created by the compiler. We don't see this function in our code but it is there. It is called a constructor. When we need to write some code to prepare an object for use, often a good place to do this is the constructor. When we want the constructor to do anything other than simply create an instance, we must replace the default (unseen) constructor provided by the compiler.

 First, we provide a constructor function declaration. Note that constructors have no return type, not even void. Also note that we can immediately see that it is the constructor function because the function name is the same as the class, Paddle.

```
public:

    // The constructor
    Paddle();

    void moveRight();
    void moveLeft();
```

```
    // Send a copy of the sprite to main
    Sprite getSprite();
```

The next code shows the new function definitions in `Paddle.cpp` (`getSprite` and the constructor, `Paddle`):

```
// The constructor
Paddle::Paddle()
{
    // Code assumes paddle.png is a real image
    m_Texture.loadFromFile("graphics/paddle.png");
    // Associate a texture with the sprite
    m_Sprite.setTexture(m_Texture);
}

// Return a copy of the sprite to main
Sprite Paddle::getSprite()
{
    return m_Sprite;
}
```

In the previous code, we use the constructor function, `Paddle`, to load the texture and associate it with the sprite. Remember that this function is called at the time that an object of type `Paddle` is declared. More specifically, when the code `Paddle paddle` is executed, the constructor is called.

In the `getSprite` function there is just one line of code that returns a copy of `m_Sprite` to the calling code. Functions like this are called **getters**.

We could do other setup work for our objects in the constructor as well and will do so when we build our first real class.

If you want to see exactly how the `getSprite` function could be used, the code in `main` would look like this:

```
window.draw(paddle.getSprite());
```

The previous line of code assumes we have an SFML `RenderWindow` object called `window`. As `getSprite` returns an object of type `Sprite`, the previous line of code works exactly as if the sprite had been declared in `main`. Now we have a neatly encapsulated class that provides controlled access via its public functions.

Jumping around in the code

I find that when I read books that jump around in the code files, it is hard to follow exactly what is going on. What follows are the complete listings for the hypothetical `Paddle.h` and `Paddle.cpp`, to get everything in context. Be sure to study them before moving on:

`Paddle.h`

```cpp
#pragma once
#include <SFML/Graphics.hpp>

using namespace sf;

class Paddle
{
    private:
        // Length of a pong paddle
        int m_Length = 100;
        // Height of a pong paddle
        int m_Height = 10;
        // Location on x axis
        int m_XPosition;
        // Location on y axis
        int m_YPosition;
        // Of course we will need a sprite
        Sprite m_Sprite;

        // And a texture
        Texture m_Texture;

    public:

        // The constructor
        Paddle();
        void moveRight();
        void moveLeft();
        // Send a copy of the sprite to main
        Sprite getSprite();
};
```

`Paddle.cpp`

```cpp
#include "stdafx.h"
#include "Paddle.h"

// The constructor
Paddle::Paddle()
{
```

```
    // Code assumes paddle.png is a real image
    m_Texture.loadFromFile("graphics/paddle.png");
    // Associate a texture with the sprite
    m_Sprite.setTexture(m_Texture);
}

// Return a copy of the sprite to main
Sprite Paddle::getSprite()
{
    return m_Sprite;
}

void Paddle::moveRight()
{
    // Move the paddle a pixel to the right
    m_XPosition ++;
}

void Paddle::moveLeft()
{
    // Move the paddle a pixel to the left
    m_XPosition --;
}
```

We will constantly be revisiting classes and OOP throughout the rest of the book. For now, however, we know enough to get started on our first real class for the Zombie Arena game.

Building Player-the first class

Let's think about what our Player class will need to do. The class will need to know how fast it can move, where in the game world it currently is, and how much health it has. As the Player class, in the player's eyes, is represented as a 2D graphical character, the class will need both a Sprite and a Texture object.

Furthermore, although the reasons might not be obvious at this point, our Player class will also benefit from knowing a few details about the overall environment the game is running in. These details are screen resolution, the size of the tiles that make up an arena, and the overall size of the current arena.

As the `Player` class will be taking full responsibility for updating itself each frame, it will need to know the player's intentions at any given moment. For example, is the player currently holding down a particular keyboard direction key? Or is the player currently holding down multiple keyboard direction keys? Boolean variables to determine the status of the *W*, *A*, *S*, and *D* keys will be essential.

It is plain we are going to need quite a selection of variables in our new class. Having learned all we have about OOP, we will, of course, be making all these variables private. This means that we must provide access, where appropriate, from the `main` function.

We will use a whole bunch of getter functions, as well as some other functions, to set up our object. These functions are quite numerous; there are actually 21 functions in this class. At first this might seem a little daunting, but we will go through them all and see that the majority of them simply set or get one of the private variables.

There are just a few fairly in-depth functions, such as `update`, which will be called once each frame from the `main` function, and `spawn`, which will handle the initializing of some of the private variables. As we will see, however, there is nothing complicated about them, and they will all be described in detail.

The best way to proceed is to code the header file. This will give us the opportunity to see all the private variables and examine all the function signatures. Pay close attention to the return values and argument types, as this will make understanding the code in the function definitions much easier.

Coding the Player class header file

Right click on **Header Files** in the **Solution Explorer** and select **Add | New Item....**. In the **Add New Item** window, highlight (by left-clicking) **Header File (.h)**, and then, in the **Name** field, type `Player.h`. Finally, click the **Add** button. We are now ready to code the header file for our first class.

Get started coding the `Player` class by adding the declaration, including the opening and closing curly braces followed by a semicolon:

```
#pragma once
#include <SFML/Graphics.hpp>

using namespace sf;

class Player
{
```

```
};
```

Now let's add all our private member variables. Based on what we have already discussed, see if you can work out what each of them will do. We will go through them individually in a minute:

```
class Player
{
private:
    const float START_SPEED = 200;
    const float START_HEALTH = 100;
    // Where is the player
    Vector2f m_Position;

    // Of course we will need a sprite
    Sprite m_Sprite;

    // And a texture
    // !!Watch this space!!
    Texture m_Texture;

    // What is the screen resolution
    Vector2f m_Resolution;

    // What size is the current arena
    IntRect m_Arena;

    // How big is each tile of the arena
    int m_TileSize;

    // Which directions is the player currently moving in
    bool m_UpPressed;
    bool m_DownPressed;
    bool m_LeftPressed;
    bool m_RightPressed;

    // How much health has the player got?
    int m_Health;

    // What is the maximum health the player can have
    int m_MaxHealth;

    // When was the player last hit
    Time m_LastHit;

    // Speed in pixels per second
    float m_Speed;
```

```
    // All our public functions will come next
};
```

The previous code declares all our member variables. Some are regular variables and some are themselves objects. Notice that they are all under the `private:` section of the class and are therefore not directly accessible from outside the class.

Also notice, we are using the naming convention of prefixing `m_` to all the names of the non-constant variables. The `m_` prefix will remind us, while coding the function definitions, that they are member variables and are distinct from some local variables we will create in some of the functions, as well as being distinct from the function parameters.

All of the variable's uses will be obvious, such as `m_Position`, `m_Texture`, and `m_Sprite`, which are for the current location, the texture, and sprite of the player. In addition, each variable (or group of variables) is commented to make their usage plain.

However, why exactly they are needed and the context they will be used in might not be so obvious. For example, `m_LastHit`, which is an object of type `Time`, is for recording the time that the player last received a hit from a zombie. The use we are putting `m_LastHit` to is plain, but at the same time, it is not obvious why we might need this information.

As we piece the rest of the game together, the context for each of the variables will become clearer. The important thing for now is to familiarize yourself with the names and types to make following along with the rest of the project trouble free.

You don't need to memorize the variable names and types as we will discuss all the code when they are used. You do need to take your time to look over them and get a little bit familiar with them. Furthermore, as we proceed it might be worth referring back to this header file if anything seems unclear.

Now we can add a whole long list of functions. Add all of the following highlighted code and see if you can work out what it all does. Pay close attention to the return types, parameters and name of each function. This is key to understanding the code we will write throughout the rest of the project. What do they tell us about each function? Add the following highlighted code and then we will examine it:

```
    // All our public functions will come next
public:
    Player();
    void spawn(IntRect arena, Vector2f resolution, int tileSize);

    // Call this at the end of every game
    void resetPlayerStats();
```

```
// Handle the player getting hit by a zombie
bool hit(Time timeHit);

// How long ago was the player last hit
Time getLastHitTime();

// Where is the player
FloatRect getPosition();

// Where is the center of the player
Vector2f getCenter();

// Which angle is the player facing
float getRotation();

// Send a copy of the sprite to main
Sprite getSprite();

// The next four functions move the player
void moveLeft();

void moveRight();

void moveUp();

void moveDown();

// Stop the player moving in a specific direction
void stopLeft();

void stopRight();

void stopUp();

void stopDown();

// We will call this function once every frame
void update(float elapsedTime, Vector2i mousePosition);

// Give player a speed boost
void upgradeSpeed();

// Give the player some health
void upgradeHealth();

// Increase the maximum amount of health the player can have
void increaseHealthLevel(int amount);
```

```
    // How much health has the player currently got?
    int getHealth();
};
```

First note, that all the functions are public. This means we can call all of these functions, using an instance of the class, from main, with code like this: player.getSprite();.

Assuming player is a fully set up instance of the Player class, the previous code will return a copy of m_Sprite. Putting this code into a real context, we could, in the main function, write code like this:

```
window.draw(player.getSprite());
```

The previous code would draw the player graphic in its correct location, just as if the sprite were declared in the main function itself. This is just like what we did with the hypothetical Paddle class previously.

Before we move on to implement (write the definitions of) these functions in a corresponding .cpp file, let's take a closer look at each of them in turn:

- void spawn(IntRect arena, Vector2f resolution, int tileSize): This function does as the name suggests. It will prepare the object ready for use, including putting it in its starting location (spawning it). Notice that it doesn't return any data, but it does have three arguments. It receives an IntRect called arena, which will be the size and location of the current level, a Vector2f that will contain the screen resolution, and an int which will hold the size of a background tile.
- void resetPlayerStats: Once we give the player the ability to level up between waves, we will need to be able to take away and reset those abilities when they die.
- Time getLastHitTime(): This function does just one thing, it returns the time when the player was last hit by a zombie. We will use this function when detecting collisions and it will enable us to make sure the player isn't punished too frequently for contact with a zombie.
- FloatRect getPosition(): This function returns a FloatRect that describes the horizontal and vertical floating point coordinates of the rectangle which contains the player graphic. This again is useful for collision detection.
- Vector2f getCenter(): This is slightly different to getPosition because it is a Vector2f and contains just the X and Y locations of the very center of the player graphic.

- `float getRotation()`: The code in main will sometimes need to know, in degrees, which way the player is currently facing. Three o'clock is zero degrees and increases clockwise.
- `Sprite getSprite()`: As previously discussed, this function returns a copy of the sprite which represents the player.
- `void moveLeft(), ...Right(), ...Up(), ...Down()`: These four functions have no return type or parameters. They will be called from the main function and the `Player` class will then be able to take action when one or more of the *W*, *A*, *S*, and *D* keys have been pressed.
- `void stopLeft(), ...Right(), ...Up(), ...Down()`: These four functions have no return type or parameters. They will be called from the main function, and the `Player` class will then be able to take action when one or more of the *W*, *A*, *S*, and *D* keys have been released.
- `void update(float elapsedTime, Vector2i mousePosition)`: This will be the only relatively long function of the entire class. It will be called once per frame from main. It will do everything necessary to make sure the player object's data is updated ready for collision detection and drawing. Notice it returns no data, but receives the amount of elapsed time since the last frame, along with a `Vector2i`, which will hold the horizontal and vertical screen location of the mouse pointer or crosshair.

 Note that these are integer screen coordinates, distinct from floating point world coordinates.

- `void upgradeSpeed()`: A function that can be called from the leveling-up screen when the player chooses to make the player faster.
- `void upgradeHealth()`: Another function that can be called from the leveling-up screen when the player chooses to make the player stronger (have more health).
- `void increaseHealthLevel(int amount)`: A subtle but important difference to the previous function in that this one will increase the amount of health the player has, up to a maximum currently set. This function will be used when the player picks up a health pick-up.

- `int getHealth()`: With the level of health being as dynamic as it is, we need to be able to determine how much health the player has at any given moment. This function returns an `int` which holds that value. As with the variables, it should now be plain what each of the functions is for. Also, as with the variables, the why and precise context of using some of these functions will only reveal itself as we progress with the project.

 You don't need to memorize the function names, return types, or parameters as we will discuss all the code when they are used. You do need to take your time to look over them, along with the previous explanations, and get a little bit more familiar with them. Furthermore, as we proceed, it might be worth referring back to this header file if anything seems unclear.

Now we can move on to the meat of our functions, the definitions.

Coding the Player class function definitions

At last we can begin to write the code which actually does the work of our class.

Right click on **Source Files** in the **Solution Explorer** and select **Add | New Item...**. In the **Add New Item** window, highlight (by left-clicking) **C++ File** (`.cpp`), and then in the **Name** field type `Player.cpp`. Finally, click the **Add** button. We are now ready to code the `.cpp` file for our first class.

Here are the necessary include directives followed by the definition of the constructor. Remember, the constructor will be called when we first instantiate an object of type `Player`. Add this code into the `Player.cpp` file and then we can take a closer look:

```
#include "stdafx.h"
#include "player.h"

Player::Player()
{
    m_Speed = START_SPEED;
    m_Health = START_HEALTH;
    m_MaxHealth = START_HEALTH;

    // Associate a texture with the sprite
    m_Texture.loadFromFile("graphics/player.png");
    m_Sprite.setTexture(m_Texture);

    // Set the origin of the sprite to the centre,
```

```
// for smooth rotation
m_Sprite.setOrigin(25, 25);
}
```

In the constructor function which, of course, has the same name as the class and no return type, we write code which begins to set up the Player object ready for use.

To be absolutely clear: This code will run when we write this code in the main function

```
Player player;
```

Don't add this previous line of code just yet.

All we do is initialize m_Speed, m_Health, and m_MaxHealth from their related constants. Then we load the player graphic in to m_Texture, associate m_Texture with m_Sprite, and set the origin of m_Sprite to the center (25, 25).

Note the cryptic comment // !!Watch this space!!, indicating that we will return to the loading of our texture and some important issues regarding it. We will eventually change how we deal with this texture once we have discovered a problem and learned a bit more C++. We will do so in Chapter 8, *Pointers, Standard Template Library, and Texture Management*.

Next, we will code the spawn function. We will only ever create one instance of the Player class. We will, however, need to spawn it into the current level, each and every wave. This is what the spawn function will handle for us. Add the following code into the Player.cpp file. Be sure to examine the detail and read the comments:

```
void Player::spawn(IntRect arena, Vector2f resolution, int tileSize)
{
    // Place the player in the middle of the arena
    m_Position.x = arena.width / 2;
    m_Position.y = arena.height / 2;

    // Copy the details of the arena to the player's m_Arena
    m_Arena.left = arena.left;
    m_Arena.width = arena.width;
    m_Arena.top = arena.top;
    m_Arena.height = arena.height;

    // Remember how big the tiles are in this arena
    m_TileSize = tileSize;

    // Store the resolution for future use
    m_Resolution.x = resolution.x;
```

```
    m_Resolution.y = resolution.y;

}
```

The previous code starts off by initializing the m_Position.x and m_Position.y values to half the height and width of the passed in arena. This has the effect of moving the player to the center of the level, regardless of its size.

Next, we copy all of the coordinates and dimensions of the passed in arena to the member object of the same type, m_Arena. The details of the size and coordinates of the current arena are used so frequently that it makes sense to do so. We can now use m_Arena for tasks such as making sure the player can't walk through walls. In addition, we copy the passed in tileSize to the member variable m_TileSize, for the same purpose. We will see m_Arena and m_TileSize in action in the update function.

The final two lines of code copy the screen resolution from the Vector2f, resolution, which is a parameter of spawn, into m_Resolution, which is a member variable of Player.

Now add the very straightforward code of the resetPlayerStats function. When the player dies, we will use it to reset any upgrades they might have used:

```cpp
void Player::resetPlayerStats()
{
    m_Speed = START_SPEED;
    m_Health = START_HEALTH;
    m_MaxHealth = START_HEALTH;
}
```

We will not write the code that actually calls the resetPlayerStats function until we have nearly completed the project, but it is there ready for when we need it.

In the next code, we will add two more functions. They will handle what happens when the player is hit by a zombie. We will be able to call player.hit() and pass in the current game time. We will also be able to query the last time that the player was hit by calling player.getLastHitTime(). Exactly how these functions will be useful will become apparent when we have some zombies!

Add the two new functions into the Player.cpp file and then we will examine the C++ a little more closely:

```cpp
Time Player::getLastHitTime()
{
    return m_LastHit;
}
```

```
bool Player::hit(Time timeHit)
{
    if (timeHit.asMilliseconds() - m_LastHit.asMilliseconds() > 200)
    {
        m_LastHit = timeHit;
        m_Health -= 10;
        return true;
    }
    else
    {
        return false;
    }

}
```

The code for `getLastHitTime` is very straightforward. Return whatever value is stored in `m_LastHit`.

The `hit` function is a bit more in-depth and nuanced. First, the `if` statement checks to see whether the time passed in is 200 milliseconds further ahead than the time stored in `m_LastHit`. If it is, `m_LastHit` is updated with the time passed in and `m_Health` has 10 deducted from its current value. The last line of code in this `if` statement is `return true`. Note that the `else` clause simply returns `false` to the calling code.

The overall effect of this function is that health will only be deducted from the player up to five times per second. Remember that our game loop might be running at thousands of iterations per second. In this scenario, without the restriction, a zombie would only need to be in contact with the player for one second and tens of thousands of health points would be deducted. The `hit` function controls and restricts this occurrence. It also lets the calling code know if a new hit has been registered (or not) by returning `true` or `false`.

This code implies that we will detect collisions between a zombie and the player in the `main` function. We will then call `player.hit()` to determine whether to deduct any health points.

Next, for the `Player` class we will implement a bunch of getter functions. They enable us to keep the data neatly encapsulated in the `Player` class, at the same time as making their values available to the `main` function.

Add the following code right after the previous block and then we will discuss exactly what each function does:

```
FloatRect Player::getPosition()
{
    return m_Sprite.getGlobalBounds();
```

```
    }

    Vector2f Player::getCenter()
    {
        return m_Position;
    }

    float Player::getRotation()
    {
        return m_Sprite.getRotation();
    }

    Sprite Player::getSprite()
    {
        return m_Sprite;
    }

    int Player::getHealth()
    {
        return m_Health;
    }
```

The previous code is very straightforward. Each and every one of the previous five functions returns the value of one of our member variables. Look carefully at each and familiarize yourself with which function returns which value.

The next eight short functions enable the keyboard controls (we will use from main) to change data contained in our object of type Player. Add the code in the Player.cpp file and then I will summarize how it all works:

```
    void Player::moveLeft()
    {
        m_LeftPressed = true;
    }

    void Player::moveRight()
    {
        m_RightPressed = true;
    }

    void Player::moveUp()
    {
        m_UpPressed = true;
    }

    void Player::moveDown()
    {
```

```
      m_DownPressed = true;
}

void Player::stopLeft()
{
   m_LeftPressed = false;
}

void Player::stopRight()
{
   m_RightPressed = false;
}

void Player::stopUp()
{
   m_UpPressed = false;
}

void Player::stopDown()
{
   m_DownPressed = false;
}
```

The previous code has four functions (moveLeft, moveRight, moveUp, moveDown) which set the related Boolean variables (m_LeftPressed, m_RightPressed, m_UpPressed, m_DownPressed) to true. The other four functions (stopLeft, stopRight, stopUp, stopDown) do the opposite and set the same Boolean variables to false. The instance of the Player class can now be kept informed of which of the *W*, *A*, *S*, and *D* keys have been pressed and which are not.

This next function is the one which does all the hard work. The update function will be called once on every single frame of our game loop. Add the code that follows and we will then examine it in detail. If you followed along with the previous eight functions and you remember how we animated the clouds for the Timber!!! project, you will probably find most of the following code quite understandable:

```
void Player::update(float elapsedTime, Vector2i mousePosition)
{
   if (m_UpPressed)
   {
      m_Position.y -= m_Speed * elapsedTime;
   }

   if (m_DownPressed)
   {
      m_Position.y += m_Speed * elapsedTime;
```

```
    }

    if (m_RightPressed)
    {
        m_Position.x += m_Speed * elapsedTime;
    }

    if (m_LeftPressed)
    {
        m_Position.x -= m_Speed * elapsedTime;
    }

    m_Sprite.setPosition(m_Position);

    // Keep the player in the arena
    if (m_Position.x > m_Arena.width - m_TileSize)
    {
        m_Position.x = m_Arena.width - m_TileSize;
    }

    if (m_Position.x < m_Arena.left + m_TileSize)
    {
        m_Position.x = m_Arena.left + m_TileSize;
    }

    if (m_Position.y > m_Arena.height - m_TileSize)
    {
        m_Position.y = m_Arena.height - m_TileSize;
    }

    if (m_Position.y < m_Arena.top + m_TileSize)
    {
        m_Position.y = m_Arena.top + m_TileSize;
    }

    // Calculate the angle the player is facing
    float angle = (atan2(mousePosition.y - m_Resolution.y / 2,
        mousePosition.x - m_Resolution.x / 2)
        * 180) / 3.141;

    m_Sprite.setRotation(angle);
}
```

The first portion of the previous code moves the player sprite. The four if statements check which of the movement-related Boolean variables (m_LeftPressed, m_RightPressed, m_UpPressed, m_DownPressed) are true and changes m_Position.x and m_Position.y accordingly. The same formula to calculate the amount to move as the Timber!!! project is used.

```
position (+ or -) speed * elapsed time.
```

After these four if statements, m_Sprite.setPosition is called and m_Position is passed in. The sprite has now been adjusted by exactly the right amount for that one frame.

The next four if statements check whether m_Position.x or m_Position.y are beyond any of the edges of the current arena. Remember that the confines of the current arena were stored in m_Arena by the spawn function. Let's look at the first of these four if statements in order to understand them all:

```
if (m_Position.x > m_Arena.width - m_TileSize)
{
    m_Position.x = m_Arena.width - m_TileSize;
}
```

The previous code tests to see if m_position.x is greater than m_Arena.width minus the size of a tile (m_TileSize). As we will see when we create the background graphics, this calculation will detect the player straying into the wall.

When the if statement is true, the calculation m_Arena.width - m_TileSize is used to initialize m_Position.x. This makes the center of the player graphic unable to stray past the left-hand edge of the right-hand wall.

The next three if statements that follow the one we have just discussed do the same thing for the other three walls.

The last two lines of code calculate and set the angle that the player sprite is rotated to (facing). The line of code might look a little complex, but it is simply using the position of the crosshair (mousePosition.x and mousePosition.y) and the center of the screen (m_Resolution.x and m_Resolution.y) in a tried and tested trigonometric function.

How atan uses these coordinates along with Pi (3.141) is quite complicated, and that is why it is wrapped up in a handy function for us. If you want to explore trigonometric functions in more detail you can do so at http://www.cplusplus.com/reference/cmath/. The last three functions for the Player class make the player 20% faster, have 20% more health, and increase the player's health by the amount passed in, respectively.

Add this code at the end of the `Player.cpp` file and then we will take a closer look:

```cpp
void Player::upgradeSpeed()
{
    // 20% speed upgrade
    m_Speed += (START_SPEED * .2);
}

void Player::upgradeHealth()
{
    // 20% max health upgrade
    m_MaxHealth += (START_HEALTH * .2);

}

void Player::increaseHealthLevel(int amount)
{
    m_Health += amount;

    // But not beyond the maximum
    if (m_Health > m_MaxHealth)
    {
        m_Health = m_MaxHealth;
    }

}
```

In the previous code, the `upgradeSpeed` and `upgradeHealth` functions increase the values stored in `m_Speed` and `m_MaxHealth`, respectively. The values are increased by 20% by multiplying the starting values by 0.2 and adding them to the current values. These functions will be called from the `main` function when the player is choosing what attributes of their character they wish to improve between levels.

The `increaseHealthLevel` takes an `int` value from `main` in the `amount` parameter. This `int` value will be provided by a class called `Pickup` that we will write in `Chapter 9`, *Collision Detection, Pick-ups, and Bullets*. The `m_Health` member variable is increased by the passed in value. There is a catch for the player, however. The `if` statement checks whether `m_Health` has exceeded `m_MaxHealth`, and if it has, sets it to `m_MaxHealth`. This means the player cannot simply gain infinite health from pick-ups. They must instead carefully balance the upgrades they choose between levels.

Of course, our `Player` class can't actually do anything until we instantiate it and put it to work in our game loop. Before we do that, let's take a look at the concept of a game camera.

Controlling the game camera with SFML View

In my opinion, the SFML `View` class is one of the neatest classes. If after finishing this book you make games without using a media or gaming library, you will really notice the absence of `View`.

The `View` class allows us to consider our game as taking place in its own world, with its own properties. What do I mean? When we create a game, we are usually trying to create a virtual world. That virtual world rarely, if ever, is measured in pixels and rarely, if ever, will that world be exactly the same number of pixels as the player's monitor. We need a way to abstract the virtual world we are building, so that it can be whatever size or shape we like.

Another way to think of SFML `View` is as a camera through which the player views a part of our virtual world. Most games will have more than one camera or view of the world.

For example, consider a split screen game where two players can be in different parts of the same world, at different times.

Or consider a game where there is a small area of the screen that represents the entire game world but at a very high level, or zoomed out, like a mini map.

Even if our games are much simpler than the previous two examples and don't need split screens or mini maps, we will likely want to create a world that is bigger than the screen it is being played on. This is, of course, the case with Zombie Arena.

And if we are constantly moving the game camera around to show different parts of the virtual world (usually tracking the player) what happens to the HUD? If we draw the score and other on-screen HUD info and then we scroll the world around to follow the player, then the score will move relative to that camera.

The SFML `View` class easily enables all these features and solves the problem with very straightforward code. The trick is to create an instance of `View` for each and every camera. Perhaps a `View` for the mini map, a `View` for the scrolling game world, and then a `View` for the HUD.

The instances of `View` can be moved around, sized, and positioned as required. So the main `View` following the game can track the player, the mini-map view can remain in a fixed zoomed-out, small corner of the screen, while the HUD can overlay the entire screen and never move, despite the fact that the main `View` can go wherever the player goes.

Let's look at some code using a few instances of View.

This code is to introduce the `View` class. Don't add this code to the Zombie Arena project.

Create and initialize a few instances of View:

```
// Create a view to fill a 1920 x 1080 monitor
View mainView(sf::FloatRect(0, 0, 1920, 1080));

// Create a view for the HUD
View hudView(sf::FloatRect(0, 0, 1920, 1080));
```

The previous code creates two `View` objects that fill a 1920 x 1080 monitor. Now we can do some magic with `mainView` while leaving `hudView` completely alone:

```
// In the update part of the game
// There are lots of things you can do with a View

// Make the view centre around the player
mainView.setCenter(player.getCenter());

// Rotate the view 45 degrees
mainView.rotate(45)

// Note that hudView is totally unaffected by the previous code
```

When we manipulate the properties of a View, we do so as shown previously. When we draw sprites, text, or other objects to a view, we must specifically set the view as the current view for the window:

```
// Set the current view
window.setView(mainView);
```

Now we can draw everything we want into that view:

```
// Do all the drawing for this view
window.draw(playerSprite);
window.draw(otherGameObject);
// etc
```

The player might be at any coordinate whatsoever. It doesn't matter because `mainView` is centered around the graphic.

Now we can draw the HUD into `hudView`. Note that, just as we draw individual elements (background, game objects, text, and so on) in layers from back to front, we also draw views from back to front as well. Hence a HUD is drawn after the main game:

```
// Switch to the hudView
window.setView(hudView);

// Do all the drawing for the HUD
window.draw(scoreText);
window.draw(healthBar);
// etc
```

Finally, we can draw or show the window and all its views for the current frame in the usual way:

```
window.display();
```

 If you want to take your understanding of SFML `View` further than is necessary for this project, including how to achieve split screen and mini maps, then the best guide on the Web is on the official SFML website at `ht tp://www.sfml-dev.org/tutorials/2.0/graphics-view.php`.

Now we have learnt about `View`, we can start coding the Zombie Arena `main` function and use our first `View` for real. In `Chapter 10`, *Layering Views and Implementing the HUD*, we will introduce a second instance of `View` for the HUD, fix it, and layer it over the top of the main `View`.

Starting the Zombie Arena game engine

In this game, we will need a slightly upgraded game engine in `main`. In particular, we will have an enumeration called `state` which will track what the current state of the game is. Then, throughout `main`, we can wrap parts of our code so that different things happen in different states.

Right-click on the `HelloSFML` file in the **Solution Explorer** and select **Rename**. Change the name to `ZombieArena.cpp`. This will be the file that contains our `main` function and the code that instantiates and controls all our classes.

We begin with the now familiar `main` function and some include directives. Note the addition of an include directive for the `Player` class.

Add the code following to the `ZombieArena.cpp` file:

```cpp
#include "stdafx.h"
#include <SFML/Graphics.hpp>
#include "Player.h"

using namespace sf;

int main()
{

    return 0;
}
```

The previous code has nothing new in it except that the `#include "Player.h"` line means we can now use the `Player` class within our code.

Let's flesh out some more of our game engine. This next code does quite a lot. Be sure to read the comments when you add the code to get an idea of what is going on. We will then go through it in detail.

Add the highlighted code at the start of the `main` function:

```cpp
int main()
{
    // The game will always be in one of four states
    enum class State
    {
        PAUSED, LEVELING_UP, GAME_OVER, PLAYING
    };
    // Start with the GAME_OVER state
    State state = State::GAME_OVER;

    // Get the screen resolution and create an SFML window
    Vector2f resolution;
    resolution.x = VideoMode::getDesktopMode().width;
    resolution.y = VideoMode::getDesktopMode().height;

    RenderWindow window(VideoMode(resolution.x, resolution.y),
        "Zombie Arena", Style::Fullscreen);

    // Create a an SFML View for the main action
    View mainView(sf::FloatRect(0, 0, resolution.x, resolution.y));
    // Here is our clock for timing everything
    Clock clock;

    // How long has the PLAYING state been active
```

```
    Time gameTimeTotal;
    // Where is the mouse in relation to world coordinates
    Vector2f mouseWorldPosition;

    // Where is the mouse in relation to screen coordinates
    Vector2i mouseScreenPosition;

    // Create an instance of the Player class
    Player player;

    // The boundaries of the arena
    IntRect arena;

    // The main game loop
    while (window.isOpen())
    {

    }

    return 0;
}
```

Let's run through each section of the code that we just entered. Just inside the main function we have this code:

```
// The game will always be in one of four states
enum class State { PAUSED, LEVELING_UP, GAME_OVER, PLAYING };
// Start with the GAME_OVER state
State state = State::GAME_OVER;
```

The previous code creates a new enumeration class called State. Then the code creates an instance of State called state. The state enumeration can now be one of four values, as defined in the declaration. Those values are PAUSED, LEVELING_UP, GAME_OVER, and PLAYING. These four values will be just what we need for keeping track and responding to the different states that the game can be in at any given time. Note that it is not possible for state to hold more than one value at a time.

Immediately after, we add the following code:

```
// Get the screen resolution and create an SFML window
Vector2f resolution;
resolution.x = VideoMode::getDesktopMode().width;
resolution.y = VideoMode::getDesktopMode().height;
RenderWindow window(VideoMode(resolution.x, resolution.y),
    "Zombie Arena", Style::Fullscreen);
```

The previous code declares a `Vector2f` called `resolution`. We initialize the two variables of `resolution` (x and y) by calling the `VideoMode::getDesktopMode` function for both `width` and `height`. The `resolution` object now holds the resolution of the monitor on which the game is running. The final line of code creates a new `RenderWindow` called `window` using the appropriate resolution.

This next code creates an SFML `View` object. The view is positioned (initially) at the exact coordinates of the pixels of the monitor. If we were to use this `View` to do some drawing in this current position it would have no effect whatsoever. However, we will eventually start to move this view to focus on the parts of our game world that the player needs to see. Then, when we start to use a second `View` that remains fixed (for the HUD), we will see how this `View` can track the action while the other remains static to display the HUD:

```
// Create a an SFML View for the main action
View mainView(sf::FloatRect(0, 0, resolution.x, resolution.y));
```

Next, we create a `Clock` to do our timing and a `Time` object called `gameTimeTotal` that will keep a running total of the game time that has elapsed. As the project progresses we will introduce more variables and objects to handle timing:

```
// Here is our clock for timing everything
Clock clock;
// How long has the PLAYING state been active
Time gameTimeTotal;
```

The next code declares two vectors. One holding two floats, called `mouseWorldPosition`, and one holding two integers, called `mouseScreenPosition`. The mouse pointer is something of an anomaly because it exists in two different coordinate spaces. You could think of these as parallel universes if you like. First, as the player moves around the world we will need to keep track of where the crosshair is in that world. These will be floating point coordinates and will be stored in `mouseWorldCoordinates`. Of course the actual pixel coordinates of the monitor itself never change. They will always be 0,0 to horizontal resolution-1, vertical resolution-1. We will track the mouse pointer position relative to this coordinate space using the integers stored in `mouseScreenPosition`:

```
// Where is the mouse in relation to world coordinates
Vector2f mouseWorldPosition;
// Where is the mouse in relation to screen coordinates
Vector2i mouseScreenPosition;
```

Finally, we get to use our `Player` class. This line of code will cause the constructor function (`Player::Player`) to execute. Refer to `Player.cpp` if you want to refresh your memory about this function:

```
// Create an instance of the Player class
Player player;
```

This `IntRect` object will hold starting horizontal and vertical coordinates as well as a width and a height. Once initialized, we will be able to access the size and location details of the current arena with code such as `arena.left`, `arena.top`, `arena.width`, and `arena.height`:

```
// The boundaries of the arena
IntRect arena;
```

The last part of the code that we added previously is, of course, our main game loop:

```
// The main game loop
while (window.isOpen())
{

}
```

You have probably noticed that the code is getting quite long. Let's talk about this inconvenience.

Managing the code files

One of the advantages of abstraction using classes and functions is that the length (number of lines) of our code files can be reduced. Even though we will be using more than a dozen code files for this project, the length of the code in `ZombieArena.cpp` will still get a little unwieldy towards the end. In the final project, we will look at even more ways to abstract and manage our code.

For now, use this tip to keep things manageable. Notice on the left hand side of the code editor in Visual Studio, there are a number of + and – signs, one of which is shown in this next image:

```
// The main game loop
while (window.isOpen())
{
```

There will be one sign for each block (if, while, for, and so on) of the code. You can expand and collapse these blocks by clicking on the + and – signs. I recommend keeping all the code not currently under discussion, collapsed. This will make things much clearer.

Furthermore, we can create our own collapsible blocks. I suggest making a collapsible block out of all the code before the start of the main game loop. To do so, highlight the code, right-click, and choose **Outlining | Hide Selection**, as shown in the next image:

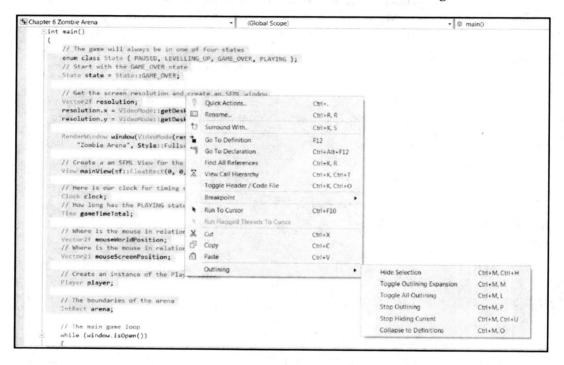

Now you can click the + and the – sign to expand and contract the block. Each time we add code before the main game loop (and that will be quite often) you can expand the code, add the new lines, and then collapse it again. This next image is what the code looks like when it is collapsed:

```
int main()
{

    // The main game loop
    while (window.isOpen())
    {
```

This is much more manageable than it was before.

Starting coding the main game loop

As you can see, the last part of the previous code is the game loop, `while (window.isOpen()){}`. It is this that we turn our attention to now. Specifically, we will be coding the input-handling section of the game loop.

The next code that we will add is quite long. There is nothing complicated about it, and we will examine it all in a minute.

Add the highlighted code only, which is shown in the following code, into the main game loop:

```
// The main game loop
while (window.isOpen())
{
    /*
    ************
    Handle input
    ************
    */

    // Handle events by polling
    Event event;
    while (window.pollEvent(event))
    {
        if (event.type == Event::KeyPressed)
        {
            // Pause a game while playing
            if (event.key.code == Keyboard::Return &&
                state == State::PLAYING)
            {
                state = State::PAUSED;
            }
            // Restart while paused
            else if (event.key.code == Keyboard::Return &&
                state == State::PAUSED)
            {
                state = State::PLAYING;
                // Reset the clock so there isn't a frame jump
                clock.restart();
            }
            // Start a new game while in GAME_OVER state
            else if (event.key.code == Keyboard::Return &&
```

```
                    state == State::GAME_OVER)
        {
            state = State::LEVELING_UP;
        }
        if (state == State::PLAYING)
        {
        }
    }
}// End event polling

}// End game loop
```

In the previous code, we instantiate an object of type `Event`. We will use `event`, as we did in the Timber!!! project, to poll for system events. To do so, we wrap the rest of the code from the previous block in a `while` loop with the condition `window.pollEvent(event)`. This will keep looping, for each frame, until there are no more events to process.

Inside this `while` loop, we handle the events we are interested in. First, we test for `Event::KeyPressed` events. If the *Enter* key is pressed while the game is in the `PLAYING` state then we switch `state` to `PAUSED`.

If the *Enter* key is pressed while the game is in the `PAUSED` state then we switch `state` to `PLAYING` and restart `clock`. The reason we restart `clock` after switching from `PAUSED` to `PLAYING` is because, while the game is paused, the elapsed time still accumulates. If we didn't restart the clock all our objects would update their locations as if the frame had just taken a very long time. This will become more apparent as we flesh out the rest of the code in this file.

We then have an `else if` test to see if the *Enter* key was pressed while the game was in the `GAME_OVER` state. If it was, then `state` is changed to `LEVELING_UP`.

Note that the `GAME_OVER` state is the state where the home screen is displayed. So the `GAME_OVER` state is the state after the player has just died and also when the player first runs the app. The first thing that the player gets to do each game is to pick an attribute to improve (level up).

In the previous code there is a final `if` condition to test if the state is `PLAYING`. This `if` block is empty, and we will add code to it throughout the project.

As we will add code to lots of different parts of this file throughout the project, it is therefore worthwhile taking time to understand the different states our game can be in and where we handle them. It will also be very beneficial to collapse and expand the different `if`, `else`, and `while` blocks as and when appropriate.

Take some time to thoroughly familiarize yourself with the `while`, `if`, and `else if` blocks we have just coded. We will be referring back to them regularly.

Next, immediately after the previous code and still inside the game loop, still dealing with handling input, add this highlighted code. Note the existing code (not highlighted) that shows exactly where the new code goes:

```cpp
}// End event polling

// Handle the player quitting
if (Keyboard::isKeyPressed(Keyboard::Escape))
{
   window.close();
}

// Handle WASD while playing
if (state == State::PLAYING)
{
   // Handle the pressing and releasing of the WASD keys
   if (Keyboard::isKeyPressed(Keyboard::W))
   {
      player.moveUp();
   }
   else
   {
      player.stopUp();
   }
   if (Keyboard::isKeyPressed(Keyboard::S))
   {
      player.moveDown();
   }
   else
   {
      player.stopDown();
   }
   if (Keyboard::isKeyPressed(Keyboard::A))
   {
      player.moveLeft();
   }
   else
   {
      player.stopLeft();
   }
   if (Keyboard::isKeyPressed(Keyboard::D))
   {
      player.moveRight();
   }
```

```
        else
        {
           player.stopRight();
        }
    }// End WASD while playing

}// End game loop
```

In the previous code, we first test to see if the player has pressed the *Esc* key. If it is pressed, the game window will be closed.

Next, within one big if(state == State::PLAYING) block we check each of the *W, A, S,* and *D* keys in turn. If a key is pressed, we call the appropriate player.move... function. If it is not, we call the related player.stop... function.

This code ensures that, in each and every frame, the player object will be updated with exactly which of the *W, A, S, D* keys are pressed and which are not. The player.move... and player.stop... functions store the information in the member Boolean variables (m_LeftPressed, m_RightPressed, m_UpPressed, and m_DownPressed). The Player class then responds to the value of these Booleans, in each frame, in the player.update function which we will call in the update section of the game loop.

Now we can handle the keyboard input to enable the player to level up at the start of each game and in between each wave. Add and study the following highlighted code and we will then discuss it:

```
    }// End WASD while playing

// Handle the LEVELING up state
if (state == State::LEVELING_UP)
{
  // Handle the player LEVELING up
  if (event.key.code == Keyboard::Num1)
  {
     state = State::PLAYING;
  }

  if (event.key.code == Keyboard::Num2)
  {
     state = State::PLAYING;
  }

  if (event.key.code == Keyboard::Num3)
  {
     state = State::PLAYING;
  }
```

```
        if (event.key.code == Keyboard::Num4)
        {
            state = State::PLAYING;
        }

        if (event.key.code == Keyboard::Num5)
        {
            state = State::PLAYING;
        }

        if (event.key.code == Keyboard::Num6)
        {
            state = State::PLAYING;
        }

        if (state == State::PLAYING)
        {
            // Prepare the level
            // We will modify the next two lines later
            arena.width = 500;
            arena.height = 500;
            arena.left = 0;
            arena.top = 0;

            // We will modify this line of code later
            int tileSize = 50;

            // Spawn the player in the middle of the arena
            player.spawn(arena, resolution, tileSize);

            // Reset the clock so there isn't a frame jump
            clock.restart();
        }
    }// End LEVELING up
}// End game loop
```

In the preceding code, which is all wrapped in a test to see if the current value of state is LEVELING_UP, we handle the keyboard keys *1, 2, 3, 4, 5,* and *6*. In the if block for each, we simply set state to State::PLAYING. We will add code to deal with each level up option later in Chapter 11, *Sound Effects, File I/O, and Finishing the Game.*

What this code does is this:

1. If the `state` is `LEVELING_UP`, wait for either the *1, 2, 3, 4, 5* or *6* key to be pressed.
2. When pressed, change `state` to `PLAYING`.
3. When the state changes, still within the `if (state == State::LEVELING_UP)` block, the nested `if(state == State::PLAYING)` block will run.
4. Within this block, we set the location and size of `arena`, the `tileSize` to 50, pass all the information in to `player.spawn`, and restart `clock`.

Now we have an actual spawned player object that is aware of its environment and can respond to key presses. We can now update the scene on each pass through the loop.

Be sure to neatly collapse the code from the input handling part of the game loop as we are done with that, for now. The next code is in the update part of the game loop. Add and study the highlighted code and then we can discuss it:

```
}// End LEVELING up

/*
****************
UPDATE THE FRAME
****************
*/
if (state == State::PLAYING)
{
  // Update the delta time
  Time dt = clock.restart();

  // Update the total game time
  gameTimeTotal += dt;

  // Make a decimal fraction of 1 from the delta time
  float dtAsSeconds = dt.asSeconds();

  // Where is the mouse pointer
  mouseScreenPosition = Mouse::getPosition();

  // Convert mouse position to world coordinates of mainView
  mouseWorldPosition = window.mapPixelToCoords(
    Mouse::getPosition(), mainView);

  // Update the player
  player.update(dtAsSeconds, Mouse::getPosition());

  // Make a note of the players new position
  Vector2f playerPosition(player.getCenter());
```

```
    // Make the view centre around the player
    mainView.setCenter(player.getCenter());
  }// End updating the scene
}// End game loop
```

First note that all the previous code is wrapped in a test to make sure the game is in the PLAYING state. We don't want this code to run if the game is paused, over, or if the player is choosing what to level up.

First, we restart the clock and store the time that the previous frame took in the dt variable:

```
// Update the delta time
Time dt = clock.restart();
```

Next, we add the time that the previous frame took onto the accumulated time the game has been running for, as held by gameTimeTotal:

```
// Update the total game time
gameTimeTotal += dt;
```

Now we initialize a float called dtAsSeconds with the value returned by the dt.AsSeconds function. For most frames this will be a fraction of one. This is perfect for passing into the player.update function to be used to calculate how much to move the player sprite.

Now we can initialize mouseScreenPosition using the function MOUSE::getPosition.

You might be wondering about the slightly unusual syntax for getting the position of the mouse? This is called a **static function**. If we define a function in a class with the static keyword, we are able to call that function using the class name and without an instance of the class. C++ OOP has loads of quirks and rules like this. We will see some more as we progress.

We then initialize mouseWorldPosition using the SFML mapPixelToCoords function on window. We discussed this function when talking about the View class earlier in the chapter.

At this point, we are now able to call player.update and pass in dtAsSeconds and the position of the mouse, as is required.

We store the player's new center in a Vector2f called playerPosition. At the moment, this is unused, but we will have a use for this later in the project.

We can then center the view around the center of the players up-to-date position with the code, mainView.setCenter(player.getCenter()).

We are now in a position to draw the player to the screen. Add this highlighted code which splits the draw section of the main game loop into different states:

```
    }// End updating the scene

    /*
    **************
    Draw the scene
    **************
    */
    if (state == State::PLAYING)
    {
        window.clear();

        // set the mainView to be displayed in the window
        // And draw everything related to it
        window.setView(mainView);

        // Draw the player
        window.draw(player.getSprite());
    }

    if (state == State::LEVELING_UP)
    {
    }
    if (state == State::PAUSED)
    {
    }
    if (state == State::GAME_OVER)
    {
    }
    window.display();

}// End game loop

return 0;
}
```

Within the `if(state == State::PLAYING)` section of the previous code, we clear the screen, set the view of the window to `mainView`, and then draw the player sprite with `window.draw(player.getSprite())`.

After all the different states have been handled, the code shows the scene in the usual manner with `window.display();`.

You can run the game and see our player character spin around in response to moving the mouse.

When you run the game, you need to press *Enter* to start the game and then a number from *1* to *6* to simulate choosing an upgrade option. Then the game will start.

You can also move the player around within the (empty) 500 x 500 pixel arena. You can see our lonely player in the center of the screen, as shown next:

You can't, however, get any sense of movement because we haven't implemented the background. We will do so in the next chapter.

FAQ

Q) I notice we have coded quite a few functions of the `Player` class that we don't use.

A) Rather than keep coming back to the `Player` class, we have added the entire code that we will need throughout the project. By the end of `Chapter 11`, *Sound Effects, File I/O, and Finishing the Game*, we will have made full use of all the functions.

Q) I have learnt other languages and OOP seems much simpler in C++.

A) This was an introduction to OOP and its basic fundamentals. There is more to it than this. We will learn more OOP concepts and details throughout the book.

Summary

Phew! That was a long one. We have learned a lot in this chapter. We have discovered the basics of OOP, including how to use encapsulation to control how code outside of our classes can access the member variables. We built our first real class, `Player`, and put it to use in the start of what will become our new game, Zombie Arena.

Don't concern yourself too much if some of the details around OOP and classes are not entirely clear. The reason I say this is because we will spend the rest of the book making classes, and the more we use them the clearer they will become.

In the next chapter, we will build our arena background by exploring what sprite sheets are. We will also learn about C++ references that allow us to manipulate variables, even when they are out of scope (in another function).

7
C++ References, Sprite Sheets, and Vertex Arrays

In Chapter 4: *Loops, Arrays, Switch, Enumerations, and Functions – Implementing Game Mechanics*, we talked about scope. The concept that variables declared in a function or inner block of code only have scope (can be seen or used) in that function or block. Using only the C++ knowledge we have at the moment, this can cause a problem. What do we do if we need to work on a number of complex objects which are needed in main? This could imply that all the code must be in main.

In this chapter we will explore **C++ references** which allow us to work on variables and objects that are otherwise out of scope. In addition, references will help us avoid having to pass large objects between functions, which is a slow process. It is a slow process because each time we do this, a copy of the variable or object must be made.

Armed with this new knowledge about references, we will take a look at the SFML VertexArray class that allows us to build up a large image that can be very quickly and efficiently drawn to the screen using multiple images from a single image file. By the end of the chapter we will have a scaleable, random, scrolling background, using references, and a VertexArray object.

We will now talk about the following topics:

- C++ references
- SFML vertex arrays
- Coding a random and scrolling background

C++ References

When we pass values to a function or return values from a function, that is exactly what we are doing. Passing/returning by **value**. What happens is that a copy of the value held by the variable is made, and sent into the function where it is used.

The significance of this is two-fold:

- If we want the function to make a permanent change to a variable, this system is no good to us.
- When a copy is made, to pass in as an argument or return from the function, processing power and memory are consumed. For a simple `int` or even perhaps a sprite, this is fairly insignificant. However, for a complex object, perhaps an entire game world (or background), the copying process will seriously affect our game's performance.

References are the solution to these two problems. A reference is a special type of variable. A reference refers to another variable. An example will be useful:

```
int numZombies = 100;
int& rNumZombies = numZombies;
```

In the code above we declare and initialize a regular `int` called `numZombies`. We then declare and initialize an `int` reference called `rNumZombies`. The reference operator `&` that follows the type, determines that a reference is being declared.

 The `r` prefix at the front of the reference name is optional but useful for remembering that we are dealing with a reference.

Now we have an `int` called `numZombies` which stores the value `100` and an `int` reference called `rNumZombies` that refers to `numZombies`.

Anything we do to `numZombies` can be seen through `rNumZombies`, and anything we do to `rNumZombies` we are actually doing to `numZombies`. Take a look at the following code:

```
int score = 10;
int& rScore = score;
score++;
rScore++;
```

In the previous code we declare an `int` called `score`. Next we declare an `int` reference called `rScore` that refers to `score`. Remember that anything we do to `score` can be seen by `rScore` and anything we do to `rScore` is actually being done to `score`.

Therefore, when we increment score like this:

```
score++;
```

The score variable now stores the value 11. In addition, if we were to output `rScore` it would also output 11. The following line of code is as follows:

```
rScore++;
```

Now `score` actually holds the value 12 because anything we do to `rScore` is actually done to `score`.

If you want to know how this works then more will be revealed in the next chapter when we discuss **pointers**. But simply put, you can consider a reference as storing a place/address in the computer's memory. That place in memory is the same place where the variable it refers to stores its value. Therefore, an operation on either the reference or the variable has exactly the same effect.

For now, it is much more important to talk more about the *why* of references. There are two reasons to use references and we have already mentioned them. Here they are summarized again:

- Changing/reading the value of a variable/object in another function which is otherwise out of scope
- Passing/returning without making a copy (and therefore more efficiently)

Study this code and then we can discuss it:

```
void add(int n1, int n2, int a);
void referenceAdd(int n1, int n2, int& a);

int main()
{
    int number1 = 2;
    int number2 = 2;
    int answer = 0;
    add(number1, number2, answer);
    // answer still equals zero because it is passed as a copy
    // Nothing happens to answer in the scope of main
```

```
        referenceAdd(number1, number2, answer);
        // Now answer equals 4 because it was passed by reference
        // When the referenceAdd funtion did this:
        // answer = num1 + num 2;
        // It is actually changing the value stored by a
        return 0;
}

// Here are the two function definitions
// They are exactly the same except that
// the second passes a reference to a
add(int n1, int n2, int a)
{
    a = n1 + n2;
    // a now equals 4
    // But when the function returns a is lost forever
}

referenceAdd(int n1, int n2, int& a)
{
    a = n1 + n2;
    // a now equals 4
    // But a is a reference!
    // So it is actually answer, back in main, that equals 4
}
```

The previous code begins with the prototypes of two functions, add and referenceAdd. The add function takes three int variables and the referenceAdd function takes two int variables and an int reference.

When the add function is called and the variables number1, number2, and answer are passed in, a copy of the values is made and new local variables to add (n1, n2, and a) are manipulated. As a result of this, answer, back in main, remains at zero.

When the referenceAdd function is called, number1 and number2 are again passed by value. However, answer is passed by reference. When the value of n1 added to n2 is assigned to the reference a, what is really happening is that the value is assigned to answer back in the main function.

It is probably obvious that we would never need to actually use a reference for something this simple. It does, however, demonstrate the mechanics of passing by reference.

References summary

The previous code demonstrated how a reference can be used to alter the value of a variable in one scope using code in another. As well as being extremely convenient, passing by reference is also very efficient because no copy is made. The example using a reference to an int is a bit ambiguous because as an int is so small there is no real efficiency gain. Later in the chapter we will use a reference to pass an entire level layout and the efficiency gain will be significant.

 There is one gotcha with references! You must assign the reference to a variable at the time you create it. This means it is not completely flexible. Don't worry about this for now. We will explore references further as well as their more flexible (and slightly more complicated) relations, pointers, in the next chapter.

This is largely irrelevant for an int but potentially significant for a large object of a class. We will use this exact technique when we implement the scrolling background of the Zombie Arena game.

SFML vertex arrays and sprite sheets

We are nearly ready to implement the scrolling background. We just need to learn about SFML vertex arrays and sprite sheets.

What is a sprite sheet?

A **sprite sheet** is a set of images, either frames of animation or totally individual graphics, contained in one image file. Take a closer look at the sprite sheet that contains four separate images that will be used to draw the background in Zombie Arena:

SFML allows us to load a sprite sheet as a regular texture in exactly the same way we have done for every texture in the book so far. When we load multiple images as a single texture, the GPU can handle it much more efficiently.

> Actually a modern PC could handle these four textures without using a sprite sheet. It is worth learning these techniques as our games are going to start getting progressively more demanding on the hardware.

What we need to do when we draw an image from the sprite sheet is make sure we refer to the precise pixel coordinates of the part of the sprite sheet we require:

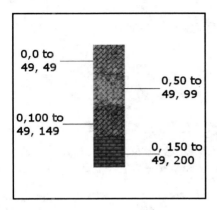

The previous image labels each part/tile with the coordinates of its position within the sprite sheet. These coordinates are called **texture coordinates**. We will use these texture coordinates in our code to draw just the right parts that we require.

What is a vertex array?

First we need to ask: what is a vertex? A **vertex** is a single graphical point, a coordinate. This point is defined by a horizontal and vertical position. The plural of vertex is vertices. A vertex array, then, is a whole collection of vertices.

In SFML, each vertex in a vertex array also has a color and a related additional vertex (pair of coordinates) called texture coordinates. Texture coordinates are the position in a sprite sheet of the image we want to use. We will see quite soon how we position graphics and choose a part of the sprite sheet to display at each position, all with a single vertex array.

The SFML `VertexArray` class can hold different types of vertex set. But each `VertexArray` should only hold one type of set. We use the type of set that suits the occasion.

Common scenarios in video games include, but are not limited to, the following **primitive** types:

- **Point**: A single vertex per point.
- **Line**: Two vertices per set that define the start and endpoint of the line.

- **Triangle**: Three vertices per point. Among the thousands used, this is probably the most common for complex 3D models or in pairs to create a simple rectangle, like a sprite.
- **Quad**: Four vertices per set, a convenient way to map rectangular areas from a sprite sheet.

We will use quads in this project.

Building a background from tiles

The Zombie Arena background will be made up of a random arrangement of square images. You can think of this arrangement like tiles on a floor.

In this project we will be using vertex arrays with **quad** sets. Each vertex will be part of a set of four (a quad). Each vertex will define one corner of a tile from our background. Each texture coordinate will hold an appropriate value based on a specific image from the sprite sheet.

Let's take a look at some code to get us started. This isn't the exact code we will use in the project but it is fairly close and enables us to study vertex arrays before we move on to the actual implementation we will use.

Building a vertex array

As we do when we create an instance of a class, we declare our new object. The following code declares a new object of type `VertexArray` called background:

```
// Create a vertex array
VertexArray background;
```

We want to let our instance of `VertexArray` know which type of primitive we will be using. Remember that points, lines, triangles, and quads all have a different number of vertices. By setting the `VertexArray` to hold a particular type, it will be possible to know the start of each primitive. In our case we want quads. Here is the code that will do this:

```
// What primitive type are we using
background.setPrimitiveType(Quads);
```

As with regular C++ arrays, a `VertexArray` needs to be set to a size. The `VertexArray` is more flexible, however. It allows us to change its size while the game is running. The size could be configured at the same time as the declaration but our background needs to expand with each wave. The `VertexArray` class provides this functionality with the `resize` function. Here is the code that would set the size of our arena to a 10 by 10 tile size:

```
// Set the size of the vertex array
background.resize(10 * 10 * 4);
```

In the previous line of code, the first 10 is the width, the second 10 is the height, and 4 is the number of vertices in a quad. We could have just passed in 400 but showing the calculation like this makes it clear what we are doing. When we code the project for real, we will go a step further and declare variables for each part of the calculation.

We now have a `VertexArray` ready to have its hundreds of vertices configured. Here is how we set the position coordinates on the first four vertices (the first quad):

```
// Position each vertex in the current quad
background[0].position = Vector2f(0, 0);
background[1].position = Vector2f(49, 0);
background[2].position = Vector2f(49,49);
background[3].position = Vector2f(0, 49);
```

Here is how we set the texture coordinates of these same vertices to the first image in the sprite sheet. These coordinates in the image file are 0, 0 (in the top left corner) to 49, 49 (in the bottom right):

```
// Set the texture coordinates of each vertex
background[0].texCoords = Vector2f(0, 0);
background[1].texCoords = Vector2f(49, 0);
background[2].texCoords = Vector2f(49, 49);
background[3].texCoords = Vector2f(0, 49);
```

If we wanted to set the texture coordinates to the second image in the sprite sheet we would have written the code like this:

```
// Set the texture coordinates of each vertex
background[0].texCoords = Vector2f(0, 50);
background[1].texCoords = Vector2f(49, 50);
background[2].texCoords = Vector2f(49, 99);
background[3].texCoords = Vector2f(0, 99);
```

Of course, if we define each and every vertex like this individually, then we are going to be configuring even a simple 10 by 10 arena for a long time.

When we implement our background for real, we will devise a set of nested `for` loops that loop through each quad, pick a random background image, and assign the appropriate texture coordinates.

The code will need to be quite smart. It will need to know when it is an edge tile so it can use the wall image from the sprite sheet. It will also need to use appropriate variables that know the position of each background tile in the sprite sheet as well as the overall size of the required arena.

We will make this complexity manageable by putting all the code in both a separate function and a separate file. We will make the `VertexArray` usable in `main` by using a C++ reference.

We will come to these details soon. You may have noticed that at no point have we associated a texture (the sprite sheet with the vertex array).

Using the vertex array to draw

We can load the sprite sheet as a texture in exactly the same way as we load any other texture, as shown in the following code:

```
// Load the texture for our background vertex array
Texture textureBackground;
textureBackground.loadFromFile("graphics/background_sheet.png");
```

We can then draw the entire `VertexArray` with one call to `draw`:

```
// Draw the background
window.draw(background, &textureBackground);
```

The previous code is many times more efficient than drawing each and every tile as an individual sprite.

 Before we move on, notice the slightly odd looking & before `textureBackground`. Your immediate thought might be that this has something to do with references. What is going on here is we are passing the address of our texture instead of the actual texture. We will learn more about this in the next chapter.

We are now in a position to use our knowledge of references and vertex arrays to implement the next stage of the Zombie Arena project.

Creating a randomly generated scrolling background

We will create the function that makes a background in a separate file. We will ensure the background will be available (in scope) to the `main` function by using a vertex array reference.

As we will be writing other functions that share data with the `main` function, we will write them all in their own `.cpp` files. We will provide prototypes for these functions in a new header file that we will include (with an include directive) in `ZombieArena.cpp`.

To achieve this, let's first make the new header file. Right-click **Header Files** in the **Solution Explorer** and select **Add | New Item...**. In the **Add New Item** window, highlight (by left-clicking) **Header File** (`.h`), and then in the **Name** field type `ZombieArena.h`. Finally click the **Add** button. We are now ready to code the header file for our new function.

In this new `ZombieArena.h` header file, add the following highlighted code including the function prototype:

```
#pragma once
using namespace sf;
int createBackground(VertexArray& rVA, IntRect arena);
```

The previous code enables us to write the definition of a function called `createBackground`. To match the prototype, the function must return an `int` value and receive as parameters a `VertexArray` reference and an `IntRect` object.

Now we can create a new `.cpp` file in which we will code the function definition. Right-click **Source Files** in the **Solution Explorer** and select **Add | New Item...**. In the **Add New Item** window, highlight (by left-clicking) **C++ File** (`.cpp`), and then in the **Name** field type `CreateBackground.cpp`. Finally click the **Add** button. We are now ready to code the function definition that will create our background.

Add the following code to the `CreateBackground.cpp` file and then we will review it:

```
#include "stdafx.h"
#include "ZombieArena.h"

int createBackground(VertexArray& rVA, IntRect arena)
{
    // Anything we do to rVA we are actually doing
    // to background (in the main function)
    // How big is each tile/texture
```

```
const int TILE_SIZE = 50;
const int TILE_TYPES = 3;
const int VERTS_IN_QUAD = 4;

int worldWidth = arena.width / TILE_SIZE;
int worldHeight = arena.height / TILE_SIZE;

// What type of primitive are we using?
rVA.setPrimitiveType(Quads);

// Set the size of the vertex array
rVA.resize(worldWidth * worldHeight * VERTS_IN_QUAD);

// Start at the beginning of the vertex array
int currentVertex = 0;

return TILE_SIZE;
}
```

In the previous code, we write the function signature as well as the opening and closing curly brackets that mark out the function body.

Within the function body we declare and initialize three new int constants to hold values that we will need to refer to throughout the rest of the function. They are TILE_SIZE, TILE_TYPES, and VERTS_IN_QUAD. The TILE_SIZE constant refers to the size in pixels of each tile within the sprite sheet. TILE_TYPES refers to the number of different tiles within the sprite sheet. We could add more tiles into our sprite sheet, change TILE_TYPES to match, and the code we are about to write would still work. VERTS_IN_QUAD refers to the fact that there are four vertices in every quad. It is less error-prone to use this constant compared to repeatedly typing the number 4, which is less clear.

We then declare and initialize two int variables, worldWidth and worldHeight. These variables might appear blindingly obvious as to their use. They are betrayed by their names but it is worth pointing out that they refer to the width and height of the world in number of tiles, not pixels. The worldWidth and worldHeight variables are initialized by dividing the height and width of the passed-in arena by the constant, TILE_SIZE.

Next, we get to use our reference for the first time. Remember that anything we do to rVA we are really doing to the variable that was passed-in which is in scope in the main function (or will be when we code it).

First we prepare the vertex array to use quads using rVA.setType, and then we make it just the right size by calling rVA.resize. To the resize function we pass in the result of worldWidth * worldHeight * VERTS_IN_QUAD, which equates to exactly the number of vertices that our vertex array will have when we are done preparing it.

The last line of code declares and initializes currentVertex to zero. We will use currentVertex as we loop through the vertex array initializing all the vertices.

We can now write the first part of a nested for loop that will prepare the vertex array. Add the following highlighted code, and based on what we have learnt about vertex arrays, try and work out what it does:

```
// Start at the beginning of the vertex array
int currentVertex = 0;

for (int w = 0; w < worldWidth; w++)
{
  for (int h = 0; h < worldHeight; h++)
  {
    // Position each vertex in the current quad
    rVA[currentVertex + 0].position =
      Vector2f(w * TILE_SIZE, h * TILE_SIZE);
    rVA[currentVertex + 1].position =
      Vector2f((w * TILE_SIZE) + TILE_SIZE, h * TILE_SIZE);

    rVA[currentVertex + 2].position =
      Vector2f((w * TILE_SIZE) + TILE_SIZE, (h * TILE_SIZE)
        + TILE_SIZE);
    rVA[currentVertex + 3].position =
      Vector2f((w * TILE_SIZE), (h * TILE_SIZE)
        + TILE_SIZE);

    // Position ready for the next for vertices
    currentVertex = currentVertex + VERTS_IN_QUAD;
  }
}

  return TILE_SIZE;
}
```

The code that we just added steps through the vertex array by using a nested for loop that first steps through the first four vertices. currentVertex + 1, currentVertex + 2, and so on.

We access each vertex in the array using array notation. rVA[currentVertex + 0].. and so on. Using array notation we call the position function rVA[currentVertex +

```
0].position....
```

Into the `position` function we pass the horizontal and vertical coordinates of each vertex. We can work these coordinates out programmatically by using a combination of `w`, `h`, and `TILE_SIZE`.

At the end of the previous code we position `currentVertex` ready for the next pass through the nested `for` loop by advancing it four places (adding four) with the code `currentVertex = currentVertex + VERTS_IN_QUAD`.

Of course, all this does is set the coordinates of our vertices; it doesn't assign a texture coordinate from the sprite sheet. This is what we will do next.

To make it absolutely clear where the new code goes I have shown it in context with all the code that we wrote a moment ago. Add and study the highlighted code:

```
for (int w = 0; w < worldWidth; w++)
    {
        for (int h = 0; h < worldHeight; h++)
        {
            // Position each vertex in the current quad
            rVA[currentVertex + 0].position =
                Vector2f(w * TILE_SIZE, h * TILE_SIZE);
            rVA[currentVertex + 1].position =
                Vector2f((w * TILE_SIZE) + TILE_SIZE, h * TILE_SIZE);
            rVA[currentVertex + 2].position =
                Vector2f((w * TILE_SIZE) + TILE_SIZE, (h * TILE_SIZE)
                + TILE_SIZE);
            rVA[currentVertex + 3].position =
                Vector2f((w * TILE_SIZE), (h * TILE_SIZE)
                + TILE_SIZE);

            // Define the position in the Texture for current quad
            // Either grass, stone, bush or wall
            if (h == 0 || h == worldHeight-1 ||
                w == 0 || w == worldWidth-1)
            {
                // Use the wall texture
                rVA[currentVertex + 0].texCoords =
                    Vector2f(0, 0 + TILE_TYPES * TILE_SIZE);
                rVA[currentVertex + 1].texCoords =
                    Vector2f(TILE_SIZE, 0 +
                    TILE_TYPES * TILE_SIZE);
                rVA[currentVertex + 2].texCoords =
                    Vector2f(TILE_SIZE, TILE_SIZE +
                    TILE_TYPES * TILE_SIZE);
```

```
        rVA[currentVertex + 3].texCoords =
            Vector2f(0, TILE_SIZE +
            TILE_TYPES * TILE_SIZE);
    }

    // Position ready for the next for vertices
    currentVertex = currentVertex + VERTS_IN_QUAD;
    }
    }

    return TILE_SIZE;
}
```

The previous code sets up the coordinates within the sprite sheet that each vertex is related to. Notice the somewhat long `if` condition. The condition checks whether the current quad is either one of the very first or the very last quads in the arena. If it is then this means it is part of the boundary. We can then use a simple formula using `TILE_SIZE` and `TILE_TYPES` to target the wall texture from the sprite sheet.

Array notation and the `texCoords` member are initialized for each vertex in turn to assign the appropriate corner of the wall texture within the sprite sheet.

The following code is wrapped in an `else` block. This means that it will run each time through the nested for loop when the quad does not represent a border/wall tile. Add the highlighted code amongst the existing code and we can then examine it:

```
// Define position in Texture for current quad
// Either grass, stone, bush or wall
if (h == 0 || h == worldHeight-1 ||
    w == 0 || w == worldWidth-1)
{
    // Use the wall texture
    rVA[currentVertex + 0].texCoords =
        Vector2f(0, 0 + TILE_TYPES * TILE_SIZE);

    rVA[currentVertex + 1].texCoords =
        Vector2f(TILE_SIZE, 0 +
        TILE_TYPES * TILE_SIZE);

    rVA[currentVertex + 2].texCoords =
        Vector2f(TILE_SIZE, TILE_SIZE +
        TILE_TYPES * TILE_SIZE);

    rVA[currentVertex + 3].texCoords =
        Vector2f(0, TILE_SIZE +
        TILE_TYPES * TILE_SIZE);
```

```
        }
        else
        {
            // Use a random floor texture
            srand((int)time(0) + h * w - h);
            int mOrG = (rand() % TILE_TYPES);
            int verticalOffset = mOrG * TILE_SIZE;

            rVA[currentVertex + 0].texCoords =
                Vector2f(0, 0 + verticalOffset);

            rVA[currentVertex + 1].texCoords =
                Vector2f(TILE_SIZE, 0 + verticalOffset);

            rVA[currentVertex + 2].texCoords =
                Vector2f(TILE_SIZE, TILE_SIZE + verticalOffset);

            rVA[currentVertex + 3].texCoords =
                Vector2f(0, TILE_SIZE + verticalOffset);
        }

        // Position ready for the next for vertices
        currentVertex = currentVertex + VERTS_IN_QUAD;
    }
}

return TILE_SIZE;
}
```

The previous new code starts by seeding the random number generator with a formula that will be different each pass through the loop. Then the mOrG variable is initialized with a number between 0 and TILE_TYPES. This is just what we need to pick one of the tile types randomly.

 mOrG stands for mud or grass. The name is arbitrary.

Now we declare and initialize a variable called verticalOffset by multiplying mOrG by TileSize. We now have a vertical reference point within the sprite sheet to the starting height of the randomly chosen texture for the current quad.

Now we use a simple formula involving TILE_SIZE and verticalOffset to assign the precise coordinates of each corner of the texture to the appropriate vertex.

Now we can put our new function to work in the game engine.

Using the background

We have done the tricky stuff, this will be simple. There are three steps:

1. Create a `VertexArray`.
2. Initialize it after leveling up each wave.
3. Draw it in each frame.

Add the code highlighted in the following to declare a `VertexArray` called background and load the `background_sheet.png` as a texture:

```
// Create an instance of the Player class
Player player;

// The boundaries of the arena
IntRect arena;

// Create the backgroundVertexArray background;
// Load the texture for our background vertex array
Texture textureBackground;
textureBackground.loadFromFile("graphics/background_sheet.png");

// The main game loop
while (window.isOpen())
```

Add the following code to call the `createBackground` function, passing in background as a reference and arena by value. Notice in the highlighted code that we have also modified the way that we initialize the `tileSize` variable. Add the highlighted code exactly as shown:

```
if (state == State::PLAYING)
{
    // Prepare thelevel
    // We will modify the next two lines later
    arena.width = 500;
    arena.height = 500;
    arena.left = 0;
    arena.top = 0;

    // Pass the vertex array by reference
    // to the createBackground function
    int tileSize = createBackground(background, arena);
```

```
    // We will modify this line of code later
    // int tileSize = 50;

    // Spawn the player in the middle of the arena
    player.spawn(arena, resolution, tileSize);

    // Reset the clock so there isn't a frame jump
    clock.restart();
}
```

Note we have replaced the `int tileSize = 50` line of code because we get the value directly from the return value of the `createBackground` function.

For the sake of future code clarity, you should delete the `int tileSize = 50` line of code and its related comment. I just commented it out to give the new code a clearer context.

Finally, it is time to do the drawing. This is really simple. All we do is call `window.draw` and pass the `VertexArray` along with the `textureBackground` texture:

```
/*
*************
Draw the scene
*************
*/

if (state == State::PLAYING)
{
    window.clear();

    // Set the mainView to be displayed in the window
    // And draw everything related to it
    window.setView(mainView);

    // Draw the background
    window.draw(background, &textureBackground);

    // Draw the player
    window.draw(player.getSprite());
}
```

If you are wondering what is going on with the odd-looking & sign in front of `textureBackground`, then all will be made clear in the next chapter.

You can now run the game as shown in this next image:

Note how the player sprite glides and rotates smoothly within the arena confines. Although the current code in main draws a small arena, the `CreateBackground` function can create an arena of any size we tell it. We will see arenas bigger than the screen in `Chapter 11`: *Sound Effects, File I/O, and Finishing the Game.*

FAQ

Here are some questions that might be on your mind:

Q) Can you summarize these references again?

A) You must initialize a reference immediately and cannot change it to reference another variable. Use references with functions so you are not working on a copy. This is good for efficiency because it avoids making copies and helps us more easily abstract our code into functions.

Q) Is there an easy way to remember the main benefit of using references?

A) To help you remember what a reference is for, consider this short rhyme:

Moving large objects can make our games choppy, passing by reference is faster than copy.

Summary

In this chapter we discovered C++ references that are special variables that act as an alias to another variable. When we pass a variable by reference instead of by value, then any work we do on the reference happens to the variable back in the calling function.

We also learnt about vertex arrays and created a vertex array full of quads to draw the tiles from a sprite sheet as a background.

The elephant in the room, of course, is that our zombie game doesn't have any zombies. Let's fix that now by learning about C++ pointers and the Standard Template Library.

8
Pointers, the Standard Template Library, and Texture Management

We will learn a lot, as well as get plenty done to the game in this chapter. We will first learn about the fundamental C++ topic of **pointers**. Pointers are variables that hold memory addresses. Typically, a pointer will hold the memory address of another variable. This sounds a bit like a reference but we will see how they are much more powerful. We will also use a pointer to handle an ever-expanding horde of zombies.

We will also learn about the **Standard Template Library** (STL) which is a collection of classes that allow us to quickly and easily implement common data management techniques.

Once we understand the basics of the STL, we will be able to use that new knowledge to manage all the textures from the game, because if we have 1000 zombies, we don't really want to load a copy of a zombie graphic into the GPU for each and every one.

We will also dig a little deeper into OOP and use a **static** function which is a function of a class that can be called without an instance of the class. At the same time, we will see how we can design a class to ensure that only one instance can ever exist. This is ideal when we need to guarantee that different parts of our code will use the same data.

In this chapter, we will learn the following topics:

- Learn about pointers
- Learn about the STL
- Implement the `Texture Holder` class using static functions and a **singleton** class
- Implement a pointer to a horde of zombies
- Edit some existing code to use the `TextureHolder` class for the player and background

Pointers

Pointers can be the cause of frustration while learning to code C++. Actually, however, the concept is simple.

A **pointer** is a variable that holds a memory address.

That's it! Nothing there to get concerned about. What probably causes the frustration to beginners is the syntax, the code we use to handle pointers. With this in mind we will step through each part of the code for using pointers. You can then begin the ongoing process of mastering them.

In this section, we will actually learn more about pointers than we need for this project. In the next project, we will make greater use of pointers. Despite this, we will only scratch the surface of the topic. Further study is definitely recommended and we will talk more about that in the final chapter.

Rarely do I suggest that memorizing facts, figures, or syntax is the best way to learn. However, memorizing the fairly brief but crucial syntax related to pointers might be worthwhile. This is so that it sinks so deep into our brains we can never forget it. We can then talk about why we need pointers and examine their relationship to references. A pointer analogy might help.

If a variable is a house and its contents are the value it holds, then a pointer is the address of the house.

We learned in the previous chapter while discussing references that when we pass values to, or return values from, a function, we are actually making a completely new house the exact same as the previous one. We are making a copy of the value passed to or from a function.

At this point, pointers are probably starting to sound a bit like references. That's because they are a bit like references. Pointers, however, are much more flexible, powerful, and have their own special and unique uses. These special and unique uses require a special and unique syntax.

Pointer syntax

There are two main operators associated with pointers. The first is the **address of** operator:

' & '

And the second is the **dereference** operator:

' * '

We will take a look now at the different ways we use these operators with pointers.

The first thing you will notice is that the address of operator is the same as the reference operator. To add to the woes of an aspiring C++ game programmer, the operators do different things in different contexts. Knowing this from the outset is valuable. If you are staring at some code involving pointers and it seems like you are going mad, know this:

You are perfectly sane! You just need to look at the detail of the context.

Now you know that if something isn't clear and immediately obvious it is not your fault. Pointers are not clear and immediately obvious, but looking carefully at the context will reveal what is going on.

Armed with the knowledge that you need to pay more attention to pointers than to previous syntax, as well as what the two operators are (address of and dereference), we can now start to actually see some real pointer code.

Make sure you have memorized the two operators before proceeding.

Declaring a pointer

To declare a new pointer, we use the dereference operator along with the type of variable the pointer will be holding the address of. Take a look at the code and we will go into it some more:

```
// Declare a pointer to hold the address of a variable of type int

int* pHealth;
```

This code declares a new pointer called `pHealth` that can hold the address of a variable of type `int`. Notice I said *can* hold a variable of type `int`. As with other variables a pointer also needs to be initialized with a value to make proper use of it. The name `pHealth` as with other variables is arbitrary.

It is common practice to prefix the names of variables that are pointers with a `p`. It is then much easier to remember when we are dealing with a pointer and to distinguish them from regular variables.

The white space used around the dereference operator is optional (because C++ rarely cares about spaces in syntax), but recommended because it aids readability. Take a look at the following three lines of code, which do exactly the same thing.

This format we have just seen, in the previous example, with the dereference operator next to the type:

```
int* pHealth;
```

White space either side of the dereference operator:

```
int * pHealth;
```

The dereference operator next to the name of the pointer:

```
int *pHealth;
```

It is worth being aware of these possibilities so that when you read code, perhaps on the Web, you will understand they are all the same. In this book, we will always use the first option with the dereference operator next to the type.

Just like a regular variable can only successfully contain data of the appropriate type, a pointer should only hold the address of a variable of the appropriate type.

A pointer to type `int` should not hold the address of a String, Zombie, Player, Sprite, float, or any other type.

Initializing a pointer

Next we can see how to get the address of a variable into a pointer. Take a look at the following code:

```
// A regular int variable called health
int health = 5;

// Declare a pointer to hold the address of a variable of type int
int* pHealth;

// Initialize pHealth to hold the address of health,
// using the "address of" operator
pHealth = &health;
```

In the previous code, we declare an `int` variable called `health` and initialize it to 5. It makes sense, although we have never discussed it before, that this variable must be somewhere in our computer's memory. It must have a memory address.

We can access this address using the address of operator. Look closely at the last line of the previous code. We initialize `pHealth` with the address of `health`, like this:

```
pHealth = &health;
```

Our `pHealth`, now holds the address of the regular `int`, `health`. In C++ terminology we say that `pHealth` points to `health`.

We can use `pHealth` by passing it to a function, so that function can work on `health`, just like we did with references. There would be no reason for pointers if that was all we were going to do with them.

Reinitializing pointers

A pointer, unlike a reference, can be reinitialized to point to a different address. Take a look at the following code:

```
// A regular int variable called health
int health = 5;
int score = 0;

// Declare a pointer to hold the address of a variable of type int
int* pHealth;

// Initialize pHealth to hold the address of health
pHealth = &health;

// Re-initialize pHealth to hold the address of score
pHealth = &score;
```

Now pHealth **points to the** int **variable,** score.

Of course the name of our pointer, pHealth, is now slightly ambiguous and should perhaps have been called pIntPointer. The key thing to understand here is that we can do this reassignment.

At this stage we haven't actually used a pointer for anything other than simply pointing (holding a memory address). Let's see how we can access the value stored at the address pointed to by a pointer. This will make them genuinely useful.

Dereferencing a pointer

So we know that a pointer holds an address in memory. If we were to output this address in our game, perhaps in our HUD, after it has been declared and initialized, it might look something like this: 9876.

It is just a value. A value that represents an address in memory. On different operating systems and hardware types, the range of these values will vary. In the context of this book we never need to manipulate an address directly. We only care what the value stored at the address that is pointed to is.

The actual addresses used by variables are determined when the game is executed (at runtime) and therefore, there is no way of knowing the address of a variable and hence the value stored in a pointer, while we are coding the game.

We access the value stored at the address pointed to by a pointer by using the dereference operator, *. The following code manipulates some variables directly, and by using a pointer. Try and follow along and then we will go through it.

 Warning! The code that follows is pointless (pun intended). It just demonstrates using pointers.

```
// Some regular int variables
int score = 0;
int hiScore = 10;

// Declare 2 pointers to hold the addresses of ints
int* pIntPointer1;
int* pIntPointer2;

// Initialize pIntPointer1 to hold the address of score
pIntPointer1 = &score;

// Initialize pIntPointer2 to hold the address of hiScore
pIntPointer2 = &hiScore;

// Add 10 to score directly
score += 10;
// Score now equals 10

// Add 10 to score using pIntPointer1
*pIntPointer1 += 10;
// score now equals 20- A new high score

// Assign the new hi score to hiScore using only pointers
*pIntPointer2 = *pIntPointer1;
// hiScore and score both equal 20
```

In the previous code, we declare two int variables, score and hiScore. We then initialize them with the values zero and ten respectively. We next declare two pointers to int. They are pIntPointer1 and pIntPointer2. We initialize them in the same step as declaring them to hold the addresses of (point to) the variables score and hiScore respectively.

Next we add ten to score in the usual way, score += 10. Then we see that by using the dereference operator on a pointer we can access the value stored at the address they point to. The following code actually changed the value stored by the variable pointed to by pIntPointer1:

```
// Add 10 to score using pIntPointer1
*pIntPointer1 += 10;
// score now equals 20, A new high score
```

The last part of the previous code dereferences both of the pointers to assign the value pointed to by pIntPointer1 as the value pointed to by pIntPointer2:

```
// Assign the new hi-score to hiScore with only pointers
*pIntPointer2 = *pIntPointer1;
// hiScore and score both equal 20
```

Both score and hiScore are now equal to 20.

Pointers are versatile and powerful

We can do so much more with pointers. Here are just a few useful things we can do.

Dynamically allocated memory

All the pointers we have seen so far point to memory addresses that have a scope limited only to the function they are created in. So if we declare and initialize a pointer to a local variable, when the function returns, the pointer, the local variable, and the memory address is gone. It is out of scope.

Up until now we have been using a fixed amount of memory that is decided in advance of the game being executed. Furthermore, the memory we have been using is controlled by the operating system and variables are lost and created as we call and return from functions. What we need is a way to use memory that is always in scope, until we are finished with it. We want to have access to memory we can call our own and take responsibility for.

When we declare variables (including pointers), they are in an area of memory known as the **stack**. There is another area of memory, which although allocated/controlled by the operating system, can be allocated at runtime. This other area of memory is called the **free store** or sometimes the **heap**.

Memory on the heap does not have scope to a particular function. Returning from a function does not delete the memory on the heap.

This gives us great power. With access to memory that is only limited by the resources of the computer our game is running on, we can plan games with a huge amount of objects. In our case we want a vast horde of zombies. As Spider-man's uncle wouldn't hesitate to remind us, however, *with great power comes great responsibility.*

Let's look at how we can use pointers to take advantage of the memory on the free store and also how we release that memory back to the operating system when we are finished with it.

To create a pointer that points to a value on the heap, first we need a pointer:

```
int* pToInt = nullptr;
```

In the previous line of code, we declare a pointer as we have seen before, but as we are not initializing it to point to a variable, we initialize it to `nullptr`. We do this because it is good practice. Consider dereferencing a pointer (changing a value at the address it points to) when you don't even know what it is pointing to. It would be the programming equivalent of going to the shooting range, blindfolding someone, spinning them around, and telling them to shoot. By pointing a pointer to nothing (`nullptr`) we can't do any harm with it.

When we are ready to request memory on the free store we use the `new` keyword as shown in the following line of code:

```
pToInt = new int;
```

The pointer `pToInt` now holds the memory address of space on the free store that is just the right size to hold an `int` value.

Any allocated memory is returned when the program ends. It is, however, important to realize that this memory will never be freed (within the execution of our game), unless we free it. If we continue to take memory from the free store without giving it back, eventually it will run out and the game will crash.

It is unlikely that we would ever run out of memory by occasionally taking `int` sized chunks of the free store. But if our program has a function or loop that requests memory, and this function or loop is executed regularly throughout the game, eventually the game will slow and then crash. Furthermore, if we allocate lots of objects on the free store and don't manage them correctly, then this situation can happen quite quickly.

The following line of code, hands back (deletes) the memory on the free store that was previously pointed to by pToInt:

```
delete pToInt;
```

Now the memory that was previously pointed to by pToInt is no longer ours to do what we like with, we must make take precautions. Although the memory has been handed back to the operating system, pToInt still holds the address of this memory, which no longer belongs to us.

The following line of code ensures that pToInt can't be used to attempt to manipulate or access this memory:

```
pToInt = nullptr;
```

 If a pointer points to an address that is invalid it is called a **wild** or **dangling** pointer. If you attempt to dereference a dangling pointer, if you are lucky the game will crash and you will get a memory access violation error. If you are unlucky you will create a bug that will be incredibly difficult to find. Furthermore, if we use memory on the free store that will persist beyond the life of a function, we must make sure to keep a pointer to it or we will have leaked memory.

Now we can declare pointers and point them to newly allocated memory on the free store. We can manipulate and access the memory they point to by dereferencing them. We can return memory to the free store when we are done with it and we know how to avoid having a dangling pointer.

Let's look at some more advantages of pointers.

Passing a pointer to a function

First we would need to write a function that has a pointer in the signature, like the following code:

```
void myFunction(int *pInt)
{
    // dereference and increment the value stored
    // at the address pointed to by the pointer
    *pInt ++
    return;
}
```

The previous function simply dereferences the pointer and adds one to the value stored at the pointed address.

Now we can use that function and pass the address of a variable or another pointer to a variable explicitly:

```
int someInt = 10;
int* pToInt = &someInt;

myFunction(&someInt);
// someInt now equals 11

myFunction(pToInt);
// someInt now equals 12
```

Now, as shown in the previous code, within the function we are actually manipulating the variable from the calling code and can do so using the address of a variable or a pointer to that variable.

Declaring and using a pointer to an object

Pointers are not just for regular variables. We can also declare pointers to user-defined types like our classes. This is how we would declare a pointer to an object of type `Player`:

```
Player player;
Player* pPlayer = &Player;
```

We can even access the member functions of a `Player` object directly from the pointer, like the following code:

```
// Call a member function of the player class
pPlayer->moveLeft()
```

We won't need to use pointers to objects in this project and we will explore them more carefully before we do, in the next project.

Pointers and arrays

Arrays and pointers have something in common. An array name is a memory address. More specifically the name of an array is the memory address of the first element in that array. To put, yet another way, an array name points to the first element of an array. The best way to understand this is to read on to see the next example.

We can create a pointer to the type that an array holds and then use the pointer in exactly the same way using exactly the same syntax that we would the array:

```
// Declare an array of ints
int arrayOfInts[100];
//  Declare a pointer to int and initialize it with the address of the
//first element of the array, arrayOfInts
int* pToIntArray = arrayOfInts;

// Use pToIntArray just as you would arrayOfInts
arrayOfInts[0] = 999;
// First element of arrayOfInts now equals 999

pToIntArray[0] = 0;
// First element of arrayOfInts now equals 0
```

This also means that a function that has a prototype that accepts a pointer, also accepts arrays of the type the pointer is pointing to. We will use this fact when we build our ever-increasing horde of zombies.

Regarding the relationship between pointers and references, the compiler actually uses pointers when implementing our references. This means that references are just a handy tool (that uses pointers under the hood). You could think of a reference as an automatic gearbox that is fine and convenient for driving around town, whereas pointers are a manual gearbox, more complicated but with the correct use, gives better results/performance/flexibility.

Summary of pointers

Pointers are a bit fiddly at times. In fact, our discussion of pointers was only an introduction to the subject. The only way to get comfortable with them is to use them as much as possible. All you need to understand about pointers in order to complete this project is the following:

- Pointers are variables that store a memory address.
- We can pass pointers to functions to directly manipulate values from the calling function's scope, within the called function. Arrays are the memory address of the first element. We can pass this address as a pointer because that is exactly what it is.
- We can use pointers to point to memory on the free store. This means we can dynamically allocate large amounts of memory while the game is running.

To further mystify the issue of pointers, C++ got upgraded fairly recently. There are now yet more ways to use pointers. If you are curious do a Web search for smart pointers.

There is just one more topic to cover and we can get coding the Zombie Arena project again.

The Standard Template Library

The STL is a collection of data containers and ways to manipulate the data we put in those containers. Or to be more specific, it is a way to store and manipulate different types of C++ variables and classes.

We can think of the different containers as customized and more advanced arrays. The STL is part of C++. It is not an optional thing that needs to be set up, such as SFML.

The STL is part of C++ because its containers and the code that manipulates them is fundamental to many types of code that many apps will need to use.

In short, the STL implements code that we and just about every C++ programmer is almost bound to need, at least at some point and probably quite regularly.

If we were to write our own code to contain and manage our data, then it is unlikely we would write it as efficiently as the people who wrote the STL.

So by using the STL we guarantee that we are using the best-written code possible to manage our data. Even SFML uses the STL. For example, under the hood, the `VertexArray` class uses the STL.

All we need to do is to choose the right type of container from those that are available. The types of container that are available through the STL include the following:

- **Vector**: Like an array with boosters. Dynamic resizing, sorting, and searching. This is probably the most useful container.
- **List**: A container that allows the ordering of data.
- **Map**: An associative container that allows the user to store data as key/value pairs. This is where one piece of data is the key to finding the other piece. A Map can also grow and shrink, as well as be searched.
- **Set**: A container that guarantees that each and every element is unique.

For a full list of STL container types and explanations, visit the following link: `http://www.tutorialspoint.com/cplusplus/cpp_stl_tutorial.htm`

In the Zombie Arena game, we will use a Map.

If you want a glimpse into the kind of complexity that the STL is sparing us, then take a look at this tutorial which implements the kind of thing that a list would do. Note that the tutorial implements only the very simplest barebones of a list: `http://www.sanfoundry.com/cpp-program-implement-single-linked-list/`.

We can easily see that we will save a lot of time and definitely end up with a better game if we explore the STL. Let's take a closer look at how to use Map and then we will see how it will be useful to us in the Zombie Arena game.

What is a Map

A **Map** is a container that is dynamically resizable. We can add and remove elements with ease. What makes a Map special compared to the other containers in the STL is the way that we access the data within it.

The data in a Map is stored in pairs. Consider the situation where you log in to an account, perhaps with a username and password. A Map would be perfect for looking up the username and then checking the value of the associated password.

A Map would also be just right for things like account names and numbers or perhaps company names and share prices.

Note that when we use Map from the STL, we decide the type of values that form the key-value pairs. The values could be data types such as `string` and `int`, such as account numbers, strings such as usernames and passwords, or user-defined types like objects.

What follows is some real code to make us familiar with Map.

Declaring a Map

This is how we could declare a Map:

```
map<string, int> accounts;
```

The previous line of code declares a new `map` called `accounts` that has a key of `string` objects, each of which will refer to a value that is `int`.

We can now store key-value-pairs of Strings that refer to data type such as `int` and we will see how next.

Adding data to a Map

Let's go ahead and add a key-value pair to accounts:

```
accounts["John"] = 1234567;
```

Now there is an entry in the `map` that can be accessed using the key of John. The following code adds two more entries to the accounts `map`:

```
accounts["Onkar"] = 7654321;
accounts["Wilson"] = 8866772;
```

Our Map has three entries in it. Let's see how we can access the account numbers.

Finding data in a Map

We would access the data in exactly the same way that we added it, by using the key. As an example, we could assign the value stored by the key `Onkar` to a new `int`, `accountNumber`, like this code:

```
int accountNumber = accounts["Onkar"];
```

The int variable `accountNumber` now stores the value `7654321`. We can do anything to a value stored in a Map that we can do to that type.

Removing data from a Map

Taking values out of our Map is also straightforward. This next line of code removes the key, John, and its associated value:

```
accounts.erase("John");
```

Let's look at a few more things we can do with a Map.

Checking the size of a Map

We might like to know how many key-value pairs we have in our Map. This next line of code does just that:

```
int size = accounts.size();
```

The int variable size now holds the value of two. This is because accounts holds values for Onkar and Wilson, we deleted John.

Checking for keys in a Map

The most relevant feature of a Map is the ability to find a value using the key. We can test for the presence or otherwise of a specific key like this:

```
if(accounts.find("John") != accounts.end())
{
    // This code won't run because John was erased
}

if(accounts.find("Onkar") != accounts.end())
{
    // This code will run because Onkar is in the map
}
```

In the previous code, the value != accounts.end is used to determine when a key doesn't exist or does exist. If the searched for key is not present in the Map, then accounts.end will be the result of the if statement.

Looping/iterating through the key-value pairs of a Map

We have seen how we can use a for loop to loop/iterate through all the values of an array. What if we want to do something similar to a Map?

The following code shows how we could loop through each key-value pair of the accounts Map and add one to each of the account numbers:

```
for (map<string,int>::iterator it = accounts.begin(); it ! =
  accounts.end();  ++ it)
{
    it->second +=1;
}
```

The condition of the for loop is probably the most interesting part of the previous code. The first part of the condition is the longest part. The `map<string,int>::iterator it = accounts.begin()` code is more understandable if we break it down.

The `map<string,int>::iterator` code is a type. We are declaring an `iterator` suitable for a `map` with key-value pairs of `string` and `int`. The iterators, name is `it`. We assign the value returned from `accounts.begin()` to it. The iterator `it` now holds the first key-value-pair in the accounts `map`.

The rest of the condition of the `for` loop works as follows. The code `it !=` `accounts.end()` means the loop will continue until the end of the `map` is reached and `it++` simply steps to the next key-value-pair in the `map`, each pass through the loop.

Inside the for loop, `it->second` accesses the second element of the key-value pair and `+=1` adds one to the value. Note that we can access the key (which is the first part of the key-value pair) with `it->first`.

The auto keyword

The code in the condition of the for loop was quite verbose, especially the `map<string,int>::iterator` type. C++ supplies a neat way to reduce verbosity with the `auto` keyword. Using the `auto` keyword, we could improve the previous code to the following:

```
for (auto it = accounts.begin(); it != accounts.end();  ++ it)
{
    it->second +=1;
```

```
}
```

The auto keyword instructs the compiler to automatically deduce the type for us. This will be especially useful with the next class that we write.

STL summary

As with almost every C++ concept that we have covered in this book, the STL is a massive topic. Whole books have been written covering just the STL. At this point, however, we know enough to build a class that uses an STL Map to store SFML `Texture` objects. We can then have textures that can be retrieved/loaded by using the filename as the key of the key-value pair.

The reason why we would go to this extra level of complexity and not just carry on using the `Texture` class as we have been so far, will become apparent as we proceed.

The TextureHolder Class

Thousands of zombies represent a new challenge. Not only would loading, storing, and manipulating thousands of copies of three different zombie textures take up a lot of memory, but also a lot of processing power. We will create a new type of class that overcomes this problem and allows us to store just one of each texture.

We will also code the class in such a way that there can only ever be one instance of it. This type of class is called a **singleton**.

A singleton is a **design pattern**, a way to structure our code that is proven to work.

Furthermore, we will also code the class so that it can be used anywhere in our game code directly through the class name, without access to an instance.

Coding the TextureHolder header file

Make the new header file. Right-click **Header Files** in the **Solution Explorer** and select **Add | New Item…**. In the **Add New Item** window, highlight (by left-clicking) **Header File (**.h**)** and then in the **Name** field type `TextureHolder.h`.

Add the code that follows into the `TextureHolder.h` file and then we can discuss it:

```
#pragma once
#ifndef TEXTURE_HOLDER_H
#define TEXTURE_HOLDER_H

#include <SFML/Graphics.hpp>
#include <map>

using namespace sf;
using namespace std;

class TextureHolder
{
private:
    // A map container from the STL,
    // that holds related pairs of String and Texture
    std::map<std::string, Texture> m_Textures;

    // A pointer of the same type as the class itself
    // the one and only instance
    static TextureHolder* m_s_Instance;


public:
    TextureHolder();
    static Texture& GetTexture(string const& filename);

};

#endif
```

In the previous code, notice that we have an include directive for `map` from the STL. We declare a `map` that holds `string` and SFML `Texture` key-value pairs. The `map` is called `m_Textures`.

In the previous code, this line is next:

```
static TextureHolder* m_s_Instance;
```

The previous line of code is quite interesting. We are declaring a `static` pointer to an object of type `TextureHolder` called `m_s_Instance`. This means that the `TextureHolder` class has an object that is the same type as itself. Not only that, but because it is `static`, it can be used through the class itself, without an instance of the class. When we code the related `.cpp` file we will see how we use this.

In the `public` part of the class we have the prototype for the constructor function, `TextureHolder`. The constructor takes no arguments and, as usual, has no return type. This is the same as the default constructor. We are going to override the default constructor with a definition that makes our singleton work how we want it to.

We have another function called `GetTexture`. Let's look at the signature again and analyze exactly what is happening:

```
static Texture& GetTexture(string const& filename);
```

First, notice that the function returns a reference to a `Texture`. This means that `GetTexture` will return a reference, which is efficient because it avoids making a copy of what could be a fairly large graphic. Also notice the function is declared as `static`. This means the function can be used without an instance of the class. The function takes a `string` as a constant reference, as a parameter. The effect of this is twofold. Firstly, the operation is efficient and secondly, because the reference is constant, it can't be changed.

Coding the TextureHolder function definitions

Now we can create a new `.cpp` file that will contain the function definition. This will enable us to see the reasons behind our new types of functions and variables. Right-click **Source Files** in the **Solution Explorer** and select **Add | New Item....** In the **Add New Item** window, highlight (by left-clicking), **C++ File (.cpp)** and then in the **Name** field type `TextureHolder.cpp`. Finally, click the **Add** button. We are now ready to code the class.

Add the following code and then we can discuss it:

```cpp
#include "stdafx.h"
#include "TextureHolder.h"

// Include the "assert feature"
#include <assert.h>

TextureHolder* TextureHolder::m_s_Instance = nullptr;

TextureHolder::TextureHolder()
{
    assert(m_s_Instance == nullptr);
    m_s_Instance = this;
}
```

In the previous code, we initialize our pointer to type `TextureHolder` to `nullptr`. In the constructor, the code `assert(m_s_Instance == nullptr)` ensures that `m_s_Instance` equals `nullptr`. If it doesn't, the game will exit execution. Then the code `m_s_Instance = this` assigns the pointer to this instance. Now consider where this code is taking place. The code is in the constructor. The constructor is the way that we create instances of objects from classes. So effectively we now have a pointer to a `TextureHolder` that points to the one and only instance of itself.

Add the final part of the code to the `TextureHolder.cpp` file. There are more comments than code next. Examine the code and read the comments as you add the code and then we can go through it:

```cpp
sf::Texture& TextureHolder::GetTexture(std::string const& filename)
{
    // Get a reference to m_Textures using m_S_Instance
    auto& m = m_s_Instance->m_Textures;
    // auto is the equivalent of map<string, Texture>

    // Create an iterator to hold a key-value-pair (kvp)
    // and search for the required kvp
    // using the passed in filename
    auto keyValuePair = m.find(filename);
    // auto is equivelant of map<string, Texture>::iterator
    // Did we find a match?
    if (keyValuePair != m.end())
    {
        // Yes
        // Return the texture,
        // the second part of the kvp, the texture
        return keyValuePair->second;
    }
    else
    {
        // Filename not found
        // Create a new key value pair using the filename
        auto& texture = m[filename];
        // Load the texture from file in the usual way
        texture.loadFromFile(filename);

        // Return the texture to the calling code
        return texture;
    }
}
```

The first thing you will probably notice about the previous code is the `auto` keyword. The `auto` keyword was explained in the previous section.

If you want to know what the actual types that have been replaced by `auto` are, then take a look at the comments immediately after each use of `auto` in the previous code.

At the start of the code we get a reference to `m_textures`. Then we attempt to get an iterator to the key-value pair represented by the passed-in filename (`filename`). If we find a matching key, we return the texture with `return keyValuePair->second`. Otherwise we add the texture to the `map` and then return it to the calling code.

Admittedly, the `TextureHolder` class introduced lots of new concepts (singletons, `static` functions, constant references, `this`, and the `auto` keyword) and syntax. Add to this the fact that we have only just learned about pointers and the STL, and this section's code might have been a little daunting.

What exactly have we achieved with TextureHolder?

The point is that now we have this class, we can go wild using textures wherever we like in our code and not worry about running out of memory or having access to a particular texture in a particular function or class. We will see how to use `TextureHolder` really soon.

Building a horde of zombies

Now we are armed with the `TextureHolder` class to make sure that our zombie textures are easily available, as well as only loaded into the GPU once, we can look into creating a whole horde of them.

We will store zombies in an array and as the process of building and spawning a horde of zombies involves quite a few lines of code, it is a good candidate for abstracting to a separate function. Soon we will code the `CreateHorde` function but first, of course, we need a `Zombie` class.

Coding the Zombie.h file

The first step to building a class to represent a zombie is to code the member variables and function prototypes in a header file.

Right-click **Header Files** in the **Solution Explorer** and select **Add | New Item...**. In the **Add New Item** window, highlight (by left-clicking) **Header File (** .h**)** and then in the **Name** field type Zombie.h.

Add the following code into the Zombie.h file:

```cpp
#pragma once
#include <SFML/Graphics.hpp>

using namespace sf;

class Zombie
{
private:
    // How fast is each zombie type?
    const float BLOATER_SPEED = 40;
    const float CHASER_SPEED = 80;
    const float CRAWLER_SPEED = 20;

    // How tough is each zombie type
    const float BLOATER_HEALTH = 5;
    const float CHASER_HEALTH = 1;
    const float CRAWLER_HEALTH = 3;

    // Make each zombie vary its speed slightly
    const int MAX_VARRIANCE = 30;
    const int OFFSET = 101 - MAX_VARRIANCE;

    // Where is this zombie?
    Vector2f m_Position;

    // A sprite for the zombie
    Sprite m_Sprite;

    // How fast can this one run/crawl?
    float m_Speed;

    // How much health has it got?
    float m_Health;

    // Is it still alive?
    bool m_Alive;
    // Public prototypes go here
};
```

The previous code declares all the private member variables of the Zombie class. At the top of the previous code, we have three constant variables to hold the speeds of each type of zombie. A very slow **Crawler**, a slightly faster **Bloater**, and a somewhat speedy **Chaser**. We can experiment with the value of these three constants to help balance the difficulty level of the game. Also worth mentioning here is that these three values are only used as a starting value for the speed of each zombie type. As we will see later in this chapter, we will vary the speed of every zombie by a small percentage from these values. This stops zombies of the same type from bunching up together as they pursue the player.

The next three constants, determine the health level for each zombie type. Note that Bloaters are the toughest followed by Crawlers. As a matter of balance, the Chaser zombies will be the easiest to kill.

Next we have two more constants MAX_VARIANCE and OFFSET; these will help us determine the individual speed of each zombie. We will see exactly how when we code the Zombie.cpp file.

After these constants we declare a bunch of variables that should look familiar because we had very similar variables in our Player class. The m_Position, m_Sprite, m_Speed, and m_Health variables are for what their names imply: the position, sprite, speed, and health of the zombie object.

Finally, in the previous code, we declare a Boolean m_Alive which will be true when the zombie is alive and hunting but false when its health gets to zero and it is just a splurge of blood on our otherwise pretty background.

Now to complete the Zombie.h file. Add the function prototypes highlighted below and then we will talk about them:

```
// Is it still alive?
bool m_Alive;
// Public prototypes go here
public:
// Handle when a bullet hits a zombie
bool hit();

// Find out if the zombie is alive
bool isAlive();

// Spawn a new zombie
void spawn(float startX, float startY, int type, int seed);

// Return a rectangle that is the position in the world
FloatRect getPosition();
```

```
// Get a copy of the sprite to draw
Sprite getSprite();

// Update the zombie each frame
void update(float elapsedTime, Vector2f playerLocation);

};
```

In the previous code, there is a hit function which we can call every time the zombie is hit by a bullet. The function can then take the necessary steps, such as taking health from the zombie (reducing the value of m_Health) or killing it dead (setting m_Alive to false).

The isAlive function returns a Boolean, which lets the calling code know whether the zombie is alive or dead. We don't want to perform collision detection or remove health from the player for walking over a blood splat.

The spawn function takes a starting position, a type (Crawler, Bloater, or Chaser, represented by an int), as well as a seed to use in some random number generation that we will see in the next section.

Just as we have in the Player class, the Zombie class has getPosition and getSprite functions to get a rectangle that represents the space occupied by the zombie and the sprite that can be drawn each frame.

The last prototype in the previous code is the update method. We could probably have guessed that it would receive the elapsed time since the last frame but also notice that it receives a Vector2f called playerLocation. This vector will indeed be the exact coordinates of the center of the player. We will see soon how we use this vector to chase after the player.

Coding the Zombie.cpp file

Next we will code the actual functionality of the Zombie class, the function definitions.

Create a new .cpp file that will contain the function definitions. Right-click **Source Files** in the **Solution Explorer** and select **Add | New Item...**. In the **Add New Item** window, highlight (by left-clicking) **C++ File** (.cpp) and then in the **Name** field type Zombie.cpp. Finally, click the **Add** button. We are now ready to code the class.

Add the following code to the Zombie.cpp file:

```
#include "stdafx.h"
#include "zombie.h"
```

```
#include "TextureHolder.h"
#include <cstdlib>
#include <ctime>

using namespace std;
```

First we add the necessary include directives and then the line `using namespace std`. You might remember a few instances when we have prefixed our object declarations with `std::`. This `using` directive means we don't need to do that for the code in this file.

Now add the following code, which is the definition of the `spawn` function. Study the code once you have added it and then we will go through it:

```
void Zombie::spawn(float startX, float startY, int type, int seed)
{
    switch (type)
    {
    case 0:
        // Bloater
        m_Sprite = Sprite(TextureHolder::GetTexture(
            "graphics/bloater.png"));

        m_Speed = 40;
        m_Health = 5;
        break;

    case 1:
        // Chaser
        m_Sprite = Sprite(TextureHolder::GetTexture(
            "graphics/chaser.png"));

        m_Speed = 70;
        m_Health = 1;
        break;

    case 2:
        // Crawler
        m_Sprite = Sprite(TextureHolder::GetTexture(
            "graphics/crawler.png"));

        m_Speed = 20;
        m_Health = 3;
        break;
    }

    // Modify the speed to make the zombie unique
    // Every zombie is unique. Create a speed modifier
    srand((int)time(0) * seed);
```

```
    // Somewhere between 80 an 100
    float modifier = (rand() % MAX_VARRIANCE) + OFFSET;

    // Express this as a fraction of 1
    modifier /= 100; // Now equals between .7 and 1
    m_Speed *= modifier;
    // Initialize its location
    m_Position.x = startX;
    m_Position.y = startY;

    // Set its origin to its center
    m_Sprite.setOrigin(25, 25);

    // Set its position
    m_Sprite.setPosition(m_Position);
}
```

The first thing the function does is `switch` based on the `int` type which is passed in as a parameter. Within the `switch`, block there is a case for each zombie type. Depending upon the type and the appropriate texture, speed and health are initialized to the relevant member variables.

Of interest here is that we use the static `TextureHolder::GetTexture` function to assign the texture. This means that no matter how many zombies we spawn, there will be a maximum of three textures in the memory of the GPU.

The next three lines of code (excluding comments) do the following:

- Seed the random number generator with the `seed` variable that was passed in as a parameter.
- Declare and initialize the `modifier` float variable using the `rand` function and the `MAX_VARIANCE` and `OFFSET` constants. The result is a fraction between zero and one which can be used to make each and every zombie's speed unique. The reason we want to do this is so that the zombies don't bunch up on top of each other too much.
- We can now multiply `m_Speed` by `modifier` and we have a zombie whose speed is within `MAX_VARRIANCE` percent of the constant defined for this particular type of zombie's speed.

After we have resolved the speed, we assign the passed in position held in `startX` and `startY` to `m_Position.x` and `m_Position.y` respectively.

The last two lines of code in the previous listing set the origin of the sprite to the center and use the `m_Position` vector to set the position of the sprite.

Now add this code for the `hit` function to the `Zombie.cpp` file:

```cpp
bool Zombie::hit()
{
    m_Health--;

    if (m_Health < 0)
    {
        // dead
        m_Alive = false;
        m_Sprite.setTexture(TextureHolder::GetTexture(
            "graphics/blood.png"));

        return true;
    }

    // injured but not dead yet
    return false;
}
```

The `hit` function is nice and simple. Reduce `m_Health` by one then check whether `m_Health` is below zero.

If it is below zero, set `m_Alive` to false, swap the zombie's texture for a blood splat, and return `true` to the calling code, so it knows the zombie is now dead.

If the zombie has survived the hit, return `false`.

Add the next three getter functions, which just return a value to the calling code:

```cpp
bool Zombie::isAlive()
{
    return m_Alive;
}

FloatRect Zombie::getPosition()
{
    return m_Sprite.getGlobalBounds();
}

Sprite Zombie::getSprite()
{
    return m_Sprite;
}
```

The previous three functions are quite self-explanatory, perhaps with the exception that the getPosition function uses the m_Sprite.getLocalBounds function to get the FloatRect, which is returned to the calling code.

Finally, for the Zombie class, add the code for the update function; look closely at the code and then we will go through it:

```cpp
void Zombie::update(float elapsedTime,
    Vector2f playerLocation)
{
    float playerX = playerLocation.x;
    float playerY = playerLocation.y;

    // Update the zombie position variables
    if (playerX > m_Position.x)
    {
        m_Position.x = m_Position.x +
            m_Speed * elapsedTime;
    }

    if (playerY > m_Position.y)
    {

        m_Position.y = m_Position.y +
            m_Speed * elapsedTime;
    }
    if (playerX < m_Position.x)
    {
        m_Position.x = m_Position.x -
            m_Speed * elapsedTime;
    }

    if (playerY < m_Position.y)
    {

        m_Position.y = m_Position.y -
            m_Speed * elapsedTime;
    }

    // Move the sprite
    m_Sprite.setPosition(m_Position);

    // Face the sprite in the correct direction
    float angle = (atan2(playerY - m_Position.y,
        playerX - m_Position.x)
        * 180) / 3.141;

    m_Sprite.setRotation(angle);
```

```
    }
```

First we copy `playerLocation.x` and `playerLocation.y` into the local variables `playerX` and `playerY`.

Next there are four `if` statements. They test to see whether the zombie is to the left, right, above, or below the current player's position. These four `if` statements, when they evaluate to `true`, adjust the zombie's `m_Position.x` and `m_Position.y` values appropriately using the usual formula, `speed * time` since last frame. More specifically, the code is `m_Speed * elapsedTime`.

After the four `if` statements, `m_Sprite` is moved to its new location.

We then use the same calculation we previously used with the player and the mouse pointer; this time, however, we do so for the zombie and the player. This calculation finds the angle needed to face the zombie toward the player.

Finally, we call `m_Sprite.setRotation` to actually rotate the zombie sprite. Remember that this function will be called for every zombie (that is alive) on every frame of the game.

Using the Zombie class to create a horde

Now we have a class to create a living, attacking, and killable zombie, we want to spawn a whole horde of them.

To achieve this, we will write a separate function and we will use a pointer so that we can refer to our horde that will be declared in `main` but configured in a different scope.

Open the `ZombieArena.h` file in Visual Studio and add the highlighted lines of code shown next:

```
#pragma once
#include "Zombie.h"

using namespace sf;

int createBackground(VertexArray& rVA, IntRect arena);
Zombie* createHorde(int numZombies, IntRect arena);
```

Now we have a prototype, we can code the function definition.

Create a new .cpp file that will contain the function definition. Right-click **Source Files** in the **Solution Explorer** and select **Add | New Item…**. In the **Add New Item** window, highlight (by left-clicking) **C++ File** (.cpp) and then in the **Name** field type CreateHorde.cpp. Finally, click the **Add** button.

Add and study the code shown next into the CreateHorde.cpp file. Afterwards, we will break it down into chunks and discuss it:

```cpp
#include "stdafx.h"
#include "ZombieArena.h"
#include "Zombie.h"

Zombie* createHorde(int numZombies, IntRect arena)
{
    Zombie* zombies = new Zombie[numZombies];

    int maxY = arena.height - 20;
    int minY = arena.top + 20;
    int maxX = arena.width - 20;
    int minX = arena.left + 20;

    for (int i = 0; i < numZombies; i++)
    {
        // Which side should the zombie spawn
        srand((int)time(0) * i);
        int side = (rand() % 4);
        float x, y;

        switch (side)
        {
        case 0:
            // left
            x = minX;
            y = (rand() % maxY) + minY;
            break;

        case 1:
            // right
            x = maxX;
            y = (rand() % maxY) + minY;
            break;

        case 2:
            // top
            x = (rand() % maxX) + minX;
            y = minY;
            break;
```

```
          case 3:
             // bottom
             x = (rand() % maxX) + minX;
             y = maxY;
             break;
          }

          // Bloater, crawler or runner
          srand((int)time(0) * i * 2);
          int type = (rand() % 3);

          // Spawn the new zombie into the array
          zombies[i].spawn(x, y, type, i);
       }
       return zombies;
    }
```

Let's look at all the previous code again, in bite-size pieces.

First we add the now familiar include directives:

```
#include "stdafx.h"
#include "ZombieArena.h"
#include "Zombie.h"
```

Next comes the function signature. Notice that the function must return a pointer to a Zombie object. We will be creating an array of Zombie objects. Once we are done creating the horde, we will return the array. When we return the array, we are actually returning the address of the first element of the array. This, as we learned in the section earlier in this chapter, is the same thing as a pointer. The signature also shows that we have two parameters. The first, numZombies, will be the number of zombies this current horde requires and the second, arena, is an IntRect that holds the size of the current arena in which to create this horde.

After the function signature, we declare a pointer to type Zombie called zombies and initialize with the memory address of the first element of an array, which we dynamically allocate on the heap:

```
Zombie* createHorde(int numZombies, IntRect arena)
{
    Zombie* zombies = new Zombie[numZombies];
```

The next code simply copies the extremities of the arena into maxY, minY, maxX, and minX. We subtract twenty pixels from the right and bottom while adding twenty pixels to the top and left. We use these four local variables to help position each of the zombies. We made the twenty-pixel adjustments to stop the zombies appearing on top of the walls:

```
int maxY = arena.height - 20;
int minY = arena.top + 20;
int maxX = arena.width - 20;
int minX = arena.left + 20;
```

Now we enter a for loop that will loop through each of the Zombie objects in the zombies array from zero through to numZombies:

```
for (int i = 0; i < numZombies; i++)
```

Inside the for loop, the first thing the code does is seed the random number generator and then generate a random number between zero and three. This number is stored in the side variable. We will use the side variable to decide whether the zombie spawns at the left, top, right, or bottom of the arena. We also declare two int variables, x and y. These two variables will temporarily hold the actual horizontal and vertical coordinates of the current zombie:

```
// Which side should the zombie spawn
srand((int)time(0) * i);
int side = (rand() % 4);
float x, y;
```

Still inside the for loop we have a switch block with four case statements. Notice the case statements are for 0, 1, 2, and 3 and the argument in the switch statement is side. Inside each of the case blocks, we initialize x and y with one predetermined value, either minX, maxX, minY, or maxY, and one randomly generated value. Look closely at the combinations of each predetermined and random value. You will see that they are appropriate for positioning the current zombie randomly across either the left side, top side, right side, or bottom side. The effect of this will be that each zombie can spawn randomly, anywhere on the outside edge of the arena:

```
switch (side)
{
    case 0:
        // left
        x = minX;
        y = (rand() % maxY) + minY;
        break;

    case 1:
```

```
        // right
        x = maxX;
        y = (rand() % maxY) + minY;
        break;

    case 2:
        // top
        x = (rand() % maxX) + minX;
        y = minY;
        break;

    case 3:
        // bottom
        x = (rand() % maxX) + minX;
        y = maxY;
        break;
    }
```

Still inside the `for` loop, we seed the random number generator again and generate a random number between 0 and 2. We store this number in the type variable. The type variable will determine whether the current zombie will be a Chaser, Bloater, or Crawler.

After the type is determined, we call the `spawn` function on the current `Zombie` object in the `zombies` array. As a reminder, the arguments sent into the `spawn` function determine the starting location of the zombie and the type of zombie it will be. The apparently arbitrary `i` is passed in as it is used as a unique seed that randomly varies the speed of a zombie within an appropriate range. This stops our zombies **bunching up** and becoming a blob rather than a horde:

```
// Bloater, crawler or runner
srand((int)time(0) * i * 2);
int type = (rand() % 3);

// Spawn the new zombie into the array
zombies[i].spawn(x, y, type, i);
```

The `for` loop repeats itself once for each zombie contained in `numZombies` and then we return the array. The array, as another reminder, is simply an address of the first element of itself. The array is dynamically allocated on the heap so it persists after the function returns:

```
return zombies;
```

Now we can bring our zombies to life.

Bringing the horde to life (back to life)

We have a `Zombie` class and a function to make a randomly spawning horde of them. We have the `TextureHolder` singleton as a neat way to hold just three textures that can be used for dozens, even thousands, of zombies. Now we can add the horde to our game engine in `main`.

Add the following highlighted code to include the `TextureHolder` class. Then, just inside `main`, we initialize the one and only instance of `TextureHolder` that can be used from anywhere within our game:

```
#include "stdafx.h"
#include <SFML/Graphics.hpp>
#include "ZombieArena.h"
#include "Player.h"
#include "TextureHolder.h"

using namespace sf;

int main()
{
    // Here is the instance of TextureHolder
    TextureHolder holder;

    // The game will always be in one of four states
    enum class State { PAUSED, LEVELING_UP, GAME_OVER, PLAYING };
    // Start with the GAME_OVER state
    State state = State::GAME_OVER;
```

The next few lines of highlighted code declare some control variables for the number of zombies at the start of the wave, the number of zombies still to be killed, and, of course, a pointer to `Zombie` called `zombies` which we initialize to `nullptr`.

Add the highlighted code:

```
    // Create the background
    VertexArray background;
    // Load the texture for our background vertex array
    Texture textureBackground;
    textureBackground.loadFromFile("graphics/background_sheet.png");

    // Prepare for a horde of zombies
    int numZombies;
    int numZombiesAlive;
    Zombie* zombies = nullptr;
```

```
// The main game loop
while (window.isOpen())
```

Next, in the PLAYING section nested inside the LEVELING_UP section, we add code that does the following:

- Initializes numZombies to 10. As the project progresses this will eventually be dynamic and based on the current wave number
- Deletes any pre-existing allocated memory, otherwise each new call to createHorde would take up progressively more memory but without freeing the previous horde's memory
- Then calls createHorde and assigns the returned memory address to zombies
- Initializes zombiesAlive with numZombies because we haven't killed any at this point

Add the highlighted code we have just discussed:

```
if (state == State::PLAYING)
{
    // Prepare thelevel
    // We will modify the next two lines later
    arena.width = 500;
    arena.height = 500;
    arena.left = 0;
    arena.top = 0;

    // Pass the vertex array by reference
    // to the createBackground function
    int tileSize = createBackground(background, arena);

    // Spawn the player in the middle of the arena
    player.spawn(arena, resolution, tileSize);

    // Create a horde of zombies
    numZombies = 10;

    // Delete the previously allocated memory (if it exists)
    delete[] zombies;
    zombies = createHorde(numZombies, arena);
    numZombiesAlive = numZombies;

    // Reset the clock so there isn't a frame jump
    clock.restart();
}
```

Now add the following highlighted code to the `ZombieArena.cpp` file:

```
/*
 ****************
 UPDATE THE FRAME
 ****************
 */
if (state == State::PLAYING)
{
    // Update the delta time
    Time dt = clock.restart();
    // Update the total game time
    gameTimeTotal += dt;
    // Make a decimal fraction of 1 from the delta time
    float dtAsSeconds = dt.asSeconds();

    // Where is the mouse pointer
    mouseScreenPosition = Mouse::getPosition();

    // Convert mouse position to world coordinates of mainView
    mouseWorldPosition = window.mapPixelToCoords(
        Mouse::getPosition(), mainView);

    // Update the player
    player.update(dtAsSeconds, Mouse::getPosition());

    // Make a note of the players new position
    Vector2f playerPosition(player.getCenter());

    // Make the view center around the player
    mainView.setCenter(player.getCenter());

    // Loop through each Zombie and update them
    for (int i = 0; i < numZombies; i++)
    {
        if (zombies[i].isAlive())
        {
            zombies[i].update(dt.asSeconds(), playerPosition);
        }
    }

}// End updating the scene
```

All that the new code does is loop through the array of zombies, check the current zombie is alive, and if it is, calls its `update` function with the necessary arguments.

Add the following code to draw all the zombies:

```
/*
**************
Draw the scene
**************
*/

if (state == State::PLAYING)
{
    window.clear();

    // set the mainView to be displayed in the window
    // And draw everything related to it
    window.setView(mainView);

    // Draw the background
    window.draw(background, &textureBackground);

    // Draw the zombies
    for (int i = 0; i < numZombies; i++)
    {
        window.draw(zombies[i].getSprite());
    }

    // Draw the player
    window.draw(player.getSprite());
}
```

The previous code loops through all the zombies and calls the `getSprite` function to allow the `draw` method to do its work. We don't check whether the zombie is alive because even if the zombie is dead we want to draw the blood splatter.

At the end of the main function, we make sure to delete our pointer, although technically this isn't essential because the game is about to exit and the operating system will reclaim all the memory used after the `return 0` statement:

```
}// End of main game loop

    // Delete the previously allocated memory (if it exists)
    delete[] zombies;

    return 0;
}
```

You can run the game and see the zombies spawn around the edge of the arena. They will immediately head straight toward the player at their various speeds. Just for fun I increased the size of the arena and increased the number of zombies to 1000.

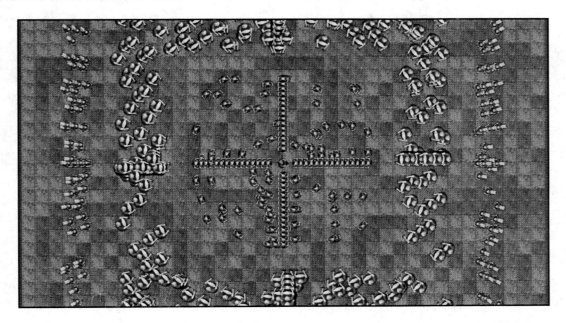

This is going to end badly!

Notice that you can also pause and resume the onslaught of the horde using the Enter key because of the code we wrote in Chapter 6: *Object-Oriented Programming, Classes, and SFML Views.*

Using the TextureHolder class for all textures

Since we have our TextureHolder class, we might as well be consistent and use it to load all our textures. Let's make some very small alterations to the existing code that loads textures for the background sprite sheet and the player.

Change the way the background gets its textures

In the `ZombieArena.cpp` file, find this code:

```
// Load the texture for our background vertex array
Texture textureBackground;
textureBackground.loadFromFile("graphics/background_sheet.png");
```

Delete the code highlighted previously and replace it with the following highlighted code, which uses our new `TextureHolder` class:

```
// Load the texture for our background vertex array
Texture textureBackground = TextureHolder::GetTexture(
    "graphics/background_sheet.png");
```

Change the way Player gets its texture

In the `Player.cpp` file, inside the constructor, find this code:

```
#include "stdafx.h"
#include "player.h"

Player::Player()
{
    m_Speed = START_SPEED;
    m_Health = START_HEALTH;
    m_MaxHealth = START_HEALTH;

    // Associate a texture with the sprite
    // !!Watch this space!!
    m_Texture.loadFromFile("graphics/player.png");
    m_Sprite.setTexture(m_Texture);


    // Set the origin of the sprite to the center,
    // for smooth rotation
    m_Sprite.setOrigin(25, 25);
}
```

Delete the code highlighted previously and replace it with this code, which uses our new `TextureHolder` class. In addition, add the include directive to add the `TextureHolder` header to the file. The new code is shown highlighted, in context:

```
#include "stdafx.h"
#include "player.h"
#include "TextureHolder.h"
```

```
Player::Player()
{
    m_Speed = START_SPEED;
    m_Health = START_HEALTH;
    m_MaxHealth = START_HEALTH;

    // Associate a texture with the sprite
    // !!Watch this space!!
    m_Sprite = Sprite(TextureHolder::GetTexture(
        "graphics/player.png"));

    // Set the origin of the sprite to the center,
    // for smooth rotation
    m_Sprite.setOrigin(25, 25);
}
```

From now on we will use the `TextureHolder` class for loading all textures.

FAQ

Here are some questions that might be on your mind:

Q) What's the difference between pointers and references?

A) Pointers are like references with boosters. Pointers can be changed to point to different variables (memory addresses), as well as point to dynamically allocated memory on the free store.

Q) What's the deal with arrays and pointers?

A) Arrays are really constant pointers to their first element.

Q) Can you remind me about the `new` keyword and memory leaks?

A) When we use memory on the free store using the `new` keyword, it persists even when the function it was created in has returned and all the local variables are gone. When we are done with using memory on the free store we must release it. So if we use memory on the free store, that we want to persist, beyond the life of a function, we must make sure to keep a pointer to it or we will have leaked memory. It would be like putting all our belongings in our house and then forgetting where we live! When we return the zombies array from `createHorde`, it is like passing the relay baton (memory address) from `createHorde` to `main`. It's like saying OK, here is your horde of zombies – they are your responsibility now. We wouldn't want any leaked zombies running around in our RAM so we must remember to call `delete` on pointers to dynamically allocated memory.

Summary

You might have noticed that the zombies don't appear to be very dangerous. They just drift through the player without leaving a scratch. At the moment this is a good thing because the player has no way to defend himself.

In the next chapter, we will make two more classes. One will be for ammo and health pickups, and one for bullets that the player can shoot. After we have done that, we will learn how to detect collisions, so that the bullets and zombies do some damage and the pickups can be collected by the player.

9
Collision Detection, Pickups, and Bullets

So far we have implemented the main visual aspects of our game. We have a controllable character running around in an arena full of zombies that chase him. The problem is that they don't interact with each other. A zombie can wander right through the player without leaving a scratch. We need to detect collisions between the zombies and the player.

If the zombies are going to be able to injure and eventually kill the player, it is only fair that we give the player some bullets for his gun. We will then need to make sure that the bullets can hit and kill the zombies.

At the same time, if we are writing collision detection code for bullets, zombies, and the player, it would be a good time to add a class for health and ammo pickups as well.

Here is what we will do and the order we will cover the topics:

- Shooting bullets
- Adding a crosshair and hiding the mouse pointer
- Spawning pickups
- Detecting collisions

Coding the Bullet class

We will use the SFML `RectangleShape` class to visually represent a bullet. We will code a `Bullet` class that has a `RectangleShape` member as well as other member data and functions. We will add bullets to our game in a few steps:

1. First we will code the `Bullet.h` file. This will reveal all the details of the member data and the prototypes for the functions.
2. Next we will code the `Bullet.cpp` file which, of course, will contain the definitions for all the functions of the `Bullet` class. As we step through it, I will explain exactly how an object of type `Bullet` will work and be controlled.
3. Finally, we will declare a whole array full of bullets in the `main` function. We will also implement a control scheme for shooting, managing the player's remaining ammo, and reloading.

Let's get started with step 1.

Coding the Bullet header file

To make the new header file, right-click on **Header Files** in the **Solution Explorer** and select **Add | New Item....** In the **Add New Item** window, highlight (by left-clicking) **Header File (.h)** and then in the **Name** field type `Bullet.h`.

Add the following private member variables along with the `Bullet` class declaration to the `Bullet.h` file. We can then run through and explain what they are for:

```
#pragma once
#include <SFML/Graphics.hpp>

using namespace sf;

class Bullet
{
private:
    // Where is the bullet?
    Vector2f m_Position;

    // What each bullet looks like
    RectangleShape m_BulletShape;

    // Is this bullet currently whizzing through the air
    bool m_InFlight = false;
```

```
// How fast does a bullet travel?
float m_BulletSpeed = 1000;

// What fraction of 1 pixel does the bullet travel,
// Horizontally and vertically each frame?
// These values will be derived from m_BulletSpeed
float m_BulletDistanceX;
float m_BulletDistanceY;
// Some boundaries so the bullet doesn't fly forever
float m_MaxX;
float m_MinX;
float m_MaxY;
float m_MinY;

// Public function prototypes go here
```

In the previous code, the first member is a `Vector2f` called `m_Position`, which will hold the bullets location in the game-world.

Next, we declare a `RectangleShape` called `m_BulletShape` as we are using a simple non-texture graphic for each bullet, a bit like we did for the time-bar in Timber!!!

The code then declares a Boolean `m_InFlight`, which will keep track of whether the bullet is currently whizzing through the air, or not. This will enable us to decide whether we need to call its `update` function each frame and whether or not we need to run collision detection checks.

The `float` variable `m_BulletSpeed` will (you can probably guess) hold the speed in pixels per second that the bullet will travel at. It is initialized to the value of `1000`, which is a little arbitrary—but it works well.

Next we have two more `float` variables, `m_BulletDistanceX` and `m_BulletDistanceY`. As the calculations to move a bullet are a little more complex than those used to move a zombie or the player, we will benefit from having these two variables that we will perform calculations on. They will be used to decide the horizontal and vertical change in the bullets position in each frame.

Finally, for the previous code, we have four more `float` variables (`m_MaxX`, `m_MinX`, `m_MaxY`, and `m_MinY`) which will later be initialized to hold the maximum and minimum, horizontal and vertical positions for the bullet.

It is likely that the need for some of these variables is not immediately apparent, but it will become clearer when we see each of them in action in the `Bullet.cpp` file.

Now add all the public function prototypes to the `Bullet.h` file:

```
// Public function prototypes go here
public:
    // The constructor
    Bullet();

    // Stop the bullet
    void stop();

    // Returns the value of m_InFlight
    bool isInFlight();

    // Launch a new bullet
    void shoot(float startX, float startY,
      float xTarget, float yTarget);

    // Tell the calling code where the bullet is in the world
    FloatRect getPosition();

    // Return the actual shape (for drawing)
    RectangleShape getShape();

    // Update the bullet each frame
    void update(float elapsedTime);
```

Let's run through each of the functions in turn, then we can move on to coding their definitions.

First we have the `Bullet` function, which is of course the constructor. In this function, we will set up each `Bullet` instance ready for action.

The `stop` function will be called when the bullet has been in action but needs to stop.

The `isInFlight` function returns a Boolean and will be used to test whether a bullet is currently in flight or not.

The `shoot` function's use is given away by its name, but how it will work deserves some discussion. For now, just note that it has four `float` parameters that will be passed in. The four values represent the starting (where the player is) horizontal and vertical position of the bullet, as well as the vertical and horizontal target position (where the crosshair is).

The `getPosition` function returns a `FloatRect` that represents the location of the bullet. This function will be used to detect collisions with zombies. You might remember from *Chapter 8: Pointers, Standard Template Library, and Texture Management* that zombies also had a `getPosition` function.

Next we have the `getShape` function, which returns an object of type `RectangleShape`. As we have discussed, each bullet is represented visually by a `RectangleShape` object. The `getShape` function, therefore, will be used to grab a copy of the current state of the `RectangleShape`, in order to draw it.

Finally, and hopefully as expected, there is the `update`, function which has a `float` parameter that represents the fraction of one second that has passed since the last time `update` was called. The `update` method will change the position of the bullet each frame.

Let's look at and code the function definitions.

Coding the Bullet source file

Now we can create a new `.cpp` file that will contain the function definitions. Right-click **Source Files** in the **Solution Explorer** and select **Add | New Item...**. In the **Add New Item** window, highlight (by left-clicking) **C++ File (`.cpp`)** and then in the **Name** field type `Bullet.cpp`. Finally, click the **Add** button. We are now ready to code the class.

Add the following code, which is the include directives and the constructor. We know it is the constructor because the function has the same name as the class:

```
#include "stdafx.h"
#include "bullet.h"


// The constructor
Bullet::Bullet()
{
    m_BulletShape.setSize(sf::Vector2f(2, 2));
}
```

The only thing that the `Bullet` constructor needs to do is set the size of `m_BulletShape`, which is the `RectangleShape` object. The code sets the size to two pixels by two pixels.

Next we have the more substantial `shoot` function. Add the following code to the `Bullet.cpp` file, study it, and then we can talk about it:

```
void Bullet::shoot(float startX, float startY,
    float targetX, float targetY)
{
    // Keep track of the bullet
    m_InFlight = true;
    m_Position.x = startX;
    m_Position.y = startY;
```

```cpp
// Calculate the gradient of the flight path
float gradient = (startX - targetX) / (startY - targetY);

// Any gradient less than 1 needs to be negative
if (gradient < 0)
{
    gradient *= -1;
}

// Calculate the ratio between x and y
float ratioXY = m_BulletSpeed / (1 + gradient);

// Set the "speed" horizontally and vertically
m_BulletDistanceY = ratioXY;
m_BulletDistanceX = ratioXY * gradient;

// Point the bullet in the right direction
if (targetX < startX)
{
    m_BulletDistanceX *= -1;
}

if (targetY < startY)
{
    m_BulletDistanceY *= -1;
}

// Set a max range of 1000 pixels
float range = 1000;
m_MinX = startX - range;
m_MaxX = startX + range;
m_MinY = startY - range;
m_MaxY = startY + range;

// Position the bullet ready to be drawn
m_BulletShape.setPosition(m_Position);
```

In order to demystify the shoot function, we will split it up and talk about the code we have just added, in chunks.

First let's remind ourselves about the signature. The shoot function receives the starting and target horizontal and vertical positions of a bullet. The calling code will supply these based on the position of the player sprite and the position of the crosshair. Here it is again:

```cpp
void Bullet::shoot(float startX, float startY, float targetX, float
targetY)
```

Inside the shoot function, we set `m_InFlight` to `true` and position the bullet using the parameters `startX` and `startY`. Here is that piece of code again:

```
// Keep track of the bullet
m_InFlight = true;
m_Position.x = startX;
m_Position.y = startY;
```

Now we use a bit of simple trigonometry to determine the gradient of travel for a bullet. The progression horizontally and vertically of a bullet must vary based on the slope of the line created by drawing between the start and target of a bullet. The rate of change cannot be the same or very steep shots will arrive at the horizontal location before the vertical location, and vice versa for shallow shots.

The following code first derives the gradient based on the equation of a line. Then it checks whether the gradient is less than zero and if it is, multiplies it by −1. This is because the start and target coordinates passed in can be negative or positive and we always want the amount of progression each frame to be positive. Multiplying by −1 simply makes the negative number into its positive equivalent, because a minus multiplied by a minus gives a positive. The actual direction of travel will be handled in the `update` function by adding or subtracting the positive values we arrive at in this function.

Next we calculate a ratio of horizontal to vertical distance by dividing our bullet's speed (`m_BulletSpeed`) by one plus the gradient. This will allow us to change the bullet's horizontal and vertical position by the correct amount each frame, based on the target the bullet is heading toward.

Finally, in this part of the code we assign the values to `m_BulletDistanceY` and `m_BulletDistanceX`:

```
// Calculate the gradient of the flight path
float gradient = (startX - targetX) / (startY - targetY);

// Any gradient less than zero needs to be negative
if (gradient < 0)
{
    gradient *= -1;
}

// Calculate the ratio between x and y
float ratioXY = m_BulletSpeed / (1 + gradient);

// Set the "speed" horizontally and vertically
m_BulletDistanceY = ratioXY;
m_BulletDistanceX = ratioXY * gradient;
```

The following code is much more straightforward. We simply set a maximum horizontal and vertical location that the bullet can reach. We don't want a bullet carrying on forever. We will see this in the update function where we test to see whether a bullet has passed its maximum or minimum locations:

```
// Set a max range of 1000 pixels in any direction
float range = 1000;
m_MinX = startX - range;
m_MaxX = startX + range;
m_MinY = startY - range;
m_MaxY = startY + range;
```

The following code moves the **RectangleShape** which represents the bullet to its starting location. We use the setPosition function as we have often done before:

```
// Position the bullet ready to be drawn
m_BulletShape.setPosition(m_Position);
```

Next we have four straightforward functions. Add the stop, isInFlight, getPosition, and getShape functions:

```
void Bullet::stop()
{
    m_InFlight = false;
}

bool Bullet::isInFlight()
{
    return m_InFlight;
}

FloatRect Bullet::getPosition()
{
    return m_BulletShape.getGlobalBounds();
}

RectangleShape Bullet::getShape()
{
    return m_BulletShape;
}
```

The stop function simply sets the m_InFlight variable to false. The isInFlight function returns whatever the value of this same variable currently is. So we can see that shoot sets the bullet going, stop makes it stop, and isInFlight let us know what the current state is.

The getPosition function returns a FloatRect and we will see how we use the FloatRect from each game object to detect collisions, soon.

Finally, for the previous code, getShape returns a RectangleShape so we can draw the bullet once each frame.

The last function we need to implement before we can start using Bullet objects is update. Add the following code, study it, and then we can talk about it:

```
void Bullet::update(float elapsedTime)
{
    // Update the bullet position variables
    m_Position.x += m_BulletDistanceX * elapsedTime;
    m_Position.y += m_BulletDistanceY * elapsedTime;

    // Move the bullet
    m_BulletShape.setPosition(m_Position);

    // Has the bullet gone out of range?
    if (m_Position.x < m_MinX || m_Position.x > m_MaxX ||
        m_Position.y < m_MinY || m_Position.y > m_MaxY)
    {
        m_InFlight = false;
    }
}
```

In the update function, we use m_BulletDistanceX and m_BulletDistanceY multiplied by the time since the last frame to move the bullet. Remember that the values of the two variables were calculated in the shoot function and represent the gradient (ratio to each other) required to move the bullet at just the right angle. Then we use the setPosition function to actually move the RectangleShape.

The last thing we do in update is test to see whether the bullet has moved beyond its maximum range. The slightly convoluted if statement checks m_Position.x and m_Position.y against the maximum and minimum values that were calculated in the shoot function. These maximum and minimum values are stored in m_MinX, m_MaxX, m_MinY, and m_MaxY. If the test is true, then m_InFlight is set to false.

The Bullet class is done. Now we can see how to shoot some in the main function.

Making the bullets fly

We will make the bullets usable with the following six steps:

1. Add the necessary include directive for the `Bullet` class.
2. Add some control variables and an array to hold some `Bullet` instances.
3. Handle the player pressing *R* to reload.
4. Handle the player pressing the left mouse button to fire a bullet.
5. Update all bullets that are in flight, in each frame.
6. Draw the bullets that are in flight, in each frame.

Including the Bullet class

Add the include directive to make the Bullet class available:

```
#include "stdafx.h"
#include <SFML/Graphics.hpp>
#include "ZombieArena.h"
#include "Player.h"
#include "TextureHolder.h"
#include "Bullet.h"
using namespace sf;
```

Let's move on to the next step.

Control variables and the bullet array

Here are some variables to keep track of bullets, clip sizes, bullets spare/remaining, bullets in the clip, the current rate of fire (starting at one per second), and the time when the last bullet was fired.

Add the highlighted code and we can move on to seeing all these variables in action in the rest of this section:

```
// Prepare for a horde of zombies
int numZombies;
int numZombiesAlive;
Zombie* zombies = NULL;

// 100 bullets should do
Bullet bullets[100];
int currentBullet = 0;
```

```
int bulletsSpare = 24;
int bulletsInClip = 6;
int clipSize = 6;
float fireRate = 1;
// When was the fire button last pressed?
Time lastPressed;

// The main game loop
while (window.isOpen())
```

Next, let's handle what happens when the player presses the *R* keyboard key, which is used for reloading a clip.

Reloading the gun

Now we handle the player input related to shooting bullets. First we will handle pressing the *R* key to reload the gun. We do so with an SFML event.

Add the code shown highlighted in the following code block. It is shown with lots of context to make sure the code goes in the right place. Study the code and then we can talk about it:

```
// Handle events
Event event;
while (window.pollEvent(event))
{
    if (event.type == Event::KeyPressed)
    {
        // Pause a game while playing
        if (event.key.code == Keyboard::Return &&
            state == State::PLAYING)
        {
            state = State::PAUSED;
        }

        // Restart while paused
        else if (event.key.code == Keyboard::Return &&
            state == State::PAUSED)
        {
            state = State::PLAYING;
            // Reset the clock so there isn't a frame jump
            clock.restart();
        }

        // Start a new game while in GAME_OVER state
        else if (event.key.code == Keyboard::Return &&
```

```
              state == State::GAME_OVER)
        {
            state = State::LEVELING_UP;
        }

        if (state == State::PLAYING)
        {
          // Reloading
          if (event.key.code == Keyboard::R)
          {
              if (bulletsSpare >= clipSize)
              {
                // Plenty of bullets. Reload.
                bulletsInClip = clipSize;
                bulletsSpare -= clipSize;
              }
              else if (bulletsSpare > 0)
              {
                // Only few bullets left
                bulletsInClip = bulletsSpare;
                bulletsSpare = 0;
              }
              else
              {
                // More here soon?!
              }
          }
        }

    }
}// End event polling
```

The previous code is nested within the event handling part of the game loop
(while(window.pollEvent)), within the block that only executes when the game is
actually being played (if(state == State::Playing)). It is obvious that we don't want
the player reloading when the game has finished or is paused and wrapping the new code
as described achieves this.

In the new code itself, the first thing we do is test for the R key being pressed, with if
(event.key.code == Keyboard::R). Once we have detected that the R key was pressed
the remaining code is executed. Here is the structure of the if, else if, and else blocks:

```
if(bulletsSpare >= clipSize)
    . . .
else if(bulletsSpare > 0)
    . . .
else
```

. . .

The previous structure allows us to handle three possible scenarios.

- The player has pressed R and they have more bullets spare than the clip can take. In this scenario, the clip is refilled and the number of spare bullets is reduced.
- The player has some spare bullets but not enough to fill the clip completely. In this scenario, the clip is filled with as many spare bullets as the player has and the number of spare bullets is set to zero.
- The player has pressed R but they have no spare bullets at all. For this scenario, we don't actually need to alter the variables. However, we will play a sound effect here when we implement our sound in Chapter 11: *Sound Effects, File I/O, and Finishing the Game*, so we leave the empty else block ready.

Let's actually shoot a bullet at last.

Shooting a bullet

Next we can handle the left mouse button being clicked to actually fire a bullet. Add the highlighted code and study it carefully:

```
if (Keyboard::isKeyPressed(Keyboard::D))
{
    player.moveRight();
}
else
{
    player.stopRight();
}

// Fire a bullet
if (Mouse::isButtonPressed(sf::Mouse::Left))
{
  if (gameTimeTotal.asMilliseconds()
    - lastPressed.asMilliseconds()
    > 1000 / fireRate && bulletsInClip > 0)
  {

    // Pass the center of the player
    // and the center of the crosshair
    // to the shoot function
    bullets[currentBullet].shoot(
        player.getCenter().x, player.getCenter().y,
        mouseWorldPosition.x, mouseWorldPosition.y);
```

```
                currentBullet++;
                if (currentBullet > 99)
                {
                    currentBullet = 0;
                }
                lastPressed = gameTimeTotal;
                bulletsInClip--;
            }
        }// End fire a bullet
    }// End WASD while playing
```

All of the previous code is wrapped in an `if` statement, which executes whenever the left mouse button is pressed, `if (Mouse::isButtonPressed(sf::Mouse::Left))`. Note that the code will execute repeatedly, even if the player just holds down the button. The code we will go through now controls the rate of fire.

In the previous code, we then check whether the total time elapsed in the game (`gameTimeTotal`), minus the time the player last shot a bullet (`lastPressed`), is greater than 1000 divided by the current rate of fire, and that the player has at least one bullet in the clip. We use 1000 because this is the number of milliseconds in a second.

If this test is successful, the code that actually fires a bullet is executed. Shooting a bullet is easy because we did all the hard work in the `Bullet` class. We simply call `shoot` on the current bullet from the `bullets` array. We pass in the player's and crosshair's current horizontal and vertical locations. The bullet will be configured and set in flight by the code in the `shoot` function of the `Bullet` class.

All we have to do is keep track of the array of bullets. First we increment the `currentBullet` variable. Then we check to see whether we fired the last bullet (99) with the statement `if (currentBullet > 99)`. If it was the last bullet, we set `currentBullet` to zero. If it wasn't the last bullet, then the next bullet is ready to go whenever the rate of fire permits it and the player presses the left mouse button.

Finally, for the previous code, we store the time that the bullet was fired in `lastPressed` and decrement `bulletsInClip`.

Now we can update every bullet, each frame.

Updating the bullets each frame

Add the highlighted code to loop through the bullets array, check whether the bullet is in flight, and if it is, call its update function:

```
// Loop through each Zombie and update them
for (int i = 0; i < numZombies; i++)
{
    if (zombies[i].isAlive())
    {
        zombies[i].update(dt.asSeconds(), playerPosition);
    }
}

// Update any bullets that are in-flight
for (int i = 0; i < 100; i++)
{
    if (bullets[i].isInFlight())
    {
        bullets[i].update(dtAsSeconds);
    }
}
}// End updating the scene
```

And lastly, we can draw all the bullets.

Drawing the bullets each frame

Add the highlighted code to loop through the `bullets` array, check whether the bullet is in flight and if it is, draw it:

```
/*
**************
Draw the scene
**************
*/

if (state == State::PLAYING)
{
    window.clear();

    // set the mainView to be displayed in the window
    // And draw everything related to it
    window.setView(mainView);

    // Draw the background
```

```
window.draw(background, &textureBackground);

// Draw the zombies
for (int i = 0; i < numZombies; i++)
{
    window.draw(zombies[i].getSprite());
}

for (int i = 0; i < 100; i++)
{
  if (bullets[i].isInFlight())
  {
      window.draw(bullets[i].getShape());
  }
}

// Draw the player
window.draw(player.getSprite());
}
```

Run the game to try out the bullets. Notice you can fire six shots before you need to press *R* to reload. The obvious things that are missing are some visual indicator of the number of bullets in the clip and the number of spare bullets. Another problem is that the player can very quickly run out of bullets, especially as the bullets have no stopping power whatsoever. They fly straight through the zombies. Add to this that the player is expected to aim at a mouse pointer instead of a precision crosshair, and it is plain we have work to do.

In the next chapter, we will give visual feedback through a HUD. We will replace the mouse cursor with a crosshair next and then spawn some pickups to replenish bullets and health after that. Finally, in this chapter, we will handle collision detection to make the bullets and the zombies do damage and make the player able to actually get the pickups.

Giving the player a crosshair

Adding a crosshair is easy and only requires one new concept. Add the highlighted code and then we can run through it:

```
// 100 bullets should do
Bullet bullets[100];
int currentBullet = 0;
int bulletsSpare = 24;
int bulletsInClip = 6;
int clipSize = 6;
```

```
float fireRate = 1;
// When was the fire button last pressed?
Time lastPressed;

// Hide the mouse pointer and replace it with crosshair
window.setMouseCursorVisible(true);
Sprite spriteCrosshair;
Texture textureCrosshair =
    TextureHolder::GetTexture("graphics/crosshair.png");

spriteCrosshair.setTexture(textureCrosshair);
spriteCrosshair.setOrigin(25, 25);
// The main game loop
while (window.isOpen())
```

First we call the `setMouseCursorVisible` function on our `window` object. We then load a `Texture`, declare a `Sprite`, and initialize it in the usual way. Furthermore, we set the sprite's origin to its center to make it convenient and simpler to make the bullets fly to the middle, as you would expect to happen.

Now we need to update the crosshair each frame with the world coordinates of the mouse. Add the highlighted line of code, which uses the `mouseWorldPosition` vector to set the crosshair position each frame:

```
/*
 ****************
 UPDATE THE FRAME
 ****************
 */
if (state == State::PLAYING)
{
    // Update the delta time
    Time dt = clock.restart();
    // Update the total game time
    gameTimeTotal += dt;
    // Make a decimal fraction of 1 from the delta time
    float dtAsSeconds = dt.asSeconds();

    // Where is the mouse pointer
    mouseScreenPosition = Mouse::getPosition();

    // Convert mouse position to world coordinates of mainView
    mouseWorldPosition = window.mapPixelToCoords(
        Mouse::getPosition(), mainView);

    // Set the crosshair to the mouse world location
    spriteCrosshair.setPosition(mouseWorldPosition);
```

```
      // Update the player
      player.update(dtAsSeconds, Mouse::getPosition());
```

Next, as you have probably come to expect, we can draw the crosshair for each frame. Add the highlighted line of code in the position shown. The line of code needs no explanation, but its position after all the other game objects is important so it is drawn on top:

```
/*
 **************
 Draw the scene
 **************
 */

if (state == State::PLAYING)
{
    window.clear();

    // set the mainView to be displayed in the window
    // And draw everything related to it
    window.setView(mainView);

    // Draw the background
    window.draw(background, &textureBackground);

    // Draw the zombies
    for (int i = 0; i < numZombies; i++)
    {
        window.draw(zombies[i].getSprite());
    }

    for (int i = 0; i < 100; i++)
    {
        if (bullets[i].isInFlight())
        {
            window.draw(bullets[i].getShape());
        }
    }

    // Draw the player
    window.draw(player.getSprite());

    //Draw the crosshair
    window.draw(spriteCrosshair);
}
```

Now you can run the game and see the cool crosshair instead of a mouse cursor:

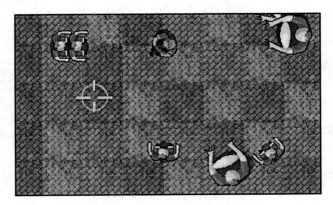

Notice how the bullet fires neatly through the center of the crosshair. The way the shooting mechanic works is analogous to allowing the player to choose to shoot from the hip or aim down the sights. If the player keeps the crosshair close to the center, he can fire and turn rapidly, yet has to carefully judge the position of distant zombies.

Alternatively, the player can hover his crosshair directly over the head of a distant zombie and score a precise hit; however, he then has much further to move the crosshair back if a zombie attacks from another direction.

An interesting improvement to the game would be to add a small random amount of inaccuracy to each shot. This inaccuracy could perhaps be mitigated with an upgrade between waves.

Coding a class for pickups

We will code a Pickup class that has a Sprite, member as well as other member data and functions. We will add pickups to our game in just a few steps:

1. First, we will code the Pickup.h file. This will reveal all the details of the member data and the prototypes for the functions.
2. Then we will code the Pickup.cpp file which, of course, will contain the definitions for all the functions of the Pickup class. As we step through it, I will explain exactly how an object of type Pickup will work and be controlled.
3. Finally, we will use the Pickup class in the main function to spawn them, update them and draw them.

Let's get started with step 1.

Coding the Pickup header file

To make the new header file, right-click **Header Files** in the **Solution Explorer** and select **Add | New Item...**. In the **Add New Item** window, highlight (by left-clicking) **Header File** (.h) and then in the **Name** field type Pickup.h.

Add and study the following code in the Pickup.h file and then we can go through it:

```
#pragma once
#include <SFML/Graphics.hpp>

using namespace sf;

class Pickup
{
private:
    //Start value for health pickups
    const int HEALTH_START_VALUE = 50;
    const int AMMO_START_VALUE = 12;
    const int START_WAIT_TIME = 10;
    const int START_SECONDS_TO_LIVE = 5;
    // The sprite that represents this pickup
    Sprite m_Sprite;

    // The arena it exists in
    IntRect m_Arena;

    // How much is this pickup worth?
    int m_Value;
    // What type of pickup is this?
    // 1 = health, 2 = ammo
    int m_Type;

    // Handle spawning and disappearing
    bool m_Spawned;
    float m_SecondsSinceSpawn;
    float m_SecondsSinceDeSpawn;
    float m_SecondsToLive;
    float m_SecondsToWait;

    // Public prototypes go here
};
```

The previous code declares all the private variables of the `Pickup` class. Although the names should be quite intuitive, it might not be obvious why many of them are needed at all. Let's go through them, starting from the top:

- `const int HEALTH_START_VALUE = 50`: This constant variable is used to set the starting value of all health pickups. The value will be used to initialize the `m_Value` variable, which will need to be manipulated throughout the course of a game.
- `const int AMMO_START_VALUE = 12`: This constant variable is used to set the starting value of all ammo pickups. The value will be used to initialize the `m_Value` variable, which will need to be manipulated throughout the course of a game.
- `const int START_WAIT_TIME = 10`: This variable is how long a pickup will wait before it re-spawns after disappearing. It will be used to initialize the `m_SecondsToWait` variable which can be manipulated throughout the game.
- `const int START_SECONDS_TO_LIVE = 5`: This variable determines how long a pickup will last between spawning and being de-spawned. Like the previous three constants, it has a non-constant associated with it that can be manipulated throughout the course of the game. The non-constant it is used to initialize is `m_SecondsToLive`.
- `Sprite m_Sprite`: This is the sprite to visually represent the object.
- `IntRect m_Arena`: This will hold the size of the current arena to help the pickup spawn in a sensible position.
- `int m_Value`: How much health or ammo is this pickup worth? This value is used when the player levels-up the value of the health or ammo pickup.
- `int m_Type`: This will be either zero or one for health or ammo. We could have used an enumeration class but that seemed like overkill for just two options.
- `bool m_Spawned`: Is the pickup currently spawned?
- `float m_SecondsSinceSpawn`: How long is it since the pickup was spawned?
- `float m_SecondsSinceDeSpawn`: How long is it since the pickup was de-spawned (disappeared)?
- `float m_SecondsToLive`: How long should this pickup stay spawned before de-spawning?
- `float m_SecondsToWait`: How long should this pickup stay de-spawned before re-spawning?

Note that most of the complexity of this class is due to the variable spawn time and its upgradeable nature. If the pickups just re-spawned when collected and had a fixed value this would be a very simple class. We need our pickups to be upgradeable, so the player is forced to develop a strategy to progress through the waves of zombies.

Next, add the following public function prototypes to the `Pickup.h` file. Be sure to familiarize yourself with the new code so we can go through it:

```
// Public prototypes go here
public:
    Pickup::Pickup(int type);

    // Prepare a new pickup
    void setArena(IntRect arena);
    void spawn();

    // Check the position of a pickup
    FloatRect getPosition();

    // Get the sprite for drawing
    Sprite getSprite();

    // Let the pickup update itself each frame
    void update(float elapsedTime);

    // Is this pickup currently spawned?
    bool isSpawned();

    // Get the goodness from the pickup
    int gotIt();

    // Upgrade the value of each pickup
    void upgrade();
};
```

Let's talk briefly about each of the function definitions:

- The first function is the constructor, named after the class. Note that it takes a single int parameter. This will be used to initialize the type of pickup it will be (health or ammo).
- The setArena function receives an IntRect. This function will be called for each Pickup instance at the start of each wave. The Pickup objects will then know the areas into which they can spawn.
- The spawn function will, of course, handle spawning the pickup.

- The getPosition function, just like in the Player, Zombie, and Bullet classes will return a FloatRect that represents the current location of the object in the game world.
- The getSprite function returns a Sprite object that enables the pickup to be drawn, once each frame.
- The update function receives the time the previous frame took. It uses this value to update its private variables and make decisions about when to spawn and de-spawn.
- The isSpawned function returns a Boolean that will let the calling code know whether or nor the pickup is currently spawned.
- The gotIt function will be called when a collision is detected with the player. The Pickup class code can then prepare itself for re-spawning at the appropriate time. Note that it returns an int so that the calling code knows how much the pickup is worth in either health or ammo.
- The upgrade function will be called when the player chooses to levelup the properties of a pickup during the levelingup phase of the game.

Now we have gone through the member variables and function prototypes, it should be quite easy to follow along as we code the function definitions.

Coding the Pickup class function definitions

Now we can create a new .cpp file that will contain the function definitions. Right-click **Source Files** in the **Solution Explorer** and select **Add | New Item....** In the **Add New Item** window, highlight (by left-clicking) **C++ File (.cpp)** and then in the **Name** field type Pickup.cpp. Finally, click the **Add** button. We are now ready to code the class.

Add the code shown here to the Pickup.cpp file. Be sure to review the code so we can discuss it:

```cpp
#include "stdafx.h"
#include "Pickup.h"
#include "TextureHolder.h"

Pickup::Pickup(int type)
{
    // Store the type of this pickup
    m_Type = type;

    // Associate the texture with the sprite
    if (m_Type == 1)
```

```
    {
        m_Sprite = Sprite(TextureHolder::GetTexture(
            "graphics/health_pickup.png"));

        // How much is pickup worth
        m_Value = HEALTH_START_VALUE;

    }
    else
    {
        m_Sprite = Sprite(TextureHolder::GetTexture(
            "graphics/ammo_pickup.png"));

        // How much is pickup worth
        m_Value = AMMO_START_VALUE;
    }

    m_Sprite.setOrigin(25, 25);

    m_SecondsToLive = START_SECONDS_TO_LIVE;
    m_SecondsToWait = START_WAIT_TIME;
}
```

In the previous code, we added the familiar include directives. Then we added the `Pickup` constructor. We know it is the constructor because it has the same name as the class.

The constructor receives an `int` called `type` and the first thing the code does is assign the value received from `type` to `m_Type`. After this, there is an `if...else` block that checks whether `m_Type` is equal to 1. If it is, `m_Sprite` is associated with the health pickup texture and `m_Value` is set to `HEALTH_START_VALUE`.

If `m_Type` is not equal to 1, the `else` block associates the ammo pickup texture with `m_Sprite` and assigns the value of `AMMO_START_VALUE` to `m_Value`.

After the `if...else` block, the code sets the origin of `m_Sprite` to the center using the `setOrigin` function and assigns `START_SECONDS_TO_LIVE` and `START_WAIT_TIME` to `m_SecondsToLive` and `m_SecondsToWait`, respectively.

The constructor has successfully prepared a `Pickup` object that is ready for use.

Next we will add the `setArena` function. Examine the code as you add it:

```
void Pickup::setArena(IntRect arena)
{

    // Copy the details of the arena to the pickup's m_Arena
```

```
    m_Arena.left = arena.left + 50;
    m_Arena.width = arena.width - 50;
    m_Arena.top = arena.top + 50;
    m_Arena.height = arena.height - 50;

    spawn();
}
```

The setArena function that we just coded simply copies the values from the passed in arena, object but varies the values by plus fifty on the left and top and minus fifty on the right and bottom. The Pickup object is now aware of the area in which it can spawn. The setArena function then calls its own spawn function to make the final preparations for being drawn and updated each frame.

The spawn function is next. Add the following code after the setArena function:

```
void Pickup::spawn()
{
    // Spawn at a random location
    srand((int)time(0) / m_Type);
    int x = (rand() % m_Arena.width);
    srand((int)time(0) * m_Type);
    int y = (rand() % m_Arena.height);

    m_SecondsSinceSpawn = 0;
    m_Spawned = true;

    m_Sprite.setPosition(x, y);
}
```

The spawn function does everything necessary to prepare the pickup. First it seeds the random number generator and gets a random number for both the horizontal and vertical position of the object. Notice that it uses m_Arena.width and m_Arena.height as the ranges for the possible horizontal and vertical positions.

The m_SecondsSinceSpawn is set to zero so the length of time allowed before it is de-spawned is reset. The m_Spawned variable is set to true so that when we call isSpawned, from main, we will get a positive response. Finally, m_Sprite is moved into position with setPosition, ready for drawing to the screen.

In the following block of code, we have three simple getter functions. The getPosition function returns a FloatRect of the current position of m_Sprite, getSprite returns a copy of m_Sprite itself, and isSpawned returns true or false depending upon whether the object is currently spawned.

Add and examine the code we have just discussed:

```
FloatRect Pickup::getPosition()
{
    return m_Sprite.getGlobalBounds();
}

Sprite Pickup::getSprite()
{
    return m_Sprite;
}

bool Pickup::isSpawned()
{
    return m_Spawned;
}
```

Next we will code the `gotIt` function. This function will be called from `main` when the player touches/collides with (gets) the pickup. Add the `gotIt` function after the `isSpawned` function:

```
int Pickup::gotIt()
{
    m_Spawned = false;
    m_SecondsSinceDeSpawn = 0;
    return m_Value;
}
```

The `gotIt` function sets `m_Spawned` to `false` so we know not to draw and check for collisions at the moment. The `m_SecondsSinceDespawn` is set to zero so the countdown to spawning begins again from the start and `m_Value` is returned to the calling code so the calling code can handle adding extra ammunition or health, as appropriate.

Next we have the `update` function, which ties together many of the variables and functions we have seen so far. Add and familiarize yourself with the `update` function and then we can talk about it:

```
void Pickup::update(float elapsedTime)
{
    if (m_Spawned)
    {
        m_SecondsSinceSpawn += elapsedTime;
    }
    else
    {
```

```
    m_SecondsSinceDeSpawn += elapsedTime;
}


// Do we need to hide a pickup?
if (m_SecondsSinceSpawn > m_SecondsToLive && m_Spawned)
{
    // Remove the pickup and put it somewhere else
    m_Spawned = false;
    m_SecondsSinceDeSpawn = 0;
}

// Do we need to spawn a pickup
if (m_SecondsSinceDeSpawn > m_SecondsToWait && !m_Spawned)
{
    // spawn the pickup and reset the timer
    spawn();
}

}
```

The update function is divided into four blocks that are considered for execution each frame:

- An `if` block that executes if `m_Spawned` is **true**—`if (m_Spawned)`. This block of code adds the time of this frame to `m_SecondsSinceSpawned`, which keeps track of how long the pickup has been spawned.
- A corresponding `else` block that executes if `m_Spawned` is `false`. This block adds the time this frame took to `m_SecondsSinceDeSpawn`, which keeps track of how long the pickup has waited since it was last de-spawned (hidden).
- Another `if` block that executes when the pickup has been spawned for longer than it should have been—`if (m_SecondsSinceSpawn > m_SecondsToLive && m_Spawned)`. This block sets `m_Spawned` to `false` and resets `m_SecondsSinceDeSpawn` to zero. Now block 2 will execute until it is time to spawn again.
- A final `if` block that executes when the time to wait since de-spawning has exceeded the necessary wait time, and the pickup is not currently spawned—`if (m_SecondsSinceDeSpawn > m_SecondsToWait && !m_Spawned)`. When this block is executed, it is time to spawn again and the spawn function is called.

These four tests and code are what controls the hiding and showing of a pickup.

Finally, add the definition for the `upgrade` function:

```
void Pickup::upgrade()
{
    if (m_Type == 1)
    {
        m_Value += (HEALTH_START_VALUE * .5);
    }
    else
    {
        m_Value += (AMMO_START_VALUE * .5);
    }

    // Make them more frequent and last longer
    m_SecondsToLive += (START_SECONDS_TO_LIVE / 10);
    m_SecondsToWait -= (START_WAIT_TIME / 10);
}
```

The `upgrade` function tests for the type of pickup, either health or ammo, and then adds 50 percent of the (appropriate) starting value on to `m_Value`. The next two lines after the `if...else` blocks increase the amount of time the pickup will remain spawned and decrease the amount of time the player has to wait between spawns.

This function is called when the player chooses to levelup the pickups during the LEVELING_UP state. Our `Pickup` class is ready for use.

Using the Pickup class

After all that hard work implementing the `Pickup` class, we can now go ahead and write code in the game engine to actually put some pickups into the game.

The first thing we do is add an include directive to the `ZombieArena.cpp` file:

```
#include "stdafx.h"
#include <SFML/Graphics.hpp>
#include "ZombieArena.h"
#include "Player.h"
#include "TextureHolder.h"
#include "Bullet.h"
#include "Pickup.h"
using namespace sf;
```

In the following code, we add two `Pickup` instances, one called `healthPickup` and the other called `ammoPickup`. We pass the values 1 and 2 respectively into the constructor so that they are initialized to the correct type of pickup. Add the highlighted code we have just discussed:

```
// Hide the mouse pointer and replace it with crosshair
window.setMouseCursorVisible(true);
Sprite spriteCrosshair;
Texture textureCrosshair =
TextureHolder::GetTexture("graphics/crosshair.png");
spriteCrosshair.setTexture(textureCrosshair);
spriteCrosshair.setOrigin(25, 25);

// Create a couple of pickups
Pickup healthPickup(1);
Pickup ammoPickup(2);

// The main game loop
while (window.isOpen())
```

In the `LEVELING_UP` state of the keyboard handling, add the highlighted lines within the nested `PLAYING` code block shown here:

```
if (state == State::PLAYING)
{
    // Prepare thelevel
    // We will modify the next two lines later
    arena.width = 500;
    arena.height = 500;
    arena.left = 0;
    arena.top = 0;

    // Pass the vertex array by reference
    // to the createBackground function
    int tileSize = createBackground(background, arena);

    // Spawn the player in the middle of the arena
    player.spawn(arena, resolution, tileSize);

    // Configure the pickups
    healthPickup.setArena(arena);
    ammoPickup.setArena(arena);

    // Create a horde of zombies
    numZombies = 10;

    // Delete the previously allocated memory (if it exists)
```

```
    delete[] zombies;
    zombies = createHorde(numZombies, arena);
    numZombiesAlive = numZombies;

    // Reset the clock so there isn't a frame jump
    clock.restart();
}
```

The previous code simply passes `arena` into the `setArena` function of each pickup. The pickups now know where they can spawn. This code executes for each new wave, so as the arena size grows, the `Pickup` objects will get updated.

The following code simply calls the `update` function for each `Pickup` object, on each frame:

```
// Loop through each Zombie and update them
for (int i = 0; i < numZombies; i++)
{
    if (zombies[i].isAlive())
    {
        zombies[i].update(dt.asSeconds(), playerPosition);
    }
}

// Update any bullets that are in-flight
for (int i = 0; i < 100; i++)
{
    if (bullets[i].isInFlight())
    {
        bullets[i].update(dtAsSeconds);
    }
}

// Update the pickups
healthPickup.update(dtAsSeconds);
ammoPickup.update(dtAsSeconds);
}// End updating the scene
```

The following code in the draw part of the game loop, checks if the pickup is currently spawned and if it is, draws it. Add the highlighted code we have just discussed:

```
// Draw the player
window.draw(player.getSprite());

// Draw the pickups, if currently spawned
if (ammoPickup.isSpawned())
{
    window.draw(ammoPickup.getSprite());
}
```

```
if (healthPickup.isSpawned())
{
   window.draw(healthPickup.getSprite());
}

//Draw the crosshair
window.draw(spriteCrosshair);
}
```

Now you can run the game and see the pickups spawn and de-spawn. You can't, however, actually pick them up yet.

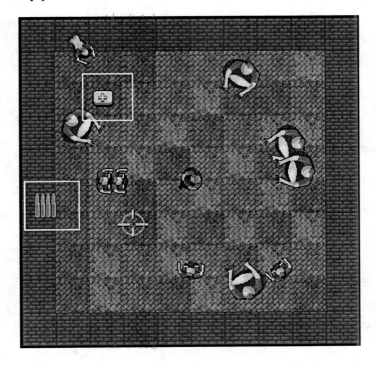

Now that we have all the objects in our game, it is a good time to make them interact (collide) with each other.

Detecting collisions

We just need to know when certain objects from our game touch certain other objects. We can then respond to that event in an appropriate manner. In our classes, we have already added functions to call when our objects collide. They are the following:

- The `Player` class has a `hit` function. We will call it when a zombie collides with the player.
- The `Zombie` class has a `hit` function. We will call it when a bullet collides with a zombie.
- The `Pickup` class has a `gotIt` function. We will call it when the player collides with a pickup.

If necessary, look back to refresh your memory on how each of those functions works. All we need to do now is detect the collisions and call the appropriate functions.

We will use **rectangle intersection** to detect collisions. This type of collision detection is really straightforward (especially with SFML). We can think of drawing an imaginary rectangle—we can call it a **hitbox** or **bounding rectangle**—around the objects we want to test for collision, and then test to see whether they intersect. If they do, we have a collision:

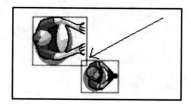

As we can see from the previous image, this is far from perfect. But in this situation it is sufficient. To implement this method, all we need to do is test for the intersection using the x and y coordinates of both object hit boxes.

The code for testing the intersection of two rectangles would look something like this. Don't use the following code. It is for demonstration purposes only:

```
if(objectA.getPosition().right > objectB.getPosition().left
    && objectA.getPosition().left < objectB.getPosition().right )
{
    // objectA is intersecting enemy on x axis
    // But they could be at different heights
    if(objectA.getPosition().top < objectB.getPosition().bottom
        && objectA.getPosition().bottom > objectB.getPosition().top )
    {
        // objectA is intersecting objectB on y axis as well
```

```
        // Collision detected
    }
}
```

We don't need to write this code, however. We will be using the SFML `intersects` function, which works on `FloatRect` objects. Think or look back to the `Zombie`, `Player`, `Bullet`, and `Pickup` classes, they all had a `getPosition` function, which returned a `FloatRect` of the object's current location. We will see how we use `getPosition` along with `intersects` to do all our collision detection.

We will deal with this in three sections of code that will all follow on from one another, and they will all go at the end of the update part of our game engine.

We need to know the answer to the following three questions, each frame:

- Has a zombie been shot?
- Has the player been touched by a zombie?
- Has the player touched a pickup?

First let's add a couple more variables for `score` and `hiscore`. We can then change them when a zombie is killed. Add the following code:

```
// Create a couple of pickups
Pickup healthPickup(1);
Pickup ammoPickup(2);

// About the game
int score = 0;
int hiScore = 0;

// The main game loop
while (window.isOpen())
```

Now let's start by detecting whether a zombie is colliding with a bullet.

Has a zombie been shot?

The following code might look complicated, but when we step through it we will see it is actually nothing we haven't seen before. Add the following code just after the call to update the pickups each frame. Then we can go through it:

```
// Update the pickups
healthPickup.update(dtAsSeconds);
ammoPickup.update(dtAsSeconds);
```

```
// Collision detection
// Have any zombies been shot?
for (int i = 0; i < 100; i++)
{
    for (int j = 0; j < numZombies; j++)
    {
      if (bullets[i].isInFlight() &&
          zombies[j].isAlive())
        {
          if (bullets[i].getPosition().intersects
            (zombies[j].getPosition()))
            {
              // Stop the bullet
              bullets[i].stop();
              // Register the hit and see if it was a kill
              if (zombies[j].hit())
              {
                // Not just a hit but a kill too
                score += 10;
                if (score >= hiScore)
                {
                    hiScore = score;
                }
                numZombiesAlive--;
                // When all the zombies are dead (again)
                if (numZombiesAlive == 0)
                {
                    state = State::LEVELING_UP;
                }
              }
            }
        }
    }
}// End zombie being shot
```

In the next section, we will see all of the zombie and bullet collision detection code again. We will do so a bit at a time so we can discuss it. First of all, notice the structure of the nested `for` loops (with the code stripped out) as follows:

```
// Collision detection
// Have any zombies been shot?
for (int i = 0; i < 100; i++)
{
    for (int j = 0; j < numZombies; j++)
    {
        ...
        ...
        ...
```

```
    }
  }
```

The code loops through each and every bullet (0 to 99) for each and every zombie (0 to < numZombies.).

Within the nested `for` loops, we do the following:

1. Check whether the current bullet is in flight and the current zombie is still alive with this code:

```
if (bullets[i].isInFlight() && zombies[j].isAlive())
```

2. Provided the zombie is alive and the bullet is in flight, we test for a rectangle intersection with this code:

```
if (bullets[i].getPosition().intersects (zombies[j].getPosition()))
```

If the current bullet and zombie have collided, then we take a number of steps.

1. Stop the bullet with this code:

```
// Stop the bullet
bullets[i].stop();
```

2. Register a hit with the current zombie by calling its `hit` function. Note that the `hit` function returns a Boolean that let's the calling code know if the zombie is dead yet. This is shown in the following line of code:

```
// Register the hit and see if it was a kill
if (zombies[j].hit()) {
```

Inside this `if` block, which detects when the zombie is dead and not just wounded, we do the following:

- Add ten to `score`
- Change `hiScore` if score has exceeded (beaten) `score`
- Reduce `numZombiesAlive` by one
- Check whether all the zombies are dead, (numZombiesAlive == 0), and if so, change `state` to LEVELING_UP

Here is the block of code inside `if(zombies[j].hit())` that we have just discussed:

```
// Not just a hit but a kill too
score += 10;
```

```
if (score >= hiScore)
{
    hiScore = score;
}

numZombiesAlive--;

// When all the zombies are dead (again)
if (numZombiesAlive == 0)
{
    state = State::LEVELING_UP;
}
```

That's the zombies and the bullets taken care of. You could run the game and see the blood. Of course you won't see the score until we implement the HUD in the next chapter.

Has the player been touched by a zombie?

This code is much shorter and simpler than the zombie and bullet collision detection. Add the highlighted code just after the previous code we wrote:

```
}// End zombie being shot

// Have any zombies touched the player
for (int i = 0; i < numZombies; i++)
{
    if (player.getPosition().intersects
        (zombies[i].getPosition()) && zombies[i].isAlive())
    {
        if (player.hit(gameTimeTotal))
        {
            // More here later
        }
        if (player.getHealth() <= 0)
        {
            state = State::GAME_OVER;
        }
    }
}// End player touched
```

We detect whether a zombie has collided with the player by using a `for` loop to loop through all the zombies. For each zombie that is alive, the code uses the `intersects` function to test for a collision with the player. When a collision has occurred, we call `player.hit`. Then we check whether the player is dead by calling `player.getHealth`. If the player's health is equal to or less than zero, then we change `state` to `GAME_OVER`.

You can run the game and collisions will be detected. However, as there is no HUD or sound effects yet, it is not clear that this is happening. In addition, we need to do some more work on resetting the game when the player dies and a new game is starting. So, although the game runs, the results are not especially satisfying at the moment. We will improve this over the next two chapters.

Has the player touched a pickup?

The collision detection code between the player and each of the two pickups follows. Add the highlighted code just after the previous code that we added:

```
}// End player touched

// Has the player touched health pickup
if (player.getPosition().intersects
   (healthPickup.getPosition()) && healthPickup.isSpawned())
{
   player.increaseHealthLevel(healthPickup.gotIt());
}

// Has the player touched ammo pickup
if (player.getPosition().intersects
   (ammoPickup.getPosition()) && ammoPickup.isSpawned())
{
   bulletsSpare += ammoPickup.gotIt();
}
}// End updating the scene
```

The previous code uses two simple if statements to see whether either healthPickup or ammoPickup has been touched by the player.

If a health pickup has been collected, then the player.increaseHealthLevel function uses the value returned from the healthPickup.gotIt function to increase the player's health.

If an ammo pickup has been collected, then bulletsSpare is increased by the value returned from ammoPickup.gotIt.

You can run the game, kill zombies, and collect pickups! Note that when your health equals zero, the game will enter the GAME_OVER state and pause. To restart it, you will need to press *Enter* followed by a number between *1* and *6*. When we implement the HUD, the home screen, and the leveling up screen, these steps will be intuitive and straightforward for the player. We will do so in the next chapter.

FAQ

Here are some questions that might be on your mind:

Q) Are there any better ways of doing collision detection?

A) Yes. There are lots more ways to do collision detection, including but not limited to the following:

- You can divide objects into multiple rectangles which better fit the shape of the sprite. It is perfectly manageable for C++ to check on thousands of rectangles each frame. This is especially true when you use techniques such as neighbor checking to reduce the number of tests that are necessary each frame.
- For circular objects, you can use the radius overlap method.
- For irregular polygons, you can use the crossing number algorithm.

    All these techniques can be investigated at the following website:

- **Neighbor checking**: `http://gamecodeschool.com/essentials/collision-detection-neighbor-checking/`
- **Radius overlap method**: `http://gamecodeschool.com/essentials/collision-detection-radius-overlap/`
- **Crossing number algorithm**: `http://gamecodeschool.com/essentials/collision-detection-crossing-number/`

Summary

That was a busy chapter but we have achieved a lot. Not only did we add bullets and pickups to the game through two new classes, but we also made all the objects interact as they should by detecting when they collide with each other.

Despite these achievements, we need to do more work to set up each new game and to give the player feedback through a HUD. In the next chapter, we will build the HUD.

10
Layering Views and Implementing the HUD

In this chapter, we will get to see the real value of SFML **Views**. We will add a large array of SFML `Text` objects and manipulate them as we did before in the **Timber!!!** project. What is new is that we will draw the HUD using a second view instance. This way, the HUD will stay neatly positioned over the top of the main game action, regardless of what the background, player, zombies, and other game objects are doing.

Here is what we will do:

- Add text and a background to the home/game over screen
- Add text to the level up screen
- Create the second view
- Add a HUD

Adding all the Text and HUD objects

We will be manipulating a few Strings in this chapter. This is so we can format the HUD and the level up screen.

Add the extra `include` directive highlighted next so we can make some `sstream` objects to achieve this:

```
#include "stdafx.h"
#include <sstream>
#include <SFML/Graphics.hpp>
#include "ZombieArena.h"
#include "Player.h"
```

```
#include "TextureHolder.h"
#include "Bullet.h"
#include "Pickup.h"

using namespace sf;
```

Next add this rather lengthy but easily explained code. To help identify where you should add the code, the new code is highlighted and the existing code is not. You may need to vary the position/size of some text/elements to suit your screen:

```
int score = 0;
int hiScore = 0;

// For the home/game over screen
Sprite spriteGameOver;
Texture textureGameOver =
TextureHolder::GetTexture("graphics/background.png");
spriteGameOver.setTexture(textureGameOver);
spriteGameOver.setPosition(0, 0);

// Create a view for the HUD
View hudView(sf::FloatRect(0, 0, resolution.x, resolution.y));

// Create a sprite for the ammo icon
Sprite spriteAmmoIcon;
Texture textureAmmoIcon =
TextureHolder::GetTexture("graphics/ammo_icon.png");
spriteAmmoIcon.setTexture(textureAmmoIcon);
spriteAmmoIcon.setPosition(20, 980);

// Load the font
Font font;
font.loadFromFile("fonts/zombiecontrol.ttf");

// Paused
Text pausedText;
pausedText.setFont(font);
pausedText.setCharacterSize(155);
pausedText.setFillColor(Color::White);
pausedText.setPosition(400, 400);
pausedText.setString("Press Enter \n to continue");

// Game Over
Text gameOverText;
gameOverText.setFont(font);
gameOverText.setCharacterSize(125);
gameOverText.setFillColor(Color::White);
gameOverText.setPosition(250, 850);
```

```cpp
gameOverText.setString("Press Enter to play");

// LEVELING up
Text levelUpText;
levelUpText.setFont(font);
levelUpText.setCharacterSize(80);
levelUpText.setFillColor(Color::White);
levelUpText.setPosition(150, 250);
std::stringstream levelUpStream;
levelUpStream <<
    "1- Increased rate of fire" <<
    "\n2- Increased clip size(next reload)" <<
    "\n3- Increased max health" <<
    "\n4- Increased run speed" <<
    "\n5- More and better health pickups" <<
    "\n6- More and better ammo pickups";
levelUpText.setString(levelUpStream.str());

// Ammo
Text ammoText;
ammoText.setFont(font);
ammoText.setCharacterSize(55);
ammoText.setFillColor(Color::White);
ammoText.setPosition(200, 980);

// Score
Text scoreText;
scoreText.setFont(font);
scoreText.setCharacterSize(55);
scoreText.setFillColor(Color::White);
scoreText.setPosition(20, 0);

// Hi Score
Text hiScoreText;
hiScoreText.setFont(font);
hiScoreText.setCharacterSize(55);
hiScoreText.setFillColor(Color::White);
hiScoreText.setPosition(1400, 0);
std::stringstream s;
s << "Hi Score:" << hiScore;
hiScoreText.setString(s.str());

// Zombies remaining
Text zombiesRemainingText;
zombiesRemainingText.setFont(font);
zombiesRemainingText.setCharacterSize(55);
zombiesRemainingText.setFillColor(Color::White);
zombiesRemainingText.setPosition(1500, 980);
```

```
zombiesRemainingText.setString("Zombies: 100");

// Wave number
int wave = 0;
Text waveNumberText;
waveNumberText.setFont(font);
waveNumberText.setCharacterSize(55);
waveNumberText.setFillColor(Color::White);
waveNumberText.setPosition(1250, 980);
waveNumberText.setString("Wave: 0");

// Health bar
RectangleShape healthBar;
healthBar.setFillColor(Color::Red);
healthBar.setPosition(450, 980);
// The main game loop
while (window.isOpen())
```

The previous code is very simple and nothing new. It basically creates a whole bunch of SFML `Text` objects. It assigns their colors and sizes, then formats their positions, using functions we have seen before.

The most important thing to note is that we create another `View` object called `hudView` and initialize it to fit the resolution of the screen.

As we have seen, the main view object scrolls around as it follows the player. In contrast, we will never move `hudView`. The result of this is that as long as we switch to this view before we draw the elements of the HUD, we will create the effect of allowing the game world to scroll by underneath while the player's HUD remains stationary.

 As an analogy, you can think of laying a transparent sheet of plastic, with some writing on it, over a TV screen. The TV will carry on as normal with moving pictures, the text on the plastic sheet will stay in the same place regardless of what goes on underneath it.

The next thing to notice, however, is that the high score is not set in any meaningful way. We will need to wait until the next chapter, when we investigate file I/O to save and retrieve the high score.

Another point worth noting is that we declare and initialize a `RectangleShape` called `healthBar` that will be a visual representation of the player's remaining health. This will work in almost exactly the same way that the time-bar worked in the last project, except of course, it will represent health instead of time.

In the previous code, there is a new sprite called `ammoIcon` that gives context to the bullet and clip statistics that we will draw next to it, in the bottom left of the screen.

Although there is nothing new or technical about the large amount of code that we just added, be sure to familiarize yourself with the details, especially the variable names, to make the rest of the chapter easier to follow.

Updating the HUD each frame

As you might expect, we will update the HUD variables in the update section of our code. We will not, however, do so every frame. The reason for this is that it is unnecessary and it also slows our game loop down.

As an example, consider the scenario where the player kills a zombie and gets some more points. It doesn't matter whether the `Text` object that holds the score is updated in a thousandth, hundredth, or even tenth of a second. The player will discern no difference. This means there is no point rebuilding strings that we set to the `Text` objects every frame.

So we can time when and how often we update the HUD, add the following variables:

```
// When did we last update the HUD?
int framesSinceLastHUDUpdate = 0;

// How often (in frames) should we update the HUD
int fpsMeasurementFrameInterval = 1000;

// The main game loop
while (window.isOpen())
```

In the previous code, we have variables to track how many frames it has been since the last time the HUD was updated and the interval, measured in frames, we would like to wait between HUD updates.

Now we can use these new variables and actually update the HUD each frame. We won't actually see all the HUD elements change, however, until we begin to manipulate the final variables, such as `wave`, in the next chapter.

Add the highlighted code in the update section of the game loop as shown:

```
// Has the player touched ammo pickup
if (player.getPosition().intersects
    (ammoPickup.getPosition()) && ammoPickup.isSpawned())
{
    bulletsSpare += ammoPickup.gotIt();
```

```
    }

    // size up the health bar
    healthBar.setSize(Vector2f(player.getHealth() * 3, 50));
    // Increment the number of frames since the previous update
    framesSinceLastHUDUpdate++;

    // re-calculate every fpsMeasurementFrameInterval frames
    if (framesSinceLastHUDUpdate > fpsMeasurementFrameInterval)
    {
        // Update game HUD text
        std::stringstream ssAmmo;
        std::stringstream ssScore;
        std::stringstream ssHiScore;
        std::stringstream ssWave;
        std::stringstream ssZombiesAlive;

        // Update the ammo text
        ssAmmo << bulletsInClip << "/" << bulletsSpare;
        ammoText.setString(ssAmmo.str());

        // Update the score text
        ssScore << "Score:" << score;
        scoreText.setString(ssScore.str());

        // Update the high score text
        ssHiScore << "Hi Score:" << hiScore;
        hiScoreText.setString(ssHiScore.str());

        // Update the wave
        ssWave << "Wave:" << wave;
        waveNumberText.setString(ssWave.str());

        // Update the high score text
        ssZombiesAlive << "Zombies:" << numZombiesAlive;
        zombiesRemainingText.setString(ssZombiesAlive.str());

        framesSinceLastHUDUpdate = 0;

    }// End HUD update

}// End updating the scene
```

In the new code, we update the size of the `healthBar` sprite, increment the `timeSinceLastUpdate` object, then increment the `framesSinceLastUpdate` variable.

Next, we start an `if` block that tests whether `framesSinceLastHUDUpdate` is greater than our preferred interval, which is stored in `fpsMeasurementFrameInterval`.

Inside this `if` block is where all the action takes place. First, we declare a string stream object for each string that we need to set to a `Text` object.

Then we use each of those string stream objects in turn, and use the `setString` function to set the result to the appropriate `Text` object.

Finally, before the `if` block is exited, the `framesSinceLastHUDUpdate` is set back to zero so that the count can begin again.

Now, when we redraw the scene, the new values will appear in the player's HUD.

Drawing the HUD, and the home and level up screens

All the code from the next three code blocks goes in the drawing phase of our game loop. All we need to do is to draw the appropriate `Text` objects during the appropriate states in the draw section of the main game loop.

In the `PLAYING` state, add the following highlighted code:

```
//Draw the crosshair
window.draw(spriteCrosshair);

// Switch to the HUD view
window.setView(hudView);

// Draw all the HUD elements
window.draw(spriteAmmoIcon);
window.draw(ammoText);
window.draw(scoreText);
window.draw(hiScoreText);
window.draw(healthBar);
window.draw(waveNumberText);
window.draw(zombiesRemainingText);
}

if (state == State::LEVELING_UP)
```

```
{
}
```

The vital thing to notice in the previous block of code is that we switch views to the HUD view. This causes everything to be drawn at the precise screen positions we gave to each of the elements of the HUD. They will never move.

In the LEVELING_UP state, add the following highlighted code:

```
if (state == State::LEVELING_UP)
{
    window.draw(spriteGameOver);
    window.draw(levelUpText);
}
```

In the PAUSED state, add the following highlighted code:

```
if (state == State::PAUSED)
{
    window.draw(pausedText);
}
```

In the GAME_OVER state, add the following highlighted code:

```
if (state == State::GAME_OVER)
{
    window.draw(spriteGameOver);
    window.draw(gameOverText);
    window.draw(scoreText);
    window.draw(hiScoreText);
}
```

Now we can run the game and see our HUD update during gameplay.

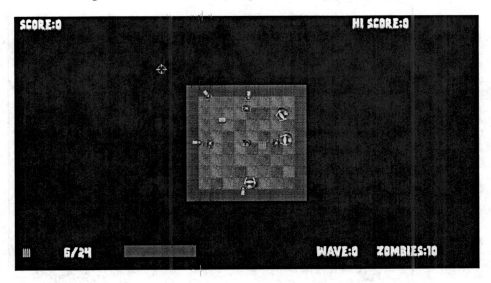

This shows the **HI SCORE** and score on the home/game over screen:

Next we see text to show what the player's level up options are, although these options don't do anything yet:

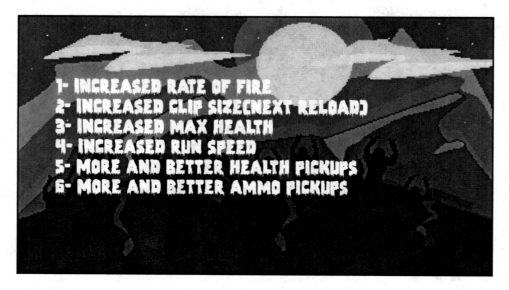

And here we see a helpful message on the pause screen:

SFML Views are more powerful than this simple HUD can demonstrate. For an insight into the potential of SFML Views and how easy to use they are, take a look at the SFML website's tutorial on `View` at `http://www.sfm l-dev.org/tutorials/2.0/graphics-view.php`.

FAQ

Here is a question that might be on your mind:

Q) Where can I see more of the power of the `View` class in action?

A) Take a look at the enhanced edition of the **Zombie Arena** game in the download bundle. You can use the keyboard cursor keys to spin and zoom the action. Warning! Spinning the scene makes the controls awkward, but you get to see some of the things that can be done with the `View` class.

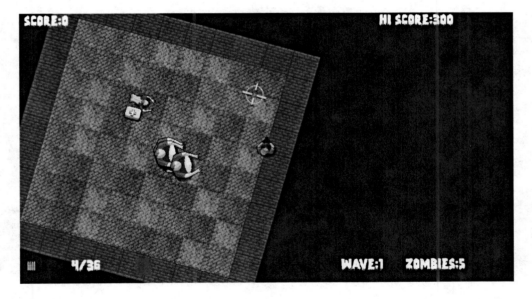

The zoom and rotate functionality was achieved with just a few lines of code in the input handling section of the main game loop. You can see the code in the `Zombie Arena Enhanced Version` folder of the download bundle or run the enhanced version from the `Runnable Games/Zombie Arena` folder.

Summary

That was a quick and simple chapter. We saw how to display the value, held by variables of different types using `sstream` and then draw them over the top of the main game action using a second SFML `View` object.

We are nearly done with Zombie Arena now. All the screenshots show a small arena that doesn't take advantage of the full monitor. In the final chapter for this project, we will put in some finishing touches such as levelingup, sound effects, and saving the high-score . The arena can then grow to the same size as the monitor and far beyond.

11
Sound Effects, File I/O, and Finishing the Game

We are nearly there. This short chapter will demonstrate how we can easily manipulate files stored on the hard drive using the C++ standard library, and we will also add sound effects. Of course, we know how to add sound effects, but we will discuss exactly where in the code the calls to play will go. We will also tie up a few loose-ends to make the game complete.

In this chapter we will learn the following topics:

- Saving and loading the high score
- Adding sound effects
- Allow the player to level up
- Create never-ending multiple waves

Saving and loading the high-score

File I/O, or input/output, is a fairly technical subject. Fortunately for us, as it is such a common requirement in programming, there is a library that handles all the complexity for us. As with concatenating strings for our HUD, it is the **Standard Library** that provides the necessary functionality through fstream.

First, we include fstream in the same way we included sstream:

```
#include "stdafx.h"
#include <sstream>
#include <fstream>
#include <SFML/Graphics.hpp>
#include "ZombieArena.h"
```

```
#include "Player.h"
#include "TextureHolder.h"
#include "Bullet.h"
#include "Pickup.h"

using namespace sf;
```

Now, add a new folder in the `ZombieArena/ZombieArena` folder called `gamedata`. Next, right-click in this folder and create a new file called `scores.txt`. It is in this file that we will save the player's high-score. You could open the file and add a score to it. If you do, make sure it is quite a low score so we can easily test whether beating that score results in the new score being added. Be sure to close the file once you are done with it or the game will not be able to access it.

In the next code, we create an `ifstream` object called `inputFile` and send the folder and file we just created as a parameter to its constructor.

The `if(InputFile.is_open())` code checks that the file exists and is ready to read from. We then put the contents of the file into `hiScore` and close the file. Add the highlighted code:

```
// Score
Text scoreText;
scoreText.setFont(font);
scoreText.setCharacterSize(55);
scoreText.setFillColor(Color::White);
scoreText.setPosition(20, 0);

// Load the high-score from a text file
std::ifstream inputFile("gamedata/scores.txt");
if (inputFile.is_open())
{
    inputFile >> hiScore;
    inputFile.close();
}

// Hi Score
Text hiScoreText;
hiScoreText.setFont(font);
hiScoreText.setCharacterSize(55);
hiScoreText.setFillColor(Color::White);
hiScoreText.setPosition(1400, 0);
std::stringstream s;
s << "Hi Score:" << hiScore;
hiScoreText.setString(s.str());
```

Now we handle saving a potentially new high-score. Within the block that handles the player's health being less than or equal to zero, we create an ofstream object called outputFile, write the value of hiScore to the text file, and then close the file:

```
// Have any zombies touched the player
for (int i = 0; i < numZombies; i++)
{
    if (player.getPosition().intersects
        (zombies[i].getPosition()) && zombies[i].isAlive())
    {

        if (player.hit(gameTimeTotal))
        {
            // More here later
        }

        if (player.getHealth() <= 0)
        {
          state = State::GAME_OVER;

          std::ofstream outputFile("gamedata/scores.txt");
          outputFile << hiScore;
          outputFile.close();
        }
    }
}// End player touched
```

You can play the game and your high-score will be saved. Quit the game and notice that your high-score is still there if you play it again.

Let's make some noise.

Preparing sound effects

In this section, we will create all the SoundBuffer and Sound objects that we need to add a range of sound effects to the game.

Start by adding the required SFML includes:

```
#include "stdafx.h"
#include <sstream>
#include <fstream>
#include <SFML/Graphics.hpp>
#include <SFML/Audio.hpp>
#include "ZombieArena.h"
```

```
#include "Player.h"
#include "TextureHolder.h"
#include "Bullet.h"
#include "Pickup.h"
```

Now go ahead and add the seven SoundBuffer and Sound objects which load and prepare the seven sound files that we prepared in Chapter 6: *Object-Oriented Programming, Classes, and SFML Views*:

```
// When did we last update the HUD?
int framesSinceLastHUDUpdate = 0;
// What time was the last update
Time timeSinceLastUpdate;
// How often (in frames) should we update the HUD
int fpsMeasurementFrameInterval = 1000;

// Prepare the hit sound
SoundBuffer hitBuffer;
hitBuffer.loadFromFile("sound/hit.wav");
Sound hit;
hit.setBuffer(hitBuffer);

// Prepare the splat sound
SoundBuffer splatBuffer;
splatBuffer.loadFromFile("sound/splat.wav");
sf::Sound splat;
splat.setBuffer(splatBuffer);

// Prepare the shoot soundSoundBuffer
shootBuffer; shootBuffer.loadFromFile("sound/shoot.wav");
Sound shoot; shoot.setBuffer(shootBuffer);

// Prepare the reload sound
SoundBuffer reloadBuffer;
reloadBuffer.loadFromFile("sound/reload.wav");
Sound reload;
reload.setBuffer(reloadBuffer);

// Prepare the failed sound
SoundBuffer reloadFailedBuffer;
reloadFailedBuffer.loadFromFile("sound/reload_failed.wav");
Sound reloadFailed;
reloadFailed.setBuffer(reloadFailedBuffer);

// Prepare the powerup sound
SoundBuffer powerupBuffer;
powerupBuffer.loadFromFile("sound/powerup.wav");
Sound powerup;
```

```
powerup.setBuffer(powerupBuffer);

// Prepare the pickup sound
SoundBuffer pickupBuffer;
pickupBuffer.loadFromFile("sound/pickup.wav");
Sound pickup;
pickup.setBuffer(pickupBuffer);

// The main game loop
while (window.isOpen())
```

Now the seven sound effects are ready to play. We just need to work out where in our code each of the calls to the `play` function will go.

Leveling up

The next code we will add enables the player to level-up between waves. Because of the work we have already done that makes, this is straightforward to achieve.

Add the highlighted code in the LEVELING_UP state where we handle player input:

```
// Handle the LEVELING up state
if (state == State::LEVELING_UP)
{
    // Handle the player LEVELING up
    if (event.key.code == Keyboard::Num1)
    {
        // Increase fire rate
        fireRate++;
        state = State::PLAYING;
    }

    if (event.key.code == Keyboard::Num2)
    {
        // Increase clip size
        clipSize += clipSize;
        state = State::PLAYING;
    }

    if (event.key.code == Keyboard::Num3)
    {
        // Increase health
        player.upgradeHealth();
        state = State::PLAYING;
    }
```

```
if (event.key.code == Keyboard::Num4)
{
  // Increase speed
  player.upgradeSpeed();
  state = State::PLAYING;
}

if (event.key.code == Keyboard::Num5)
{
  // Upgrade pickup
  healthPickup.upgrade();
  state = State::PLAYING;
}

if (event.key.code == Keyboard::Num6)
{
  // Upgrade pickup
  ammoPickup.upgrade();
  state = State::PLAYING;
}

if (state == State::PLAYING)
{
```

The player can now level-up each time a wave of zombies is cleared. We can't, however, increase the number of zombies or the size of the level yet.

In the next part of the LEVELING_UP state, right after the code we have just added, amend the code that runs when the state changes from LEVELING_UP to PLAYING.

Here is the code in full. I have highlighted the lines that are either new or have been slightly amended.

Add or amend the highlighted code:

```
if (event.key.code == Keyboard::Num6)
{
  ammoPickup.upgrade();
  state = State::PLAYING;
}

if (state == State::PLAYING)
{
  // Increase the wave number
  wave++;

  // Prepare thelevel
  // We will modify the next two lines later
```

```
arena.width = 500 * wave;
arena.height = 500 * wave;
arena.left = 0;
arena.top = 0;

// Pass the vertex array by reference
// to the createBackground function
int tileSize = createBackground(background, arena);

// Spawn the player in the middle of the arena
player.spawn(arena, resolution, tileSize);

// Configure the pickups
healthPickup.setArena(arena);
ammoPickup.setArena(arena);

// Create a horde of zombies
numZombies = 5 * wave;

// Delete the previously allocated memory (if it exists)
delete[] zombies;
zombies = createHorde(numZombies, arena);
numZombiesAlive = numZombies;

// Play the powerup sound
powerup.play();

// Reset the clock so there isn't a frame jump
clock.restart();
    }
}// End LEVELING up
```

The previous code starts by incrementing the wave variable. Then the code is amended to make the number of zombies and size of the arena relative to the new value of wave. Finally, we add the call to powerup.play() to play the leveling up sound effect.

Restarting the game

We already determine the size of the arena and the number of zombies by the value of the wave variable. We must also reset the ammo, gun, wave, and score to zero at the start of each new game. Find the following code in the event handling section of the game loop and add the highlighted code:

```
// Start a new game while in GAME_OVER state
else if (event.key.code == Keyboard::Return &&
```

```
            state == State::GAME_OVER)
    {
        state = State::LEVELING_UP;
        wave = 0;
        score = 0;

        // Prepare the gun and ammo for next game
        currentBullet = 0;
        bulletsSpare = 24;
        bulletsInClip = 6;
        clipSize = 6;
        fireRate = 1;

        // Reset the player's stats
        player.resetPlayerStats();
    }
```

Now we can play the game, the player can get ever more powerful and the zombies will get ever more numerous within an arena of increasing size – until he dies then it all starts again.

Playing the rest of the sounds

Now we will add the rest of the calls to the `play` function. We deal with each of them individually as locating exactly where they go is key to playing them at the right moment.

Adding sound effects while the player is reloading

Add the highlighted code in three places to play the appropriate `reload` or `reloadFailed` sound when the player presses the *R* key to attempt to reload their gun:

```
if (state == State::PLAYING)
{
    // Reloading
    if (event.key.code == Keyboard::R)
    {
        if (bulletsSpare >= clipSize)
        {
            // Plenty of bullets. Reload.
            bulletsInClip = clipSize;
            bulletsSpare -= clipSize;
            reload.play();
        }
```

```
        else if (bulletsSpare > 0)
        {
            // Only few bullets left
            bulletsInClip = bulletsSpare;
            bulletsSpare = 0;
            reload.play();
        }
        else
        {
            // More here soon?!
            reloadFailed.play();
        }
    }
}
```

Make a shooting sound

Add the highlighted call to `shoot.play()` near the end of the code that handles the player clicking the left mouse button:

```
// Fire a bullet
if (sf::Mouse::isButtonPressed(sf::Mouse::Left))
{

    if (gameTimeTotal.asMilliseconds()
        - lastPressed.asMilliseconds()
      > 1000 / fireRate && bulletsInClip > 0)
    {

        // Pass the centre of the player and crosshair
        // to the shoot function
        bullets[currentBullet].shoot(
            player.getCenter().x, player.getCenter().y,
            mouseWorldPosition.x, mouseWorldPosition.y);

        currentBullet++;
        if (currentBullet > 99)
        {
            currentBullet = 0;
        }
        lastPressed = gameTimeTotal;

        shoot.play();

        bulletsInClip--;
    }
```

```
}// End fire a bullet
```

Play a sound when the player is hit

In this next code, we wrap the call to hit.play in a test to see whether the player.hit function returns true. Remember that the player.hit function tests to see whether a hit has been recorded in the previous 100 milliseconds. This will have the effect of playing a fast, repeating, thudding sound, but not so fast that the sound blurs into one noise.

Add the call to hit.play, as highlighted here:

```
// Have any zombies touched the player
for (int i = 0; i < numZombies; i++)
{
    if (player.getPosition().intersects
        (zombies[i].getPosition()) && zombies[i].isAlive())
    {

        if (player.hit(gameTimeTotal))
        {
            // More here later
            hit.play();
        }

        if (player.getHealth() <= 0)
        {
            state = State::GAME_OVER;

            std::ofstream OutputFile("gamedata/scores.txt");
            OutputFile << hiScore;
            OutputFile.close();
        }
    }
}// End player touched
```

Play a sound when getting a pickup

When the player picks up a health pickup, we will play the regular pickup sound, but when the player gets an ammo pickup we play the reload sound effect.

Add the two calls to play sounds as highlighted here, within the appropriate collision detection code:

```
// Has the player touched health pickup
if (player.getPosition().intersects
    (healthPickup.getPosition()) && healthPickup.isSpawned())
{
    player.increaseHealthLevel(healthPickup.gotIt());
    // Play a sound
    pickup.play();
}

// Has the player touched ammo pickup
if (player.getPosition().intersects
    (ammoPickup.getPosition()) && ammoPickup.isSpawned())
{
    bulletsSpare += ammoPickup.gotIt();
    // Play a sound
    reload.play();
}
```

Make a splat sound when a zombie is shot

Add a call to `splat.play` at the end of the section of code that detects a bullet colliding with a zombie:

```
// Have any zombies been shot?
for (int i = 0; i < 100; i++)
{
    for (int j = 0; j < numZombies; j++)
    {
        if (bullets[i].isInFlight() &&
            zombies[j].isAlive())
        {
            if (bullets[i].getPosition().intersects
                (zombies[j].getPosition()))
            {
                // Stop the bullet
                bullets[i].stop();

                // Register the hit and see if it was a kill
                if (zombies[j].hit()) {
                    // Not just a hit but a kill too
                    score += 10;
                    if (score >= hiScore)
                    {
```

```
                hiScore = score;
            }

            numZombiesAlive--;

            // When all the zombies are dead (again)
            if (numZombiesAlive == 0) {
                state = State::LEVELING_UP;
            }
        }

        // Make a splat sound
        splat.play();
    }
}

}
}// End zombie being shot
```

You can now play the completed game and watch the number of zombies and the arena increase with each wave. Choose your level-ups carefully:

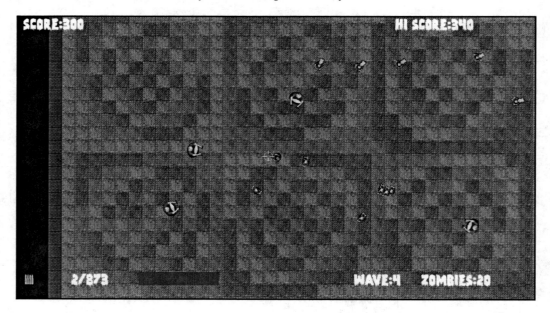

Congratulations!

FAQ

Here are some questions that might be on your mind:

Q) Despite using classes, I am finding that the code is getting really long and unmanageable, again.

A) One of the biggest issues is the structure of our code. As we learn more C++, we will also learn ways to make the code more manageable and generally less lengthy.

Q) The sound effects seem a bit flat and unrealistic. How can they be improved?

A) One way to significantly improve the feeling the player gets from sound is to make the sound directional, as well as change the volume based on the distance from the sound source to the player character. We will use SFML's advanced sound features in the next project.

Summary

We are finished with the Zombie Arena game. It has been quite a journey. We have learned a whole bunch of C++ fundamentals such as references, pointers, OOP, and classes. In addition, we have used SFML for managing cameras, vertex arrays, and collision detection as well. We learned how to use sprite sheets to reduce the number of calls to `window.draw` and speed up the frame rate. Using C++ pointers, the STL, and a little bit of OOP, we built a singleton class to manage our textures and in the next project we will extend this idea to manage all of our game's assets.

Coming up in the closing project of the book we will discover particle effects, directional sound, and split-screen multiplayer gaming. In C++, we will encounter inheritance, polymorphism, and a few more new concepts as well.

12
Abstraction and Code Management – Making Better Use of OOP

In this chapter, we will take a first look at the final project of the book. The project will have advanced features such as directional sound, which comes out of the speakers relative to the position of the player. It will also have split screen cooperative gameplay. In addition, this project will introduce the concept of **Shaders**, which are programs written in another language that run directly on the graphics card. By the end of Chapter 16, *Extending SFML Classes, Particle Systems, and Shaders*, you will have a fully functioning multiplayer platform game built in the style of the hit classic **Thomas Was Alone**.

This chapter's main focus will be getting the project started—in particular, exploring how the code will be structured to make better use of OOP. The following topics will be covered:

- An introduction to the final project, **Thomas Was Late**, including the gameplay features and project assets
- A detailed discussion of how we will improve the structure of the code compared to previous projects
- Coding the Thomas Was Late game engine
- Implementing split screen functionality

The Thomas Was Late game

At this point, if you haven't already, I would suggest you go and watch a video of Thomas Was Alone at `http://store.steampowered.com/app/220780/`. Notice the really simple but aesthetically excellent graphics. The video also shows a variety of gameplay challenges such as using the character's different attributes (height, jump, power, and so on). To keep our game simple without losing the challenge, we will have fewer puzzle features than Thomas Was Alone, but will have the additional challenge of creating the need for two players to play cooperatively. Just to make sure the game is not too easy, we will also make the players race against the clock, hence why the name of our game is Thomas Was Late.

Features of Thomas Was Late

Our game will not be nearly as advanced as the masterpiece that we are attempting to emulate, but it will have a good selection of exciting gameplay features:

- A clock that count downs from a time appropriate to the challenge of the level.
- Fire pits that emit a roar relative to the position of the player and re-spawn the player at the start if they fall in. Water pits have the same effect but without the directional sound effects.
- Cooperative gameplay—both the players will have to get their characters to the goal within the allotted time. They will frequently need to work together, for example the shorter, lower-jumping Bob will need to stand on his friend's (Thomas's) head.
- The player will have the option of switching between full and split screen, so he can attempt to control both characters himself.
- Each level will be designed in and loaded from a text file. This will make it really easy to design varied and numerous levels.

Take a look at this annotated screenshot of the game to see some of the features in action and the components/assets that make up the game:

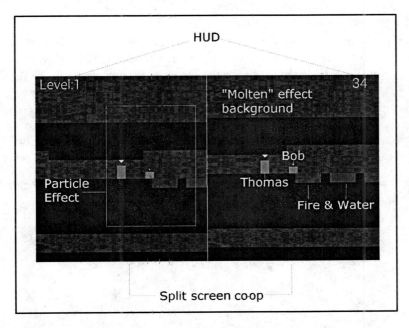

Let's look at each of those features and describe a few more:

- The screenshot shows a simple HUD that details the level number and the number of seconds remaining until the players fail and have to restart the level.
- You can also clearly see the split screen co-op in action. Remember that this is optional. A single player can take on the game, fullscreen, while switching the camera focus between Thomas and Bob.
- It is not very clear in the screenshot (especially in print), but when a character dies, he will explode in a starburst/firework-like particle effect.

- The water and fire tiles can be strategically placed to make the level fun and force cooperation between the characters. More on this in `Chapter 14`, *Building Playable Levels and Collision Detection.*
- Notice Thomas and Bob—not only are they different in heights, but they also have significantly different jumping abilities. This means that Bob is dependent upon Thomas for big jumps, and levels can be designed to force Thomas to take a route that avoids him banging his head.

- In addition, the fire tiles will emit a roaring sound. These will be relative to the position of Thomas. Not only will they be directional and come from either the left or right speaker, they will also get louder and quieter as Thomas moves closer or further away from the source.
- Finally, in the annotated screenshot, you can see the background. If you compare how that looks to the `background.png` file (shown later in this chapter), you will see it is quite different. We will use OpenGL shader effects in Chapter 16, *Extending SFML Classes, Particle Systems, and Shaders*, to achieve the moving—almost bubbling—effect in the background.

All those features warrant a few more screenshots so we can keep the finished product in mind as we write the C++ code.

The following screenshot shows Thomas and Bob arriving at a fire pit that Bob has no chance of jumping over without help:

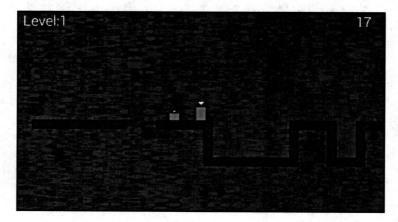

The following screenshot shows Bob and Thomas collaborating to clear a precarious jump:

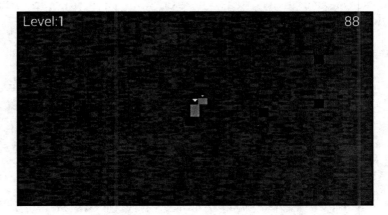

The following screenshot shows how we can design puzzles where a "leap of faith" is required in order to reach the goal:

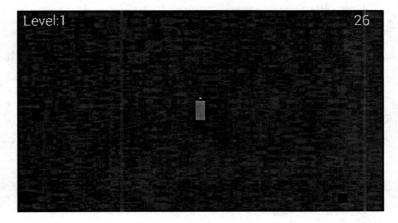

The following screenshot demonstrates how we can design oppressive cave systems of almost any size. We can also devise levels where Bob and Thomas are forced to split up and go different routes:

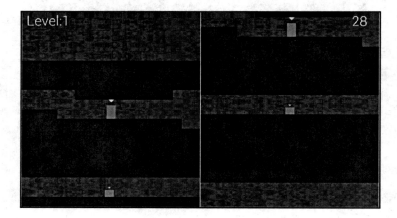

Creating a project from the template

Creating the Thomas Was Late project is the same as the other two projects. Just follow these straightforward steps in Visual Studio:

1. Select **File | New Project** from the main menu.
2. Make sure that **Visual C++** is selected in the left-hand menu and then select **HelloSFML** from the list of presented options. The following screenshot should make this clear:

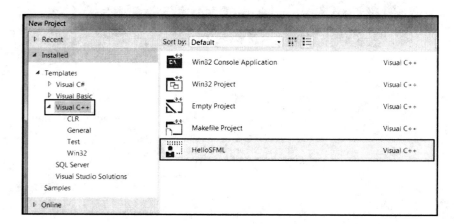

3. In the **Name:** field, type TWL and also make sure that the **Create directory for solution** option is checked. Now click **OK**.

4. Now we need to copy the SFML .dll files into the main project directory. My main project directory is D:\Visual Studio Stuff\Projects\ TWL\TWL. This folder was created by Visual Studio in the previous step. If you put your Projects folder somewhere else, perform this step there instead. The files we need to copy into the project folder are located in your SFML\bin folder. Open a window for each of the two locations and highlight the required .dll files.

5. Now copy and paste the highlighted files into the project.

The project is now set up and ready to go.

The project assets

The assets in this project are even more numerous and diverse than the Zombie Arena game. As usual, the assets include a font for the writing on the screen, sound effects for different actions such as jumping, reaching the goal, or the distant roar of fire, and, of course, graphics for Thomas and Bob as well as a sprite sheet for all the background tiles.

All the assets required for the game are included in the download bundle. They can be found in the Chapter 12/graphics and Chapter 12/sound folders, respectively.

The font that is required has not been supplied. This is because I wanted to avoid any possible ambiguity regarding the license. This will not cause a problem though, as I will show you exactly where and how to choose and download fonts for yourself.

Although I will provide either the assets themselves or information on where to get them, you might like to create and acquire them for yourself.

In addition to the graphics, sound, and fonts that we have come to expect, this game has two new asset types. They are level design files and GLSL shader programs. Let's find out about each of them next.

Game level designs

Levels are all created in a text file. By using the numbers 0 through 3, we can build level designs to challenge players. All the level designs are in the levels folder in the same directory as the other assets. Feel free to take a peek at one now, but we will look at them in detail in Chapter 14, *Building Playable Levels and Collision Detection*.

In addition to these level design assets, we have a special type of graphical asset, called shaders.

GLSL Shaders

Shaders are programs written in **GLSL (Graphics Library Shading Language)**. Don't worry about having to learn another language, as we don't need to get too in-depth to take advantage of shaders. Shaders are special, as they are entire programs, separate from our C++ code, which are executed by the GPU each and every frame. In fact, some of these shader programs are run every frame, for every pixel! We will find out more details in Chapter 16, *Extending SFML Classes, Particle Systems, and Shaders*. If you can't wait that long, take a look at the files in the Chapter 12/shaders folder of the download bundle.

The graphical assets close-up

The graphical assets make up the parts of the scene of our game. Take a look at the graphical assets and it should be clear where in our game they will be used:

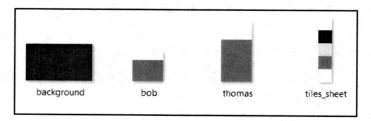

If the tiles on the tiles_sheet graphic look a little different to the screenshots of the game, this is because they are partly transparent and the background showing through changes them a little. If the background graphic looks totally different to the actual background in the game screenshots, that is because the shader programs we will write will manipulate each and every pixel, each and every frame, to create a kind of "molten" effect.

The sound assets close-up

The sound files are all `.wav` format. These are files that contain the sound effects we will play at certain events throughout the game. They are as follows:

- `fallinfire.wav`: A sound that will be played when the player's head goes into fire and the player has no chance of escape.
- `fallinwater.wav`: Water has the same end effect as fire: death. This sound effect notifies the player they need to start from the beginning of the level.
- `fire1.wav`: This sound effect is recorded in mono. It will be played at different volumes based on the player's distance from fire tiles, and from different speakers based on whether the player is to the left or the right of the fire tile. Clearly, we will need to learn a few more tricks to implement this functionality.
- `jump.wav`: A pleasing (slightly predictable) whooping sound for when the player jumps.
- `reachgoal.wav`: A pleasing victory sound for when the player (or players) gets both characters (Thomas and Bob) to the goal tile.

The sound effects are very straightforward and you can easily create your own. If you intend to replace the `fire1.wav` file, be sure to save your sound in a mono (not stereo) format. The reasons for this will be explained in `Chapter 15`, *Sound Spacialization and HUD*.

Adding the assets to the project

Once you have decided which assets you will use, it is time to add them to the project. The following instructions will assume you are using all the assets supplied in the book's download bundle.

Where you are using your own, simply replace the appropriate sound or graphic file with your chosen file, using exactly the same filename:

1. Browse to the Visual `D:\Visual Studio Stuff\Projects\TWL\TWL` directory.
2. Create five new folders within this folder and name them as `graphics`, `sound`, `fonts`, `shaders`, and `levels`.
3. From the download bundle, copy the entire contents of `Chapter 12/graphics` into the `D:\Visual Studio Stuff\Projects\TWL\TWL\graphics` folder.
4. From the download bundle, copy the entire contents of `Chapter 12/sound` into the `D:\Visual Studio Stuff\Projects\TWL\TWL\sound` folder.

5. Now visit `http://www.dafont.com/roboto.font` in your web browser and download the **Roboto Light** font.

6. Extract the contents of the zipped download and add the `Roboto-Light.ttf` file to the `D:\Visual Studio Stuff\Projects\TWL\TWL\fonts` folder.

7. From the download bundle, copy the entire contents of `Chapter 12/levels` into the `D:\Visual Studio Stuff\Projects\TWL\TWL\levels` folder.

8. From the download bundle, copy the entire contents of `Chapter 12/shaders` into the `D:\Visual Studio Stuff\Projects\TWL\TWL\shaders` folder.

Now that we have a new project, along with all the assets we will need for the entire project, we can talk about how we will structure the game engine code.

Structuring the Thomas Was Late code

One of the problems that has been quite pronounced in both projects so far is how long and unwieldy the code gets. OOP allows us to break our projects up into logical and manageable chunks called classes.

We will make a big improvement to the manageability of the code in this project with the introduction of an **Engine class**. Among other functions, the Engine class will have three private functions. They are `input`, `update`, and `draw`. This should sound very familiar. Each of these functions will hold a chunk of the code that was previously all in the `main` function. Each of these functions will be in a code file of its own, `Input.cpp`, `Update.cpp`, and `Draw.cpp` respectively.

There will also be one public function in the `Engine` class, which can be called with an instance of `Engine`. This function is `run` and will be responsible for calling `input`, `update`, and `draw`, once for each frame of the game:

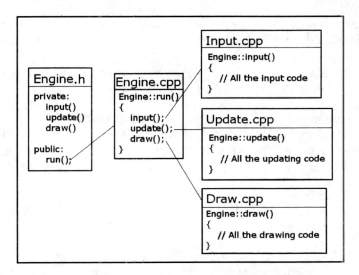

Furthermore, because we have abstracted the major parts of the game engine to the `Engine` class, we can also move many of the variables from `main` and make them members of `Engine`. All we need to do to get our game engine fired up is create an instance of `Engine` and call its `run` function. Here is a sneak preview of the super-simple main function:

```
int main()
{
    // Declare an instance of Engine
    Engine engine;

    // Start the engine
    engine.run();

    // Quit in the usual way when the engine is stopped
    return 0;
}
```

 Don't add the preceding code just yet.

To make our code even more manageable and readable, we will also abstract responsibility for big tasks, such as loading a level and collision detection, to separate functions (in separate code files). These two functions are `loadLevel` and `detectCollisions`. We will also code other functions to handle some of the new features of the Thomas Was Late project. We will cover them in detail as and when they occur.

To further take advantage of OOP, we will delegate responsibility for particular areas of the game entirely to new classes. You probably remember that the sound and HUD code was quite lengthy in previous projects. We will build a `SoundManager` and `HUD` class to handle these aspects in a cleaner manner. Exactly how they work will be explored in depth when we implement them.

The game levels themselves are much more in-depth than previous games, so we will also code a `LevelManager` class.

As you would expect, the playable characters will be made with classes as well. For this project, however, we will learn some more C++ and implement a `PlayableCharacter` class with all the common functionality of Thomas and Bob, and then `Thomas` and `Bob` classes, which will inherit this common functionality as well as implement their own unique functions and abilities. This, perhaps unsurprisingly, is called **inheritance**. I will go into more detail about inheritance in the following `Chapter 13`, *Advanced OOP, Inheritance, and Polymorphism*.

We will also implement a number of other classes to perform specific responsibilities. For example, we will make some neat explosions using particle systems. You might be able to guess that to do this, we will code a `Particle` class and a `ParticleSystem` class. All of these classes will have instances that are members of the `Engine` class. Doing things this way will make all the features of the game accessible from the game engine, but encapsulate the details into appropriate classes.

The last thing to mention before we move on to see the actual code that will make the Engine class is that we will reuse, without any changes whatsoever, the `TextureHolder` class, which we discussed and coded for the Zombie Arena game.

Building the game engine

As suggested in the previous discussion, we will code a class called `Engine` that will control and bind together the different parts of the Thomas Was Late game.

The first thing we will do is make the `TextureHolder` class from the previous project available in this one.

Reusing the TextureHolder class

The TextureHolder class that we discussed and coded for the Zombie Arena game will also be useful in this project. While it is possible to add the files (TextureHolder.h and TextureHolder.cpp) directly from the previous project without recoding them or recreating the files, I don't want to make the assumption that you haven't jumped straight to this project. What follows is very brief instructions, along with the complete code listing to create the TextureHolder class. If you want the class or the code explained, please see Chapter 8, *Pointers, Standard Template Library, and Texture Management*.

If you did complete the previous project and you *do* want to add the class from the Zombie Arena project, simply do the following: in the **Solution Explorer** window, right-click **Header Files** and select **Add | Existing Item…**. Browse to TextureHolder.h from the previous project and select it. In the **Solution Explorer** window, right-click on **Source Files** and select **Add | Existing Item…**. Browse to TextureHolder.cpp from the previous project and select it. You can now use the TextureHolder class in this project. Note that the files are shared between projects and any changes will take effect in both projects.

To create the TextureHolder class from scratch, right-click **Header Files** in the **Solution Explorer** and select **Add | New Item…**. In the **Add New Item** window, highlight (by left-clicking) **Header File (.h)** and then in the **Name** field, type TextureHolder.h. Finally, click the **Add** button.

Add the following code to TextureHolder.h:

```
#pragma once
#ifndef TEXTURE_HOLDER_H
#define TEXTURE_HOLDER_H

#include <SFML/Graphics.hpp>
#include <map>

class TextureHolder
{
private:
    // A map container from the STL,
    // that holds related pairs of String and Texture
    std::map<std::string, sf::Texture> m_Textures;

    // A pointer of the same type as the class itself
    // the one and only instance
    static TextureHolder* m_s_Instance;
```

```
public:
    TextureHolder();
    static sf::Texture& GetTexture(std::string const& filename);

};

#endif
```

Right-click **Source Files** in the **Solution Explorer** and select **Add | New Item….** In the **Add New Item** window, highlight (by left-clicking) **C++ File (**.cpp**)** and then, in the **Name** field, type TextureHolder.cpp. Finally, click the **Add** button.

Add the following code to TextureHolder.cpp:

```
#include "stdafx.h"
#include "TextureHolder.h"
#include <assert.h>

using namespace sf;
using namespace std;

TextureHolder* TextureHolder::m_s_Instance = nullptr;

TextureHolder::TextureHolder()
{
    assert(m_s_Instance == nullptr);
    m_s_Instance = this;
}

sf::Texture& TextureHolder::GetTexture(std::string const& filename)
{
    // Get a reference to m_Textures using m_S_Instance
    auto& m = m_s_Instance->m_Textures;
    // auto is the equivalent of map<string, Texture>

    // Create an iterator to hold a key-value-pair (kvp)
    // and search for the required kvp
    // using the passed in file name
    auto keyValuePair = m.find(filename);
    // auto is equivalent of map<string, Texture>::iterator


    // Did we find a match?
    if (keyValuePair != m.end())
    {
        // Yes
        // Return the texture,
        // the second part of the kvp, the texture
```

```
        return keyValuePair->second;
    }
    else
    {
        // File name not found
        // Create a new key value pair using the filename
        auto& texture = m[filename];
        // Load the texture from file in the usual way
        texture.loadFromFile(filename);

        // Return the texture to the calling code
        return texture;
    }
}
```

We can now get on with our new `Engine` class.

Coding Engine.h

As usual, we will start with the header file, which holds the function declarations and member variables. Note that we will revisit this file throughout the project to add more functions and member variables. For now, we will add just the code that is necessary at this stage.

Right-click **Header Files** in the **Solution Explorer** and select **Add | New Item...**. In the **Add New Item** window, highlight (by left-clicking) **Header File (**.h**)** and then in the **Name** field, type Engine.h. Finally, click the **Add** button. We are now ready to code the header file for the `Engine` class.

Add the following member variables as well as the function declarations. Many of them we have seen before in the other projects, and some of them we discussed in the *Structuring the Thomas Was Late* code section. Take note of the function and variable names, as well as whether they are private or public. Add the following code to the `Engine.h` file, and then we will talk about it:

```
#pragma once
#include <SFML/Graphics.hpp>
#include "TextureHolder.h"

using namespace sf;

class Engine
{
private:
```

```
// The texture holder
TextureHolder th;

const int TILE_SIZE = 50;
const int VERTS_IN_QUAD = 4;

// The force pushing the characters down
const int GRAVITY = 300;

// A regular RenderWindow
RenderWindow m_Window;

// The main Views
View m_MainView;
View m_LeftView;
View m_RightView;

// Three views for the background
View m_BGMainView;
View m_BGLeftView;
View m_BGRightView;

View m_HudView;

// Declare a sprite and a Texture
// for the background
Sprite m_BackgroundSprite;
Texture m_BackgroundTexture;

// Is the game currently playing?
bool m_Playing = false;

// Is character 1 or 2 the current focus?
bool m_Character1 = true;

// Start in fullscreen mode
bool m_SplitScreen = false;

// How much time is left in the current level
float m_TimeRemaining = 10;
Time m_GameTimeTotal;

// Is it time for a new/first level?
bool m_NewLevelRequired = true;
// Private functions for internal use only
void input();
void update(float dtAsSeconds);
void draw();
```

```
public:
    // The Engine constructor
    Engine();

    // Run will call all the private functions
    void run();

};
```

Here is a complete run-down of all the private variables and functions. Where appropriate, I spend a little longer on the explanation:

- `TextureHolder th`: The one and only instance of the `TextureHolder` class.
- `TILE_SIZE`: A useful constant to remind us that each tile in the sprite sheet is fifty pixels wide and fifty pixels high.
- `VERTS_IN_QUAD`: A useful constant to make our manipulation of a `VertexArray` less error prone. There are, in fact, four vertices in a quad. Now we can't forget it.
- `GRAVITY`: A constant `int` value representing the number of pixels by which the game characters will be pushed downward each second. This is quite a fun value to play with once the game is done. We initialize it to `300`, as this works well for our initial level designs.
- `m_Window`: The usual `RenderWindow` object, like we have had in all our projects.
- The SFML `View` objects, `m_MainView`, `m_LeftView`, `m_RightView`, `m_BGMainView`, `m_BGLeftView`, `m_BGRightView`, and `m_HudView`: The first three `View` objects are for the fullscreen view, and left and right split screen views of the game. We also have a separate SFML `View` object for each of those three, which will draw the background behind. The last `View` object, `m_HudView`, will be drawn on top of the appropriate combination of the other six views to display the score, the remaining time, and any messages to the players. Having seven different `View` objects might imply complexity, but when you see how we deal with them as the chapter progresses, you will see they are quite straightforward. We will have the whole split screen/fullscreen conundrum sorted out by the end of this chapter.
- `Sprite m_BackgroundSprite` and `Texture m_BackgroundTexture`: Somewhat predictably, this combination of SFML `Sprite` and `Texture` will be for showing and holding the background graphic from the graphics assets folder.
- `m_Playing`: This Boolean will keep the game engine informed about whether the level has started yet (by pressing the *Enter* key). The player does not have the option to pause the game once they have started it.

- `m_Character1`: When the screen is fullscreen, should it center on Thomas (m_Character1 = true), or Bob (m_Character1 = false)? Initially, it is initialized to true, to center on Thomas.

- `m_SplitScreen`: Is the game currently being played in split screen mode or not? We will use this variable to decide how exactly to use all the View objects we declared a few steps ago.

- `m_TimeRemaining` variable: This `float` variable holds how much time is remaining to get to the goal of the current level. In the previous code, it is set to `10` for the purposes of testing, until we actually get to set a specific time for each level.

- `m_GameTimeTotal` variable: This variable is an SFML Time object. It keeps track of how long the game has been played for.

- `m_NewLevelRequired` Boolean variable: This variable keeps a check on whether the player has just completed or failed a level. We can then use it to trigger the loading of the next level or the restarting of the current level.

- The `input` function: This function will handle all of the player's input, which in this game is entirely from the keyboard. At first glance, it would appear that it handles all the keyboard input directly. In this game, however, we will be handling keyboard input that directly affects Thomas or Bob within the `Thomas` and `Bob` classes directly. We will call the `input` function, and this function will directly handle keyboard inputs such as quitting, switching to split screen, and any other keyboard input.

- The `update` function: This function will do all the work that we previously did in the update section of the `main` function. We will also call some other functions from the `update` function in order to keep the code organized. If you look back at the code, you will see that it receives a `float` parameter, which will hold the fraction of a second that has passed since the previous frame. This, of course, is just what we need to update all our game objects.

- The `draw` function: This function will hold all the code that used to go in the drawing section of the main function in previous projects. We will, however, have some drawing code that is not kept in this function when we look at other ways to draw with SFML. We will see this new code when we learn about particle systems in Chapter 16, *Extending SFML Classes, Particle Systems, and Shaders*.

Now let's run through all the public functions:

- The `Engine` constructor function: As we have come to expect, this function will be called when we first declare an instance of `Engine`. It will do all the setup and initialization of the class. We will see exactly what when we code the `Engine.cpp` file shortly.
- The `run` function: This is the only public function that we need to call. It will trigger the execution of input, update, and draw, which will do all the work.

Next, we will see the definition of all these functions and some of the variables in action.

Coding Engine.cpp

In all our previous classes, we have put all the function definitions into the `.cpp` file, prefixed with the class name. As our aim for this project is to make the code more manageable, we are doing things a little differently.

In the `Engine.cpp` file, we will put the constructor (`Engine`) and the public `run` function. All the rest of the functions will go in their own `.cpp` file, with a name that makes it clear what function goes where. This will not be a problem for the compiler as long as we add the appropriate include directive (`#include "Engine.h"`) at the top of all the files that contain function definitions from the `Engine` class.

Let's get started by coding `Engine` and run it in `Engine.cpp`. Right-click **Source Files** in the **Solution Explorer** and select **Add | New Item...**. In the **Add New Item** window, highlight (by left-clicking) **C++ File (.cpp)** and then in the **Name** field, type `Engine.cpp`. Finally, click the **Add** button. We are now ready to code the `.cpp` file for the `Engine` class.

Coding the Engine class constructor definition

The code for this function will go in the `Engine.cpp` file we have recently created.

Add the following code and then we can discuss it:

```
#include "stdafx.h"
#include "Engine.h"

Engine::Engine()
{
    // Get the screen resolution
    // and create an SFML window and View
```

```
        Vector2f resolution;
        resolution.x = VideoMode::getDesktopMode().width;
        resolution.y = VideoMode::getDesktopMode().height;

        m_Window.create(VideoMode(resolution.x, resolution.y),
            "Thomas was late",
            Style::Fullscreen);

        // Initialize the fullscreen view
        m_MainView.setSize(resolution);
        m_HudView.reset(
            FloatRect(0, 0, resolution.x, resolution.y));

        // Initialize the split screen Views
        m_LeftView.setViewport(
            FloatRect(0.001f, 0.001f, 0.498f, 0.998f));

        m_RightView.setViewport(
            FloatRect(0.5f, 0.001f, 0.499f, 0.998f));

        m_BGLeftView.setViewport(
            FloatRect(0.001f, 0.001f, 0.498f, 0.998f));

        m_BGRightView.setViewport(
            FloatRect(0.5f, 0.001f, 0.499f, 0.998f));
        m_BackgroundTexture = TextureHolder::GetTexture(
            "graphics/background.png");

        // Associate the sprite with the texture
        m_BackgroundSprite.setTexture(m_BackgroundTexture);

    }
```

Much of the code we have seen before. For example, there are the usual lines of code to get the screen resolution as well as to create a RenderWindow. At the end of the previous code we use the now familiar code to load a texture and assign it to a Sprite. In this case we are loading the background.png texture and assigning it to m_BackgroundSprite.

It is the code in between, the four calls to the setViewport function, that needs some explanation. The setViewport function assigns a portion of the screen to an SFML View object. It doesn't work using pixel coordinates, however. It works using a ratio. Where "1" is the entire screen (width or height), the first two values in each call to setViewport are the starting position (horizontally, then vertically) and the last two are the ending position.

Notice that the m_LeftView and m_BGLeftView are placed in exactly the same place, starting at virtually the far left (0.001) of the screen, and ending two 1,000ths from the center (0.498).

The m_RightView and m_BGRightView are also in exactly the same position, starting just left of the previous two View objects (0.5) and extending to almost the far right-hand side (0.998) of the screen.

Furthermore, all the views leave a tiny sliver of a gap at the top and bottom of the screen. When we draw these View objects on the screen on top of a white background, it will have the effect of splitting the screen with a thin white line between the two sides of the screen, as well as a thin white border around the edges.

I have tried to represent this effect in the following diagram:

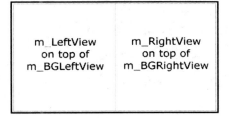

The best way to understand it is to finish this chapter, run the code, and see it in action.

Coding the run function definition

The code for this function will go in the Engine.cpp file we have recently created.

Add the following code immediately after the previous constructor code:

```
void Engine::run()
{
    // Timing
    Clock clock;

    while (m_Window.isOpen())
    {
        Time dt = clock.restart();
        // Update the total game time
        m_GameTimeTotal += dt;
        // Make a decimal fraction from the delta time
        float dtAsSeconds = dt.asSeconds();
```

```
        // Call each part of the game loop in turn
        input();
        update(dtAsSeconds);
        draw();
    }
}
```

The run function is the center of our engine—it initiates all the other parts. First, we declare a Clock object. Next, we have the familiar `while(window.isOpen())` loop, which creates the game loop. Inside this while loop, we do the following:

1. Restart `clock` and save the time that the previous loop took in `dt`.
2. Keep track of the total time elapsed in `m_GameTimeTotal`.
3. Declare and initialize a `float` to represent the fraction of a second that elapsed during the previous frame.
4. Call `input`.
5. Call `update` passing in the elapsed time (`dtAsSeconds`).
6. Call `draw`.

All of this should look very familiar. What is new is that it is wrapped in the `run` function.

Coding the input function definition

As explained previously, the code for this function will go in its own file because it is more extensive than the constructor or the `run` function. We will use `#include "Engine.h"` and prefix the function signature with `Engine::` to make sure the compiler is aware of our intentions.

Right-click **Source Files** in the **Solution Explorer** and select **Add** | **New Item...**. In the **Add New Item** window, highlight (by left-clicking) **C++ File (.cpp)** and then in the **Name** field, type `Input.cpp`. Finally, click the **Add** button. We are now ready to code the `input` function.

Add the following code:

```
void Engine::input()
{
    Event event;
    while (m_Window.pollEvent(event))
    {
        if (event.type == Event::KeyPressed)
        {
```

```
    // Handle the player quitting
    if (Keyboard::isKeyPressed(Keyboard::Escape))
    {
        m_Window.close();
    }

    // Handle the player starting the game
    if (Keyboard::isKeyPressed(Keyboard::Return))
    {
        m_Playing = true;
    }

    // Switch between Thomas and Bob
    if (Keyboard::isKeyPressed(Keyboard::Q))
    {
        m_Character1 = !m_Character1;
    }

    // Switch between full and split screen
    if (Keyboard::isKeyPressed(Keyboard::E))
    {
        m_SplitScreen = !m_SplitScreen;
    }
    }
    }
    }
```

As with both of the previous projects, we check the RenderWindow event queue each frame. Also, as we have done before, we detect specific keyboard keys using if (Keyboard::isKeyPressed(Keyboard::E)). What is most relevant in the code we just added is what the keys actually do:

- As usual, the *Esc* key closes the window and the game will quit.
- The *Enter* key sets m_Playing to true, and eventually, this will have the effect of starting the level.
- The *Q* key alternates the value of m_Character1 between true and false. This key only has an effect in fullscreen mode. It will switch between Thomas and Bob being the center of the main View.
- The *E* key switches m_SplitScreen between true and false. This will have the effect of switching between fullscreen and split screen views.

The majority of this keyboard functionality will be fully working by the end of the chapter. We are getting close to being able to run our game engine. Next, let's code the `update` function.

Coding the update function definition

As explained previously, the code for this function will go in its own file because it is more extensive than the constructor or the `run` function. We will use `#include "Engine.h"` and prefix the function signature with `Engine::` to make sure the compiler is aware of our intentions.

Right-click **Source Files** in the **Solution Explorer** and select **Add** | **New Item…**. In the **Add New Item** window, highlight (by left-clicking) **C++ File (**.cpp**)** and then in the **Name** field, type `Update.cpp`. Finally, click the **Add** button. We are now ready to write some code for the `update` function.

Add the following code to the `Update.cpp` file to implement the `update` function:

```cpp
#include "stdafx.h"
#include "Engine.h"
#include <SFML/Graphics.hpp>
#include <sstream>

using namespace sf;

void Engine::update(float dtAsSeconds)
{

    if (m_Playing)
    {
        // Count down the time the player has left
        m_TimeRemaining -= dtAsSeconds;

        // Have Thomas and Bob run out of time?
        if (m_TimeRemaining <= 0)
        {
            m_NewLevelRequired = true;
        }

    }// End if playing
}
```

First of all, notice that the `update` function receives the time the previous frame took as a parameter. This, of course, will be essential for the update function to fulfill its role.

The preceding code doesn't achieve anything visible at this stage. It does put in the structure that we will require for future chapters. It subtracts the time the previous frame took from `m_TimeRemaining`. It checks whether time has run out, and if it has, it sets `m_NewLevelRequired` to `true`. All this code is wrapped in an `if` statement that only executes when `m_Playing` is `true`. The reason for this is because, as with the previous projects, we don't want time advancing and objects updating when the game has not started.

We will build on this code as the project continues.

Coding the draw function definition

As explained previously, the code for this function will go in its own file, because it is more extensive than the constructor or the `run` function. We will use `#include "Engine.h"` and prefix the function signature with `Engine::` to make sure the compiler is aware of our intentions.

Right-click **Source Files** in the **Solution Explorer** and select **Add | New Item....** In the **Add New Item** window, highlight (by left-clicking) **C++ File (.**cpp**)** and then in the **Name** field, type `Draw.cpp`. Finally, click the **Add** button. We are now ready to add some code to the `draw` function.

Add the following code to the `Draw.cpp` file to implement the `draw` function:

```cpp
#include "stdafx.h"
#include "Engine.h"

void Engine::draw()
{
    // Rub out the last frame
    m_Window.clear(Color::White);

    if (!m_SplitScreen)
    {
        // Switch to background view
        m_Window.setView(m_BGMainView);
        // Draw the background
        m_Window.draw(m_BackgroundSprite);
        // Switch to m_MainView
        m_Window.setView(m_MainView);
    }
```

```
        else
        {
            // Split screen view is active

            // First draw Thomas' side of the screen

            // Switch to background view
            m_Window.setView(m_BGLeftView);
            // Draw the background
            m_Window.draw(m_BackgroundSprite);
            // Switch to m_LeftView
            m_Window.setView(m_LeftView);
            // Now draw Bob's side of the screen

            // Switch to background view
            m_Window.setView(m_BGRightView);
            // Draw the background
            m_Window.draw(m_BackgroundSprite);
            // Switch to m_RightView
            m_Window.setView(m_RightView);
        }

        // Draw the HUD
        // Switch to m_HudView
        m_Window.setView(m_HudView);
        // Show everything we have just drawn
        m_Window.display();
    }
```

In the preceding code, there is nothing we haven't seen before. The code starts, as usual, by clearing the screen. In this project, we clear the screen with white. What is new is the way the different drawing options are separated by a condition, which checks whether the screen is currently split or full:

```
if (!m_SplitScreen)
{
}
else
{
}
```

If the screen is not split, we draw the background sprite in the background View (m_BGView) and then switch to the main fullscreen View (m_MainView). Note that at the moment, we don't actually do any drawing in m_MainView.

If, on the other hand, the screen is split, the code in the `else` block is executed and we draw `m_BGLeftView` with the background sprite on the left of the screen, followed by switching to `m_LeftView`.

Then, still in the `else` block, we draw `m_BGRightView` with the background sprite on the right of the screen, followed by switching to `m_RightView`.

Outside of the `if...else` structure just described, we switch to `m_HUDView`. At this stage, we are not actually drawing anything in `m_HUDView`.

As with the other two (`input`, `update`) of the three most significant functions, we will be back here at the `draw` function often. We will add new elements of our game that need to be drawn. You will notice that each time we do, we will add code into each of the main, left, and right sections.

Let's quickly recap the `Engine` class and then we can fire it up.

The Engine class so far

What we have achieved is the abstraction of all the code that used to be in the `main` function into the `input`, `update`, and `draw` functions. The continuous looping of these functions, as well as the timing, is handled by the `run` function.

Consider leaving the **Input.cpp**, **Update.cpp**, and **Draw.cpp** tabs open in Visual Studio, perhaps organized in order, as shown in the following screenshot:

We will revisit each of these functions throughout the course of the project to add more code. Now that we have the basic structure and functionality of the `Engine` class, we can create an instance of it in the `main` function and see it in action.

Coding the main function

Let's rename the HelloSFML.cpp file as Main.cpp. Right-click on the HelloSFML file in the **Solution Explorer** and select **Rename**. Change the name to Main.cpp. This will be the file that contains our main function and the code that instantiates the Engine class.

Add the following code to Main.cpp:

```
#include "stdafx.h"
#include "Engine.h"

int main()
{
    // Declare an instance of Engine
    Engine engine;

    // Start the engine VRRrrrrmmm
    engine.run();

    // Quit in the usual way when the engine is stopped
    return 0;
}
```

All we do is add an include directive for the Engine class, declare an instance of Engine, then call its run function. Everything will be handled by the Engine class until the player quits and the execution returns to main and the return 0 statement.

That was easy. Now we can run the game and see the empty background, either fullscreen or split screen, which will eventually contain all the action.

Here is the game so far, in fullscreen mode, showing just the background:

Now tap the *E* key, and you will be able to see the screen neatly partitioned into two halves, ready for split screen co-op gameplay:

Here are some questions that might be on your mind.

FAQ

Q) I don't fully understand the structure of the code files.

A) It is true that abstraction can make the structure of our code less clear, but the actual code itself becomes so much easier. Instead of cramming everything into the main function as we did in previous projects, we will split the code up into `Input.cpp`, `Update.cpp`, and `Draw.cpp`. Furthermore, we will use more classes to group together related code as we proceed. Study the Structuring the Thomas Was Late code section again, especially the diagrams.

Summary

In this chapter, we introduced the Thomas Was Late game and laid the foundations of understanding, as well as the code structure, for the rest of the project. It is certainly true that there are a lot of files in the Solution Explorer, but as long as we understand the purpose of each we will find the implementation of the rest of the project much more easy going.

In the following chapter, we will learn two more fundamental C++ topics, inheritance and polymorphism. We will also begin to put them to use, building three classes to represent two playable characters.

13

Advanced OOP – Inheritance and Polymorphism

In this chapter, we will further extend our knowledge of OOP by looking at the slightly more advanced concepts of **inheritance** and **polymorphism**. We will then be able to use this new knowledge to implement the star characters of our game, Thomas and Bob. Here is what we will cover in this chapter in a little more detail:

- How to extend and modify a class using inheritance?
- Treating an object of a class as if it is more than one type of class by using polymorphism
- Abstract classes and how designing classes that are never instantiated can actually be useful
- Building an abstract `PlayableCharacter` class
- Puting inheritance to work with `Thomas` and `Bob` classes
- Adding Thomas and Bob to the game project

Inheritance

We have seen how we can use other people's hard work by instantiating/creating objects from the classes of the SFML library. But this whole OOP thing goes even further than that.

What if there is a class that has loads of useful functionality in it, but is not quite what we want? In this situation we can **inherit** from the other class. Just like it sounds, **inheritance** means we can harness all the features and benefits of other people's classes, including the encapsulation, while further refining or extending the code specifically to our situation. In this project, we will inherit from and extend some SFML classes. We will also do so with our own classes.

Let's look at some code that uses inheritance,

Extending a class

With all this in mind, let's look at an example class and see how we can extend it, just to see the syntax and as a first step.

First, we define a class to inherit from. This is no different from how we created any of our other classes. Take a look at this hypothetical `Soldier` class declaration:

```
class Soldier
{
    private:
        // How much damage can the soldier take
        int m_Health;
        int m_Armour;
        int m_Range;
        int m_ShotPower;
    Public:
        void setHealth(int h);
        void setArmour(int a);
        void setRange(int r);
        void setShotPower(int p);
};
```

In the previous code, we define a `Soldier` class. It has four private variables, `m_Health`, `m_Armour`, `m_Range`, and `m_ShotPower`. It has four public functions `setHealth`, `setArmour`, `setRange`, and `setShotPower`. We don't need to see the definition of the functions, they will simply initialize the appropriate variable that their name makes obvious.

We can also imagine that a fully implemented `Soldier` class would be much more in-depth than this. It would probably have functions such as `shoot`, `goProne`, and others. If we implemented a `Soldier` class in an SFML project, it would likely have a `Sprite` object, as well as an `update` and a `getPostion` function.

The simple scenario presented here is suitable for learning about inheritance. Now let's look at something new, actually inheriting from the `Soldier` class. Look at this code, especially the highlighted part:

```
class Sniper : public Soldier
{
public:
    // A constructor specific to Sniper
    Sniper::Sniper();
};
```

By adding the : `public Soldier` code to the `Sniper` class declaration, `Sniper` inherits from `Soldier`. But what does this mean, exactly? `Sniper` is a `Soldier`. It has all the variables and functions of `Soldier`. Inheritance is more than this, however.

Notice also that in the previous code, we declare a `Sniper` constructor. This constructor is unique to `Sniper`. We have not only inherited from`Soldier`, we have **extended** `Soldier`. All the functionality (definitions) of the `Soldier` class are handled by the `Soldier` class, but the definition of the `Sniper` constructor must be handled by the `Sniper` class.

This is what the hypothetical `Sniper` constructor definition might look like:

```
// In Sniper.cpp
Sniper::Sniper()
{
    setHealth(10);
    setArmour(10);
    setRange(1000);
    setShotPower(100);
}
```

We could go ahead and write a bunch of other classes that are an extension of the `Soldier` class, perhaps `Commando` and `Infantryman`. Each would have the exact same variables and functions, but each could also have a unique constructor that initializes those variables appropriate to the type of `Soldier`. `Commando` might have very high `m_Health` and `m_ShotPower` but really puny `m_Range`. `Infantryman` might be in between `Commando` and `Sniper`, with mediocre values for each variable.

As if OOP were not useful enough already, we can now model real-world objects, including their hierarchies. We achieve this by sub-classing, extending, and inheriting from other classes.

The terminology we might like to learn here is that the class that is extended from is the **super-class**, and the class that inherits from the super-class is the **sub-class**. We can also say **parent** and **child** class.

You might find yourself asking this question about inheritance: Why? The reason is something like this: we can write common code once; in the parent class, we can update that common code and all classes that inherit from it are also updated. Furthermore, a sub-class only gets to use public and **protected** instance variables and functions. So, designed properly, this also further enhances the goals of encapsulation.

Did you say protected? Yes. There is an access specifier for class variables and functions called **protected**. You can think of protected variables as being somewhere between public and private. Here is a quick summary of access specifiers, along with more details about the protected specifier:

- Public variables and functions can be accessed and used by anyone.
- Private variables and functions can only be accessed/used by the internal code of the class. This is good for encapsulation, and when we need to access/change private variables, we can provide public getter and setter functions (such as getSprite and so on). If we extend a class that has private variables and functions, that child class *cannot* directly access the private data of its parent.
- Protected variables and functions are almost the same as private. They cannot be accessed/used directly by an instance of the class. However, they *can* be used directly by any class that extends the class they are declared in. So it is like they are private, except to child classes.

To fully understand what protected variables and functions are and how they can be useful, let's look at another topic first and then we can see them in action.

Polymorphism

Polymorphism allows us to write code that is less dependent on the types we are trying to manipulate. This can make our code clearer and more efficient. Polymorphism means different forms. If the objects that we code can be more than one type of thing, then we can take advantage of this.

What does polymorphism mean to us? Boiled down to its simplest definition, polymorphism is this: any sub-class can be used as part of the code that uses the super-class. This means we can write code that is simpler and easier to understand and also easier to modify or change. Also, we can write code for the super-class and rely on the fact that no matter how many times it is sub-classed, within certain parameters, the code will still work.

Let's discuss an example.

Suppose we want to use polymorphism to help write a zoo management game where we have to feed and tend to the needs of animals. We will probably want to have a function such as `feed`. We will also probably want to pass an instance of the Animal to be fed into the `feed` function.

A zoo, of course, has lots of types of animal—`Lion`, `Elephant`, and `ThreeToedSloth`. With our new knowledge of C++ inheritance, it will make sense to code an `Animal` class and have all the different types of animal inherit from it.

If we want to write a function (`feed`) that we can pass Lion, Elephant, and ThreeToedSloth into as a parameter, it might seem like we need to write a `feed` function for each and every type of `Animal`. However, we can write polymorphic functions, with polymorphic return types and arguments. Take a look at this definition of the hypothetical `feed` function:

```
void feed(Animal& a)
{
    a.decreaseHunger();
}
```

The preceding function has the `Animal` reference as a parameter, meaning that any object that is built from a class that extends `Animal` can be passed into it.

So, you can even write code today and make another sub-class in a week, month, or year, and the very same functions and data structures will still work. Also, we can enforce upon our sub-classes a set of rules for what they can and cannot do, as well as how they do it. So, good design in one stage can influence it at other stages.

But will we ever really want to instantiate an actual Animal?

Abstract classes – virtual and pure virtual functions

An **abstract class** is a class that cannot be instantiated and therefore cannot be made into an object.

 Some terminology we might like to learn here is concrete class. A **concrete class** is any class that isn't abstract. In other words, all the classes we have written so far have been concrete classes and can be instantiated into usable objects.

So, it's code that will never be used, then? But that's like paying an architect to design your home and then never building it!

If we, or the designer of a class, want to force its users to inherit it before using their class, they can make a class **abstract**. Then, we cannot make an object from it; therefore, we must extend it first and make an object from the sub-class.

To do so, we can make a function **pure virtual** and not provide any definition. Then that function must be **overridden** (re-written) in any class that extends it.

Let's look at an example; it will help. We make a class abstract by adding a pure virtual function such as this abstract `Animal` class that can only perform the generic action of makeNoise:

```
Class Animal
    private:
        // Private stuff here

    public:

        void virtual makeNoise() = 0;

        // More public stuff here
};
```

As you can see, we add the C++ keyword, `virtual`, before, and `= 0` after the function declaration. Now, any class that extends/inherits from `Animal` must override the `makeNoise` function. This might make sense, since different types of animal make very different types of noise. We could perhaps have assumed that anybody who extends the `Animal` class is smart enough to notice that the `Animal` class cannot make a noise and that they will need to handle it, but what if they don't notice? The point is that by making a pure virtual function we guarantee that they will, because they have to.

Abstract classes are also useful because sometimes, we want a class that can be used as a polymorphic type, but we need to guarantee it can never be used as an object. For example, `Animal` doesn't really make sense on its own. We don't talk about animals; we talk about types of animal. We don't say, *"Ooh, look at that lovely, fluffy, white animal!"* or, *"Yesterday we went to the pet shop and got an animal and an animal bed"*. It's just too, well, abstract.

So, an abstract class is kind of like a **template** to be used by any class that extends it (inherits from it). If we were building an *Industrial Empire*-type game where the player manages businesses and their employees, we might want a `Worker` class, for example, and extend it to make `Miner`, `Steelworker`, `OfficeWorker`, and, of course, `Programmer`. But what exactly does a plain `Worker` do? Why would we ever want to instantiate one?

The answer is we wouldn't want to instantiate one, but we might want to use it as a polymorphic type so we can pass multiple `Worker` sub-classes between functions and have data structures that can hold all types of workers.

All pure virtual functions must be overridden by any class that extends the parent class that contains the pure virtual function. This means that the abstract class can provide some of the common functionality that would be available in all its sub-classes. For example, the `Worker` class might have the `m_AnnualSalary`, `m_Productivity`, and `m_Age` member variables. It might also have the `getPayCheck` function, which is not pure virtual and is the same in all the sub-classes, but it might have a `doWork` function, which is pure virtual and must be overridden, because all the different types of `Worker` will `doWork` very differently.

 By the way, **virtual**, as opposed to pure virtual, is a function that can be **optionally overridden**. You declare a virtual function the same way as a pure virtual function, but leave the `= 0` off the end. In the current game project, we will use a pure virtual function.

If any of this virtual, pure virtual, or abstract stuff is unclear, using it is probably the best way to understand it.

Building the PlayableCharacter class

Now we know the basics about inheritance, polymorphism, and pure virtual functions, we will put them to use. We will build a `PlayableCharacter` class that has the vast majority of the functionality that any character from our game is going to need. It will have one pure virtual function, `handleInput`. The `handleInput` function will need to be quite different in the sub-classes, so this makes sense.

As `PlayableCharacter` will have a pure virtual function, it will be an abstract class and no objects of it will be possible. We will then build both `Thomas` and `Bob` classes, which will inherit from `PlayableCharacter`, implement the definition of the pure virtual function, and allow us to instantiate `Bob` and `Thomas` objects in our game.

Coding PlayableCharacter.h

As usual, when creating a class, we will start off with the header file that will contain the member variables and function declarations. What is new is that in this class, we will declare some **protected** member variables. Remember that protected variables can be used as if they are `Public` by classes, which inherit from the class with the protected variables.

Right-click **Header Files** in the **Solution Explorer** and select **Add | New Item....** In the **Add New Item** window, highlight (by left-clicking) **Header File (.h)** and then in the **Name** field, type `PlayableCharacter.h`. Finally, click the **Add** button. We are now ready to code the header file for the `PlayableCharacter` class.

We will add and discuss the contents of the `PlayableCharacter.h` file in three sections. First, the **protected** section, followed by **private**, then **public**.

Add the code shown next to the `PlayableCharacter.h` file:

```
#pragma once
#include <SFML/Graphics.hpp>

using namespace sf;

class PlayableCharacter
{
protected:
    // Of course we will need a sprite
    Sprite m_Sprite;

    // How long does a jump last
    float m_JumpDuration;
```

```
// Is character currently jumping or falling
bool m_IsJumping;
bool m_IsFalling;

// Which directions is the character currently moving in
bool m_LeftPressed;
bool m_RightPressed;

// How long has this jump lasted so far
float m_TimeThisJump;

// Has the player just initialted a jump
bool m_JustJumped = false;

// Private variables and functions come next
```

The first thing to notice in the code we just wrote is that all the variables are `protected`. This means that when we extend the class, all the variables we just wrote will be accessible to those classes that extend it. We will extend this class with `Thomas` and `Bob` classes.

Apart from the `protected` access specification, there is nothing new or complicated about the previous code. It is worth paying attention to some of the details, however. Then it will be easy to understand how the class works as we progress. So, let's run through those `protected` variables, one at a time.

We have our somewhat predictable `Sprite`, `m_Sprite`. We have a float called `m_JumpDuration`, which will hold a value representing the time that the character is able to jump for. The greater the value, the further/higher the character will be able to jump.

Next, we have a Boolean, `m_IsJumping`, which is `true` when the character is jumping and `false` otherwise. This will be useful for making sure that the character can't jump while in mid-air.

The `m_IsFalling` variable has a similar use to `m_IsJumping`. It will be useful to know when a character is falling.

Next, we have two Booleans that will be true if the character's left or right keyboard buttons are currently being pressed. These are relative depending upon the character (*A* and *D* for Thomas, Left and Right arrow keys for Bob). How we respond to these Booleans will be seen in the `Thomas` and `Bob` classes.

The m_TimeThisJump **float variable is updated each and every frame that** m_IsJumping **is** true. **We can then know when** m_JumpDuration **has been reached.**

The final protected **variable is the Boolean** m_JustJumped. **This will be** true **if a jump was initiated in the current frame. It will be useful for knowing when to play a jump sound effect.**

Next, add the following private **variables to the** PlayableCharacter.h **file:**

```
private:
    // What is the gravity
    float m_Gravity;

    // How fast is the character
    float m_Speed = 400;

    // Where is the player
    Vector2f m_Position;

    // Where are the characters various body parts?
    FloatRect m_Feet;
    FloatRect m_Head;
    FloatRect m_Right;
    FloatRect m_Left;

    // And a texture
    Texture m_Texture;

    // All our public functions will come next
```

In the previous code, we have some interesting private **variables. Remember that these variables will only be directly accessible to the code in the** PlayableCharacter **class. The** Thomas **and** Bob **classes will not be able to access them directly.**

The m_Gravity **variable will hold the number of pixels per second that the character will fall. The** m_Speed **variable will hold the number of pixels per second that the character can move left or right.**

The Vector2f, m_Position **variable is the position in the world (not the screen) where the center of the character is.**

The next four `FloatRect` objects are important to discuss. When we did collision detection in the *Zombie Arena* game, we simply checked to see if two `FloatRect` objects intersected. Each `FloatRect` object represented an entire character, a pick-up, or a bullet. For the non-rectangular shaped objects (zombies and the player), this was a little bit inaccurate.

In this game, we will need to be more precise. The `m_Feet`, `m_Head`, `m_Right`, and `m_Left` `FloatRect` objects will hold the coordinates of the different parts of a character's body. These coordinates will be updated in each and every frame.

Through these coordinates, we will be able to tell exactly when a character lands on a platform, bumps his head during a jump, or rubs shoulders with a tile to his side.

Lastly, we have `Texture`. `Texture` is `private` as it is not used directly by the `Thomas` or `Bob` classes but, as we saw, `Sprite` is `protected` because it is used directly.

Now add all the `public` functions to the `PlayableCharacter.h` file and then we will discuss them:

```
public:

    void spawn(Vector2f startPosition, float gravity);

    // This is a pure virtual function
    bool virtual handleInput() = 0;
    // This class is now abstract and cannot be instanciated

    // Where is the player
    FloatRect getPosition();

    // A rectangle representing the position
    // of different parts of the sprite
    FloatRect getFeet();
    FloatRect getHead();
    FloatRect getRight();
    FloatRect getLeft();

    // Send a copy of the sprite to main
    Sprite getSprite();

    // Make the character stand firm
    void stopFalling(float position);
    void stopRight(float position);
    void stopLeft(float position);
    void stopJump();

    // Where is the center of the character
```

```
        Vector2f getCenter();

    // We will call this function once every frame
    void update(float elapsedTime);
};// End of the class
```

Let's talk about each of the function declarations that we just added. This will make coding their definitions easier to follow.

- The `spawn` function receives a `Vector2f` called `startPosition` and a `float` called `gravity`. As the names suggest, `startPosition` will be the coordinates in the level at which the character will start and `gravity` will be the number of pixels per second at which the character will fall.

- The `bool virtual handleInput() = 0` is, of course, our pure virtual function. As `PlayableCharacter` has this function, any class that extends it, if we want to instantiate it, must provide a definition for this function. Therefore, when we write all the function definitions for `PlayableCharacter` in a minute, we will not provide a definition for `handleInput`. There will of course need to be definitions in both the `Thomas` and `Bob` classes.

- The `getPosition` function returns a `FloatRect` that represents the position of the whole character.

- The `getFeet()` function, as well as `getHead`, `getRight`, and `getLeft`, each return a `FloatRect` that represents the location of a specific part of the character's body. This is just what we need for detailed collision detection.

- The `getSprite` function, as usual, returns a copy of `m_Sprite` to the calling code.

- The `stopFalling`, `stopRight`, `stopLeft`, and `stopJump` function receive a single `float` value, which the function will use to reposition the character and stop it walking or jumping through a solid tile.

- The `getCenter` function returns a `Vector2f` to the calling code to let it know exactly where the center of the character is. This value is, of course, held in `m_Position`. We will see later that it is used by the `Engine` class to center the appropriate `View` around the appropriate character.

- The `update` function we have seen many times before and as usual, it takes a `float` parameter, which is the fraction of a second that the current frame has taken. This `update` function will need to do more work than previous `update` functions (from other projects), however. It will need to handle jumping, as well as updating the `FloatRect` objects that represent the head, feet, left, and right.

Now we can write the definitions for all the functions, except, of course, `handleInput`.

Coding PlayableCharacter.cpp

Right-click **Source Files** in the **Solution Explorer** and select **Add | New Item....** In the **Add New Item** window, highlight (by left-clicking) **C++ File (**.cpp**)** and then in the **Name** field, type `PlayableCharacter.cpp`. Finally, click the **Add** button. We are now ready to code the .cpp file for the `PlayableCharacter` class.

We will break up the code and discussion into a number of chunks. First, add the include directives and the definition of the `spawn` function:

```cpp
#include "stdafx.h"
#include "PlayableCharacter.h"

void PlayableCharacter::spawn(Vector2f startPosition, float gravity)
{
    // Place the player at the starting point
    m_Position.x = startPosition.x;
    m_Position.y = startPosition.y;

    // Initialize the gravity
    m_Gravity = gravity;

    // Move the sprite in to position
    m_Sprite.setPosition(m_Position);

}
```

The `spawn` function initializes `m_Position` with the passed-in position, as well as initializing `m_Gravity`. The final line of code moves `m_Sprite` to its starting position.

Next, add the definition for the `update` function, immediately after the preceding code:

```cpp
void PlayableCharacter::update(float elapsedTime)
{

    if (m_RightPressed)
```

```
{
    m_Position.x += m_Speed * elapsedTime;
}

if (m_LeftPressed)
{
    m_Position.x -= m_Speed * elapsedTime;
}


// Handle Jumping
if (m_IsJumping)
{
    // Update how long the jump has been going
    m_TimeThisJump += elapsedTime;

    // Is the jump going upwards
    if (m_TimeThisJump < m_JumpDuration)
    {
        // Move up at twice gravity
        m_Position.y -= m_Gravity * 2 * elapsedTime;
    }
    else
    {
        m_IsJumping = false;
        m_IsFalling = true;
    }

}

// Apply gravity
if (m_IsFalling)
{
    m_Position.y += m_Gravity * elapsedTime;
}

// Update the rect for all body parts
FloatRect r = getPosition();

// Feet
m_Feet.left = r.left + 3;
m_Feet.top = r.top + r.height - 1;
m_Feet.width = r.width - 6;
m_Feet.height = 1;

// Head
m_Head.left = r.left;
m_Head.top = r.top + (r.height * .3);
```

```
m_Head.width = r.width;
m_Head.height = 1;

// Right
m_Right.left = r.left + r.width - 2;
m_Right.top = r.top + r.height * .35;
m_Right.width = 1;
m_Right.height = r.height * .3;

// Left
m_Left.left = r.left;
m_Left.top = r.top + r.height * .5;
m_Left.width = 1;
m_Left.height = r.height * .3;

// Move the sprite into position
m_Sprite.setPosition(m_Position);

}
```

The first two parts of the code check whether m_RightPressed or m_LeftPressed is true. If either of them is, m_Position is changed using the same formula as the previous project (elapsed time multiplied by speed).

Next, we see whether or not the character is currently executing a jump. We know this from if(m_IsJumping). If this if statement is true, these are the steps the code takes:

1. Update m_TimeThisJump with elapsedTime.
2. Check if m_TimeThisJump is still less than m_JumpDuration. If it is, change the y coordinate of m_Position by twice gravity multiplied by the elapsed time.
3. In the else clause that executes when m_TimeThisJump is not lower than m_JumpDuration, then m_Falling is set to true. The effect of doing this will be seen next. Also, m_Jumping is set to false. This prevents the code we have just been discussing from executing, because if(m_IsJumping) is now false.

The if(m_IsFalling) block moves m_Position down each frame. It is moved using the current value of m_Gravity and the elapsed time.

The following code (almost all of the remaining code) updates the body parts of the character, relative to the current position of the sprite as a whole. Take a look at the following diagram to see how the code calculates the position of the virtual head, feet, left, and right sides of the character:

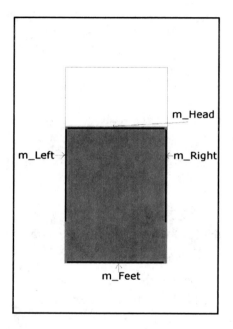

The final line of code uses the setPosition function to move the sprite to its correct location after all of the possibilities of the update function.

Now add the definition for the getPosition, getCenter, getFeet, getHead, getLeft, getRight, and getSprite functions, immediately after the previous code:

```
FloatRect PlayableCharacter::getPosition()
{
    return m_Sprite.getGlobalBounds();
}

Vector2f PlayableCharacter::getCenter()
{
    return Vector2f(
        m_Position.x + m_Sprite.getGlobalBounds().width / 2,
        m_Position.y + m_Sprite.getGlobalBounds().height / 2
```

```
            );
    }

    FloatRect PlayableCharacter::getFeet()
    {
        return m_Feet;
    }

    FloatRect PlayableCharacter::getHead()
    {
        return m_Head;
    }

    FloatRect PlayableCharacter::getLeft()
    {
        return m_Left;
    }

    FloatRect PlayableCharacter::getRight()
    {
        return m_Right;
    }

    Sprite PlayableCharacter::getSprite()
    {
        return m_Sprite;
    }
```

The getPosition function returns a FloatRect that wraps the entire sprite, and getCenter returns a Vector2f, which contains the center of the sprite. Notice that we divide the height and width of the sprite by two in order to dynamically arrive at this result. This is because Thomas and Bob will be of different heights.

The getFeet, getHead, getLeft, and getRight functions return the FloatRect objects that represent the body parts of the character that we update each frame in the update function. We will write the **collision detection code** that uses these functions in the following chapter.

The getSprite function, as usual, returns a copy of m_Sprite.

Finally, for the PlayableCharacter class, add the definitions for the stopFalling, stopRight, stopLeft, and stopJump functions. Do so immediately after the previous code:

```
    void PlayableCharacter::stopFalling(float position)
    {
```

```
    m_Position.y = position - getPosition().height;
    m_Sprite.setPosition(m_Position);
    m_IsFalling = false;
}

void PlayableCharacter::stopRight(float position)
{
    m_Position.x = position - m_Sprite.getGlobalBounds().width;
    m_Sprite.setPosition(m_Position);
}

void PlayableCharacter::stopLeft(float position)
{
    m_Position.x = position + m_Sprite.getGlobalBounds().width;
    m_Sprite.setPosition(m_Position);
}

void PlayableCharacter::stopJump()
{
    // Stop a jump early
    m_IsJumping = false;
    m_IsFalling = true;
}
```

Each of the previous functions receives a value as a parameter that is used to reposition either the top, bottom, left, or right of the sprite. Exactly what these values are and how they are obtained will be seen in the following chapter. Each of the previous functions also repositions the sprite.

The final function is the stopJump function that will also be used in collision detection. It sets the necessary values for m_IsJumping and m_IsFalling to end a jump.

Building the Thomas and Bob classes

Now we get to use inheritance for real. We will build a class for Thomas and a class for Bob. They will both inherit from the PlayableCharacter class we just coded. They will then have all the functionality of the PlayableCharacter class, including direct access to its protected variables. We will also add the definition for the pure virtual function handleInput. You will notice that the handleInput functions for Thomas and Bob will be different.

Coding Thomas.h

Right-click **Header Files** in the **Solution Explorer** and select **Add | New Item…**. In the **Add New Item** window, highlight (by left-clicking) **Header File** (.h) and then in the **Name** field, type Thomas.h. Finally, click the **Add** button. We are now ready to code the header file for the Thomas class.

Now add this code to the Thomas.h class:

```
#pragma once
#include "PlayableCharacter.h"

class Thomas : public PlayableCharacter
{
public:
    // A constructor specific to Thomas
    Thomas::Thomas();

    // The overridden input handler for Thomas
    bool virtual handleInput();

};
```

The previous code is very short and sweet. We can see that we have a constructor and that we are going to implement the pure virtual handleInput function, so let's do that now.

Coding Thomas.cpp

Right-click **Source Files** in the **Solution Explorer** and select **Add | New Item…**. In the **Add New Item** window, highlight (by left-clicking) **C++ File** (.cpp) and then in the **Name** field, type Thomas.cpp. Finally, click the **Add** button. We are now ready to code the .cpp file for the Thomas class.

Add the Thomas constructor to the Thomas.cpp file, as shown in the following snippet:

```
#include "stdafx.h"
#include "Thomas.h"
#include "TextureHolder.h"

Thomas::Thomas()
{
    // Associate a texture with the sprite
    m_Sprite = Sprite(TextureHolder::GetTexture(
        "graphics/thomas.png"));
```

```
      m_JumpDuration = .45;
  }
```

All we need to do is load the `thomas.png` graphic and set the duration of a jump (`m_JumpDuration`) to `.45` (nearly half a second).

Add the definition of the `handleInput` function, as shown in the following snippet:

```
// A virtual function
bool Thomas::handleInput()
{
    m_JustJumped = false;

    if (Keyboard::isKeyPressed(Keyboard::W))
    {

        // Start a jump if not already jumping
        // but only if standing on a block (not falling)
        if (!m_IsJumping && !m_IsFalling)
        {
            m_IsJumping = true;
            m_TimeThisJump = 0;
            m_JustJumped = true;
        }
    }
    else
    {
        m_IsJumping = false;
        m_IsFalling = true;

    }
    if (Keyboard::isKeyPressed(Keyboard::A))
    {
        m_LeftPressed = true;
    }
    else
    {
        m_LeftPressed = false;
    }

    if (Keyboard::isKeyPressed(Keyboard::D))
    {
        m_RightPressed = true;
    }
    else
    {
        m_RightPressed = false;
```

```
    }

    return m_JustJumped;
}
```

This code should look quite familiar. We are using the SFML isKeyPressed function to see whether any of the *W*, *A*, or *D* keys are pressed.

When *W* is pressed, the player is attempting to jump. The code then uses the if(!m_IsJumping && !m_IsFalling) code, which checks that the character is not already jumping and that it is not falling either. When these tests are both true, m_IsJumping is set to true, m_TimeThisJump is set to zero, and m_JustJumped is set to true.

When the previous two tests don't evaluate to true, the else clause is executed and m_Jumping is set to false and m_IsFalling is set to true.

The handling of the *A* and *D* keys being pressed is as simple as setting m_LeftPressed and/or m_RightPressed to true or false. The update function will now be able to handle moving the character.

The last line of code in the function returns the value of m_JustJumped. This will let the calling code know if it needs to play a jumping sound effect.

We will now code the Bob class, although this is nearly identical to the Thomas class, except it has different jumping abilities, a different Texture, and uses different keys on the keyboard.

Coding Bob.h

The Bob class is identical in structure to the Thomas class. It inherits from PlayableCharacter, it has a constructor, and it provides the definition of the handleInput function. The difference compared to Thomas is that we initialize some of Bob's member variables differently and we handle input (in the handleInput function) differently as well. Let's code the class and see the details.

Right-click **Header Files** in the **Solution Explorer** and select **Add | New Item....**. In the **Add New Item** window, highlight (by left-clicking) **Header File (.h)** and then in the **Name** field, type Bob.h. Finally, click the **Add** button. We are now ready to code the header file for the Bob class.

Add the following code to the `Bob.h` file:

```
#pragma once
#include "PlayableCharacter.h"

class Bob : public PlayableCharacter
{
public:
    // A constructor specific to Bob
    Bob::Bob();

    // The overriden input handler for Bob
    bool virtual handleInput();

};
```

The previous code is identical to the `Thomas.h` file apart from the class name, and therefore, the constructor name.

Coding Bob.cpp

Right-click **Source Files** in the **Solution Explorer** and select **Add | New Item…**. In the **Add New Item** window, highlight (by left-clicking) **C++ File (**`.cpp`**)** and then in the **Name** field, type `Thomas.cpp`. Finally, click the **Add** button. We are now ready to code the `.cpp` file for the `Bob` class.

Add the code for the `Bob` constructor to the `Bob.cpp` file. Notice that the texture is different (`bob.png`) and that `m_JumpDuration` is initialized to a significantly smaller value. Bob is now his own, unique self:

```
#include "stdafx.h"
#include "Bob.h"
#include "TextureHolder.h"

Bob::Bob()
{
    // Associate a texture with the sprite
    m_Sprite = Sprite(TextureHolder::GetTexture(
        "graphics/bob.png"));

    m_JumpDuration = .25;
}
```

Add the `handleInput` **code immediately after the** `Bob` **constructor:**

```
bool Bob::handleInput()
{
    m_JustJumped = false;

    if (Keyboard::isKeyPressed(Keyboard::Up))
    {

        // Start a jump if not already jumping
        // but only if standing on a block (not falling)
        if (!m_IsJumping && !m_IsFalling)
        {
            m_IsJumping = true;
            m_TimeThisJump = 0;
            m_JustJumped = true;
        }

    }
    else
    {
        m_IsJumping = false;
        m_IsFalling = true;

    }
    if (Keyboard::isKeyPressed(Keyboard::Left))
    {
        m_LeftPressed = true;

    }
    else
    {
        m_LeftPressed = false;
    }


    if (Keyboard::isKeyPressed(Keyboard::Right))
    {

        m_RightPressed = true;;

    }
    else
    {
        m_RightPressed = false;
    }

    return m_JustJumped;
```

```
    }
```

Notice that the code is nearly identical to the code in the `handleInput` function of the `Thomas` class. The only difference is that we respond to different keys (Left arrow key, Right arrow key, and Up arrow key for jump.)

Now we have a `PlayableCharacter` class that has been extended by `Bob` and `Thomas`, we can add a `Bob` and a `Thomas` instance to the game.

Updating the game engine to use Thomas and Bob

In order to be able to run the game and see our new characters, we have to declare instances of them, call their `spawn` functions, update them each frame, and draw them each frame. Let's do that now.

Updating Engine.h to add an instance of Bob and Thomas

Open up the `Engine.h` file and add the highlighted lines of code, as shown in the following:

```
#pragma once
#include <SFML/Graphics.hpp>
#include "TextureHolder.h"
#include "Thomas.h"
#include "Bob.h"

using namespace sf;

class Engine
{
private:
    // The texture holder
    TextureHolder th;

    // Thomas and his friend, Bob
    Thomas m_Thomas;
    Bob m_Bob;

    const int TILE_SIZE = 50;
```

```
const int VERTS_IN_QUAD = 4;
...
...
```

Now we have an instance of both Thomas and Bob, which are derived from
PlayableCharacter.

Updating the input function to control Thomas and Bob

Now we will add the ability to control the two characters. This code will go in the input
part of the code. Of course, for this project, we have a dedicated input function. Open up
Input.cpp and add this highlighted code:

```cpp
void Engine::input()
{
    Event event;
    while (m_Window.pollEvent(event))
    {
        if (event.type == Event::KeyPressed)
        {
            // Handle the player quitting
            if (Keyboard::isKeyPressed(Keyboard::Escape))
            {
                m_Window.close();
            }

            // Handle the player starting the game
            if (Keyboard::isKeyPressed(Keyboard::Return))
            {
                m_Playing = true;
            }

            // Switch between Thomas and Bob
            if (Keyboard::isKeyPressed(Keyboard::Q))
            {
                m_Character1 = !m_Character1;
            }

            // Switch between full and split-screen
            if (Keyboard::isKeyPressed(Keyboard::E))
            {
                m_SplitScreen = !m_SplitScreen;
            }
        }
```

```
        }

        // Handle input specific to Thomas
        if(m_Thomas.handleInput())
        {
            // Play a jump sound
        }

        // Handle input specific to Bob
        if(m_Bob.handleInput())
        {
            // Play a jump sound
        }
    }
```

Note how simple the previous code is, as all the functionality is contained within the Thomas and Bob classes. All the code has to do is add an include directive for each of the Thomas and Bob classes. Then, within the input function, the code just calls the pure virtual handleInput functions on m_Thomas and m_Bob. The reason we wrap each of the calls in an if statement is because they return true or false based upon whether a new jump has just been successfully initiated. We will handle playing the jump sound effects in Chapter 15, *Sound Spacialization and HUD*.

Updating the update function to spawn and update the PlayableCharacter instances

This is broken down into two parts. First, we need to spawn Bob and Thomas at the start of a new level, and second, we need to update (by calling their update functions) each frame.

Spawning Thomas and Bob

We need to call the spawn functions of our Thomas and Bob objects in a few different places as the project progresses. Most obviously, we need to spawn the two characters when a new level begins. In the following chapter, as the number of tasks we need to perform at the beginning of a level increases, we will write a loadLevel function. For now, lets just call spawn on m_Thomas and m_Bob in the update function, as shown in the following highlighted code. Add the code, but keep in mind that this code will eventually be deleted and replaced:

```
void Engine::update(float dtAsSeconds)
{
```

```
if (m_NewLevelRequired)
{
  // These calls to spawn will be moved to a new
  // loadLevel() function soon
  // Spawn Thomas and Bob
  m_Thomas.spawn(Vector2f(0,0), GRAVITY);
  m_Bob.spawn(Vector2f(100, 0), GRAVITY);

  // Make sure spawn is called only once
  m_TimeRemaining = 10;
  m_NewLevelRequired = false;
}

if (m_Playing)
{
    // Count down the time the player has left
    m_TimeRemaining -= dtAsSeconds;

    // Have Thomas and Bob run out of time?
    if (m_TimeRemaining <= 0)
    {
        m_NewLevelRequired = true;
    }

}// End if playing
}
```

The previous code simply calls spawn and passes in a location in the game world, along with the gravity. The code is wrapped in an if statement that checks whether a new level is required. The actual spawning code will be moved to a dedicated loadLevel function, but the if condition will be part of the finished project. Also, m_TimeRemaining is set to a somewhat arbitrary 10 seconds.

Updating Thomas and Bob each frame

Next, we will update Thomas and Bob. All we need to do is call their update functions and pass in the time this frame has taken.

Add the following highlighted code:

```
void Engine::update(float dtAsSeconds)
{
    if (m_NewLevelRequired)
    {
        // These calls to spawn will be moved to a new
        // LoadLevel function soon
```

```
        // Spawn Thomas and Bob
        m_Thomas.spawn(Vector2f(0,0), GRAVITY);
        m_Bob.spawn(Vector2f(100, 0), GRAVITY);

        // Make sure spawn is called only once
        m_NewLevelRequired = false;
    }

    if (m_Playing)
    {
        // Update Thomas
        m_Thomas.update(dtAsSeconds);

        // Update Bob
        m_Bob.update(dtAsSeconds);

        // Count down the time the player has left
        m_TimeRemaining -= dtAsSeconds;

        // Have Thomas and Bob run out of time?
        if (m_TimeRemaining <= 0)
        {
            m_NewLevelRequired = true;
        }

    }// End if playing
}
```

Now that the characters can move, we need to update the appropriate `View` objects to center around the characters and make them the center of attention. Of course, until we have some objects in our game world, the sensation of actual movement will not be achieved.

Add the highlighted code, as shown in the following snippet:

```
void Engine::update(float dtAsSeconds)
{
    if (m_NewLevelRequired)
    {
        // These calls to spawn will be moved to a new
        // LoadLevel function soon
        // Spawn Thomas and Bob
        m_Thomas.spawn(Vector2f(0,0), GRAVITY);
        m_Bob.spawn(Vector2f(100, 0), GRAVITY);

        // Make sure spawn is called only once
        m_NewLevelRequired = false;
    }
```

```
if (m_Playing)
{
    // Update Thomas
    m_Thomas.update(dtAsSeconds);

    // Update Bob
    m_Bob.update(dtAsSeconds);

    // Count down the time the player has left
    m_TimeRemaining -= dtAsSeconds;

    // Have Thomas and Bob run out of time?
    if (m_TimeRemaining <= 0)
    {
        m_NewLevelRequired = true;
    }

}// End if playing
// Set the appropriate view around the appropriate character
if (m_SplitScreen)
{
  m_LeftView.setCenter(m_Thomas.getCenter());
  m_RightView.setCenter(m_Bob.getCenter());
}
else
{
  // Centre full screen around appropriate character
  if (m_Character1)
  {
      m_MainView.setCenter(m_Thomas.getCenter());
  }
  else
  {
      m_MainView.setCenter(m_Bob.getCenter());
  }
}
}
```

The previous code handles the two possible situations. First,
the if(mSplitScreen) condition positions the left-hand view around m_Thomas and the
right-hand view around m_Bob. The else clause that executes when the game is in
fullscreen mode tests to see if m_Character1 is true. If it is, then the fullscreen view
(m_MainView) is centered around Thomas, otherwise it is centered around Bob. You
probably remember that the player can use the *E* key to toggle split screen mode and the *Q*
key to toggle between Bob and Thomas, in fullscreen mode. We coded this in the input
function of the Engine class, back in Chapter 12, *Abstraction and Code Management – Making
Better Use of OOP*.

Drawing Bob and Thomas

Make sure the Draw.cpp file is open and add the highlighted code, as shown in the
following snippet:

```
void Engine::draw()
{
    // Rub out the last frame
    m_Window.clear(Color::White);

    if (!m_SplitScreen)
    {
        // Switch to background view
        m_Window.setView(m_BGMainView);
        // Draw the background
        m_Window.draw(m_BackgroundSprite);
        // Switch to m_MainView
        m_Window.setView(m_MainView);

        // Draw thomas
        m_Window.draw(m_Thomas.getSprite());

        // Draw bob
        m_Window.draw(m_Bob.getSprite());
    }
    else
    {
        // Split-screen view is active

        // First draw Thomas' side of the screen

        // Switch to background view
        m_Window.setView(m_BGLeftView);
        // Draw the background
```

```
m_Window.draw(m_BackgroundSprite);
// Switch to m_LeftView
m_Window.setView(m_LeftView);

// Draw bob
m_Window.draw(m_Bob.getSprite());

// Draw thomas
m_Window.draw(m_Thomas.getSprite());
// Now draw Bob's side of the screen

// Switch to background view
m_Window.setView(m_BGRightView);
// Draw the background
m_Window.draw(m_BackgroundSprite);
// Switch to m_RightView
m_Window.setView(m_RightView);

// Draw thomas
m_Window.draw(m_Thomas.getSprite());

// Draw bob
m_Window.draw(m_Bob.getSprite());
}

// Draw the HUD
// Switch to m_HudView
m_Window.setView(m_HudView);
// Show everything we have just drawn
m_Window.display();
}
```

Notice that we draw both Thomas and Bob for the full screen, the left, and the right. Also note the very subtle difference in the way that we draw the characters in split screen mode. When drawing the left side of the screen, we switch the order the characters are drawn and draw Thomas after Bob. So, Thomas will always be on top on the left, and Bob on the right. This is because the player controlling Thomas is catered for on the left and Bob the right.

You can run the game and see Thomas and Bob in the center of the screen:

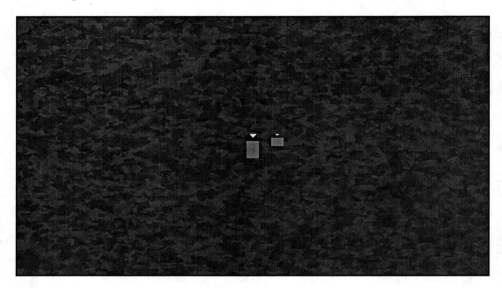

If you press the *Q* key to switch focus from Thomas to Bob, you will see the `View` make the slight adjustment. If you move either of the characters left or right (Thomas with *A* and *D*, Bob with the arrow keys) you will see them move relative to each other.

Try pressing the *E* key to toggle between fullscreen and split-screen. Then try moving both characters again to see the effect. In the following screenshot, you can see that Thomas is always centered in the left-hand window and Bob is always centered in the right-hand window:

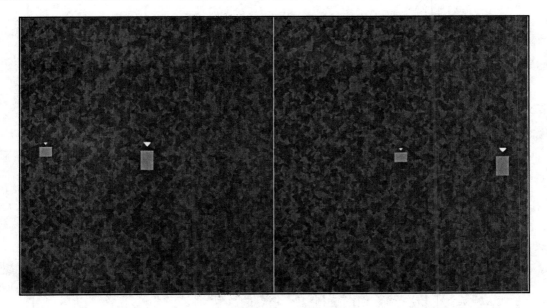

If you leave the game running long enough, the characters will re-spawn in their original positions every ten seconds. This is the beginnings of the functionality we will need for the finished game. This behavior is caused by m_TimeRemaining going below zero and then setting the m_NewLevelRequired variable to true.

Also note that we can't see the full effect of movement until we draw the details of the level. In fact, although it can't be seen, both characters are continuously falling at 300 pixels per second. As the camera is centering around them every frame and there are no other objects in the game-world, we cannot see this downward movement.

If you want to demonstrate this to yourself, just change the call to m_Bob.spawn, as shown in the following code:

```
m_Bob.spawn(Vector2f(0,0), 0);
```

Now that Bob has no gravitational effect, Thomas will visibly fall away from him. This is shown in the following screenshot:

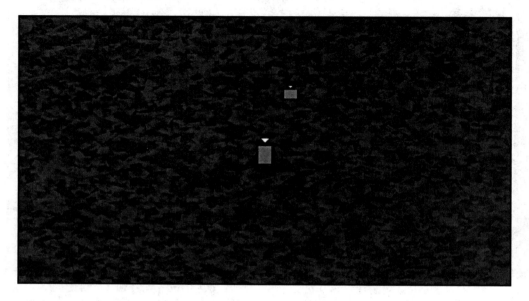

We will add some playable levels to interact with in the following chapter.

FAQ

Q) We learned about polymorphism, but I didn't notice anything polymorphic in the game code so far.

A) We will see polymorphism in action in the following chapter, when we write a function that takes a `PlayableCharacter` as a parameter. We will see how we can pass either Bob or Thomas to this new function and it will work the same with either of them.

Summary

In this chapter, we learned some new C++ concepts. First, Inheritance allows us to extend a class and gain all of its functionality. We also learned that we can declare variables as protected, and that will give the child class access to them, but they will still be encapsulated (hidden) from all other code. We also used pure virtual functions, which make a class abstract, meaning that the class cannot be instantiated and must therefore be inherited/extended from. We were also introduced to the concept of polymorphism, but will need to wait until the following chapter to use it in our game.

Next up, we will add some major functionality to the game. By the end of the following chapter, Thomas and Bob will be walking, jumping, and falling. They will even be able to jump on each other's heads, as well as explore some level designs that are loaded from a text file.

14
Building Playable Levels and Collision Detection

This chapter will probably be one of the most satisfying of this project. The reason for this is that by the end of it, we will have a playable game. Although there will still be features to implement (sound, particle effects, HUD, and shader effects), Bob and Thomas will be able to run, jump, and explore the world. Furthermore, you will be able to create your very own level designs of almost any size or complexity by simply making platforms and obstacles in a text file.

We will achieve all this by covering following topics in this chapter:

- Exploring how to design levels in a text file
- Building a `LevelManager` class that will load levels from a text file, convert them into data our game can use, and keep track of the level details, such as spawn position, current level, and allowed time limit
- Updating the game engine to use `LevelManager`
- Coding a polymorphic function to handle the collision detection for both Bob and Thomas

Designing some levels

Remember our sprite sheet that we introduced in `Chapter 12`, *Abstraction and Code Management – Making Better Use of OOP*. Here it is again, annotated with numbers that represent each tile that we will build our levels from:

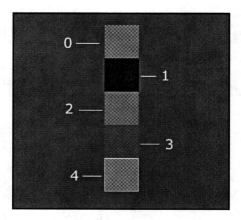

I placed the screenshot on a gray background so you could see clearly the different details of the sprite sheet. The checkered background represents the level of transparency. So, all of the tiles except for number 1 will reveal at least a little of the background behind them:

- Tile 0 is completely transparent and will be used to fill in the gaps where there aren't any other tiles
- Tile 1 is for the platforms that Thomas and Bob will walk on
- Tile 2 is for fire tiles and tile 3 is for water tiles
- Tile 4 you might need to look quite closely to see. It has a white, square outline. This is the goal of the level where Thomas and Bob must get to together.

Keep this screenshot in mind as we discuss designing the levels.

We will enter combinations of these tile numbers into text files to design the layouts. An example will help:

```
00000000000000000000000000000000000000000000000
00000000000000000000000000000000000000000000000
00000000000000000000000000000000000000000000000
00000000000000000000000000000000000000000000000
00000000000000000000000000000000000000000000000
00000000000000000000000000000000000000000000000
11111111110001111122222222111133111111111411
```

```
000000000000000000122222222100013310000001110
000000000000000000122222222100013310000000000
000000000000000000122222222100013310000000000
000000000000000000111111111100011110000000000
```

The previous code translates to the following level layout:

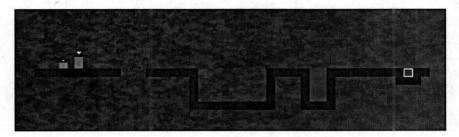

Note that to get the view shown in the previous screenshot, I had to zoom out the `View`. Also, the screenshot is cropped. The actual start of the level would look like the following screenshot:

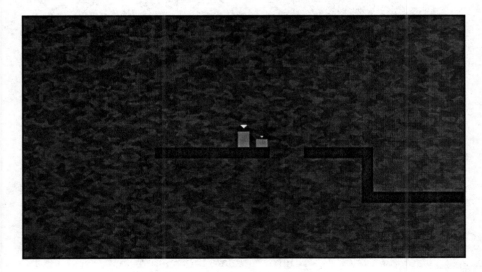

The point of showing you these screenshots is two fold. Firstly, you can see how you can quickly construct level designs using a simple and free text editor.

Just make sure you use a monospace font so that all the numbers are the same size. This makes designing the levels much easier.

Secondly, the screenshots demonstrate the gameplay aspects of the design. From left to right in the level, Thomas and Bob first need to jump a small hole or they will fall to their deaths (re-spawn). Then they have a large expanse of fire to traverse. It is actually impossible for Bob to jump that many tiles. The players will need to work together for the solution. The only way that Bob will clear the fire tiles is by standing on Thomas's head and jumping from there, as shown in the following screenshot:

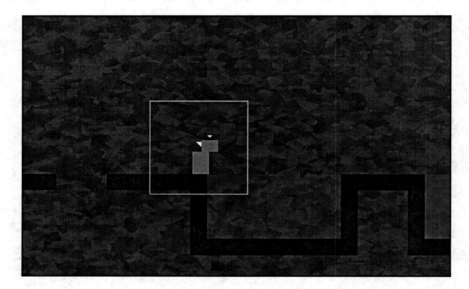

It is then quite simple to get to the goal and move on to the next level.

I strongly encourage you to complete this chapter and then spend some time designing your own levels.

I have included a few level designs to get you started. They are in the `levels` folder that we added to the project back in `Chapter 12`, *Abstraction and Code Management – Making Better Use of OOP*.

What follows are some zoomed out views of the game, along with a screenshot of the code of the level design. The screenshot of the code is probably more useful than reproducing the actual textual content. If you do want to see the code, just open up the files in the `levels` folder.

This is what the code looks like:

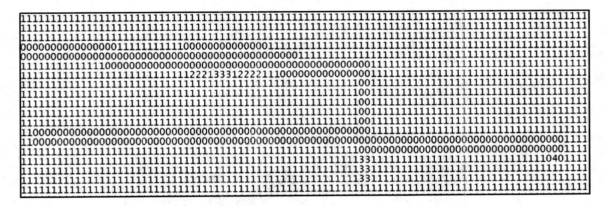

This is level layout that the previous code will produce:

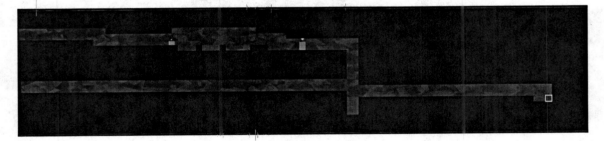

This level is the "leap of faith" level I referred to in Chapter 12, *Abstraction and Code Management – Making Better Use of OOP*:

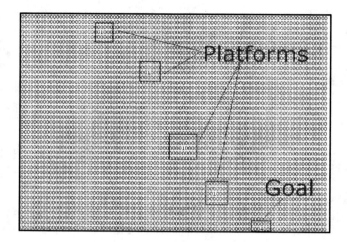

I have highlighted the platforms, as they are not very clear in the zoomed-out screenshot:

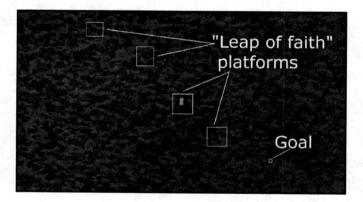

The provided designs are simple. The game engine will be able to handle very large designs, however. You have the freedom to use your imagination and build some really big and hard-to-complete levels.

Of course, these designs won't actually do anything until we learn how to load them and convert the text into a playable level. Additionally, it won't be possible to stand on any platforms until we have implemented the collision detection.

First, let's handle loading the level designs.

Building the LevelManager class

It will take several phases of coding to make our level designs work. The first thing we will do is code the `LevelManager` header file. This will allow us to look at and discuss the member variables and functions that will be in the `LevelManger` class.

Next, we will code the `LevelManager.cpp` file, which will have all the function definitions in it. As this is a long file, we will break it up into several sections, to code and discuss them.

Once the `LevelManager` class is complete, we will add an instance of it to the game engine (`Engine` class). We will also add a new function to the `Engine` class, `loadLevel`, which we can call from the `update` function whenever a new level is required. The `loadLevel` function will not only use the `LevelManager` instance to load the appropriate level but it will also take care of aspects such as spawning the player characters and preparing the clock.

As already mentioned, let's get an overview of `LevelManager` by coding the `LevelManager.h` file.

Coding LevelManager.h

Right-click **Header Files** in the **Solution Explorer** and select **Add | New Item...**. In the **Add New Item** window, highlight (by left-clicking) **Header File (.h)** and then in the **Name** field, type `LevelManager.h`. Finally, click the **Add** button. We are now ready to code the header file for the `LevelManager` class.

Add the following include directives and private variables, and then we will discuss them:

```
#pragma once

#include <SFML/Graphics.hpp>
using namespace sf;
using namespace std;
```

```
class LevelManager
{
private:
    Vector2i m_LevelSize;
    Vector2f m_StartPosition;
    float m_TimeModifier = 1;
    float m_BaseTimeLimit = 0;
    int m_CurrentLevel = 0;
    const int NUM_LEVELS = 4;

    // public declarations go here
```

The code declares `Vector2i m_LevelSize` to hold two integer values that will hold the horizontal and vertical number of tiles that the current map contains. `Vector2f, m_StartPosition` contains the coordinates in the world where Bob and Thomas should be spawned. Note that this is not a tile position relatable to `m_LevelSize` units, but a horizontal and vertical pixel position in the level.

The `m_TimeModifier` member variable is a float that will be used to multiply the time available in the current level. The reason we want to do this is so that by changing (decreasing) this value, we will shorten the time available each time the player attempts the same level. As an example, if the player gets 60 seconds for the first time they attempt level one then 60 multiplied by 1 is, of course, 60. When the player completes all the levels and comes back to level 1 for the second time, `m_TimeModifier` will have been reduced by 10 percent. Then, when the time available is multiplied by 0.9, the amount of time available to the player will be 54 seconds. This is 10 percent less than 60. The game will get steadily harder.

The float variable, `m_BaseTimeLimit`, holds the original, unmodified time limit we have just been discussing.

You can probably guess that `m_CurrentLevel` will hold the current level number that is being played.

The `int NUM_LEVELS` constant will be used to flag when it is appropriate to go back to level one again and reduce the value of `m_TimeModifier`.

Now add the following public variables and function declarations:

```
public:

    const int TILE_SIZE = 50;
    const int VERTS_IN_QUAD = 4;

    float getTimeLimit();
```

```
    Vector2f getStartPosition();

    int** nextLevel(VertexArray& rVaLevel);

    Vector2i getLevelSize();

    int getCurrentLevel();

};
```

In the previous code, there are two constant `int` members. `TILE_SIZE` is a useful constant to remind us that each tile in the sprite sheet is fifty pixels wide and fifty pixels high. `VERTS_IN_QUAD` is a useful constant to make our manipulation of a `VertexArray` less error-prone. There are, in fact, four vertices in a quad. Now we can't forget it.

The `getTimeLimit`, `getStartPosition`, `getLevelSize`, and `getCurrentLevel` functions are simple getter functions, that return the current value of the private member variables we declared in the previous block of code.

A function that deserves a closer look is `nextLevel`. This function receives a `VertexArray` reference, just like we used in the Zombie Arena game. The function can then work on the `VertexArray`, and all the changes will be present in the `VertexArray` from the calling code. The `nextLevel` function returns a pointer to a pointer, which means we can return an address that is the first element of a two-dimensional array of `int` values. We will be building a two-dimensional array of `int` values that will represent the layout of each level. Of course, these int values will be read from the level design text files.

Coding the LevelManager.cpp file

Right-click **Source Files** in the **Solution Explorer** and select **Add | New Item....** In the **Add New Item** window, highlight (by left-clicking) **C++ File (** `.cpp` **)** and then in the **Name** field, type `LevelManager.cpp`. Finally, click the **Add** button. We are now ready to code the `.cpp` file for the `LevelManager` class.

As this is quite a long class, we will break it up to discuss it in six chunks. The first five will cover the `nextLevel` function, and the sixth, all the rest.

Add the following include directives and the first (of five) part of the `nextLevel` function:

```cpp
#include "stdafx.h"
#include <SFML/Graphics.hpp>
#include <SFML/Audio.hpp>
#include "TextureHolder.h"
#include <sstream>
#include <fstream>
#include "LevelManager.h"

using namespace sf;
using namespace std;

int** LevelManager::nextLevel(VertexArray& rVaLevel)
{
    m_LevelSize.x = 0;
    m_LevelSize.y = 0;

    // Get the next level
    m_CurrentLevel++;
    if (m_CurrentLevel > NUM_LEVELS)
    {
        m_CurrentLevel = 1;
        m_TimeModifier -= .1f;
    }

    // Load the appropriate level from a text file
    string levelToLoad;
    switch (m_CurrentLevel)
    {

    case 1:
        levelToLoad = "levels/level1.txt";
        m_StartPosition.x = 100;
        m_StartPosition.y = 100;
        m_BaseTimeLimit = 30.0f;
        break;

    case 2:
        levelToLoad = "levels/level2.txt";
        m_StartPosition.x = 100;
        m_StartPosition.y = 3600;
        m_BaseTimeLimit = 100.0f;
        break;

    case 3:
        levelToLoad = "levels/level3.txt";
        m_StartPosition.x = 1250;
```

```
        m_StartPosition.y = 0;
        m_BaseTimeLimit = 30.0f;
        break;

    case 4:
        levelToLoad = "levels/level4.txt";
        m_StartPosition.x = 50;
        m_StartPosition.y = 200;
        m_BaseTimeLimit = 50.0f;
        break;

    }// End switch
```

After the include directives, the code initializes m_LevelSize.x and m_LevelSize.y to zero.

Next, m_CurrentLevel is incremented. The if statement that follows checks whether m_CurrentLevel is greater than NUM_LEVELS. If it is, m_CurrentLevel is set back to 1 and m_TimeModifier is reduced by .1f in order to shorten the time allowed for all levels.

The code then switches based on the value held by m_CurrentLevel. Each case statement initializes the name of the text file, which holds the level design and the starting position for Thomas and Bob, as well as m_BaseTimeLimit, which is the unmodified time limit for the level in question.

 If you design your own levels, add a case statement and the appropriate values for it here. Also edit the NUM_LEVELS constant in the LevelManager.h file.

Now add the second part of the nextLevel function, as shown. Add the code immediately after the previous code. Study the code as you add it so we can discuss it:

```
ifstream inputFile(levelToLoad);
string s;

// Count the number of rows in the file
while (getline(inputFile, s))
{
    ++m_LevelSize.y;
}

// Store the length of the rows
m_LevelSize.x = s.length();
```

In the previous (second part) we have just coded, we declare an ifstream object called inputFile, which opens a stream to the filename contained in levelToLoad.

The code loops through each line of the file using getline, but doesn't record any of its content. All it does is count the number of lines by incrementing m_LevelSize.y. After the for loop, the width of the level is saved in m_LevelSize.x using s.length. This implies that the length of all the lines must be the same or we would run in to trouble.

At this point, we know and have saved the length and width of the current level in m_LevelSize.

Now add the third part of the nextLevel function, as shown. Add the code immediately after the previous code. Study the code as you add it so we can discuss it:

```
// Go back to the start of the file
inputFile.clear();
inputFile.seekg(0, ios::beg);

// Prepare the 2d array to hold the int values from the file
int** arrayLevel = new int*[m_LevelSize.y];
for (int i = 0; i < m_LevelSize.y; ++i)
{
    // Add a new array into each array element
    arrayLevel[i] = new int[m_LevelSize.x];
}
```

First, we clear inputFile using its clear function. The seekg function called with the 0, ios::beg parameters resets the stream back to before the first character.

Next, we declare a pointer to a pointer called arrayLevel. Note that this is done on the free store/heap using the new keyword. Once we have initialized this two-dimensional array, we will be able to return its address to the calling code and it will persist until we either delete it or the game is closed.

for loops from 0 to m_LevelSize.y −1. In each pass, it adds a new array of int values to the heap to match the value of m_LevelSize.x. We now have a perfectly configured (for the current level) two-dimensional array. The only problem is that there is nothing in it.

Now add the fourth part of the nextLevel function, as shown. Add the code immediately after the previous code. Study the code as you add it so we can discuss it:

```
 // Loop through the file and store all the values in the 2d array
string row;
int y = 0;
while (inputFile >> row)
{
    for (int x = 0; x < row.length(); x++) {

        const char val = row[x];
        arrayLevel[y][x] = atoi(&val);
    }

    y++;
}

// close the file
inputFile.close();
```

First, the code initializes a string, called row, which will hold one row of the level design at a time. We also declare and initialize an int called y that will help us count the rows.

The while loop executes repeatedly until inputFile gets past the last row. Inside the while loop there is a for loop, which goes through each character of the current row and stores it in the two-dimensional array, arrayLevel. Notice that we access exactly the right element of the two-dimensional array with arrayLevel[y][x] =. The atoi function converts char val to int. This is what is required, because we have a two-dimensional array for int, not char.

Now add the fifth part of the nextLevel function, as shown. Add the code immediately after the previous code. Study the code as you add it so we can discuss it:

```
// What type of primitive are we using?
rVaLevel.setPrimitiveType(Quads);

// Set the size of the vertex array
rVaLevel.resize(m_LevelSize.x * m_LevelSize.y * VERTS_IN_QUAD);

// Start at the beginning of the vertex array
int currentVertex = 0;

for (int x = 0; x < m_LevelSize.x; x++)
{
    for (int y = 0; y < m_LevelSize.y; y++)
    {
```

```
        // Position each vertex in the current quad
        rVaLevel[currentVertex + 0].position =
           Vector2f(x * TILE_SIZE,
           y * TILE_SIZE);

        rVaLevel[currentVertex + 1].position =
           Vector2f((x * TILE_SIZE) + TILE_SIZE,
           y * TILE_SIZE);

        rVaLevel[currentVertex + 2].position =
           Vector2f((x * TILE_SIZE) + TILE_SIZE,
           (y * TILE_SIZE) + TILE_SIZE);

        rVaLevel[currentVertex + 3].position =
           Vector2f((x * TILE_SIZE),
           (y * TILE_SIZE) + TILE_SIZE);

        // Which tile from the sprite sheet should we use
        int verticalOffset = arrayLevel[y][x] * TILE_SIZE;

        rVaLevel[currentVertex + 0].texCoords =
           Vector2f(0, 0 + verticalOffset);

        rVaLevel[currentVertex + 1].texCoords =
           Vector2f(TILE_SIZE, 0 + verticalOffset);

        rVaLevel[currentVertex + 2].texCoords =
           Vector2f(TILE_SIZE, TILE_SIZE + verticalOffset);

        rVaLevel[currentVertex + 3].texCoords =
           Vector2f(0, TILE_SIZE + verticalOffset);

        // Position ready for the next four vertices
        currentVertex = currentVertex + VERTS_IN_QUAD;
    }
  }

   return arrayLevel;
  } // End of nextLevel function
```

Although this is the longest section of code from the five sections we divided nextLevel into, it is also the most straightforward. This is because we have seen very similar code in the Zombie Arena project.

What happens is that the nested `for` loop loops from zero through to the width and height of the level. For each position in the array, four vertices are put into `VertexArray` and four texture coordinates are assigned from the sprite sheet. The positions of the vertices and texture coordinates are calculated using the `currentVertex` variable, the `TILE SIZE`, and `VERTS_IN_QUAD` constants. At the end of each loop of the inner `for` loop, `currentVertex` is increased by `VERTS_IN_QUAD`, moving nicely on to the next tile.

The important thing to remember about this `VertexArray` is that it was passed into `nextLevel` by reference. Therefore, the `VertexArray` will be available in the calling code. We will call `nextLevel` from the code in the `Engine` class.

Once this function has been called, the `Engine` class will have a `VertexArray` to represent the level graphically, and a two-dimensional array of `int` values as a numerical representation of all the platforms and obstacles in the level.

The rest of the `LevelManager` functions are all simple getter functions, but do take the time to familiarize yourself with what private value is returned by which function. Add the remaining functions from the `LevelManager` class:

```
Vector2i LevelManager::getLevelSize()
{
    return m_LevelSize;
}

int LevelManager::getCurrentLevel()
{
    return m_CurrentLevel;
}

float LevelManager::getTimeLimit()
{
    return m_BaseTimeLimit * m_TimeModifier;

}
Vector2f LevelManager::getStartPosition()
{
    return m_StartPosition;
}
```

Now that the `LevelManager` class is complete, we can move on to using it. We will code another function in the Engine class to do so.

Coding the loadLevel function

To be clear, this function is part of the `Engine` class, although it will delegate much of its work to other functions, including those of the `LevelManager` class that we just built.

First, let's add the declaration for the new function, along with some other new code, to the `Engine.h` file. Open the `Engine.h` file and add the highlighted lines of code shown in the following abbreviated snapshot of the `Engine.h` file:

```cpp
#pragma once
#include <SFML/Graphics.hpp>
#include "TextureHolder.h"
#include "Thomas.h"
#include "Bob.h"
#include "LevelManager.h"

using namespace sf;

class Engine
{
private:
    // The texture holder
    TextureHolder th;

    // Thomas and his friend, Bob
    Thomas m_Thomas;
    Bob m_Bob;

    // A class to manage all the levels
    LevelManager m_LM;

    const int TILE_SIZE = 50;
    const int VERTS_IN_QUAD = 4;

    // The force pushing the characters down
    const int GRAVITY = 300;

    // A regular RenderWindow
    RenderWindow m_Window;

    // The main Views
    View m_MainView;
    View m_LeftView;
    View m_RightView;

    // Three views for the background
    View m_BGMainView;
```

```
    View m_BGLeftView;
    View m_BGRightView;

    View m_HudView;

    // Declare a sprite and a Texture for the background
    Sprite m_BackgroundSprite;
    Texture m_BackgroundTexture;

    // Is the game currently playing?
    bool m_Playing = false;

    // Is character 1 or 2 the current focus?
    bool m_Character1 = true;

    // Start in full screen mode
    bool m_SplitScreen = false;

    // How much time is left in the current level
    float m_TimeRemaining = 10;
    Time m_GameTimeTotal;

    // Is it time for a new/first level?
    bool m_NewLevelRequired = true;

    // The vertex array for the level tiles
    VertexArray m_VALevel;
    // The 2d array with the map for the level
    // A pointer to a pointer
    int** m_ArrayLevel =  NULL;
    // Texture for the level tiles
    Texture m_TextureTiles;

    // Private functions for internal use only
    void input();
    void update(float dtAsSeconds);
    void draw();

    // Load a new level
    void loadLevel();

public:
    // The Engine constructor
    Engine();

    ...
    ...
    ...
```

You can see the following in the previous code:

- We included the `LevelManager.h` file
- We added an instance of `LevelManager` called `m_LM`
- We added a `VertexArray` called `m_VALevel`
- We added a pointer to a pointer to an `int` that will hold the two-dimensional array that is returned from `nextLevel`
- We added a new `Texture` object for the sprite sheet
- We added the declaration for the `loadLevel` function that we will write now

Right-click **Source Files** in the **Solution Explorer** and select **Add | New Item....** In the **Add New Item** window, highlight (by left-clicking) **C++ File (**.cpp**)** and then in the **Name** field, type `LoadLevel.cpp`. Finally, click the **Add** button. We are now ready to code the `loadLevel` function.

Add the code for the `loadLevel` function to the `LoadLevel.cpp` file, and then we can discuss it:

```cpp
#include "stdafx.h"
#include "Engine.h"

void Engine::loadLevel()
{
    m_Playing = false;

    // Delete the previously allocated memory
    for (int i = 0; i < m_LM.getLevelSize().y; ++i)
    {
        delete[] m_ArrayLevel[i];

    }
    delete[] m_ArrayLevel;

    // Load the next 2d array with the map for the level
    // And repopulate the vertex array as well
    m_ArrayLevel = m_LM.nextLevel(m_VALevel);

    // How long is this new time limit
    m_TimeRemaining = m_LM.getTimeLimit();

    // Spawn Thomas and Bob
    m_Thomas.spawn(m_LM.getStartPosition(), GRAVITY);
    m_Bob.spawn(m_LM.getStartPosition(), GRAVITY);
```

```
    // Make sure this code isn't run again
    m_NewLevelRequired = false;
}
```

First, we set m_Playing to false to stop parts of the update function from executing. Next, we loop through all the horizontal arrays within m_ArrayLevel and delete them. After the for loop, we delete m_ArrayLevel.

The code, m_ArrayLevel = m_LM.nextLevel(m_VALevel), calls nextLevel and prepares both the VertexArray and m_VALevel, as well as the two-dimensional m_ArrayLevel array. The level is set up and ready to go.

m_TimeRemaining is initialized by calling getTimeLimit, and Thomas and Bob are spawned using the spawn function along with the value returned from getStartPosition.

Finally, m_NewLevelRequired is set to false. As we will see in a few page's time, m_NewLevelRequired being set to true is what causes loadLevel to be called. We only want to run this function once.

Updating the engine

Open the Engine.cpp file and add the highlighted code to load the sprite sheet texture at the end of the Engine constructor:

```
Engine::Engine()
{
    // Get the screen resolution and create an SFML window and View
    Vector2f resolution;
    resolution.x = VideoMode::getDesktopMode().width;
    resolution.y = VideoMode::getDesktopMode().height;

    m_Window.create(VideoMode(resolution.x, resolution.y),
        "Thomas was late",
        Style::Fullscreen);

    // Initialize the full screen view
    m_MainView.setSize(resolution);
    m_HudView.reset(
        FloatRect(0, 0, resolution.x, resolution.y));

    // Inititialize the split-screen Views
    m_LeftView.setViewport(
        FloatRect(0.001f, 0.001f, 0.498f, 0.998f));
```

```
    m_RightView.setViewport(
        FloatRect(0.5f, 0.001f, 0.499f, 0.998f));

    m_BGLeftView.setViewport(
        FloatRect(0.001f, 0.001f, 0.498f, 0.998f));

    m_BGRightView.setViewport(
        FloatRect(0.5f, 0.001f, 0.499f, 0.998f));

    // Can this graphics card use shaders?
    if (!sf::Shader::isAvailable())
    {
        // Time to get a new PC
        m_Window.close();
    }

    m_BackgroundTexture = TextureHolder::GetTexture(
        "graphics/background.png");

    // Associate the sprite with the texture
    m_BackgroundSprite.setTexture(m_BackgroundTexture);

    // Load the texture for the background vertex array
    m_TextureTiles = TextureHolder::GetTexture("graphics/tiles_sheet.png");
}
```

All we do in the previous code is load the sprite sheet into m_TextureTiles.

Open the Update.cpp file and make the following highlighted changes and additions:

```
void Engine::update(float dtAsSeconds)
{
    if (m_NewLevelRequired)
    {
        // These calls to spawn will be moved to a new
        // LoadLevel function soon
        // Spawn Thomas and Bob
        //m_Thomas.spawn(Vector2f(0,0), GRAVITY);
        //m_Bob.spawn(Vector2f(100, 0), GRAVITY);

        // Make sure spawn is called only once
        //m_TimeRemaining = 10;
        //m_NewLevelRequired = false;

        // Load a level
        loadLevel();
    }
```

Actually, you should delete, rather than comment out, the lines we are no longer using. I have just shown it to you this way so that the changes are clear. All there should be in the previous `if` statement is the call to `loadLevel`.

Finally, before we can see the results of the work so far this chapter, open the `Draw.cpp` file and make the following highlighted additions to draw the vertex array that represents a level:

```
void Engine::draw()
{
    // Rub out the last frame
    m_Window.clear(Color::White);

    if (!m_SplitScreen)
    {
        // Switch to background view
        m_Window.setView(m_BGMainView);
        // Draw the background
        m_Window.draw(m_BackgroundSprite);
        // Switch to m_MainView
        m_Window.setView(m_MainView);

        // Draw the Level
        m_Window.draw(m_VALevel, &m_TextureTiles);

        // Draw thomas
        m_Window.draw(m_Thomas.getSprite());

        // Draw thomas
        m_Window.draw(m_Bob.getSprite());
    }
    else
    {
        // Split-screen view is active

        // First draw Thomas' side of the screen

        // Switch to background view
        m_Window.setView(m_BGLeftView);
        // Draw the background
        m_Window.draw(m_BackgroundSprite);
        // Switch to m_LeftView
        m_Window.setView(m_LeftView);

        // Draw the Level
        m_Window.draw(m_VALevel, &m_TextureTiles);
        // Draw thomas
```

```
        m_Window.draw(m_Bob.getSprite());

        // Draw thomas
        m_Window.draw(m_Thomas.getSprite());
        // Now draw Bob's side of the screen

        // Switch to background view
        m_Window.setView(m_BGRightView);
        // Draw the background
        m_Window.draw(m_BackgroundSprite);
        // Switch to m_RightView
        m_Window.setView(m_RightView);

        // Draw the Level
        m_Window.draw(m_VALevel, &m_TextureTiles);

        // Draw thomas
        m_Window.draw(m_Thomas.getSprite());

        // Draw bob
        m_Window.draw(m_Bob.getSprite());
    }

    // Draw the HUD
    // Switch to m_HudView
    m_Window.setView(m_HudView);
    // Show everything we have just drawn
    m_Window.display();
}
```

Notice we need to draw the `VertexArray` for all screen options (full, left, and right.)

Now you can run the game. Unfortunately, however, Thomas and Bob fall straight through all our lovingly-designed platforms. For this reason, we can't try and progress through the levels and beat the clock.

Collision detection

We will handle collision detection using rectangle intersection and the SFML intersects function. What will be different in this project is that we will abstract the collision detection code into its own function and Thomas and Bob, as we have already seen, have multiple rectangles (`m_Head`, `m_Feet`, `m_Left`, `m_Right`) that we need to check for collisions.

Coding the detectCollisions function

To be clear, this function is part of the Engine class. Open up the `Engine.h` file and add a declaration for a function called `detectCollisions`. This is shown highlighted in the following code snippet:

```
// Private functions for internal use only
void input();
void update(float dtAsSeconds);
void draw();

// Load a new level
void loadLevel();

// Run will call all the private functions
bool detectCollisions(PlayableCharacter& character);
public:
    // The Engine constructor
    Engine();
```

Notice from the signature that the `detectCollision` function takes a polymorphic argument, a `PlayerCharacter` object. As we know, `PlayerCharacter` is abstract and can never be instantiated. We do, however, inherit from it with the `Thomas` and `Bob` classes. We will be able to pass either m_Thomas or m_Bob to `detectCollisions`.

Right-click **Source Files** in the **Solution Explorer** and select **Add | New Item...**. In the **Add New Item** window, highlight (by left-clicking) **C++ File (**.cpp**)** and then in the **Name** field, type `DetectCollisions.cpp`. Finally, click the **Add** button. We are now ready to code the `detectCollisions` function.

Add the following code to `DetectCollisions.cpp`. Note that this is just the first part of this function:

```
#include "stdafx.h"
#include "Engine.h"

bool Engine::detectCollisions(PlayableCharacter& character)
{
    bool reachedGoal = false;
    // Make a rect for all his parts
    FloatRect detectionZone = character.getPosition();

    // Make a FloatRect to test each block
    FloatRect block;

    block.width = TILE_SIZE;
```

```
block.height = TILE_SIZE;

// Build a zone around thomas to detect collisions
int startX = (int)(detectionZone.left / TILE_SIZE) - 1;
int startY = (int)(detectionZone.top / TILE_SIZE) - 1;
int endX = (int)(detectionZone.left / TILE_SIZE) + 2;

// Thomas is quite tall so check a few tiles vertically
int endY = (int)(detectionZone.top / TILE_SIZE) + 3;

// Make sure we don't test positions lower than zero
// Or higher than the end of the array
if (startX < 0)startX = 0;
if (startY < 0)startY = 0;
if (endX >= m_LM.getLevelSize().x)
    endX = m_LM.getLevelSize().x;
if (endY >= m_LM.getLevelSize().y)
    endY = m_LM.getLevelSize().y;
```

The first thing that happens is that we declare a Boolean called reachedGoal. This is the value that the detectCollisions function returns to the calling code. It is initialized to false.

Next we declare a FloatRect called detectionZone and initialize it with the same rectangle that represents the entire rectangle of the character sprite. Note that we will not actually do intersection tests with this rectangle. After that, we declare another FloatRect called block. We initialize block as a 50 by 50 rectangle. We will see block in use shortly.

Next we see how we will use detectionZone. We initialize four int variables, startX, startY, endX, and endY by expanding the area around detectionZone a few blocks. In the four if statements that follow, we check that it is not possible to try and do collision detection on a tile that does not exist. We achieve this by making sure we never check positions less than zero or greater than the value returned by getLevelSize().x or .y.

What all this previous code has done is to create an area with which to do collision detection. There is no point doing collision detection on a block that is hundreds or thousands of pixels away from the character. In addition, if we try and do collision detection where an array position doesn't exist (less than zero or greater than getLevelSize()...), the game will crash.

Next, add this code, which handles the player falling out of the level:

```
// Has the character fallen out of the map?
FloatRect level(0, 0,
    m_LM.getLevelSize().x * TILE_SIZE,
    m_LM.getLevelSize().y * TILE_SIZE);
if (!character.getPosition().intersects(level))
{
    // respawn the character
    character.spawn(m_LM.getStartPosition(), GRAVITY);
}
```

For a character to stop falling, it must collide with a platform. Therefore, if the player moves out of the map (where there are no platforms) it will continuously fall. The previous code checks whether the character *does not* intersect with the `FloatRect`, `level`. If it does not, then it has fallen out of the level and the `spawn` function sends it back to the start.

Add the following, quite large code, and then we will go through what it does:

```
// Loop through all the local blocks
for (int x = startX; x < endX; x++)
{
    for (int y = startY; y < endY; y++)
    {
        // Initialize the starting position of the current block
        block.left = x * TILE_SIZE;
        block.top = y * TILE_SIZE;

        // Has character been burnt or drowned?
        // Use head as this allows him to sink a bit
        if (m_ArrayLevel[y][x] == 2 || m_ArrayLevel[y][x] == 3)
        {
            if (character.getHead().intersects(block))
            {
                character.spawn(m_LM.getStartPosition(), GRAVITY);
                // Which sound should be played?
                if (m_ArrayLevel[y][x] == 2)// Fire, ouch!
                {
                    // Play a sound

                }
                else // Water
                {
                    // Play a sound
                }
            }
        }
        // Is character colliding with a regular block
```

```
if (m_ArrayLevel[y][x] == 1)
{

    if (character.getRight().intersects(block))
    {
        character.stopRight(block.left);
    }
    else if (character.getLeft().intersects(block))
    {
        character.stopLeft(block.left);
    }


    if (character.getFeet().intersects(block))
    {
        character.stopFalling(block.top);
    }
    else if (character.getHead().intersects(block))
    {
        character.stopJump();
    }
}
// More collision detection here once we have
// learned about particle effects

// Has the character reached the goal?
if (m_ArrayLevel[y][x] == 4)
{
    // Character has reached the goal
    reachedGoal = true;
}

}

}
```

The previous code does three things using the same techniques. It loops through all the values contained between startX, endX and startY, endY. For each pass, it checks and does the following:

- Has the character burned or drowned? The code if (m_ArrayLevel[y][x] == 2 || m_ArrayLevel[y][x] == 3) determines if the current position being checked is a fire or a water tile. If the character's head intersects with one of these tiles, the player is re-spawned. We also code an empty if...else block in preparation for adding sound in the following chapter.

- Has the character touched a regular tile? The code `if (m_ArrayLevel[y][x] == 1)` determines if the current position being checked holds a regular tile. If it intersects with any of the rectangles that represent the various body parts of the character, the related function is called (`stopRight`, `stopLeft`, `stopFalling`, and `stopJump`). The value that is passed to each of these functions and how the function uses the value to reposition the character is quite nuanced. While it is not necessary to closely examine these values to understand the code, you might like to look at the values passed in and then refer back to the appropriate function of the `PlayableCharacter` class in the previous chapter. This will help you appreciate exactly what is going on.

- Has the character touched the goal tile? This is determined with the code `if (m_ArrayLevel[y][x] == 4)`. All we need to do is set `reachedGoal` to `true`. The `update` function of the `Engine` class will keep track of whether both characters (Thomas and Bob) have reached the goal simultaneously. We will write this code in `update` in just a minute.

Add the last line of code to the `detectCollisions` function:

```
// All done, return, whether or not a new level might be required
return reachedGoal;
}
```

The previous line of code returns `reachedGoal` so that the calling code can keep track and respond appropriately if both characters reach the goal simultaneously.

All we need to do now is call the `detectCollision` function once per character per frame. Add the following highlighted code in the `Update.cpp` file within the `if(m_Playing)` block of code:

```
if (m_Playing)
{
    // Update Thomas
    m_Thomas.update(dtAsSeconds);

    // Update Bob
    m_Bob.update(dtAsSeconds);

    // Detect collisions and see if characters
    // have reached the goal tile
    // The second part of the if condition is only executed
    // when thomas is touching the home tile
    if (detectCollisions(m_Thomas) && detectCollisions(m_Bob))
    {
        // New level required
```

```
        m_NewLevelRequired = true;
        // Play the reach goal sound
    }
    else
    {
      // Run bobs collision detection
      detectCollisions(m_Bob);
    }

    // Count down the time the player has left
    m_TimeRemaining -= dtAsSeconds;

    // Have Thomas and Bob run out of time?
    if (m_TimeRemaining <= 0)
    {
        m_NewLevelRequired = true;
    }

}// End if playing
```

The previous code calls the detectCollision function and checks if both Bob and Thomas have simultaneously reached the goal. If they have, the next level is prepared by setting m_NewLevelRequired to true.

You can run the game and walk on the platforms. You can reach the goal and start a new level. Also, for the first time, the jump buttons (*W* or Arrow Up) will work.

If you reach the goal, the next level will load. If you reach the goal of the last level, then the first level will load with a 10% reduced time limit. Of course, there is no visual feedback for the time or the current level because we haven't built a HUD yet. We will do so in the following chapter.

Many of the levels, however, require Thomas and Bob to work as a team. More specifically, Thomas and Bob need to be able to climb on each other's heads.

More collision detection

Add this code just after the previous code you added in the Update.cpp file, within the if (m_Playing) section:

```
if (m_Playing)
{
   // Update Thomas
   m_Thomas.update(dtAsSeconds);
```

```
    // Update Bob
    m_Bob.update(dtAsSeconds);

    // Detect collisions and see if characters
    // have reached the goal tile
    // The second part of the if condition is only executed
    // when thomas is touching the home tile
    if (detectCollisions(m_Thomas) && detectCollisions(m_Bob))
    {
        // New level required
        m_NewLevelRequired = true;

        // Play the reach goal sound

    }
    else
    {
        // Run bobs collision detection
        detectCollisions(m_Bob);
    }

    // Let bob and thomas jump on each others heads
    if (m_Bob.getFeet().intersects(m_Thomas.getHead()))
    {
      m_Bob.stopFalling(m_Thomas.getHead().top);
    }
    else if (m_Thomas.getFeet().intersects(m_Bob.getHead()))
    {
      m_Thomas.stopFalling(m_Bob.getHead().top);
    }

    // Count down the time the player has left
    m_TimeRemaining -= dtAsSeconds;

    // Have Thomas and Bob run out of time?
    if (m_TimeRemaining <= 0)
    {
        m_NewLevelRequired = true;
    }

}// End if playing
```

You can run the game again and stand on the heads of Thomas and Bob to get to the hard-to-reach places that were previously not attainable:

Summary

There was quite a lot of code in this chapter. We learned how to read from a file and convert strings of text into char and then `int`. Once we had a two-dimensional array of `int`, we were able to populate a `VertexArray` to actually show the level on the screen. We then used exactly the same two-dimensional array of int to implement collision detection. We used rectangle intersection, just as we did in the Zombie Arena project, although this time, for more precision, we gave each character four collision zones, one each to represent their head, feet, and their left and right sides.

Now that the game is totally playable, we need to represent the state of the game (score and time) on the screen. In the following chapter, we will implement the HUD, along with some much more advanced sound effects than we have used so far.

15
Sound Spatialization and HUD

In this chapter, we will be adding all the sound effects and the HUD. We have done this in both of the previous projects, but we will do things a bit differently this time. We will explore the concept of sound **spatialization** and how SFML makes this otherwise complicated concept nice and easy; in addition, we will build a HUD class to encapsulate the code that draws information to the screen.

We will complete these tasks in the following order:

- What is spatialization?
- How SFML handles spatialization
- Building a `SoundManager` class
- Deploying emitters
- Using the `SoundManager` class
- Building a `HUD` class
- Using the `HUD` class

What is Spatialization?

Spatialization is the act of making something relative to the space it is a part of, or within. In our daily lives, everything in the natural world, by default, is spatialized. If a motorbike whizzes past from left to right we will hear the sound grow from faint to loud from one side and as it passes by, it will become more prominent in the other ear, before fading into the distance once more. If we woke up one morning and the world was no longer spatialized, it would be exceptionally weird.

If we can make our video games a little bit more like the real world, our players can become more immersed. Our zombie game would have been a lot more fun if the player could have heard them faintly in the distance and their inhuman wailing grew louder as they drew closer, from one direction or another.

It is probably obvious that the mathematics of spatialization will be complex. How do we calculate how loud a given sound will be in a specific speaker, based on the direction the sound is coming from, and the distance from the player (the hearer of the sound) to the object that is making the sound (the emitter)?

Fortunately, SFML does all the complicated stuff for us. All we need to do is get familiar with a few technical terms and then we can start using SFML to spatialize our sound effects.

Emitters, attenuation, and listeners

We will need to be aware of a few pieces of information in order to give SFML what it needs to do its work. We will need to be aware of where the sound is coming from in our game world. This source of the sound is called an **emitter**. In a game, the emitter could be a Zombie, a vehicle, or in the case of our current project, a fire tile. We already keep track of the position of objects in our game, so giving SFML the emitter location will be quite straightforward.

The next factor we need to be aware of is **attenuation**. Attenuation is the rate at which a wave deteriorates. You could simplify that statement and make it specific to sound by saying that attenuation is how quickly the sound reduces in volume. That isn't technically exact, but it is a good enough description for the purposes of this chapter.

The final factor we need to consider is the **listener**. When SFML spatializes the sound, where is it spatializing it relative to? In most games, the logical thing to do is use the player character. In our game, we will use Thomas.

How SFML handles spatialization

SFML has a number of functions that allow us to handle emitters, attenuation, and listeners. Let's take a look at them hypothetically, and then we will write some code to add spatialized sound to our project for real.

We can set up a sound effect ready to be played, as we have done so often, as follows:

```
// Declare SoundBuffer in the usual way
SoundBuffer zombieBuffer;
```

```
// Declare a Sound object as-per-usual
Sound zombieSound;
// Load the sound from a file like we have done so often
zombieBuffer.loadFromFile("sound/zombie_growl.wav");
// Associate the Sound object with the Buffer
zombieSound.setBuffer(zombieBuffer);
```

We can set the position of the emitter using the `setPosition` function, as shown in the following code:

```
// Set the horizontal and vertical positions of the emitter
// In this case the emitter is a zombie
// In the Zombie Arena project we could have used
// getPosition().x and getPosition().y
// These values are arbitrary
float x = 500;
float y = 500;
zombieSound.setPosition(x, y, 0.0f);
```

As suggested in the comments of the previous code, how exactly you obtain the coordinates of the emitter will probably be dependent upon the type of game. As shown in the previous code, this would be quite simple in the Zombie Arena project. We will have a few challenges to overcome when we set the position in this project.

We can set the attenuation level using the following code:

```
zombieSound.setAttenuation(15);
```

The actual attenuation level can be a little ambiguous. The effect that you want the player to get might be different from the accurate scientific formula used to reduce the volume over distance based on attenuation. Getting the right attenuation level is usually achieved by experimenting. Generally speaking, the higher the level of attenuation, the quicker the sound level reduces to silence.

Also, you might want to set a zone around the emitter where the volume is not attenuated at all. You might do this if the feature isn't appropriate beyond a certain range, or you have a large number of sound sources and don't want to overdo the feature. To do so, we can use the `setMinimumDistance` function, as shown here:

```
zombieSound.setMinDistance(150);
```

With the previous line of code, attenuation would not begin to be calculated until the listener is `150` pixels/units away from the emitter.

Some other useful functions from the SFML library include the `setLoop` function. This function will tell SFML to keep playing the sound over and over when true is passed in as a parameter, as demonstrated by the following code:

```
zombieSound.setLoop(true);
```

The sound will continue to play until we ended it with the following code:

```
zombieSound.stop();
```

From time to time, we will want to know the status of a sound (playing or stopped). We can achieve this with the `getStatus` function, as demonstrated in the following code:

```
if (zombieSound.getStatus() == Sound::Status::Stopped)
{
    // The sound is NOT playing
    // Take whatever action here
}

if (zombieSound.getStatus() == Sound::Status::Playing)
{
    // The sound IS playing
    // Take whatever action here
}
```

There is just one more aspect of using sound spatialization with SFML that we need to cover. Where is the listener? We can set the position of the listener with the following code:

```
// Where is the listener?
// How we get the values of x and y varies depending upon the game
// In the Zombie Arena game or the Thomas Was Late game
// We can use getPosition()
Listener::setPosition(m_Thomas.getPosition().x,
    m_Thomas.getPosition().y, 0.0f);
```

The preceding code will make all sounds play relative to that location. This is just what we need for the distant roar of a fire tile or incoming zombie, but for regular sound effects such as jumping, this is a problem. We could start handling an emitter for the location of the player, but SFML makes things simple for us. Whenever we want to play a *normal* sound, we simply call `setRelativeToListener`, as shown in the following code, and then play the sound in the exact same way we have done so far. Here is how we might play a *normal*, un-spatialized jump sound effect:

```
jumpSound.setRelativeToListener(true);
jumpSound.play();
```

All we need to do is call `Listener::setPosition` again before we play any spatialized sounds.

We now have a wide repertoire of SFML sound functions and we are ready to make some spatialized noise for real.

Building the SoundManager class

You might recall that in the previous project, all the sound code took up quite a few lines of code. Now consider that with spatialization, it's going to get longer still. To keep our code manageable, we will code a class to manage the playing of all our sound effects. In addition, to help us with spatialization, we will add a function to the Engine class as well, but we will discuss that when we come to it, later in the chapter.

Coding SoundManager.h

Let's get started by coding and examining the header file.

Right-click **Header Files** in the **Solution Explorer** and select **Add | New Item....** In the **Add New Item** window, highlight (by left-clicking) **Header File (.h)** and then in the **Name** field, type `SoundManager.h`. Finally, click the **Add** button. We are now ready to code the header file for the `SoundManager` class.

Add and examine the following code:

```
#pragma once
#include <SFML/Audio.hpp>

using namespace sf;

class SoundManager
{
    private:
        // The buffers
        SoundBuffer m_FireBuffer;
        SoundBuffer m_FallInFireBuffer;
        SoundBuffer m_FallInWaterBuffer;
        SoundBuffer m_JumpBuffer;
        SoundBuffer m_ReachGoalBuffer;

        // The Sounds
        Sound m_Fire1Sound;
```

```
        Sound m_Fire2Sound;
        Sound m_Fire3Sound;
        Sound m_FallInFireSound;
        Sound m_FallInWaterSound;
        Sound m_JumpSound;
        Sound m_ReachGoalSound;

        // Which sound should we use next, fire 1, 2 or 3
        int m_NextSound = 1;

    public:

        SoundManager();

        void playFire(Vector2f emitterLocation,
            Vector2f listenerLocation);

        void playFallInFire();
        void playFallInWater();
        void playJump();
        void playReachGoal();
};
```

There is nothing tricky in the code we just added. There are five SoundBuffer objects and eight Sound objects. Three of the Sound objects will play the same SoundBuffer. This explains the reason for the different number of Sound/SoundBuffer objects. We do this so that we can have multiple roaring sound effects playing, with different spatialized parameters, simultaneously.

Notice there is the m_NextSound variable that will help us keep track of which of these potentially simultaneous sounds we should use next.

There is a constructor, SoundManager, where we will set up all our sound effects, and there are five functions that will play the sound effects. Four of these functions simply play *normal* sound effects and their code will be really simple.

One of the functions, playFire, will handle the spatialized sound effects and will be a bit more in-depth. Notice the parameters of the playFire function. It receives a Vector2f, which is the location of the emitter, and a second Vector2f, which is the location of the listener.

Coding the SoundManager.cpp file

Now we can code the function definitions. The constructor and the `playFire` functions have a fair amount of code, so we will look at them individually. The other functions are short and sweet so we will handle them all at once.

Right-click **Source Files** in the **Solution Explorer** and select **Add | New Item....** In the **Add New Item** window, highlight (by left-clicking) **C++ File (**`.cpp`**)** and then in the **Name** field, type `SoundManager.cpp`. Finally, click the **Add** button. We are now ready to code the `.cpp` file for the `SoundManager` class.

Coding the constructor

Add the following code for the include directives and the constructor to `SoundManager.cpp`:

```
#include "stdafx.h"
#include "SoundManager.h"
#include <SFML/Audio.hpp>

using namespace sf;

SoundManager::SoundManager()
{
    // Load the sound in to the buffers
    m_FireBuffer.loadFromFile("sound/fire1.wav");
    m_FallInFireBuffer.loadFromFile("sound/fallinfire.wav");
    m_FallInWaterBuffer.loadFromFile("sound/fallinwater.wav");
    m_JumpBuffer.loadFromFile("sound/jump.wav");
    m_ReachGoalBuffer.loadFromFile("sound/reachgoal.wav");

    // Associate the sounds with the buffers
    m_Fire1Sound.setBuffer(m_FireBuffer);
    m_Fire2Sound.setBuffer(m_FireBuffer);
    m_Fire3Sound.setBuffer(m_FireBuffer);
    m_FallInFireSound.setBuffer(m_FallInFireBuffer);
    m_FallInWaterSound.setBuffer(m_FallInWaterBuffer);
    m_JumpSound.setBuffer(m_JumpBuffer);
    m_ReachGoalSound.setBuffer(m_ReachGoalBuffer);
    // When the player is 50 pixels away sound is full volume
    float minDistance = 150;
    // The sound reduces steadily as the player moves further away
    float attenuation = 15;

    // Set all the attenuation levels
```

```
m_Fire1Sound.setAttenuation(attenuation);
m_Fire2Sound.setAttenuation(attenuation);
m_Fire3Sound.setAttenuation(attenuation);

// Set all the minimum distance levels
m_Fire1Sound.setMinDistance(minDistance);
m_Fire2Sound.setMinDistance(minDistance);
m_Fire3Sound.setMinDistance(minDistance);

// Loop all the fire sounds
// when they are played
m_Fire1Sound.setLoop(true);
m_Fire2Sound.setLoop(true);
m_Fire3Sound.setLoop(true);
}
```

In the previous code, we loaded five sound files into the five `SoundBuffer` objects. Next, we associated the eight `Sound` objects with one of the `SoundBuffer` objects. Notice that `m_Fire1Sound`, `m_Fire2Sound`, and `m_Fire3Sound` are all going to be playing from the same `SoundBuffer`, `m_FireBuffer`.

Next, we set the attenuation and minimum distance for the three fire sounds.

The values of `150` and `15`, respectively, were arrived at through experimentation. Once the game is running, I encourage you to experiment with these values by changing them around and seeing (or rather hearing) the difference.

Finally, for the constructor, we used the `setLoop` function on each of the fire-related `Sound` objects. Now when we call `play`, they will play continuously.

Coding the playFire function

Add the `playFire` function shown in the following code, and then we can discuss it:

```
void SoundManager::playFire(
    Vector2f emitterLocation, Vector2f listenerLocation)
{
    // Where is the listener? Thomas.
    Listener::setPosition(listenerLocation.x,
        listenerLocation.y, 0.0f);

    switch(m_NextSound)
    {
```

```
case 1:
    // Locate/move the source of the sound
    m_Fire1Sound.setPosition(emitterLocation.x,
        emitterLocation.y, 0.0f);

    if (m_Fire1Sound.getStatus() == Sound::Status::Stopped)
    {
        // Play the sound, if its not already
        m_Fire1Sound.play();
    }
    break;

case 2:
    // Do the same as previous for the second sound
    m_Fire2Sound.setPosition(emitterLocation.x,
        emitterLocation.y, 0.0f);

    if (m_Fire2Sound.getStatus() == Sound::Status::Stopped)
    {
        m_Fire2Sound.play();
    }
    break;

case 3:
    // Do the same as previous for the third sound
    m_Fire3Sound.setPosition(emitterLocation.x,
        emitterLocation.y, 0.0f);

    if (m_Fire3Sound.getStatus() == Sound::Status::Stopped)
    {
        m_Fire3Sound.play();
    }
    break;
}

// Increment to the next fire sound
m_NextSound++;

// Go back to 1 when the third sound has been started
if (m_NextSound > 3)
{
    m_NextSound = 1;
}
}
```

The first thing we do is call `Listener::setPosition` and set the location of the listener based on the `Vector2f` that is passed in as a parameter.

Next, the code enters a `switch` block based on the value of `m_NextSound`. Each of the `case` statements does the exact same thing, but to either `m_Fire1Sound`, `m_Fire2Sound`, or `m_Fire3Sound`.

In each of the `case` blocks, we set the position of the emitter using the passed-in parameter with the `setPosition` function. The next part of the code in each `case` block checks whether the sound is currently stopped, and if it is, plays the sound. We will see quite soon how we arrive at the positions for the emitter and listener that are passed into this function.

The final part of the `playFire` function increments `m_NextSound` and ensures that it can only be equal to 1, 2, or 3, as required by the `switch` block.

Coding the rest of the SoundManager functions

Add these four simple functions:

```
void SoundManager::playFallInFire()
{
    m_FallInFireSound.setRelativeToListener(true);
    m_FallInFireSound.play();
}

void SoundManager::playFallInWater()
{
    m_FallInWaterSound.setRelativeToListener(true);
    m_FallInWaterSound.play();
}

void SoundManager::playJump()
{
    m_JumpSound.setRelativeToListener(true);
    m_JumpSound.play();
}

void SoundManager::playReachGoal()
{
    m_ReachGoalSound.setRelativeToListener(true);
    m_ReachGoalSound.play();
}
```

The playFallInFire, playFallInWater, and playReachGoal functions do just two things. First, they each call setRelativeToListener, so the sound effect is not spatialized, making the sound effect *normal*, not directional, and then they call play on the appropriate Sound object.

That concludes the SoundManager class. Now we can use it in the Engine class.

Adding SoundManager to the game engine

Open the Engine.h file and add an instance of the new SoundManager class, as shown in the following highlighted code:

```
#pragma once
#include <SFML/Graphics.hpp>
#include "TextureHolder.h"
#include "Thomas.h"
#include "Bob.h"
#include "LevelManager.h"
#include "SoundManager.h"

using namespace sf;

class Engine
{
private:
    // The texture holder
    TextureHolder th;

    // Thomas and his friend, Bob
    Thomas m_Thomas;
    Bob m_Bob;

    // A class to manage all the levels
    LevelManager m_LM;

    // Create a SoundManager
    SoundManager m_SM;

    const int TILE_SIZE = 50;
    const int VERTS_IN_QUAD = 4;
```

At this point, we could use m_SM to call the various play... functions. Unfortunately, there is still a bit more work to be done in order to manage the locations of the emitters (fire tiles).

Populating the sound emitters

Open the `Engine.h` file and add a new prototype for a `populateEmitters` function and a new STL `vector` of `Vector2f` objects:

```
    . . .
    . . .
    . . .
    // Run will call all the private functions
    bool detectCollisions(PlayableCharacter& character);

    // Make a vector of the best places to emit sounds from
    void populateEmitters(vector <Vector2f>& vSoundEmitters,
      int** arrayLevel);

    // A vector of Vector2f for the fire emitter locations
    vector <Vector2f> m_FireEmitters;
public:
    . . .
    . . .
    . . .
```

The `populateEmitters` function takes as a parameter a `vector` of `Vector2f` objects, as well as a pointer to `int` (a two-dimensional array). The `vector` will hold the location of each emitter in a level and the array is our two-dimensional array, which holds the layout of a level.

Coding the populateEmitters function

The job of the `populateEmitters` function is to scan through all the elements of `arrayLevel` and decide where to put the emitters. It will store its results in `m_FireEmitters`.

Right-click **Source Files** in the **Solution Explorer** and select **Add | New Item...** In the **Add New Item** window, highlight (by left-clicking) **C++ File** (`.cpp`) and then in the **Name** field, type `PopulateEmitters.cpp`. Finally, click the **Add** button. Now we can code the new function, `populateEmitters`.

Add the code in its entirety; be sure to study the code as you do, and then we can discuss it:

```
#include "stdafx.h"
#include "Engine.h"

using namespace sf;
```

```cpp
using namespace std;

void Engine::populateEmitters(
    vector <Vector2f>& vSoundEmitters, int** arrayLevel)
{

    // Make sure the vector is empty
    vSoundEmitters.empty();

    // Keep track of the previous emitter
    // so we don't make too many
    FloatRect previousEmitter;

    // Search for fire in the level
    for (int x = 0; x < (int)m_LM.getLevelSize().x; x++)
    {
        for (int y = 0; y < (int)m_LM.getLevelSize().y; y++)
        {
            if (arrayLevel[y][x] == 2)// fire is present
            {
                // Skip over any fire tiles too
                // near a previous emitter
                if (!FloatRect(x * TILE_SIZE,
                    y * TILE_SIZE,
                    TILE_SIZE,
                    TILE_SIZE).intersects(previousEmitter))
                {
                    // Add the coordiantes of this water block
                    vSoundEmitters.push_back(
                        Vector2f(x * TILE_SIZE, y * TILE_SIZE));

                    // Make a rectangle 6 blocks x 6 blocks,
                    // so we don't make any more emitters
                    // too close to this one
                    previousEmitter.left = x * TILE_SIZE;
                    previousEmitter.top = y * TILE_SIZE;
                    previousEmitter.width = TILE_SIZE * 6;
                    previousEmitter.height = TILE_SIZE * 6;
                }

            }

        }

    }
    return;

}
```

Some of the code might appear complex at first glance. Understanding the technique we use to choose where an emitter will make it simpler. In our levels, there are, regularly, large blocks of fire tiles. In one of the levels I designed there are more than 30 fire tiles together. The code makes sure that there is only one emitter within a given rectangle. This rectangle is stored in previousEmitter and is 300 pixels by 300 pixels (TILE_SIZE * 6).

The code sets up a nested for loop that loops through arrayLevel looking for fire tiles. When it finds one, it makes sure that it does not intersect with previousEmitter. Only then does it use the pushBack function to add another emitter to vSoundEmitters. After doing so, it also updates previousEmitter to avoid getting large clusters of sound emitters.

Let's make some noise.

Playing sounds

Open up the LoadLevel.cpp file and add the call to the new populateEmitters function, as highlighted in the following code:

```
void Engine::loadLevel()
{
    m_Playing = false;

    // Delete the previously allocated memory
    for (int i = 0; i < m_LM.getLevelSize().y; ++i)
    {
        delete[] m_ArrayLevel[i];

    }
    delete[] m_ArrayLevel;

    // Load the next 2d array with the map for the level
    // And repopulate the vertex array as well
    m_ArrayLevel = m_LM.nextLevel(m_VALevel);

    // Prepare the sound emitters
    populateEmitters(m_FireEmitters, m_ArrayLevel);

    // How long is this new time limit
    m_TimeRemaining = m_LM.getTimeLimit();

    // Spawn Thomas and Bob
    m_Thomas.spawn(m_LM.getStartPosition(), GRAVITY);
    m_Bob.spawn(m_LM.getStartPosition(), GRAVITY);
```

```
    // Make sure this code isn't run again
    m_NewLevelRequired = false;
}
```

The first sound to add is the jump sound. You might remember that the keyboard handling code is in the pure virtual functions within both the `Bob` and `Thomas` classes, and that the `handleInput` function returns `true` when a jump has been successfully initiated.

Open up the `Input.cpp` file and add the highlighted lines of code to play a jump sound when either Thomas or Bob successfully begins a jump:

```
// Handle input specific to Thomas
if (m_Thomas.handleInput())
{
    // Play a jump sound
    m_SM.playJump();
}

// Handle input specific to Bob
if (m_Bob.handleInput())
{
    // Play a jump sound
    m_SM.playJump();
}
```

Open up the `Update.cpp` file and add the highlighted line of code to play a success sound when both Thomas and Bob have simultaneously reached the goal for the current level:

```
// Detect collisions and see if characters have reached the goal tile
// The second part of the if condition is only executed
// when thomas is touching the home tile
if (detectCollisions(m_Thomas) && detectCollisions(m_Bob))
{
    // New level required
    m_NewLevelRequired = true;

    // Play the reach goal sound
    m_SM.playReachGoal();

}
else
{
    // Run bobs collision detection
    detectCollisions(m_Bob);
}
```

Also within the `Update.cpp` file, we will add code to loop through the `m_FireEmitters` vector and decide when we need to call the `playFire` function of the `SoundManager` class.

Look closely at the small amount of context around the new highlighted code. It is essential to add this code in exactly the right place:

```
}// End if playing

// Check if a fire sound needs to be played
vector<Vector2f>::iterator it;

// Iterate through the vector of Vector2f objects
for (it = m_FireEmitters.begin();it != m_FireEmitters.end(); it++)
{
    // Where is this emitter?
    // Store the location in pos
    float posX = (*it).x;
    float posY = (*it).y;
    // is the emiter near the player?
    // Make a 500 pixel rectangle around the emitter
    FloatRect localRect(posX - 250, posY - 250, 500, 500);

    // Is the player inside localRect?
    if (m_Thomas.getPosition().intersects(localRect))
    {
        // Play the sound and pass in the location as well
        m_SM.playFire(Vector2f(posX, posY), m_Thomas.getCenter());
    }
}
// Set the appropriate view around the appropriate character
```

The previous code is a bit like collision detection for sound. Whenever Thomas stays within a 500-by-500 pixel rectangle surrounding a fire emitter, the `playFire` function is called, passing in the coordinates of the emitter and of Thomas. The `playFire` function does the rest of the work and sets off a spatialized, looping sound effect.

Open up the `DetectCollisions.cpp` file, find the appropriate place, and add the highlighted code as shown in the following. The two highlighted lines of code trigger the playing of a sound effect when either character falls into a water or fire tile:

```
// Has character been burnt or drowned?
// Use head as this allows him to sink a bit
if (m_ArrayLevel[y][x] == 2 || m_ArrayLevel[y][x] == 3)
{
    if (character.getHead().intersects(block))
    {
        character.spawn(m_LM.getStartPosition(), GRAVITY);
```

```
      // Which sound should be played?
      if (m_ArrayLevel[y][x] == 2)// Fire, ouch!
      {
        // Play a sound
        m_SM.playFallInFire();

      }
      else // Water
      {
        // Play a sound
        m_SM.playFallInWater();
      }
    }
  }
```

Playing the game will allow you to hear all the sounds, including cool spatialization, when near a fire tile.

The HUD class

The HUD is super-simple and not really anything different compared to the other two projects in the book. What we will do that is different is wrap all the code up in a new HUD class. If we declare all the Font, Text, and other variables as members of this new class, we can then initialize them in the constructor and provide getter functions to all their values. This will keep the Engine class clear from loads of declarations and initializations.

Coding HUD.h

First, we will code the HUD.h file with all the member variables and function declarations. Right-click **Header Files** in the **Solution Explorer** and select **Add | New Item....** In the **Add New Item** window, highlight (by left-clicking) **Header File** (.h) and then in the **Name** field, type HUD.h. Finally, click the **Add** button. We are now ready to code the header file for the HUD class.

Add the following code to HUD.h:

```
#pragma once
#include <SFML/Graphics.hpp>

using namespace sf;

class Hud
```

```
{
private:
    Font m_Font;
    Text m_StartText;
    Text m_TimeText;
    Text m_LevelText;

public:
    Hud();
    Text getMessage();
    Text getLevel();
    Text getTime();

    void setLevel(String text);
    void setTime(String text);
};
```

In the previous code, we added one Font instance and three Text instances. The Text objects will be used to show a message prompting the user to start, the time remaining, and the current level number.

The public functions are more interesting. First, there is the constructor, where most of the code will go. The constructor will initialize the Font and Text objects, as well as position them on the screen relative to the current screen resolution.

The three getter functions, getMessage, getLevel, and getTime will return a Text object to the calling code in order to be able to draw them to the screen.

The setLevel and setTime functions will be used to update the text shown in m_LevelText and m_TimeText, respectively.

Now we can code all the definitions for the functions we have just outlined.

Coding the HUD.cpp file

Right-click **Source Files** in the **Solution Explorer** and select **Add | New Item....** In the **Add New Item** window, highlight (by left-clicking) **C++ File (**.cpp**)** and then in the **Name** field, type HUD.cpp. Finally, click the **Add** button. We are now ready to code the .cpp file for the HUD class.

Add the include directives and the following code, and then we will discuss it:

```
#include "stdafx.h"
#include "Hud.h"
```

```
Hud::Hud()
{
    Vector2u resolution;
    resolution.x = VideoMode::getDesktopMode().width;
    resolution.y = VideoMode::getDesktopMode().height;

    // Load the font
    m_Font.loadFromFile("fonts/Roboto-Light.ttf");

    // when Paused
    m_StartText.setFont(m_Font);
    m_StartText.setCharacterSize(100);
    m_StartText.setFillColor(Color::White);
    m_StartText.setString("Press Enter when ready!");

    // Position the text
    FloatRect textRect = m_StartText.getLocalBounds();

    m_StartText.setOrigin(textRect.left +
        textRect.width / 2.0f,
        textRect.top +
        textRect.height / 2.0f);

    m_StartText.setPosition(
        resolution.x / 2.0f, resolution.y / 2.0f);

    // Time
    m_TimeText.setFont(m_Font);
    m_TimeText.setCharacterSize(75);
    m_TimeText.setFillColor(Color::White);
    m_TimeText.setPosition(resolution.x - 150, 0);
    m_TimeText.setString("------");

    // Level
    m_LevelText.setFont(m_Font);
    m_LevelText.setCharacterSize(75);
    m_LevelText.setFillColor(Color::White);
    m_LevelText.setPosition(25, 0);
    m_LevelText.setString("1");
}
```

First, we store the horizontal and vertical resolution in a `Vector2u` called `resolution`. Next, we load the font from the `fonts` directory that we added back in `Chapter 12, Abstraction and Code Management – Making Better Use of OOP`.

The next four lines of code set the font, the color, the size, and the text of m_StartText. The block of code after this captures the size of the rectangle that wraps m_StartText and performs a calculation to work out how to position it centrally on the screen. If you want a more thorough explanation of this part of the code, refer back to Chapter 3: *C++ Strings, SFML Time – Player Input and HUD*.

The final two blocks of code in the constructor set the font, text size, color, position, and actual text for m_TimeText and m_LevelText. We will see in a moment, however, that these two Text objects will be updatable through two setter functions, whenever it is required.

Add the following getter and setter functions immediately after the code we have just added:

```
Text Hud::getMessage()
{
    return m_StartText;
}

Text Hud::getLevel()
{
    return m_LevelText;
}

Text Hud::getTime()
{
    return m_TimeText;
}

void Hud::setLevel(String text)
{
    m_LevelText.setString(text);
}

void Hud::setTime(String text)
{
    m_TimeText.setString(text);
}
```

The first three functions in the previous code simply return the appropriate Text object, m_StartText, m_LevelText, and m_TimeText. We will use these functions shortly, when drawing the HUD on the screen. The final two functions, setLevel and setTime, use the setString functions to update the appropriate Text object with the value that will be passed in from the update function of the Engine class every 500 frames.

With all that done, we can put the HUD class to work in our game engine.

Using the HUD class

Open `Engine.h`, add an include for our new class, declare an instance of the new HUD class, and also declare and initialize two new member variables that will keep track of how often we update the HUD. As we have learned in the two previous projects, we don't need to do this for every frame.

Add the highlighted code to `Engine.h`:

```
#pragma once
#include <SFML/Graphics.hpp>
#include "TextureHolder.h"
#include "Thomas.h"
#include "Bob.h"
#include "LevelManager.h"
#include "SoundManager.h"
#include "HUD.h"

using namespace sf;

class Engine
{
private:
    // The texture holder
    TextureHolder th;

    // Thomas and his friend, Bob
    Thomas m_Thomas;
    Bob m_Bob;

    // A class to manage all the levels
    LevelManager m_LM;

    // Create a SoundManager
    SoundManager m_SM;

    // The Hud    Hud m_Hud;
    int m_FramesSinceLastHUDUpdate = 0;
    int m_TargetFramesPerHUDUpdate = 500;

    const int TILE_SIZE = 50;
```

Next, we need to add some code to the update function of the Engine class. Open Update.cpp and add the highlighted code to update the HUD once every 500 frames:

```cpp
// Set the appropriate view around the appropriate character
if (m_SplitScreen)
{
    m_LeftView.setCenter(m_Thomas.getCenter());
    m_RightView.setCenter(m_Bob.getCenter());
}
else
{
    // Centre full screen around appropriate character
    if (m_Character1)
    {
        m_MainView.setCenter(m_Thomas.getCenter());
    }
    else
    {
        m_MainView.setCenter(m_Bob.getCenter());
    }
}

// Time to update the HUD?
// Increment the number of frames since the last HUD calculation
m_FramesSinceLastHUDUpdate++;

// Update the HUD every m_TargetFramesPerHUDUpdate frames
if (m_FramesSinceLastHUDUpdate > m_TargetFramesPerHUDUpdate)
{
    // Update game HUD text
    stringstream ssTime;
    stringstream ssLevel;
    // Update the time text
    ssTime << (int)m_TimeRemaining;
    m_Hud.setTime(ssTime.str());
    // Update the level text
    ssLevel << "Level:" << m_LM.getCurrentLevel();
    m_Hud.setLevel(ssLevel.str());
    m_FramesSinceLastHUDUpdate = 0;
}
}// End of update function
```

In the previous code, `m_FramesSinceLastUpdate` is incremented each frame. When `m_FramesSinceLastUpdate` exceeds `m_TargetFramesPerHUDUpdate`, execution enters the `if` block. Inside the `if` block, we use `stringstream` objects to update our `Text`, as we have done in both previous projects. As you probably expected, however, in this project we are using the `HUD` class, so we call the `setTime` and `setLevel` functions, passing in the current values that the `Text` objects need to be set to.

The final step in the `if` block is to set `m_FramesSinceLastUpdate` back to zero so it can start counting toward the next update.

Finally, open the `Draw.cpp` file and add the highlighted code to draw the HUD, each frame:

```
    else
    {
        // Split-screen view is active

        // First draw Thomas' side of the screen

        // Switch to background view
        m_Window.setView(m_BGLeftView);
        // Draw the background
        m_Window.draw(m_BackgroundSprite);
        // Switch to m_LeftView
        m_Window.setView(m_LeftView);

        // Draw the Level
        m_Window.draw(m_VALevel, &m_TextureTiles);
        // Draw thomas
        m_Window.draw(m_Bob.getSprite());

        // Draw thomas
        m_Window.draw(m_Thomas.getSprite());
        // Now draw Bob's side of the screen

        // Switch to background view
        m_Window.setView(m_BGRightView);
        // Draw the background
        m_Window.draw(m_BackgroundSprite);
        // Switch to m_RightView
        m_Window.setView(m_RightView);

        // Draw the Level
        m_Window.draw(m_VALevel, &m_TextureTiles);

        // Draw thomas
        m_Window.draw(m_Thomas.getSprite());
```

```
    // Draw bob
    m_Window.draw(m_Bob.getSprite());
}

// Draw the HUD
// Switch to m_HudView
m_Window.setView(m_HudView);
m_Window.draw(m_Hud.getLevel());
m_Window.draw(m_Hud.getTime());
if (!m_Playing)
{
  m_Window.draw(m_Hud.getMessage());
}
// Show everything we have just drawn
m_Window.display();
}// End of draw
```

The previous code draws the HUD by using the getter functions from the HUD class. Notice that the call to draw the message to that prompts the player to start is only used when the game is not currently playing (!m_Playing).

Run the game and play a few levels to see the time tick down and the levels tick up. When you get back to level one again, notice that you have 10% less time than before.

Summary

Our Thomas Was Late game is not only fully playable, with directional sound effects and a simple but informative HUD, but we also have the capability to add new levels with ease. At this point, we could call it done.

It would be nice to add a bit more sparkle. In the following chapter, we will look into two gaming concepts. Firstly we will look at particle systems, which are how we can handle things such as explosions or other special effects. To achieve this, we will need to learn a bit more C++, look at a way we might radically rethink how we structure our game code.

After that, we will add the final flourish to the game when we learn about OpenGL and the programmable graphics pipeline. We will then be in a position to dip our toes into the **GLSL** language, which allows us to write code that executes directly on the GPU, to create some special effects.

16

Extending SFML Classes, Particle Systems, and Shaders

In this final chapter, we will explore the C++ concept of extending other people's classes. More specifically, we will look at the SFML `Drawable` class and the benefits of using it as a base class for our own classes. We will also scratch the surface of the topic of OpenGL shaders and see how writing code in another language **OpenGL Shading Language (GLSL)**, which can be run directly on the graphics card, can lead to smooth graphical effects that might otherwise be impossible. As usual, we will also use our new skills and knowledge to enhance the current project.

Here is a list of the topics in the order we will cover them:

- The SFML Drawable class
- Building a particle system
- OpenGl shaders and GLSL
- Using shaders in the Thomas Was Late game

The SFML Drawable class

The `Drawable` class has just one function. It has no variables either. Furthermore, its one and only function is pure virtual. This means that if we inherit from `Drawable`, we must implement its one and only function. The purpose of this, which you may remember from `Chapter 12`, *Abstraction and Code Management – Making Better Use of OOP*, is that we can then use our class, which inherits from `drawable`, as a polymorphic type. Put more simply, anything that SFML allows us to do with a `Drawable` object, we will be able to do with our class that inherits from it. The only requirement is that we must provide a definition for the pure virtual function, `draw`.

Some classes that inherit from `Drawable` already include `Sprite` and `VertexArray` (among others). Whenever we have used `Sprite` or `VertexArray`, we have passed them to the `draw` function of the `RenderWindow` class.

The reason that we have been able to draw every object we have drawn in this book is that they have all inherited from `Drawable`. We can use this knowledge to our advantage.

We can inherit from `Drawable` with any object we like, as long as we implement the pure virtual `draw` function. This is also a straightforward process. The header file (`SpaceShip.h`) of a hypothetical `SpaceShip` class that inherits from `Drawable` would look as follows:

```
class SpaceShip : public Drawable
{
private:
    Sprite m_Sprite;
    // More private members
public:

    virtual void draw(RenderTarget& target,
        RenderStates states) const;

    // More public members

};
```

In the previous code, we can see the pure virtual `draw` function and a Sprite. Notice there is no way to access the private `Sprite` outside of the class, not even a `getSprite` function!

The `SpaceShip.cpp` file would then look something like the following:

```
void SpaceShip::SpaceShip
{
    // Set up the spaceship
}

void SpaceShip::draw(RenderTarget& target, RenderStates states) const
{
    target.draw(m_Sprite, states);
}

// Any other functions
```

In the previous code, notice the simple implementation of the draw function. The parameters are beyond the scope of the book. Just note that the target parameter is used to call draw and passes in m_Sprite as well as states, the other parameter.

 While it is not necessary to understand the parameters to take full advantage of Drawable, in the context of the book, you might be intrigued. You can read more about the SFML Drawable class on the SFML website: http://www.sfml-dev.org/tutorials/2.3/graphics-ve rtex-array.php#creating-an-sfml-like-entity

In the main game loop, we could now treat a SpaceShip instance as if it were a Sprite, or any other class that inherits from Drawable:

```
SpaceShip m_SpaceShip;
// create other objects here
// ...

// In the draw function
// Rub out the last frame
m_Window.clear(Color::Black);

// Draw the spaceship
m_Window.draw(m_SpaceShip);
// More drawing here
// ...

// Show everything we have just drawn
m_Window.display();
```

It is because SpaceShip is a Drawable that we can treat it like a Sprite or VertexArray, and because we overrode the pure virtual draw function, everything just works as we want it to. Let's look at an alternative way of encapsulating the drawing code into the game object.

An alternative to inheriting from Drawable

It is also possible to keep all the drawing functionality within the class that is the object to be drawn by implementing our own function, within our class, perhaps like the following code:

```
void drawThisObject(RenderWindow window)
{
    window.draw(m_Sprite)
}
```

The previous code assumes that `m_Sprite` represents the visual appearance of the current class we are drawing, as it has throughout this and the previous project. Assuming that the instance of the class that contains the `drawThisObject` function is called `playerHero`, and further assuming we have an instance of `RenderWindow` called `m_Window`, we could then draw the object from the main game loop with the following code:

```
playerHero.draw(m_Window);
```

In this solution, we pass the `RenderWindow`, `m_Window`, into the `drawThisObject` function as a parameter. The `drawThisObject` function then uses the `RenderWindow` to draw the Sprite, `m_Sprite`.

This solution certainly seems simpler than extending `Drawable`. The reason we do things the way suggested (extending Drawable) isn't really of any great benefit, in its own right, for this project. The actual reason we will soon draw a neat explosion using this method is because it is a good technique to learn.

Why it is best to inherit from Drawable?

With each project we have completed throughout the book, we have learned more about games, C++, and SFML. Possibly the biggest improvements we have made from one game to the next is in the structure of our code—the programming **patterns** that we have used.

If there were a fourth project to this book, we could take things even further. Unfortunately, there isn't, but have a think about the following idea for improving our code.

Imagine every object in our game is derived from a single, simple, abstract base class. Let's call it GameObject. Game object would probably have concrete functions for getPosition and others. It would likely have a pure virtual update function (because every object updates differently). Furthermore, consider that GameObject inherits from Drawable.

Now look at this hypothetical code:

```
vector<GameObject> m_GameObjects;
// Code to initialise all game objects
// Including tiles, characters, enemies, bullets and anything else

// In the update function
for (i = m_GameObjects.begin(); i != m_GameObjects.end(); i++)
{
    (*i).update(elapsedTime);
}
// That's it!

// In the draw function
// Rub out the last frame
m_Window.clear(Color::Black);

for (i = m_GameObjects.begin(); i != m_GameObjects.end(); i++)
{
    m_Window.draw(*i);
}

// Show everything we have just drawn
m_Window.display();
// That's it!
```

The preceding code is a big step up in terms of encapsulation, code manageability, and elegance when compared to even this final project. If you look at the previous code, you will notice there are, however, unanswered questions, such as where collision detection fits in, for example. Hopefully, however, you can see that further study (by building lots of games) will be necessary to master C++.

Although we will not be implementing an entire game in this manner, we will see how we can design a class (ParticleSystem) and pass it directly to m_Window.draw(m_MyParticleSystemInstance).

Building a particle system

Before we start coding, it will be helpful to see exactly what it is we are trying to achieve. Take a look at the following screenshot:

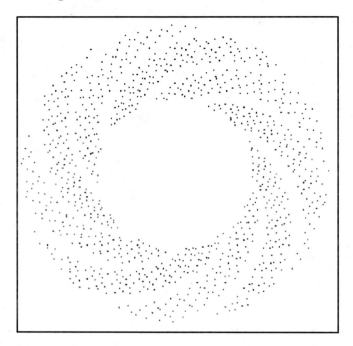

This is a screenshot of the particle effect on a plain background. We will use the effect in our game.

The way we achieve the effect is as follows:

1. Spawn 1,000 dots (particles), one on top of the other, at a chosen pixel position.
2. In each frame of the game, move each of the 1,000 particles outward at a predetermined, but random, speed and angle.
3. Repeat step two for two seconds and then make the particles disappear.

We will use a VertexArray to draw all the dots and the primitive type of Point to represent each particle visually. Furthermore, we will inherit from Drawable so that our particle system can take care of drawing itself.

Coding the Particle class

The `Particle` class will be a simple class that represents just one of the 1,000 particles. Let's get coding.

Coding Particle.h

Right-click **Header Files** in the **Solution Explorer** and select **Add | New Item....** In the **Add New Item** window, highlight (by left-clicking) **Header File** (`.h`) and then in the **Name** field, type `Particle.h`. Finally, click the **Add** button. We are now ready to code the header file for the `Particle` class.

Add the following code to the `Particle.h` file:

```
#pragma once
#include <SFML/Graphics.hpp>

using namespace sf;

class Particle
{
private:
    Vector2f m_Position;
    Vector2f m_Velocity;

public:
    Particle(Vector2f direction);

    void update(float dt);

    void setPosition(Vector2f position);

    Vector2f getPosition();
};
```

In the preceding code, we have two `Vector2f` objects. One will represent the horizontal and vertical coordinates of the particle and the other will represent the horizontal and vertical speed.

When you have a rate of change (speed) in more than one direction, the combined values also define a direction. This is called **velocity**; hence, the `Vector2f` is called `m_Velocity`.

We also have a number of public functions. First is the constructor. It takes a `Vector2f`, which will be used to let it know what direction/velocity this particle will have. This implies that the system, not the particle itself, will be choosing the velocity.

Next is the `update` function, which takes the time the previous frame has taken. We will use this to move the particle by precisely the correct amount.

The final two functions, `setPosition` and `getPosition`, are used to move the particle into position and find out its position, respectively.

All these functions will make complete sense when we code them.

Coding the Particle.cpp file

Right-click **Source Files** in the **Solution Explorer** and select **Add** | **New Item....** In the **Add New Item** window, highlight (by left-clicking) **C++ File** (`.cpp`) and then in the **Name** field, type `Particle.cpp`. Finally, click the **Add** button. We are now ready to code the `.cpp` file for the `Particle` class.

Add the following code to `Particle.cpp`:

```
#include "stdafx.h"
#include "Particle.h"

Particle::Particle(Vector2f direction)
{

   // Determine the direction
   //m_Velocity = direction;
   m_Velocity.x = direction.x;
   m_Velocity.y = direction.y;
}

void Particle::update(float dtAsSeconds)
{
   // Move the particle
   m_Position += m_Velocity * dtAsSeconds;
}

void Particle::setPosition(Vector2f position)
{
   m_Position = position;

}
```

```
Vector2f Particle::getPosition()
{
    return m_Position;
}
```

All these functions use concepts we have seen before. The constructor sets up the m_Velocity.x and m_Velocity.y values using the passed-in Vector2f object.

The update function moves the horizontal and vertical positions of the particle by multiplying m_Velocity by the elapsed time (dtAsSeconds). Notice that to achieve this, we simply add the two Vector2f objects together. There is no need to perform calculations for both the *x* and *y* members separately.

The setPosition function, as previously explained, initializes the m_Position object with the passed-in values. The getPosition function returns m_Position to the calling code.

We now have a fully functioning Particle class. Next, we will code a ParticleSystem class to spawn and control the particles.

Coding the ParticleSystem class

The ParticleSystem class does most of the work for our particle effects. It is this class that we will create an instance of in the Engine class.

Coding ParticleSystem.h

Right-click **Header Files** in the **Solution Explorer** and select **Add | New Item....** In the **Add New Item** window, highlight (by left-clicking) **Header File** (.h) and then in the **Name** field, type ParticleSystem.h. Finally, click the **Add** button. We are now ready to code the header file for the ParticleSystem class.

Add the code for the ParticleSystem class to ParticleSystem.h:

```
#pragma once
#include <SFML/Graphics.hpp>
#include "Particle.h"

using namespace sf;
using namespace std;

class ParticleSystem : public Drawable
{
private:
```

```
        vector<Particle> m_Particles;
        VertexArray m_Vertices;
        float m_Duration;
        bool m_IsRunning = false;

    public:

        virtual void draw(RenderTarget& target, RenderStates states) const;
        void init(int count);

        void emitParticles(Vector2f position);

        void update(float elapsed);

        bool running();

    };
```

Let's go through this a bit at a time. Firstly, notice that we are inheriting from `Drawable`. This is what will enable us to pass our `ParticleSystem` instance to `m_Window.draw`, because `ParticleSystem` is a `Drawable`.

There is a vector named `m_Particles`, of type `Particle`. This vector will hold each and every instance of `Particle`. Next we have a `VertexArray` called `m_Vertices`. This will be used to draw all the particles in the form of a whole bunch of `Point` primitives.

The `m_Duration`, `float` variable is how long each effect will last. We will initialize it in the constructor function.

The Boolean `m_IsRunning` variable will be used to indicate whether the particle system is currently in use or not.

Next, in the public section, we have the pure virtual function, `draw`, that we will soon implement to handle what happens when we pass our instance of `ParticleSystem` to `m_Window.draw`.

The `init` function will prepare the `VertexArray` and the `vector`. It will also initialize all the `Particle` objects (held by the `vector`) with their velocities and initial positions.

The `update` function will loop through each and every `Particle` instance in the `vector` and call their individual `update` functions.

The `running` function provides access to the `m_IsRunning` variable so that the game engine can query whether or not the `ParticleSystem` is currently in use.

Let's code the function definitions to see what goes on inside `ParticleSystem`.

Coding the ParticleSystem.cpp file

Right-click **Source Files** in the **Solution Explorer** and select **Add | New Item....** In the **Add New Item** window, highlight (by left-clicking) **C++ File (**`.cpp`**)** and then in the **Name** field, type `ParticleSystem.cpp`. Finally, click the **Add** button. We are now ready to code the `.cpp` file for the `ParticleSystem` class.

We will split this file into five sections to code and discuss it better. Add the first section of code as shown here:

```cpp
#include "stdafx.h"
#include <SFML/Graphics.hpp>
#include "ParticleSystem.h"

using namespace sf;
using namespace std;

void ParticleSystem::init(int numParticles)
{
    m_Vertices.setPrimitiveType(Points);
    m_Vertices.resize(numParticles);

    // Create the particles

    for (int i = 0; i < numParticles; i++)
    {
        srand(time(0) + i);
        float angle = (rand() % 360) * 3.14f / 180.f;
        float speed = (rand() % 600) + 600.f;

        Vector2f direction;

        direction = Vector2f(cos(angle) * speed,
            sin(angle) * speed);

        m_Particles.push_back(Particle(direction));

    }

}
```

After the necessary `includes`, we have the definition of the `init` function. We call `setPrimitiveType` with `Points` as the argument so that `m_VertexArray` knows what types of primitive it will be dealing with. We resize `m_Vertices` with `numParticles`, which was passed in to the `init` function when it was called.

The `for` loop creates random values for speed and angle. It then uses trigonometric functions to convert those values into a vector, which is stored in the `Vector2f`, `direction`.

If you want to know more about how the trigonometric functions (`cos`, `sin`, and `tan`) convert angles and speeds into a vector, you can take a look at this article series: http://gamecodeschool.com/essentials/calculating-heading-in-2d-games-using-trigonometric-functions-part-1/

The last thing that happens in the `for` loop (and the `init` function) is that the vector is passed in to the `Particle` constructor. The new `Particle` instance is stored in `m_Particles` using the `push_back` function. Therefore, a call to `init` with a value of `1000` would mean we have one thousand instances of `Particle`, with random velocity, stashed away in `m_Particles` just waiting to blow!

Next, add the `update` function to `ParticleSysytem.cpp`:

```cpp
void ParticleSystem::update(float dt)
{
    m_Duration -= dt;
    vector<Particle>::iterator i;
    int currentVertex = 0;

    for (i = m_Particles.begin(); i != m_Particles.end(); i++)
    {
        // Move the particle
        (*i).update(dt);

        // Update the vertex array
        m_Vertices[currentVertex].position = (*i).getPosition();

        // Move to the next vertex
        currentVertex++;
    }

    if (m_Duration < 0)
    {
        m_IsRunning = false;
    }
```

```
}
```

The update function is simpler than it looks at first glance. First of all, m_Duration is reduced by the passed-in time, dt. This is so we know when the two seconds have elapsed. A vector iterator, i, is declared for use with m_Particles.

The for loop goes through each of the Particle instances in m_Particles. For each and every one it calls its update function and passes in dt. Each particle will update its position. After the particle has updated itself, the appropriate vertex in m_Vertices is updated by using the particle's getPosition function. At the end of each pass through, the for loop currentVertex is incremented, ready for the next vertex.

After the for loop has completed, if(m_Duration < 0) checks whether it is time to switch off the effect. If two seconds have elapsed, m_IsRunning is set to false.

Next, add the emitParticles function:

```
void ParticleSystem::emitParticles(Vector2f startPosition)
{
    m_IsRunning = true;
    m_Duration = 2;

    vector<Particle>::iterator i;
    int currentVertex = 0;

    for (i = m_Particles.begin(); i != m_Particles.end(); i++)
    {
        m_Vertices[currentVertex].color = Color::Yellow;
        (*i).setPosition(startPosition);

        currentVertex++;
    }

}
```

This is the function we will call to start the particle system running. So, predictably, we set m_IsRunning to true and m_Duration to 2. We declare an iterator, i, to iterate through all the Particle objects in m_Particles, and then we do so in a for loop.

Inside the for loop, we set each particle in the vertex array to yellow and set each position to startPosition, which was passed in as a parameter. Remember that each particle starts life in exactly the same position, but they are each assigned a different velocity.

Next, add the pure virtual draw function definition:

```
void ParticleSystem::draw(RenderTarget& target, RenderStates states) const
{
    target.draw(m_Vertices, states);
}
```

In the previous code, we simply use `target` to call `draw`, passing in `m_Vertices` and `states`. This is exactly as we discussed when talking about `Drawable` earlier in the chapter, except we pass in our `VertexArray`, which holds 1,000 point primitives instead of the hypothetical spaceship Sprite.

Finally, add the running function:

```
bool ParticleSystem::running()
{
    return m_IsRunning;
}
```

The `running` function is a simple getter function that returns the value of `m_IsRunning`. We will see where this is useful to determine the current state of the particle system.

Using ParticleSystem

To put our particle system to work is very straightforward, especially because we inherited from `Drawable`.

Adding a ParticleSystem object to the Engine class

Open `Engine.h` and add a `ParticleSystem` object, as shown in the following highlighted code:

```
#pragma once
#include <SFML/Graphics.hpp>
#include "TextureHolder.h"
#include "Thomas.h"
#include "Bob.h"
#include "LevelManager.h"
#include "SoundManager.h"
#include "HUD.h"
#include "ParticleSystem.h"

using namespace sf;
```

```
class Engine
{
private:
    // The texture holder
    TextureHolder th;

    // create a particle system
    ParticleSystem m_PS;

    // Thomas and his friend, Bob
    Thomas m_Thomas;
    Bob m_Bob;
```

Next, initialize the system.

Initializing ParticleSystem

Open the `Engine.cpp` file and add the short highlighted code right at the end of the Engine constructor:

```
Engine::Engine()
{
    // Get the screen resolution and create an SFML window and View
    Vector2f resolution;
    resolution.x = VideoMode::getDesktopMode().width;
    resolution.y = VideoMode::getDesktopMode().height;

    m_Window.create(VideoMode(resolution.x, resolution.y),
        "Thomas was late",
        Style::Fullscreen);

    // Initialize the full screen view
    m_MainView.setSize(resolution);
    m_HudView.reset(
        FloatRect(0, 0, resolution.x, resolution.y));

    // Inititialize the split-screen Views
    m_LeftView.setViewport(
        FloatRect(0.001f, 0.001f, 0.498f, 0.998f));

    m_RightView.setViewport(
        FloatRect(0.5f, 0.001f, 0.499f, 0.998f));

    m_BGLeftView.setViewport(
        FloatRect(0.001f, 0.001f, 0.498f, 0.998f));

    m_BGRightView.setViewport(
```

```
        FloatRect(0.5f, 0.001f, 0.499f, 0.998f));

    // Can this graphics card use shaders?
    if (!sf::Shader::isAvailable())
    {
        // Time to get a new PC
        m_Window.close();
    }

    m_BackgroundTexture = TextureHolder::GetTexture(
        "graphics/background.png");

    // Associate the sprite with the texture
    m_BackgroundSprite.setTexture(m_BackgroundTexture);

    // Load the texture for the background vertex array
    m_TextureTiles = TextureHolder::GetTexture(
        "graphics/tiles_sheet.png");

    // Initialize the particle system
    m_PS.init(1000);

}// End Engine constructor
```

The `VertexArray` and the `vector` of `Particle` instances are ready for action.

Updating the particle system in each frame

Open the `Update.cpp` file and add the following highlighted code. It can go right at the end of the `update` function:

```
    // Update the HUD every m_TargetFramesPerHUDUpdate frames
    if (m_FramesSinceLastHUDUpdate > m_TargetFramesPerHUDUpdate)
    {
        // Update game HUD text
        stringstream ssTime;
        stringstream ssLevel;

        // Update the time text
        ssTime << (int)m_TimeRemaining;
        m_Hud.setTime(ssTime.str());

        // Update the level text
        ssLevel << "Level:" << m_LM.getCurrentLevel();
        m_Hud.setLevel(ssLevel.str());

        m_FramesSinceLastHUDUpdate = 0;
```

```
    }

    // Update the particles
    if (m_PS.running())
    {
      m_PS.update(dtAsSeconds);
    }

}// End of update function
```

All that is needed in the previous code is the call to update. Notice that it is wrapped in a check to make sure the system is currently running. If it isn't running, there is no point updating it.

Starting the particle system

Open the DetectCollisions.cpp file, which has the detectCollisions function in it. We left a comment in it when we originally coded it back in Chapter 15, *Building Playable Levels and Collision Detection*.

Identify the correct place from the context and add the highlighted code, as shown:

```
// Is character colliding with a regular block
if (m_ArrayLevel[y][x] == 1)
{

    if (character.getRight().intersects(block))
    {
        character.stopRight(block.left);
    }
    else if (character.getLeft().intersects(block))
    {
        character.stopLeft(block.left);
    }


    if (character.getFeet().intersects(block))
    {
        character.stopFalling(block.top);
    }
    else if (character.getHead().intersects(block))
    {
        character.stopJump();
    }
}
```

```
// More collision detection here once
// we have learned about particle effects

// Has the character's feet touched fire or water?
// If so, start a particle effect
// Make sure this is the first time we have detected this
// by seeing if an effect is already running
if (!m_PS.running())
{
    if (m_ArrayLevel[y][x] == 2 || m_ArrayLevel[y][x] == 3)
    {
      if (character.getFeet().intersects(block))
      {
        // position and start the particle system
        m_PS.emitParticles(character.getCenter());
      }
    }
}

// Has the character reached the goal?
if (m_ArrayLevel[y][x] == 4)
{
    // Character has reached the goal
    reachedGoal = true;
}
```

First the code checks if the particle system is already running. If it isn't, it checks if the current tile being checked is either a water or a fire tile. If either is the case, it checks whether the character's feet are in contact. When each of these if statements is true, the particle system is started by calling the emitParticles function and passing in the location of the center of the character as the coordinates to start the effect.

Drawing the particle system

This is the best bit. See how easy it is to draw the ParticleSystem. We pass our instance directly to the m_Window.draw function after checking that the particle system is actually running.

Open the Draw.cpp file and add the highlighted code in all the places shown in the following code:

```
void Engine::draw()
{
    // Rub out the last frame
    m_Window.clear(Color::White);
```

```
if (!m_SplitScreen)
{
    // Switch to background view
    m_Window.setView(m_BGMainView);
    // Draw the background
    m_Window.draw(m_BackgroundSprite);
    // Switch to m_MainView
    m_Window.setView(m_MainView);

    // Draw the Level
    m_Window.draw(m_VALevel, &m_TextureTiles);

    // Draw thomas
    m_Window.draw(m_Thomas.getSprite());

    // Draw thomas
    m_Window.draw(m_Bob.getSprite());

    // Draw the particle system
    if (m_PS.running())
    {
        m_Window.draw(m_PS);
    }
}
else
{
    // Split-screen view is active

    // First draw Thomas' side of the screen

    // Switch to background view
    m_Window.setView(m_BGLeftView);
    // Draw the background
    m_Window.draw(m_BackgroundSprite);
    // Switch to m_LeftView
    m_Window.setView(m_LeftView);

    // Draw the Level
    m_Window.draw(m_VALevel, &m_TextureTiles);
    // Draw thomas
    m_Window.draw(m_Bob.getSprite());

    // Draw thomas
    m_Window.draw(m_Thomas.getSprite());

    // Draw the particle system
    if (m_PS.running())
    {
```

```
        m_Window.draw(m_PS);
    }
    // Now draw Bob's side of the screen

    // Switch to background view
    m_Window.setView(m_BGRightView);
    // Draw the background
    m_Window.draw(m_BackgroundSprite);
    // Switch to m_RightView
    m_Window.setView(m_RightView);

    // Draw the Level
    m_Window.draw(m_VALevel, &m_TextureTiles);

    // Draw thomas
    m_Window.draw(m_Thomas.getSprite());

    // Draw bob
    m_Window.draw(m_Bob.getSprite());

    // Draw the particle system
    if (m_PS.running())
    {
        m_Window.draw(m_PS);
    }
}
// Draw the HUD
// Switch to m_HudView
m_Window.setView(m_HudView);
m_Window.draw(m_Hud.getLevel());
m_Window.draw(m_Hud.getTime());
if (!m_Playing)
{
    m_Window.draw(m_Hud.getMessage());
}
// Show everything we have just drawn
m_Window.display();
}
```

Notice in the previous code that we have to draw the particle system in all of the left, right, and full-screen code blocks.

Run the game and move one of the character's feet over the edge of a fire tile. Notice the particle system burst into life:

Now for something else that is new.

OpenGL, shaders, and GLSL

Open Graphics Library (OpenGL) is a programming library that handles 2D and 3D graphics. OpenGL works on all major desktop operating systems and there is also a version, OpenGL ES, that works on mobile devices.

OpenGL was originally released in 1992. It has been refined and improved over more than twenty years. Furthermore, graphics cards manufacturers design their hardware to make it work well with OpenGL. The point of telling you this is not for the history lesson, but to explain that it would be a fool's errand to try and improve upon OpenGL, and using it in 2D (and 3D) games on the desktop, especially if you want your game to run on more than just Windows, is the obvious choice. We are already using OpenGL because SFML uses OpenGL. Shaders are programs that run on the GPU itself, so let's find out more about them next.

The programmable pipeline and shaders

Through OpenGL we have access to what is called a **programmable pipeline**. We can send our graphics off to be drawn, each frame, with the `RenderWindow draw` function. We can also write code that runs on the GPU, which is capable of manipulating each and every pixel independently, after the call to `draw`. This is a very powerful feature.

This extra code that runs on the GPU is called a **shader program**. We can write code to manipulate the geometry (position) of our graphics in what is called a **vertex shader**. We can also write code that manipulates the appearance of each and every pixel individually, in code called a **fragment shader**.

Although we will not be exploring shaders in any great depth, we will write some shader code using GLSL and we will get a glimpse of the possibilities offered.

In OpenGL, everything is a point, a line, or a triangle. In addition, we can attach colors and textures to this basic geometry and we can also combine these elements to make the complex graphics that we see in today's modern games. These are collectively known as **primitives**. We have access to OpenGL primitives through the SFML primitives and `VertexArray`, as well as the `Sprite` and `Shape` classes we have seen.

In addition to primitives, OpenGL uses matrices. Matrices are a method and structure for performing arithmetic. This arithmetic can range from extremely simple high school-level calculations to move (translate) a coordinate, or it can be quite complex, to perform more advanced mathematics; such as, converting our game world coordinates into OpenGL screen coordinates that the GPU can use. Fortunately, it is this complexity that SFML handles for us behind the scenes.

SFML also allows us to handle OpenGL directly. If you want to find out more about OpenGL, you can get started here: `http://learnopengl.com/#!Introduction`. If you want to use OpenGL directly alongside SFML, you can read the following article: `http://www.sfml-dev.org/tutorials/2.3/window-opengl.php`.

An application can have many shaders. We can then *attach* different shaders to different game objects to create the desired effects. We will only have one vertex and one fragment shader in this game. We will apply it, each frame, to the background.

However, when you see how to attach a shader to a `draw` call, it will be plain that it is trivial to add more shaders.

We will follow these steps:

1. First of all, we need the code for the shader that will be executed on the GPU.
2. Then we need to compile that code.
3. Finally, we need to attach the shader to the appropriate draw call in the draw function of our game engine.

GLSL is a language in its own right and it also has its own types, and variables of those types can be declared and utilized. Furthermore, we can interact with the shader program's variables from our C++ code.

> If gaining further knowledge about the power of programmable graphics pipelines and shaders is just too exciting to leave for another day, then I can highly recommend GLSL Essentials by Jacobo Rodríguez: `https://www.packtpub.com/hardware-and-creative/glsl-essentials`. The book explores OpenGL shaders on the desktop and is highly accessible to any reader with decent C++ programming knowledge and a willingness to learn a different language.

As we will see, GLSL has some syntax similarities to C++.

Coding a fragment shader

Here is the code from the `rippleShader.frag` file in the `shaders` folder. You don't need to code this as it was in the assets we added back in Chapter 12, *Abstraction and Code Management – Making Better Use of OOP*:

```
// attributes from vertShader.vert
varying vec4 vColor;
varying vec2 vTexCoord;

// uniforms
uniform sampler2D uTexture;
uniform float uTime;

void main() {
```

```
    float coef = sin(gl_FragCoord.y * 0.1 + 1 * uTime);
    vTexCoord.y +=  coef * 0.03;
    gl_FragColor = vColor * texture2D(uTexture, vTexCoord);
}
```

The first four lines (excluding comments) are the variables that the fragment shader will use. However, they are not ordinary variables. The first type we see is `varying`. These are variables which are in scope between both `shaders`. Next, we have the `uniform` variables. These variables can be manipulated directly from our C++ code. We will see how we do this soon.

In addition to the `varying` and `uniform` types, each of the variables also has a more conventional type, which defines the actual data:

- `vec4` is a vector with four values
- `vec2` is a vector with two values
- `sampler2d` will hold a texture
- `float` is just like a `float` in C++

The code inside the `main` function is what is actually executed. If you look closely at the code in `main`, you will see each of the variables in use. Exactly what this code does is beyond the scope of this book. In summary, however, the texture coordinates (`vTexCoord`) and the color of the pixels/fragments (`glFragColor`) are manipulated by a number of mathematical functions and operations. Remember that this executes for each and every pixel involved in the draw call, on each and every frame of our game. Furthermore, be aware that `uTime` is passed in as a different value, each and every frame. The result, as we will soon see, will be a rippling effect.

Coding a vertex shader

Here is the code from the `vertShader.vert` file. You don't need to code this as it was in the assets we added back in Chapter 12, *Abstraction and Code Management – Making Better Use of OOP*:

```
//varying "out" variables to be used in the fragment shader
varying vec4 vColor;
varying vec2 vTexCoord;
void main() {
    vColor = gl_Color;
    vTexCoord = (gl_TextureMatrix[0] * gl_MultiTexCoord0).xy;
    gl_Position = gl_ModelViewProjectionMatrix * gl_Vertex;
}
```

First of all, notice the two `varying` variables. These are the very same variables that we manipulated back in the fragment shader. In the `main` function, the code manipulates the position of each and every vertex. How the code works is beyond the scope of this book, but there is some quite in-depth math going on behind the scenes and if it interests you, then exploring GLSL will be fascinating (see the previous tip).

Now we have two shaders (one fragment and one vertex). We can use them in our game.

Adding shaders to the Engine class

Open the `Engine.h` file. Add the highlighted line of code, which adds an SFML `Shader` instance called `m_RippleShader` to the `Engine` class:

```
// Three views for the background
View m_BGMainView;
View m_BGLeftView;
View m_BGRightView;

View m_HudView;

// Declare a sprite and a Texture for the background
Sprite m_BackgroundSprite;
Texture m_BackgroundTexture;

// Declare a shader for the background
Shader m_RippleShader;

// Is the game currently playing?
bool m_Playing = false;

// Is character 1 or 2 the current focus?
bool m_Character1 = true;
```

The engine object and all its functions now have access to `m_RippleShadder`. Note that an SFML `Shader` object will be comprised of both shader code files.

Loading the shaders

Add the following code, which checks whether the player's GPU can handle shaders. The game will quit if it can't.

You will have to have an exceptionally old PC for this not to work. If you do have a GPU that doesn't handle shaders, please accept my apologies.

Next we will add an else clause that actually loads the shaders if the system can handle them. Open the `Engine.cpp` file and add the following code to the constructor:

```
// Can this graphics card use shaders?
if (!sf::Shader::isAvailable())
{
    // Time to get a new PC
    m_Window.close();
}
else
{
    // Load two shaders (1 vertex, 1 fragment)
    m_RippleShader.loadFromFile("shaders/vertShader.vert",
      "shaders/rippleShader.frag");
}

m_BackgroundTexture = TextureHolder::GetTexture(
    "graphics/background.png");
```

Now we are nearly ready to see our ripple effect in action.

Updating and drawing the shader in each frame

Open the `Draw.cpp` file. As we discussed when we coded the shaders, we will update the uTime variable directly from our C++ code each frame. We do so with the `Uniform` function.

Add the highlighted code to update the shader's `uTime` variable and change the call to `draw` for `m_BackgroundSprite` in each of the possible drawing scenarios:

```
void Engine::draw()
{
    // Rub out the last frame
    m_Window.clear(Color::White);

    // Update the shader parameters
    m_RippleShader.setUniform("uTime", m_GameTimeTotal.asSeconds());

    if (!m_SplitScreen)
    {
```

```
    // Switch to background view
    m_Window.setView(m_BGMainView);
    // Draw the background
    //m_Window.draw(m_BackgroundSprite);

    // Draw the background, complete with shader effect
    m_Window.draw(m_BackgroundSprite, &m_RippleShader);

    // Switch to m_MainView
    m_Window.setView(m_MainView);

    // Draw the Level
    m_Window.draw(m_VALevel, &m_TextureTiles);

    // Draw thomas
    m_Window.draw(m_Thomas.getSprite());

    // Draw thomas
    m_Window.draw(m_Bob.getSprite());

    // Draw the particle system
    if (m_PS.running())
    {
        m_Window.draw(m_PS);
    }
}
else
{
    // Split-screen view is active

    // First draw Thomas' side of the screen

    // Switch to background view
    m_Window.setView(m_BGLeftView);
    // Draw the background
    //m_Window.draw(m_BackgroundSprite);

    // Draw the background, complete with shader effect
    m_Window.draw(m_BackgroundSprite, &m_RippleShader);

    // Switch to m_LeftView
    m_Window.setView(m_LeftView);

    // Draw the Level
    m_Window.draw(m_VALevel, &m_TextureTiles);
    // Draw thomas
    m_Window.draw(m_Bob.getSprite());
```

```
    // Draw thomas
    m_Window.draw(m_Thomas.getSprite());

    // Draw the particle system
    if (m_PS.running())
    {
        m_Window.draw(m_PS);
    }
    // Now draw Bob's side of the screen

    // Switch to background view
    m_Window.setView(m_BGRightView);
    // Draw the background
    //m_Window.draw(m_BackgroundSprite);
    // Draw the background, complete with shader effect
    m_Window.draw(m_BackgroundSprite, &m_RippleShader);

    // Switch to m_RightView
    m_Window.setView(m_RightView);

    // Draw the Level
    m_Window.draw(m_VALevel, &m_TextureTiles);

    // Draw thomas
    m_Window.draw(m_Thomas.getSprite());

    // Draw bob
    m_Window.draw(m_Bob.getSprite());

    // Draw the particle system
    if (m_PS.running())
    {
        m_Window.draw(m_PS);
    }
}
// Draw the HUD
// Switch to m_HudView
m_Window.setView(m_HudView);
m_Window.draw(m_Hud.getLevel());
m_Window.draw(m_Hud.getTime());
if (!m_Playing)
{
    m_Window.draw(m_Hud.getMessage());
}
// Show everything we have just drawn
m_Window.display();
}
```

It would be best to actually delete the lines of code that I have shown commented out. I just did it this way to make it clear which lines of code are being replaced.

Run the game, and you get an eerie kind of molten-rock effect. Experiment with changing the background image if you want to have some fun:

That's it! Our third and final game is done.

Summary

In the grand finale, we explored the concepts of particle systems and shaders. Although we looked at probably the simplest possible case for each, we still managed to create a simple explosion and an eerie molten-rock effect.

Please take a look at the final, short chapter, which discusses what to do next.

17
Before you go...

When you first opened this big doorstop of a book, the back page probably seemed like a long way off. But it wasn't too tough, I hope!

The point is, you are here now, and hopefully you have a good insight into how to build games in C++.

The point of this chapter is not only to congratulate you on a fine achievement, but also to point out that this page probably shouldn't be the end of your journey. If, like me, you get a bit of a buzz whenever you make a new game feature come to life, then you probably want to learn more.

It might surprise you to hear, that even after all these hundreds of pages, we have only dipped our toes into C++. Even the topics we did cover could be covered in more depth and there are numerous, some quite significant, topics that we haven't even mentioned. With this in mind, let's take a look at what might be next.

If you absolutely must have a formal qualification, then the only way to proceed is a formal education. This, of course, is expensive and time consuming, and I can't really help any further.

On the other hand, if you want to learn on the job, perhaps while starting work on a game you will eventually release, then what follows is a discussion of what you might like to do next.

Possibly the toughest decision we face with each project is how to structure our code. In my opinion, the absolute best source of information on how to structure your C++ game code is `http://gameprogrammingpatterns.com/`. Some of the discussion is around concepts not covered in this book, but much of it will be completely accessible. If you understand classes, encapsulation, pure virtual functions, and singletons, dive in to this website.

I have already pointed out the SFML website throughout the book. In case you haven't visited yet, please take a look at this URL: `http://www.sfml-dev.org/`.

When you come across C++ topics you don't understand (or have never even heard of), the most concise and best-organized C++ tutorials can be found at this URL: `http://www.cplusplus.com/doc/tutorial/`

In addition to this, there are four more SFML books you might like to look into. They are all good books, but vary greatly in who they are suitable for. Here is a list of the books, in ascending order, from most beginner-focused to most technical:

- SFML Essentials, by Milcho G. Milchev: `https://www.packtpub.com/game-development/sfml-essentials`
- SFML Blueprints, by Maxime Barbier: `https://www.packtpub.com/game-development/sfml-blueprints`
- SFML Game Development by Example, by Raimondas Pupius: `https://www.packtpub.com/game-development/sfml-game-development-example`
- SFML Game Development, by Jan Haller, Henrik Vogelius Hansson, and Artur Moreira: `https://www.packtpub.com/game-development/sfml-game-development`
- You might also like to consider adding lifelike 2D physics to your game. SFML works perfectly with the Box2D physics engine. This URL is the official website: http://box2d.org/. This next URL is probably the best guide to using it with C++: `http://www.iforce2d.net/`.
- Lastly, may I shamelessly plug my own website for beginner game programmers: `http://gamecodeschool.com`.

Thanks!

Most importantly, thanks very much for buying this book, and keep making games!

Index

CPSIA information can be obtained
at www.ICGtesting.com
Printed in the USA
FSOW02n1432031217
41730FS